D1571559

ABOLITIONIST, ACTUARY, ATHEIST

Elizur Wright, 1879. (Reprinted from Philip Green Wright and Elizabeth Q. Wright, *Elizur Wright: The Father of Life Insurance* [Chicago: The University of Chicago Press, 1937]. © 1937 by The University of Chicago Press. Reprinted by permission.)

Abolitionist, Actuary, Atheist

ELIZUR WRIGHT AND THE REFORM IMPULSE

Lawrence B. Goodheart

THE KENT STATE UNIVERSITY PRESS
Kent, Ohio, and London, England

© 1990 by The Kent State University Press, Kent, Ohio 44242
All rights reserved
Library of Congress Catalog Card Number 89-20011
ISBN 0-87338-397-4
Manufactured in the United States of America

E
449
,W 9373
G 66
1990

Library of Congress Cataloging-in-Publication Data

Goodheart, Lawrence B., 1944–
   Abolitionist, actuary, atheist: Elizur Wright and the reform
impulse/Lawrence B. Goodheart.
     p. cm.
   Includes bibliographical references.
   ISBN 0-87338-397-4 (alk. paper) ∞
   1. Wright, Elizur, 1804–1885. 2. Abolitionists—United States—Biography.
3. Actuaries—United States—Biography. 4. Atheists—United
States—Biography. 5. Slavery—United States—Anti-slavery movements.
6. Insurance, Life—United States—History—19th century. I. Title.
E449.W9373G66 1990
973.7'114'092—dc20
[B]   89-20011
                                                                          CIP

British Library Cataloging-in-Publication data are available

For
Richard O. Curry
and
Ellen E. Embardo

Contents

Preface and Acknowledgments

Elizur Wright was a remarkable reformer. One of the most influential immediate abolitionists, he played a major role during the 1830s in the organization of the American Anti-Slavery Society and in the formation of what became the Liberty party. His reputation in business circles was established at midcentury as America's foremost actuary and leading advocate of state regulation of life insurance. During the 1870s as president of the National Liberal League he directed opposition to the Comstock Law, Victorian anti-vice legislation that restricted First Amendment freedoms. His last crusade after 1880 was for the preservation of the Middlesex Fells, a forested region of glaciated hills and ponds just north of Boston. He was also a devoted husband and the father of eighteen children.

At first glance the central concerns of Elizur's reform career appear wholly disparate. His commitments to abolitionism, life insurance, free thought, and conservation seem to have little in common. There were, indeed, important transitions in his life. As a young man he aspired to the ministry; during old age he was an avowed atheist. Despite significant changes over time, there was a fundamental continuity underlying his protean endeavors. He broke with the Congregationalism of his parents, but retained an evangelical belief in self-reliance, in an ethic of good works, and in social melioration. As a second-generation republican, he kept the revolutionary faith that an intelligent and virtuous citizenry could govern itself. He shared the Enlightenment reverence for reason, science, justice, and progress. A rigorously analytical mind, moral intensity, and abrasive individualism well suited him for the reformer's role during an age of major structural change and shifting patterns of thought.

Like many of his contemporaries, Elizur interpreted the disruptive economic change and social dislocation taking place in American society after 1815—the harbinger of industrialization—in the imagery of evangelical Protestantism and the American Revolution. He shared with other antebellum reformers a strong sense of religious righteousness and republican responsibility that differentiated them from their more complacent peers. He was very much a part of the phenomenon that Ralph Waldo Emerson described in his 1840 essay "New England Reformers." "The Church, or religious party," Emerson wrote, "is falling from the Church nominal, and is appearing in . . . a fertility of projects for the salvation of the world."[1] What was particularly distinctive about Elizur was the degree of his alienation from the "Church nominal." His epic journey across the nineteenth century was an odyssey of secularization, culminating in his rejection of God and creed. He was also set apart by the "fertility of projects" in which he was engaged from the Jacksonian Era to the Gilded Age.

There was a creative tension in Elizur's character and activities that resonated with the changing culture of nineteenth-century America. He was paradoxically an evangelical atheist, an impassioned actuary, a liberal who advocated state regulation, an individualist who championed social cooperation, and a very private public crusader. At the core of his long and versatile reform career was a dynamic interconnection between the individual, society, and the historical moment. In historian David Brion Davis's words, "By showing how cultural tensions and contradictions may be internalized, struggled with, and resolved within actual individuals, biography offers the most promising key to the synthesis of culture and history."[2] Since cultural dilemmas are first clarified in individual minds, Elizur's life history raises intriguing questions about personal social engagement.

This book focuses on five major topics of Elizur Wright's reform career which have been arranged thematically and chronologically. Each section seeks to integrate issues of motivation and perception with the wider social and historical context in order to understand why and how Elizur sought to change his world. The availability and nature of relevant primary documents so critically shapes the biographer's portrait of a subject that a brief comment on sources is included with the following overview of each section.

Part I, "The Making of an Evangelical," examines the influence of childrearing practices, conversion experience, and career choice on reform commitment during the first decades of the new century. Family letters, some memoirs, and other material—housed principally at the Library of Congress, Case Western Reserve University, the Western Reserve Historical Society, and Yale University—are abundant and valuable.

Part II, "Abolitionist," describes Elizur's highly significant role in the immediatist struggle against slavery during the 1830s, including the issues of motivation, organization, and ideology. During the period of almost a decade of full-time abolitionist activity, Elizur left a wealth of letters, reports, newspaper articles, and essays that chronicle the early years of the antislavery struggle. This section is longer than the others because of the historical importance of abolitionism and the richness of the sources.

Part III, "Transitions," deals with the fundamental reorientation of his reform career after the abolitionist schism of 1837–40, and his public advocacy by the mid-1840s of a "sisterhood of reforms," most significantly in his provocative Boston newspaper, *The Chronotype*. But after 1845 the sources on the private man are noticeably fewer. Elizur was more guarded about his personal life after the rancor and recrimination of the schism. He felt vulnerable, and increasingly turned to his large family for emotional sustenance, a relationship which, except for some private poetry and letters, remains only partially recorded. Both his parents were now dead, he was alienated from his siblings over the issue of religion, and he was rarely absent from home, which further diminished his previously rich personal correspondence.

Part IV, "Actuary," discusses his forty-year involvement in life insurance reform with an emphasis on his effort to make the business mathematically exact and just for the policyholder. Life insurance was in large part for Elizur a direct continuation of his antebellum reform concerns. In addition to actuarial journals, state reports, and pamphlets, the Baker Library of the Harvard University Business School contains his extensive insurance correspondence, which has generally been overlooked by scholars.

Part V, "Atheist," focuses on the secularization of his thought, his presidency of the National Liberal League, and his opposition to the Comstock Law of 1873. His principled defense of First Amendment freedoms foreshadowed by nearly half a century the formation of the American Civil Liberties Union. It is also argued, based on a thesis derived from psychiatrist Robert Jay Lifton, that the old man's devoted effort to preserve the Middlesex Fells after 1880 was closely tied to numerous deaths in his large family. The Wright Papers at the Library of Congress are the main source for much of the material on the National Liberal League and the Middlesex Fells. The book concludes with a short epilogue.

The evolution from a youthful ministerial aspirant to a militant atheist in old age is an example of the dramatic transformation possible in one life during the nineteenth century. The key to Elizur's lifelong championship of public causes is that, though he ultimately rejected formal religion, he had internalized from childhood an evangelical ethic, an imperative to moral stewardship. His evolution from a Congregationalist to a freethinker occurred gradually over the decades. If he had been born even a generation earlier, he probably would have devoted himself to the ministry. But the rapid economic growth and accompanying social disruption of his century formed the material base for a challenge to the conventional wisdom and traditional institutions which his parents' age-group found a natural part of their world. For Elizur, the failure of so many churchmen to act forthrightly on Christian principles in regard to the heinous sin of slavery first exposed organized religion as not only morally bankrupt but an anachronistic impediment to social progress.

Elizur's ethical indictment of Protestantism cleared the way for him to spurn the church, while he retained an allegiance to a personal social gospel. He turned his talents from the overtly spiritual to the ostensibly secular. The immediatism of the 1830s, an alternative holy vocation to the ministry, was a way station between the sacred and the profane. His life insurance reforms represented a full-borne secular commitment, an actuarial solution to the inadequate existing means of coping with the economic consequences of death in an urbanizing society. Contrary to what one might first think about the business world, life insurance was for Elizur a continuation of the antebellum reform impulse, a mathematically exact way to harmonize the needs of the individual with the interests of society. Having rejected Christian eschatology and survived most of his large family, the crusade to save the Middlesex Fells represented in emotional terms the effort to achieve a metaphoric triumph over death through identification with the survival of nature itself.

His reform career embodied the tension between Christianity and culture in the nineteenth century. In order to fulfill the missionary calling of his youth, he left the church at midlife, and in old age became its vocal critic. The evolution of an evangelical over nine decades followed a secular path that ironically contained an inherently sacred orientation. His ideals were formed in the church. Circumstances and conscience, however, led him to renounce the religion of his pious parents, so that he could honor their commandment to act on what he called his "sense of justice." Over time Elizur reduced religion to its moral principles which rendered formal theology irrelevant, if not an impediment, to the pursuit of good works, a situation that he first confronted in the struggle against slavery.

This book has been made possible through the valuable assistance of a number of people. Librarians at several institutions provided much-needed help, including: the Boston Public Library, the Boston Atheneum, Case Western Reserve University, Connecticut Historical Society, Connecticut State Library, Cornell University, the Baker and Pusey Libraries of Harvard University, Library of Congress, Massachusetts Historical Society, Syracuse University, Vanderbilt University, Western Reserve Historical Society, and the Sterling and Beinecke Libraries of Yale University. Special thanks are due to the skilled staff of the Homer Babbidge Library at the University of Connecticut on whom I have relied over a number of years.

I am indebted to the following people who offered important suggestions about the manuscript in its various forms: Robert Asher, J. David Cummins, David Brion Davis, Stanley Engerman, Lawrence J. Friedman, Ralph D. Gray, John T. Hubbell, Edward Pessen, Allen Ward, and Bertram Wyatt-Brown. The book is dedicated to Richard O. Curry and Ellen E. Embardo, the two people on whom I relied most in completing this work. I have greatly benefited from not only Dick's probing intellect and personal generosity, but from what has become a long friendship and scholarly collaboration. Ellen's editorial talents greatly helped to improve the style and clarity of the final product.

Part One

The Making of an Evangelical

Chapter 1

The Wright Family

The bright colors of the autumn trees on the New Haven common provided little cheer as a slightly built, dark-haired youth anxiously read a letter from home. Elizur Wright, Jr., had recently written his parents. Ought he not be back on the farm instead of at Yale, he wondered? There was illness in Ohio as well as persistent financial problems. The familiar handwriting sought to reassure him. "It is a source of great consolation in my dark hours," his father wrote, to see "your advancement as a Christian, your celebrity as a scholar, and your enjoyment as a dear child."[1] As he put the letter away, Elizur reflected on his family's sacrifice and returned to his studies with a feeling of added responsibility.

The young man well knew the hopes that went with him. Ever since he could remember his parents had encouraged him in their loving but exacting way. What the college senior could not foresee in 1825 was that his commitment to their ideals was the basic motivation for what would be a lifelong career devoted to social reform. His father's letter was representative of a national trend after 1750 toward an affectionate style of child-rearing. Evangelical families such as the Wrights sought to instill self-reliance in their children, a trait appropriate to the changing nature of the early republic. Moral development corresponded to recognized stages of physical maturation. Pious parents stressed the formation of conscience in children, religious conversion during youth, and career choice for the young men. In keeping with the lingering Puritan tradition, they prepared their offspring to honor God in their pursuit of a worldly calling.[2]

As Elizur sat in his stark college room, he had at best an incomplete understanding of the latent forces that bound his life. He aspired to the ministry. Such a vocation, he hoped, would realize his spiritual mission, satisfy his intellectual ambitions, and meet his parents' high expectations. But he was part of a transitional generation born at the turn of the century that would help transform their parents' world. By 1850 no major institution would bear close resemblance to any of its eighteenth-century counterparts. Undermined by the dormant forces that exploded in the American Revolution, the social virtue of deference gave way to ideals of egalitarianism, personal freedom, and the repudiation of arbitrary authority. Elizur was already experiencing the anxiety of attending college far from home. He would also marry and pursue a career apart from his boyhood community. He would break a centuries-old tradition and leave the farm for the city. Above all, the devout twenty-one-year-old would have failed to appreciate the irony that his commitment to Christian benevolence would eventually result in the secularization of his religious values.[3]

The origins of Elizur's reform career began with his family. There was a close correspondence between the Wrights' childrearing practices—especially the internalization of conscience and high expectations—and his commitment to reform. Parental responsibility was heightened by fundamental economic, demographic, and cultural changes that affected their lives. Population pressures and rising land costs that forced the New England family westward were but one tangible measure of the social flux for which they had to prepare their children. More generally, the erosion of the norms of a traditional society in the aftermath of the American Revolution lessened restraints on thought and behavior. The evangelical stress on conscience reflected the intuitive parental realization that moral self-reliance was an essential virtue for a more autonomous age.

In a farmhouse nestled among the snow-covered hills of northwestern Connecticut, Deacon Wright's second wife, Clarissa, gave birth to her first child on February 12, 1804. The infant joined five brothers and sisters from his father's first marriage. The proud parents honored the event by naming the baby Elizur after his father and grandfather. Constancy in naming was a means of maintaining their family legacy, of remembering ancestral ties. By name alone that child, among what would become ten siblings, was marked with a special relationship to the patrimonial heritage. A family tradition of piety set the context in which Elizur, Jr., sought his place in the world. (With his father's death in 1845, he dropped "junior" from his name.)[4]

The Wrights were yeoman farmers who had lived in Connecticut since the late seventeenth century. Less expensive land west of Wethersfield lured the grandfather from the fertile Connecticut River valley to South Canaan on the edge of the scenic Berkshires. His only child was the first family member to attend college, graduating a Phi Beta Kappa from Yale in 1781, despite the disruption caused by the British invasion. Responsibility for the South Canaan farm, marriage at age twenty-two, a growing family, and the care of his widowed mother tied this talented young man to the land. In 1802 (four years after the death of his first wife), Elizur, Sr., married the daughter of a revolutionary war veteran, Clarissa Richards, with whom he had five additional children.[5]

Despite a large family and financial woes, Elizur, Sr., aspired to public service and pursued scholarly interests. Like his father, he was deacon of the local Congregational church. He was also a schoolteacher, justice of the peace, and town representative in the state general assembly for seven

WRIGHT FAMILY GENEALOGY

First Marriage Of Elizur, Sr.

Elizur, Sr. (1762–1845) m. (1784) Rhoda Hanmer (d. 1798)

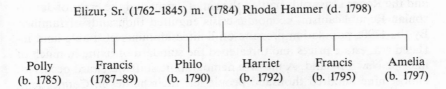

Polly	Francis	Philo	Harriet	Francis	Amelia
(b. 1785)	(1787–89)	(b. 1790)	(b. 1792)	(b. 1795)	(b. 1797)

Second Marriage Of Elizur, Sr.

Elizur, Sr. m. (1802) Clarissa Richards (d. 1843)

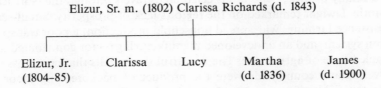

Elizur, Jr.	Clarissa	Lucy	Martha	James
(1804–85)			(d. 1836)	(d. 1900)

terms between 1799 and 1805. Adept at mathematics and science, he taught for a semester at Yale and was a founding member of the Connecticut Academy of Arts and Sciences, along with Timothy Dwight and Eli Whitney. He published two articles on physics, including the description of an air pump he invented in 1803, and wrote a treatise on mathematics. Circumstances, however, would limit the opportunities for this extraordinary man. Through the achievement of his children, especially his namesake who shared similar intellectual interests and benevolent concerns, Elizur, Sr., would vicariously seek the personal fulfillment denied to him.[6]

In Connecticut, the land of steady habits, Litchfield County was a citadel of tradition. The Congregational church and Federalist party dominated the religion and politics of the people, while Yale educated their worthy sons. The church was not disestablished in Connecticut until 1818, and as late as the election of 1806 not one Jeffersonian Republican was elected in Litchfield County. The citizenry spontaneously deferred to men of merit, such as Elizur, Sr., for leadership. Ties of church, community, and family closely bound these rural residents of the interior mountain valleys of northwestern Connecticut about the values of social order and religious conformity.

Yet, life in the Nutmeg State at the turn of the nineteenth century was not placid. While the ministers and the politicians, the Timothy Dwights and the Roger Griswolds battled the sin of deism and the error of Jeffersonian Republicanism, economic crisis engulfed thousands of families. By the 1790s population pressure on limited amounts of arable land inflated real estate prices and threatened the standard of living in much of interior New England. A massive demographic shift westward occurred: almost nine hundred thousand people left their homes in Connecticut, Rhode Island, and Massachusetts between 1790 and 1820. The population of Litchfield County in 1810 was a steady 41,375, up a miniscule 161 from the 1800 census. In 1822, on a nostalgic visit to his family's deserted South Canaan homestead, Elizur, Jr., found "the old house fast fitting for a family of owls," and in his celebrated travels through the Northeast Timothy Dwight remarked on the region's lack of prosperity. Small-scale subsistence farming, widespread household production, a poor transportation system, and an undeveloped manufacturing sector contributed to a crippled state of agriculture. The beautiful stone walls that crisscross the New England countryside were the product of backbreaking labor to clear the fields of the rocky, glacial debris so farmers could plow and plant. Like the weary sons in playwright Eugene O'Neill's *Desire under the Elms,* Connecticut yeomen looked with relief to the richer soils of the West.[7]

Jeffersonian foreign policy, culminating in the embargo of 1808 and the War of 1812, was a plot to ruin the Northeast economically, or so New England Federalists thought. Agricultural exports piled up on the docks as the commercial fleet rested at anchor despite the best Yankee efforts at smuggling. Elizur, Sr., had had enough: there were now eight children to feed and high taxes to pay, and he faced the continued prospect of inflated real estate and a depressed economy. Cheaper land and fertile soil, opportunity and hope, beckoned in the West. His mother died in 1803, so that filial obligations no longer tied him to South Canaan. By 1808 the Connecticut Missionary Society already had nineteen representatives in the Western Reserve, an area in northeastern Ohio to which the Nutmeg State ceded a long-standing claim to the national government in 1800. In addition to the economic motivation for emigration, there was the strong incentive to spread the faith.[8]

David Bacon, a missionary to the Indians in the Western Reserve, persuaded Wright to settle in the town of Tallmadge, which Bacon had founded in 1805 and named in honor of Benjamin Tallmadge, a Litchfield grantor of Ohio land. With the lure of some twelve thousand acres of wilderness that he had purchased at the low price of $1.50 per acre, Bacon solicited pious settlers who would help him establish a godly community in Ohio. At the center of the five-mile square plot of land was the church, accessible to the major roads and supported by an annual tax of $2.00 per one hundred acres. These New England emigrants were the western extension of a Puritan migration that had originally landed in eastern Massachusetts in the early seventeenth century.[9]

For the yeoman, ownership of land was all-important. Survival was linked to the land—the more acreage, the greater chance of economic viability. Elizur, Sr., inherited some 237 acres from his father, and by 1802 had acquired a total of 403.5 acres in South Canaan, a sizable freehold but little security in an uncertain economy. The prologue to the migration of his family in the spring of 1810 required Elizur, Sr.'s journey to Ohio in 1809 to arrange for the clearing of several acres of land and the erection of a log cabin, plus the divestiture in 1809 and 1810 of his South Canaan land for three thousand acres in Tallmadge.[10]

The economic incentive for migration was apparent in Elizur, Sr.'s real estate transactions. Connecticut land prices were high and rising higher.

The average price per acre for six parcels of land that he sold in 1809 and 1810 was $31.50, with one choice tract selling for $61.00, $20.00 more per acre than he had paid for it only seven years before. In contrast he purchased 1,745.17 acres in Ohio in 1810 for less than $3.00 per acre. With the $12,722.54 he realized from the sale of his Connecticut land, he acquired a total of 3,000 acres in Ohio, increasing his landholdings by more than sevenfold at less than one-tenth the cost per acre. By selling small lots of his land to other settlers in some forty-six transactions between 1812 and 1838, he tied the economic well-being of his large family to real estate values.[11]

With the arrival of spring, the parents, eight children (including six-year-old Elizur, Jr.), and two hired men left South Canaan on May 22, 1810. Yokes of oxen pulled two sturdy wagons that carried the family's possessions, while Clarissa tended the children in a large, horse-drawn carriage. The six-hundred-mile journey wound through southeastern New York, over Pennsylvania's rugged mountains, across the Allegheny River at Pittsburgh, and among dense beech forests in Ohio, before ending thirty-nine days later on June 30 at Tallmadge. At the conclusion of the arduous trek, the young Elizur, Jr., beheld his exhausted mother collapse in tears on a tree stump before their crude log cabin.[12]

In spite of hardship, the Connecticut pioneers transformed the Ohio wilderness into a model New England community. The Wrights cleared the land, erected a frame dwelling, and became a leading family of Tallmadge. They were the first to establish a Sunday school, and their home was used for religious services. Clarissa taught the Bible to young women; Elizur, Sr., founded the Western Reserve Bible Society, for which he served as president from 1814 to 1839. Because David Bacon spent much of his time struggling to pay off the credit on which he had purchased land, Elizur, Sr., assumed an even greater role in shaping the community. During the War of 1812 he made arrangements with the American military to protect Tallmadge from British invasion along the Great Lakes. In addition to farming, he taught school, helped educate the deaf and dumb, and was a founding trustee of Western Reserve College. A scholar in the wilderness, he wrote a treatise on pedagogy, published three articles on calculus, and corresponded with Yale's president Jeremiah Day and the prominent New Haven scientist Benjamin Silliman.[13]

As population pressure and rising land costs forced New Englanders westward, they translated their hopes and fears into religious terms. Social transformation was understood in the imagery of evangelical Protestantism. The challenge of Enlightenment thought and political upheaval, the perceived threat of Jeffersonian infidelity and Jacobian anarchy added a greater sense of disorder to the actual disruption of economic hardship and demographic shifts. Revivals that began in Connecticut in 1797, the formation of the Connecticut Missionary Society in 1798, and the organization of the Connecticut Bible Society in 1809 were efforts to maintain social order and to reaffirm faith in an era of cultural stress and personal difficulty.[14]

Under the dynamic leadership of the Reverend Timothy Dwight, grandson of Jonathan Edwards and president of Yale from 1795 to 1817, the Yale college faculty consciously revitalized the old faith for the rigors of the new age. Dwight argued for a practical combination of dependence on God and individual responsibility, a balance between the prerogative of divine will and the power of human ability. More concerned with spurring sinners to salvation than theological consistency, he preached personal initiative in spiritual regeneration and the necessity of Christian service to the community. He encouraged revivals, of which there were four during his tenure, as a means to individual redemption and group unity in the face of social change and intellectual challenge. In 1802 he appointed his devout student Benjamin Silliman to the chair of chemistry in order to neutralize the secular thrust of the French philosophes through the reconciliation of religion and science, faith and reason. Dwight's emphasis on a functional theology and his enduring influence on the faculty made Yale the center of a movement within Congregationalism away from Calvinism and toward Arminianism, an increased appreciation for the role of human agency in salvation.[15]

In Connecticut and the Western Reserve, the New Haven theology gave ministerial authorization for what economic change and social flux had already prepared the people—a series of periodic revivals during the first third of the nineteenth century that constituted the Second Great Awakening. With heightened interest in religion, evangelical Protestantism flourished. Broadly defined, evangelicals were orthodox Christians of the Congregational, Presbyterian, Methodist, and Baptist denominations who held some distinguishing doctrines in common. They believed that postlapsarian man was inherently flawed. There existed, however, an immediate, intimate relationship between a loving God and sinful man. All who truly repented of sin would probably be saved. In addition, the practice of good works was essential, especially the duty to proselytize. What characterized the style of the Second Great Awakening was the belief in a greatly enhanced moral ability and a contagious desire to eradicate sin throughout society. As the leading New England preacher, the Reverend Lyman Beecher explained, sinners were "complete moral agents" accountable to God for their actions. According to Beecher, it was not likely that a beneficent God would overlook the repentant sinner. Evangelicals also worked together to some extent. They shared pulpits and ministers, as did the Congregationalists and Presbyterians after the 1801 Plan of Union in such places as the Western Reserve. And they created a united front of benevolent societies after 1815.[16]

During the Second Great Awakening, the Wright family represented a microcosm of evangelical enthusiasm. Religion rooted them in time and space. It linked them to their pious progenitors as it connected them to their Connecticut origins. The parents oriented the family toward the world in what their son Elizur, Jr., remembered (albeit with hyperbole) as "the strictest Calvinist faith," for his parents modified some doctrines. He described his childhood as that of a "son of a deacon, brought up in a sort of a minister's home, [and] taught to the letter Cowper's 'solemn awe' for the pulpit as soon as we could lisp." The children committed to memory the 107 questions and answers in the Shorter Westminster Confession. The parents taught that the church was "the salvation of the world" and "sole depository of truth." The father declared that the Bible was "a sure guide to future happiness."[17]

The childrearing practices of the Wright family were strict and authoritative, but not severe and authoritarian. The children revered and loved their parents, an affectionate child nurture that the Reverend Cotton Mather had set as a goal as early as 1710 in his essay *Bonifacius*. Elizur, Jr., characteristically spoke of his "beloved parents" and thought them "thoroughly good." He expressed his gratitude for "those dear parents [who] shall have my thanks *now*—and they do have more from day-to-day." Upon the death of Elizur, Sr., on December 11, 1845 at the age of eighty-three, his namesake memorialized not only his parent's Christian piety and Enlightenment intellect but also his love and gentleness in the poem "My Father":

> My father! Yesterday his pen and plough
> Were equal claimants of his strength and time;
> Newton and Nature shared his thoughts sublime,
> And talk with God, as near almost as now.
> O, I remember his manly brow,

His peaceful look, and words so few and mild
And how he showed me, then a prattling child,
His tables vast of logarithms, and how
He called them Napier's army, rank and file,
To conquer worlds with in the noblest style,
And bade me climb the height whereon he stood,
And eased its steepness with the kindest smile.
My Father! I could face life's roughest mood,
Could I but be as thou wast, WISE and GOOD.

Father and mother sought to bend, not break, their children's will, unlike the techniques their seventeenth-century Puritan progenitors practiced and some evangelicals employed as late as the Age of Jackson. Love and duty, not awe and fear, characterized the child nurture of the Wright family at the turn of the nineteenth century.[18]

Enlightenment thought had important implications for childrearing, even for evangelicals. John Locke's *Some Thoughts Concerning Education* (1690) described the mind as tabula rasa at birth and stressed the importance of education on human development—reason judiciously applied could shape the child. And Scottish common sense philosophy postulated the existence of an innate moral sense that could be cultivated. As a schoolmaster, Elizur, Sr., adopted Enlightenment environmentalism in the form of the Lancaster system of education. He believed that most students would exercise self-control in the classroom when properly instructed. "If the teacher is kind and conciliatory in his manner," Elizur, Sr., explained, "he can generally get the good will of most of the scholars, so that they will obey from love." He advocated corporal punishment only as a last resort, a discipline reserved for recalcitrant rowdies. He cautioned, however, never to punish out of spite or in a passion. "Incline every child to have an affectionate regard for you" was his guiding rule.[19]

Lockean concepts of pedagogy complemented the New Haven theology's emphasis on the human responsibility for salvation. Parents had a special obligation to raise their children so they would willingly accept the gift of grace—a changing theology and the manner of training youngsters were interconnected. In the hands of the tyrannical God of seventeenth-century New England, Puritan parents suppressed their children's willfulness and autonomy at an early age in conformity with a religion that taught predestination and infant damnation. The deity of the Second Great Awakening was, however, beneficent and comforting, a Protestant appropriation of the Catholic Virgin, the *mater lactans,* in the male form of Jesus, the succoring son of God. During a lecture at the Tallmadge academy, Elizur, Sr., exclaimed, "How powerful! How wise! How good! must be that Being, who is able to create such a world." A wonderous world, indeed, where the sinner chose salvation and the yeoman expanded his landholdings.[20]

What the schoolmaster taught, the father practiced. Love-oriented methods of parental guidance instilled the concepts of justice and moral obligation in children. "They will attend to you because they love you," Elizur, Sr., proffered. The use of praise and reasonable explanation with the threat of withdrawal of love and rational chastisement stimulated the child's capacity for self-judgment and guilt. Although practical parents kept a birch handy, the child's conscience was a reliable psychological gyroscope guiding behavior from within. The father of ten observed, "Conscience whispers no in the ear of the child when he is first tempted to tell a lie, or take even a pin that is not his, and that it chokes his utterance and agitates his nerves as he commits the deed." The parents who inculcated self-criticism and self-reliance in their offspring had well prepared them for evangelical soul-searching and the individual's obligation for his salvation. At home and school, for his father was also his teacher, Elizur, Jr., developed the heightened sense of conscience that was the emotional foundation for a lifetime of social reform. The son thanked his father "for the pains he took to cultivate in me that reverence for truth."[21]

In addition to the father's significant influence on his son, the burden of child care, especially during the formative first years of life, fell typically upon the mother and her stepdaughters. Though largely unrecorded, the female sphere within the Wright family appears highly important. Elizur, Jr., warmly remembered the "sisterly affection and charity" of his trio of elder half sisters, Polly, Harriet, and Amelia. From her solicitous letters to her eldest son at Yale, it is clear that Clarissa shared her husband's views on childrearing. She, too, bore the responsibility for shaping impressionable minds and preparing young hearts to receive saving grace. Religious duty defined her demanding role as wife and mother on the frontier. Her maternal bonding with her firstborn may well have provided him early in life with a sense of special destiny that set him apart from his siblings. Not unlike other evangelical mothers at this time, she expected her boy to do the Lord's work.[22]

Despite affectionate parents, agonizing moral tension was still a fact of life for dutiful young people growing up in devout New England homes during the early part of the nineteenth century. At an early age their lessons taught children that they were eternally damned because of Adam's transgression, unless, as the Shorter Westminster Confession taught, God's spirit "doth persuade and enable us to embrace Jesus Christ, freely offered to us in the gospel." The opportunity for conversion rarely occurred, however, before the middle teenage years. Young people reared with a strong sense of moral commitment during a period of increased religious concern were made aware of their "sin and misery," but they had to wait anxiously a decade before they could hope to gain "assurance of God's love [and] peace of conscience," as their catechism told them. Such children were subject to intense psychological pressure.[23]

A sensitive and conscientious child, Elizur, Jr., agonized about the condition of his soul. Unlike his older half brothers, Francis and Philo, he did not enjoy the bloody sport of hunting, a common juvenile activity on the frontier. The vivid impression made by an iron forge near his South Canaan home forced him to question his catechism. Like the fiendish imagery of the lime kiln in Nathaniel Hawthorne's "Ethan Brand," the six-year-old associated the furnace with the hell fire of religion. He could not believe that a merciful God would cast him into such a fiery pit. He even refused to say the word *hell* in his recitations, a behavior to which his compassionate parents acquiesced. As he later put it, "The first moral idea that I conceived was an intense disgust at the Shorter Confession of the Westminster Assembly of Divines." The son recalled that his father smoothed over "the horrid points of Calvinism"—total human deformity, the bloody atonement, and hell fire. These adult recollections of childhood, fueled by a growing religious skepticism, are probably overstated. Nevertheless they should not be dismissed without consideration. They demonstrate at least one important psychological reality: love-oriented childrearing practices were eroding the emotional foundation for a faith based on hell fire and brimstone.[24]

The boy had intuitively resolved a theological paradox which the New Haven clergy and his kindly parents had brought to the fore. If God was good, why did he condemn children to a fiery fate? Elizur, Jr., solved the riddle of theodicy by positing the existence of a benevolent God and rejecting the concept of eternal damnation. His logic was an emotional extension of his relationship to his parents in the metaphoric sense that the Reverend Samuel Spring astutely recognized at this time: "The voice of the parents is the voice of God." A close correspondence existed between the child's perception of his parents and his personification of the deity.

Through identification with the parents, the child incorporated their authority in the form of conscience, while projecting upon the divinity infantile conceptions of the parents. On the one hand, a wrathful God and avenging conscience were appropriate to Puritan childrearing practices that relentlessly broke the child's will. On the other hand, a loving God and the imperatives of conscience balanced with ego strength were compatible with a child nurture that stressed love and respect instead of awe and fear, self-control rather than self-suppression. Change in theology and parental discipline created the psychological mandate to dethrone the tyrannical Father of the Puritans and to elevate his compassionate Son who proffered salvation.[25]

Elizur, Jr., became the eligible son to train for the ministry. If two generations of Wrights were deacons, one of four boys ought to become a preacher. The oldest male child, Francis, remained embarrassingly unlettered and unregenerate. In the fall of 1817, the father sadly advised his twenty-seven-year-old son, Philo, that the poor condition of the young man's health was such that "it will not be advisable to pursue the study of divinity." Philo appropriately turned to a medical career, and Elizur, Jr., the next eldest, assumed his half brother's role. During revivals in the summer and fall of 1820, the sixteen-year-old converted, joined the Tallmadge church, and declared interest in preparing for the ministry.[26]

During the Second Great Awakening, most converts were in their late teens or early twenties. Conversion was a rite of passage into adulthood, a means of resolving religious anxieties and asserting vocational goals. The circumstances of Elizur's conversion were of great significance for his emotional development and career choice. Despite his father's exhortations, the son stayed away from the revivals, apparently because of doubts about the doctrine of hell fire and eternal damnation. One workday Elizur, Sr., took over his son's chore of cutting corn so that he could attend the camp meeting. On returning from the preaching, Elizur, Jr., found to his distress that his father had badly cut himself with a sickle. Guilt over his parent's injury, which reversed the roles of father and son in the imagery of the Christian atonement, spurred the young man to conversion. The father's sacrifice gained the son's redemption. Because of unsatisfactory answers to some questions on church doctrine, a close vote, swayed by his father's prominence, admitted Elizur, Jr., to church membership. Although his conversion and aspiration for the ministry were ostensibly his own decisions, emotional coercion prompted his actions, which he later realized were accomplished by "a sort of flank movement... [of]

parents and friends infinitely kinder and juster than the catechism they sedulously taught."[27]

Revivals permitted youth to unburden themselves of the moral tension they had long borne, to become integrated into adult religious fellowship, and to declare their future goals. Elizur, Jr., joined the church, committed himself to the ministry, and pleased his grateful parents. However, his inability to accept the doctrine of eternal damnation presented a major dilemma. He aspired to a career in which he rejected a major tenet of belief. While he taught school in a nearby community during 1821 in preparation for matriculation at Yale, he blamed himself for a persistent feeling of discontent. "And I begin to find," he wrote to his parents, "that the fault lies in my own bosom, which no change of place can alter." Conversion had not quieted doubt, which like Banquo's ghost would not down. His family's expectations, guilt over his father's accident, and a strong sense of filial duty committed him to an inappropriate life's work. He was self-conscious of his anxiety without being fully self-aware of its origin or self-confident enough at the moment to resolve the tension. The burden of the young man lay in formulating a clearer self-definition, in choosing a compatible career, and in clarifying his own goals in relation to his parents' expectations.[28]

Chapter 2

Yale Years

After three weeks of walking and sharing rides on their one horse, Elizur, Jr., and two Ohio companions arrived in New Haven on September 16, 1822, in time for the fall college semester. Well tutored by his father in Greek and Latin, the eighteen-year-old easily passed the entrance requirements for admission to Yale. For Congregationalists in the Western Reserve, Yale University was an important institutional link with their Connecticut origins. Four years of undergraduate education there provided excellent preparation for the seminary. An exemplary student and solemnly pious, Elizur, Jr., nevertheless worried about his worthiness for a clerical career.

Part of the problem was financial. Land rich but cash poor, Elizur, Sr., was unable to provide the nearly $200 necessary to support his son for one academic year. He confided to President Jeremiah Day of Yale, "I feel a considerable anxiety in sending my son so great a distance for an education without being able to give him an immediate support." The family pastor commended the young man to his New Haven friends for financial aid. Elizur, Jr., began his freshman term with three dollars in hand, a sick horse that he later sold for twenty-five dollars, and title to one hundred acres of Ohio wilderness, which served as security for the tuition. His mother and sisters sent homespun clothing. "I have a great desire," his father lamented, "to send you a little money but my hands are tied." Destitute students, such as Elizur, Jr., earned an income by ringing the school bell, sawing wood, and waiting on tables in the dining hall. He also taught school in New London for two winter terms but missed classes at Yale. "You will better earn the money afterward," his father cautioned, "than leave college now to earn it." He began his studies with the consolation that "were it not for the considerations that the earth is the Lord's and the fulness thereof, and that if He has need of me in his vineyard, He will qualify me for his service, I might well despair."[1]

His parents' letters reveal the persistence of an intense emotional bond and continued high expectations for their son. The evangelical concern for piety and the injunction to do good works remained unabated. The Wrights shared concerns, though couched in religious language, with modern parents who have children away at college. His parents not only genuinely missed him and worried about the cost of a college education, but hoped that he would prove himself now that he was on his own. In addition, Yale had a student body which included northern yeomen and wealthy slaveholders, the pious and the pleasure-loving. Even then some students were more interested in drinking, athletics, and socializing than scholarship. The city of New Haven offered an innocent country lad the further lure of taverns, bad companionship, and loose women.

Clarissa had "many fears" for her son, because life was "full of snares, temptations, [and] false promises which end in disappointment." She stressed regular Bible reading and the virtue of humility. She "put up many prayers" that he would remain "faithful." Clarissa missed her son greatly, and on one occasion spent "two hours weeping" over his hardships. She worried about his health and maternally pleaded, "Be careful of your eyes and don't study by candlelight too late." His half sister Harriet, who had married a preacher, also enjoined him to stay true to his religious calling.[2]

His father similarly stressed the topic of religion. Let "this stand first in our inquiries, in our communications, and in our affections," he wrote. He reminded his son "to lay up a good stock of knowledge seasoned with piety," and pointed to the Bible as "the only safe guide to conduct." Elizur, Sr., spoke of the shortness of life, the boundlessness of eternity, and devotion to Christ. He even gave credence to a prophecy current among evangelicals that linked the political unification of Jewry with the coming of the millennium. He predicted that before 1865 "astonishing events will take place" and exhorted his son to join the "heroes of the cross rather than heroes of the world."[3]

The parents merged spiritual faith with social benevolence. Clarissa's "most ardent desire" was that her children "may be heavenly minded— that they may be ready to give up all for Christ." Instead of participating in college frivolities, she urged her son to aid "destitute widows and orphans" in New Haven. The father instructed Elizur, Jr., and his classmates "to let your souls be filled with benevolent plans for ameliorating the condition of mankind." Above all the useful callings in life, the "humble Minister of Christ had the distinct advantage," he emphasized. Unlike the farmer, merchant, or scholar, the minister could devote his entire effort to religion, "the goal to which all things tend."[4]

Father and son also carried on an active correspondence involving the mutual solution of calculus problems. Like his parent, Elizur, Jr., excelled in mathematics, ranking first in his class. He was also inclined toward the sciences, which Professor Silliman successfully promoted at Yale. Although Elizur, Sr., stressed the harmony of religion and science, as did the Yale faculty, he warned against "an intemperate attention to science." "Let your soul, enlarged by science," he wrote, "be brought to a nearer view of the wonderful perfections of God, and may devotion and holy zeal keep equal pace with every scientific pursuit." Despite the parental emphasis on the ministry, the father correctly anticipated that his talented son's calling might be in the sciences and cautioned him to remain pious. "Whether you are destined to fill the place of Professor of Mathematics and Natural Philosophy or of Chemistry...," he advised, "it is by faith alone that we overcome the world."[5]

Much later in life, Elizur, Jr., did renounce revealed religion for scientific skepticism. But his dilemma at Yale was how best to meet his deeply held religious obligations. Duty pointed to the ministry. Yet, his intellectual interests were scientific, not theological. In his senior year he even complained of "a want...of intellect" in theological instruction at Yale. There was also an emerging generational difference in the way father and son harmonized faith and reason. In orthodox fashion, Elizur, Sr., ultimately accepted the Bible as inerrant. Elizur, Jr., however, could not accept the scriptural account of creation as literally true and sought to reconcile the Book of Genesis with the new geological knowledge learned in Silliman's class. For the father, faith was the foundation of religion; for the son, religion must be rational. Much of the young man's burden was in resolving the conflicting evangelical demands of spiritual self-abnegation and worldly self-fulfillment, which were personified in his father, the deacon and mathematician.[6]

His parents' anticipation that he become a minister and return home to preach in the Western Reserve did little to ease their son's feeling of inadequacy. At the start of his college years, Elizur, Jr., typically denigrated himself: "When I reflect how little I deserve the blessings I enjoy, how remiss I am in duty, it almost seems as though I was enjoying too many good things in this world." Scholastic problems did not contribute to his anxiety. He found the Yale examinations offered "not much to fear." But he reproached himself for having left the farm to attend college at a time of economic hardship. His father reassured him that the sacrifice was essential, because Elizur, Jr., was "preparing to fill a useful station in public life." The dutiful son pledged that he would "requite the kindness and expense of my parents."[7]

Within the ritualistic context of evangelical soul-searching, the young man expressed the dissonance between his ideal image and his actual perception, between the goal of the self-assured clergyman and the reality of the self-doubting undergraduate. His concern with humankind's unregenerate state despite a loving God's offer of grace mirrored his personal situation. "Sin has cast its deadening influence over our natures," he lamented, "and because we do not love the truths of the Bible, its glories excite in our breast no emotions." The spirituality of the Yale community was distressingly deficient. Even though he was a member in good standing of the Yale congregation, he woefully noted, "The members of our church seem to be alive to everything but the welfare of their souls. I would not except myself from this remark." In further self-directed words, he added, "I shudder to think of the young men that are yearly ruined here,—some of them alas from within the pale of Christ's visible church."[8]

At the close of his college years, a sense of spiritual malaise still haunted him. He reflected, "I wish that many things in my college years had been otherwise—but it is too late to alter. . . . By all along neglecting the present moment, with perhaps high intentions for the future, I have miserably failed to serve my redeemer in college." He also expressed fear of vice, of being ruined, of being lost to Christ. Couched in conventional religious rhetoric was a young man's partial awareness that he was not inclined for his professed career of the ministry.[9]

The high spiritual standards to which Elizur, Jr., aspired were reinforced by the persuasive articulation that his distinguished professors gave to enhanced moral ability. In addition to President Jeremiah Day and Nathaniel William Taylor, Dwight Professor of Didactic Theory, other clerical luminaries included Chauncey A. Goodrich, professor of rhetoric and oratory, and Eleazar Thompson Fitch, professor of divinity. The preeminent preacher, Lyman Beecher, Taylor's close friend, and the Reverend Ashel Nettleton, a Yale graduate, promoted the New Divinity through local revivals. In an effort to undercut the challenge of Unitarianism, the disestablishment of Congregationalism in Connecticut in 1818, and the appeal of popular sects, the Yale theologians, most notably Taylor, restated Calvinism to make it more acceptable to the age. Elizur, Jr.'s teachers stressed free agency and the individual's responsibility for the choice to sin. They fashioned a doctrine conducive to revivalism.[10]

During the 1820s evangelical Protestantism spread the message of redemption—as Taylor put it, "whosoever will, may come"—throughout New England and its diaspora in New York and Ohio. Beecher preached that "men are free agents, in the possession of such faculties, and placed in such circumstances as practicable for them to do whatever God requires." In western New York, the soul-stirring sermons of the Reverend Charles Grandison Finney sparked mass conversions to Christ that left that religiously inflamed region with the apt name of "the burned-over district." In the nearby Western Reserve the "loud" preaching of the Reverend J. A. Pepoon, a young man with a "very bold and commanding" pulpit style, impressed Elizur, Sr., and Clarissa in 1827. The father wrote his son:

> Leaving the abstruse doctrines of the decrees, moral inability, and others of a like nature, [Pepoon] fixes upon the duties of repentance and faith, charges home upon the sinner, his sins, and his liability every moment to be sent to hell; the dying love of the Savior; the offers of salvation freely made to perishing sinners; and the criminality of not forsaking sin immediately and returning to the Lord by doing works meant for repentance.

During the Second Great Awakening the triumph of Arminianism over Calvinism was the theological equivalent of the ongoing political shift during the Age of Jackson from deferential politics to popular democracy.[11]

The New Haven theology left an indelible mark on Elizur, Jr. Shortly after arriving at New Haven, he and friends made a pilgrimage to Litchfield County for an audience with the renowned Lyman Beecher, who encouraged them in their studies. Beecher's son Edward was a tutor at Yale during 1825–26. Professor Goodrich sparked campus revivals in which Elizur participated; he also attended the daily prayer meetings at the college chapel officiated at by the faculty. Much impressed with his distinguished instructors, Elizur acclaimed that Reverend Taylor had not had his equal "in theology since the days of Edwards."[12]

The message of immediate repentance of sin and the immediate restoration of grace was an inspiration to the young man intent on a career of social benevolence. A buoyant doctrine empowering the individual was appropriate to the seemingly unlimited possibilities of the young republic and to the rising generation who was preparing to take a place in it. In contrast, older evangelicals such as Elizur, Sr., were hesitant about the theological innovations. He warned his son to judge carefully whether "certain philosophical and metaphysical refinements in divinity...gaining ground in Connecticut" were "weighted by the standard to truth. The Holy Scripture." The father eventually accepted the "metaphysical subtleties." The generational difference was that his son had been an ardent admirer of Taylor and the New Divinity from the beginning.[13]

Yet, the individualistic emphasis of the New Haven theology placed an added burden on the young Wright. He alone was responsible for his soul. The tension between divine aspirations and human inclinations, between the state of grace and sin, played on his strong sense of conscience in a creative way. He was able to translate some of his evangelical ideals into concrete social action. The performance of Christian duty was not only a catharsis for anxiety but an objective proof of moral commitment. The practice of good works at Yale marked the start of his reform career.

Like his father, Elizur, Jr., was a member of Phi Beta Kappa. In keeping with his temperance principles, he succeeded in prohibiting alcohol from the functions of Yale's chapter. He was appalled that a society dedicated to scholarship spent half of its budget for its annual banquet on liquor which was imbibed to such excess that one student passed out drunk.

On another occasion, Elizur, Jr., successfully challenged Edward Laurens, the scion of a prominent South Carolina family. He protested that Laurens's proposal to raise a student tax to one dollar for the support of athletics would work a hardship on poor students like himself. In response Laurens ridiculed his plebian status, and in return Elizur mocked Laurens's patrician airs. During one heated moment, he pushed the haughty Laurens out of his room. With the backing of fellow students, his opposition to the fee increase was sustained.[14]

Class confrontation and sectional strife were common among Yale students during Elizur's undergraduate years. The student body of some 370 included the sons of affluent merchants, aristocratic slaveholders, and plain yeomen. Elizur, Jr., associated mainly with his Ohio friends. Clad in homespun, their dress contrasted sharply with the fine clothes of the well-to-do students. In his class of 1826, 10 percent hailed from the South and the West Indies; some students were even attended by their personal slaves. Disturbances were common, often involving confrontations between southern planters and northern yeomen. Windows were broken, firecrackers exploded, and sometimes firearms were brandished in the dormitories. In 1823 President Day expelled two students for violent behavior, and the next year a student from Charleston killed another in a duel.

Although Elizur had been reluctant to report students for petty pranks, he declared in a statement of principles that "every man ought to lend his influence to suppress disorder and immorality by giving information to proper authority." He and other northerners banded together to suppress hooliganism perpetrated by southerners and their friends. After a dismissed student exploded six pounds of gunpowder in the chapel, breaking three hundred windows and setting fire to the building in March 1824, they organized the Blue Skin Society with the pledge to report any infraction of college rules to the appropriate authorities. "Blue Skin" was a term of reproach for students who cooperated with the college officials. The number of members increased to one hundred, and the society pressed for the expulsion of those guilty of misconduct. Elizur, Sr., urged his son's vigilance and instructed him to "keep in the strait path of duty let the consequences be what they may."[15]

Contention developed among factions of the students over the issue of expelling some troublemakers. A fellow undergraduate observed that in a meeting on that subject, "No tongue was more potent than that of Elizur Wright. His remarkable power of sarcasm and ridicule was effectively employed in behalf of righteousness." The rowdies were expelled but discord remained. Yeomen's children, such as Elizur, who worked their way through school, were considered mudsills by the southern elite. Any opposition to slavery invited insult, if not physical assault. Elizur's firsthand experience with the planter class at Yale acquainted him with the arrogance of slaveholders, a group whom he would later castigate.[16]

Chapter 3

Career Choices

Before graduation in the summer of 1826, Elizur, Jr., accepted an appointment from the Reverend John Todd to head the local school (now Lawrence Academy) at Groton, Massachusetts, at the attractive salary of seven hundred dollars a year. Although Elizur privately worried that his orthodoxy might not be sufficient for his devout employer, the recommendation of the Yale faculty satisfied Todd. Schoolteaching was a necessity for the impecunious college graduate. As soon as he gained financial solvency, Elizur hoped to pursue divinity studies at nearby Andover Theological Seminary.[1]

Continued money problems, a love affair, and persistent qualms about a clerical calling led him to abandon his original plan. His two-year stay at Groton amounted to a career moratorium during which he grappled with the identity-defining choices of vocation and marriage. He had somehow to reconcile his long-standing and largely repressed religious doubts with his family's desires and his conscientious commitment to evangelical principles. A romance with one of his pupils quickly turned toward marriage. And he also found himself in the midst of an acrimonious dispute between local Congregationalists and Unitarians that heightened his own spiritual insecurity.[2]

During the first two decades of the nineteenth century, many Congregational churches in eastern Massachusetts not only experienced sharp doctrinal divisions in their ranks, but also divided into warring factions—"orthodox" Trinitarians versus "liberal" Unitarians—which engaged in bitter legal controversies over the selection of ministers and the ownership of ecclesiastical property. These quarrels culminated in 1820 in the landmark decision, *Baker v. Fales,* handed down by the

Unitarian-dominated Massachusetts Supreme Court. Although the Trinitarians held decided majorities in terms of church membership, that advantage was negated by this case involving litigants from the town of Dedham. The high court ruled that the parish, rather than the church, not only had the right to select ministers, but also held legal title to all ecclesiastical property. The parish, in contrast to the church, was comprised of all taxpayers required by law to support the Congregational establishment whether they were church members or not. Traditionally, church membership was limited to those who had demonstrated their religiosity to the satisfaction of other church members. Until the Dedham case, churches had chosen ministers without being challenged by the parishes.

The Dedham decision had enormous ramifications. In scores of towns located within a thirty-five-mile radius of Boston, Congregational churches that attempted to choose orthodox ministers were overruled by majorities in the parishes that preferred Unitarian ministers instead. By the end of the 1820s eighty church divisions occurred in eastern Massachusetts in which 3,900 seceding Trinitarians forfeited more than six hundred thousand dollars worth of ecclesiastical property to the parishes and the remaining 1,282 Unitarian church members. In essence, the Dedham decision forced the Trinitarians to form new congregations. By seceding, the orthodox had honored their religious principles, but at an enormous financial sacrifice accompanied by wrenching emotional turmoil.[3]

Shocked by the havoc wrought by the Dedham case, the eminent evangelical, Lyman Beecher, accepted a call in 1826 to the Park Street Church in Boston. He declared, "By means of those decisions the Unitarians had been playing the mischief with our churches, and I was as eager to get at them as a hound on a fox's track." In addition to the revival launched by Beecher, he founded the journal *The Spirit of the Pilgrims* so that "the orthodox should have some regular channel of communicating with the public."[4]

The Spirit of the Pilgrims highlighted the doctrinal differences between the disputants. The Trinitarians believed man entered the world depraved, while the Unitarians renounced original sin. The Unitarians rejected the conventional Christology that Jesus was one with the Father, that the Son suffered as a surrogate for sinners, and that there was justification by faith in the Savior. Unitarians no longer accepted the orthodox belief in eternal damnation nor believed in all cases that the Bible was written under infallible inspiration. In addition, Trinitarians perceived Unitarians as a serious threat to traditional social values already challenged by modernizing influences in eastern Massachusetts. They accused the Unitarians of cavorting at bowling alleys, frequenting taverns, and patronizing the theater.[5]

During the latter part of the 1820s, the village of Groton, some thirty miles northwest of Boston, was embroiled in the Unitarian controversy. Following the precedent established at Dedham, the liberal and orthodox factions divided over the question of a successor to the elderly local minister, the Reverend Daniel Chaplin. While the predominantly liberal parish preferred a Unitarian cleric from Boston, the majority of the church remained Trinitarian and concurred with Chaplin's choice of the orthodox minister, John Todd, a recent Andover graduate, as the new appointee. The meetinghouse and ecclesiastical property came into possession of the minority Unitarian church members in accord with the ruling of *Baker v. Fales*. The Unitarians barred Chaplin from the church and forced the Trinitarians to worship elsewhere. Groton Academy stayed in orthodox hands, for the school was common property and the orthodox had a majority on the board of trustees.[6]

Elizur had children of both factions in his classes. He boarded at Chaplin's home, where Todd also roomed for a while. With the completion on January 1, 1827, of a new meetinghouse for the seceders, Elizur, like other devout parishioners, purchased a pew in order to defray the considerable cost involved in financing the new church. As he later remarked, "I was orthodox enough to pay over $50 for one." When the church lights for the public examination of Todd were not yet hung, Elizur dismissed school early and completed the task himself. On January 3 the redoubtable Lyman Beecher, fresh from his successful Boston revivals, preached the ordination sermon, adding spiritual illumination to Elizur's handiwork.[7]

During the bitter schism, Elizur lambasted the Unitarians. Much later in life, he recalled being curious about Unitarianism, even to the point of attending their rival ordination and banquet, which displeased his orthodox friends. The open-mindedness and rationality of Unitarianism must have offered a strong temptation to Elizur with his scientific interests and his own doctrinal doubts about orthodoxy. For the young man, however, Unitarianism provided a negative reference group on which he could project his own theological uncertainties, especially in his letters to his pious parents.[8]

The youth from backwoods Ohio denounced the Unitarians as corrupt urbanites. A teetotaler and nonsmoker, Elizur was shocked by the drinking, smoking, and party-going he associated with Boston's Unitarians.

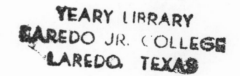

His piety and ostensible orthodoxy contrasted clearly with the Unitarians' impiety and blatant heterodoxy. Whatever his private doctrinal questions, the Unitarians publicly denied the very redemption of Christ. "The leading Unitarians here are," he railed, "as completely shut out from the truth, and the influence of those means by which God usually works, as though they lived in Japan." Their dissolution was so ignominious that a drunken Unitarian judge, he scoffed, "was obliged about a year ago to hold himself up by the side of a pew at town meeting to make a speech against orthodoxy."[9]

Elizur lashed out at the Unitarians as a privileged elite. "All the rich and great of the community [are] conspiring," he believed, "to crush the church of Christ and hoot out of the world the idea of the regeneration of the world by the Holy Spirit." Furthermore, a "phalanx of judges and counsellors...has driven the little band of Christians from their altar and has offered unholy fire upon it," a reference to *Baker v. Fales* that Trinitarians saw as a judicial machination by a Unitarian-dominated court. He linked the well-born of Groton to the worldly influence of Boston. When the Unitarians settled their minister at the First Church at Groton, he scornfully noted, "Boston poured forth its whole host of false, smooth-tongued prophets on the occasion."[10]

The Unitarians were seen as temptors. Elizur protested their seductive charms: "There is an extensive nobility here that would bestow on me the choicest of the caresses if I would step a little aside from that rigid old fashioned religion of Paul. But I hope I shall not step aside to please either the honorable legislators and judges, or their smiling daughters." The sensual imagery betrayed the young man's aroused sexual desires, which he cast on the devious Unitarians. He thought the Unitarians would be pleased if he would attend parties instead of religious meetings and quote from the liberal *North American Review* instead of the orthodox *Spirit of the Pilgrims*. When invited by an eminent Unitarian to Sunday dinner, Elizur replied, "He must excuse me for not dining out on the Sabbath." He wrote his parents that "never before had the depravity of man [been] so clearly demonstrated to me." The great danger of Unitarianism was its "fascinating, bewitching sophistry." He damned them in order to ward off temptation.[11]

In Groton, Elizur viewed the frequent prayer meetings, the growth of a revival, and the well-attended ordination of Todd as spiritual triumphs over Unitarianism. "Revivals of religion torment them exceedingly," he gloated; "we have the pleasure of seeing them writhe like snakes in fire."

He claimed that the new Congregational church drew over twice as many parishioners as the Unitarians. Even Boston, the seat of apostasy, was "shaken to its center" by Beecher's orthodox assault. Elizur exclaimed, "The Unitarians shrink before him like mice before a lion." While Andover flourished under orthodoxy, he believed Harvard was deteriorating under Unitarian control. He praised the publicized return of Lewis Tappan (a future abolitionist colleague) to the Trinitarian fold after he had strayed into Unitarian pastures.[12]

Elizur's parents spurred their son's indictment of Unitarianism from afar. Clarissa and Elizur, Sr., called Unitarianism the "enemy." His mother remarked of the religious struggle in Groton: "I hope the strong fortifications of the grand enemy may be all demolished, and the kingdom of our Lord Jesus built on the ruins." Comparing Unitarianism to a "fit of insanity," the father warned, "Remember that you are on an enemy's ground—watch—and pray for wisdom to direct."[13]

The excitement of sectarian strife contrasted with the boredom of schoolteaching. Many of Elizur's forty-six students, whom he ridiculed as "blockheads," could barely spell their names, so he claimed. Lacking his father's patience, the short-tempered schoolmaster beat his hapless charges with a rawhide strap or handy ruler. "On the whole my labors," he confessed, "are rather unproductive and I am disposed to lay a large share of the blame to my timber." Yet, after two years under his tutelage, enrollment tripled, the library expanded, and a girls' section was added. Neither Elizur's dislike of teaching nor the religious controversy detracted from the educational success of the school. He also solicited two hundred dollars' worth of chemical apparatus with which he delighted in performing experiments. "I can imagine," he wrote, betraying his scientific inclinations, "how a chemical enthusiasm may creep over a man."[14]

As a respite from drilling sluggish scholars, Elizur continued his temperance work, part of an evangelical crusade to dry up what historian William J. Rorabaugh has called "the alcoholic republic." He sought to stem the flow of rum at Groton, which he calculated was awash with annual sales of twenty-eight thousand gallons. Inspired by Beecher's celebrated *Six Sermons on Intemperance,* which in 1826 called for total abstinence, Elizur gathered numerous cold-water pledges from the townspeople.[15]

Parental pressure on their son to fulfill their great expectations continued. Detecting a hint in one of Elizur's letters that too much was asked of him, Clarissa chided, "Being a beloved son I would warn you, and hold up an example sometimes, that would be worthy of imitation, for there is nothing I desire so much as your advancement in the divine life." She pointedly asked, "My dear E. do you feel ready to deny yourself, to take up the cross, and follow Jesus?" The father similarly exhorted his son to pursue the ministerial calling.[16]

As late as the spring of 1827, Elizur still expressed hopes of attending Andover, as his parents wished. A friend aptly named him the "parson" because of his intended career. Elizur lectured a former Yale roommate, "Let your soul be swallowed up in preparation for the ministry." He visited Andover Seminary and pronounced himself "well satisfied" with what he saw. "That mint of the church is," he reported, "on a very cold and dreary hill, but it turns out some genuine silver, warm stamped with orthodoxy." He entreated his friends to join him there for three years of theological studies.[17]

Elizur's hectoring may well have masked a reluctance to attend Andover that he displaced onto his Yale classmates who had embarked on other career plans. Moreover, he would have been disingenuous not to have been aware of the serious theological dissension existing at nearby Andover, a part of the general Calvinist declension in the early nineteenth century. Despite apparent unity against the common Unitarian foe, the orthodox were divided over important issues involving the nature of human ability, revivalism, and biblical criticism. The New Haven theology received a mixed reception from two of Andover's most prominent faculty members. Moses Stuart was sympathetic, while Leonard Wood was antagonistic. Elizur's disinclination for metaphysics and personal questions about specific theological issues would have been sorely tried by the abstruse arguments between Old Calvinists and Hopkinsians that constituted an Andover education.[18]

The transformation of the ministry itself since the Revolution also acted to deter a clerical career. A decline in deference threatened the standing of the clergy, not to mention the disestablishment of the Congregational church throughout New England. Insufficient salaries, insecure pulpit tenure, doctrinal divisions, competing popular sects, itinerant preachers, and erosion of a stable community base lessened their former power and authority. The religious hullabaloo that the young John Todd faced in Groton was a point not lost on Elizur.[19]

What troubled Elizur the most was the social isolation and sterile scholasticism of the seminary. In his frankest statement on the matter, he admitted to a friend: "To tell the truth I should have delighted to go to

Andover fresh from college, but now I am grown old, and am become so confirmed in the habit of living among folks, that I cannot bear to think of shutting myself up three years to Hebrew roots and the company of theological spectres in black coats." Andover had a well-deserved reputation among students as an austere Protestant monastery. Set, as Elizur described, on "a very cold and dreary hill," the dormitory rooms were drafty and the lecture halls unheated. The work load was as arduous as seminary life was ascetic. Beriah Green and Theodore Weld, two future abolitionist colleagues of Elizur, suffered physical and emotional breakdowns under the Andover regimen. Elizur's intellectual interests were, moreover, in science and mathematics, not theology and Hebrew. "I find many things to do pleasanter," he complained, "than to unearth Hebrew roots."[20]

The most pleasant thing was the courtship of Susan Clark, a sixteen-year-old student at Groton Academy when love first smote the schoolmaster. A friend teased him: "I am a little suspicious you are not so entirely insensible to the charms of the Groton Ladies." And Todd noticed that Susan was "a pretty wee bit of a thing...[who] bewitches the little fellow." Her thin, dark-haired suitor, some five feet, seven inches tall, was completely enamored with this daughter of a prominent Groton family. A diffident Elizur confided to his sister that for nearly a year "I kept a curious eye upon her." Their mutual infatuation soon became a serious romance with impending plans for marriage.[21]

In contrast to what biographer Robert Abzug has called Theodore Weld's "guilt-ridden struggle for love and against desire," Elizur revealed that evangelicals could be love-struck romantics. Though at times he sternly lectured her on religious duty, he was deeply in love. "The thoughts of you crowd into my mind continually," he longingly wrote her during an absence, "so that I often lose my place when I undertake to hear my boys recite Latin." He blissfully daydreamed about her even in church and would be disappointed to find a letter from his parents instead of his sweetheart. In Susan, he found a young woman to whom he could express emotions and affections that were usually masked in a dutiful, evangelical persona. "Recollect that you are everything to me," he told her. "I am another being from what I was a year ago." More than any other factor, Elizur's love for Susan barred the door to Andover.[22]

The pressure on Elizur to decide his future mounted. In the spring of 1827, the Reverend William Hanford, his brother-in-law and an officer of Western Reserve College, offered him an appointment there for one year as a tutor at an annual salary of two hundred dollars. The job provided an opportunity to return to Ohio with enough free time to devote to personal divinity studies. Despite his father's urging, he declined the offer. The substantial cut in salary was less a factor than his reluctance to break off his courtship of Susan. Elizur also decided not to matriculate at Andover. "I had rather lay out my scanty means in theological books," he explained to his wondering parents, "and trust to my own efforts, than to spend them on a course of study, and then go into the wilderness without books or the prospect of having any." After five months of solitary study, he fell ill and abandoned self-instruction.[23]

Recovering his health during the summer of 1828, Elizur was prepared to act. He could not bear another year schoolteaching, but he and Susan planned to marry and needed an income. In lieu of formal study at Andover, which precluded marriage for three years, he chose to enroll as a colporteur for the American Tract Society in the trans-Appalachian West and eventually become licensed "for preaching in the wilderness." In such a way, he would be able to support a family, devote himself to religion, and please his parents.[24]

Bidding a sad adieu to Susan, Elizur left for Ohio on August 30, 1828 to await his assignment in the West from the American Tract Society. Staying with his parents, he poured over the religious tracts that he would soon be distributing. This popular literature contained evangelical melodramas replete with endless variations on the theme of sin, faith, and redemption. Elizur found the tracts inspirational, noting that *The Conversion of Mrs. Eleanor Emerson* persuasively showed "the benefit of humbling the soul and taking up the cross."[25]

Compared to the "deathful languor" of schoolteaching, Elizur looked forward to active, missionary work. "I rejoice that Divine Providence has opened the way for me," he wrote Susan, "in which I can be more useful and at the same time be better prepared for the work of the ministry." He cited the example of the English clergyman, Legh Richmond, author of the popular tract *The Dairyman's Daughter,* which was credited with bringing about numerous conversions. "Who would not wish to be such a humble, devoted minister," he asked, "as that same Richmond even if his name were never to be known beyond his own parish in this world?"[26]

The American Tract Society was an appropriate agency to engage an energetic, young evangelical. Between 1815 and 1830, Protestants united to form nearly a dozen voluntary benevolent societies. Ambivalent about the significant changes shaping the Republic, they sought to buttress their value system. Although the Benevolent Empire was intolerant of other religions and damned deviation from traditional morality, evangelicals were not simply backward-looking bigots. They optimistically believed that through moral stewardship they could effect constructive social change.[27]

The rapidly expanding frontier had a special fascination for the benevolent societies. If the West was won, Lyman Beecher prophesied, "the millennium would commence in America." He warned, however, that an un-Christianized frontier would harbor "a poor uneducated mass of infuriated animalism." Without a sufficient number of churches or preachers to minister to the pioneers, some might stray from orthodoxy, and others might abandon religion altogether. Adding to Protestant fears was the revelation during the 1820s of a putative, papist plot aided by Prince Metternich, the Austrian reactionary, to Catholicize the Mississippi River Valley and subvert the American republic. Reports of priests and nuns converting Protestant frontiersmen and their children made evangelicals ready to do spiritual battle in the face of a new European Counter-Reformation. For evangelicals, the future development of the West held no less than the religious and political fate of the world.[28]

No organization of the United Front did more to proselytize the frontiersman than the American Tract Society. Founded in 1825, the New York City–based organization blended revivalistic religion with the latest printing technology and an enviable distribution system. Auxiliary societies and systematic colportage blanketed the nation with the evangelical word. The society handed out an astonishing sixty-five million tracts within its first six years of existence. They were sold at cost, ten pages for a penny, and given free to the poor. Paid $150 per year, the western colporteur distributed tracts to the backwoodsmen whose rapid pace of settlement had outdistanced the uplifting influence of church and clergy. Evangelicals in the East could readily imagine a rough woodsman in a crude cabin being moved to tears of piety after reading in the glow of firelight a tract about a misfortunate little girl who had accepted Jesus Christ on her deathbed, a melodramatic theme typical of the literature.[29]

In November 1828 the American Tract Society ordered Elizur to canvass a large territory in western Pennsylvania, not far from his boyhood home in Ohio. The region included a potpourri of religious and ethnic groups: congregations of Presbyterians, Methodists, Baptists, Lutherans, and Catholics; and communities of English, Welsh, Scotch-Irish, Irish, and Germans. He wrote Susan that "so vast is this country that a hundred

miles makes but a small figure on any map you see." Neighbors were un-
likely to live as close as a mile apart and were separated by dense maple
and beech forests. The "Pennsylvania way of settling" was to make a
clearing in the woods, erect a log cabin near a source of water, and remain
well back from the main road. The frontier city of Pittsburgh also needed
spiritual regeneration. He complained that the commercial concerns of
the smoky "Black City" were such that "men are too much engaged for
themselves to mind the welfare of others. Every man here seems to be
straining every nerve to get rich." But he was also awed by Pittsburgh's
rapid economic expansion and the bustle of steamboat traffic on its con-
fluence of rivers.[30]

Another challenge was the substantial number of Irish immigrants,
many of whom were Roman Catholics. Elizur found them "very ignorant" and "little above the half civilized state." He depicted their homes
as hovels crowded with children of all ages. Having spent the night with a
hospitable Irish family living in the remote forest, he breakfasted on a
large stack of honeyed pancakes. The dirty utensils and begrimed smoked
pork lessened his appetite, however. He thought his work went well, even
if the impoverished Irish at first confused religious tracts with tracts of
land. On one occasion, he called on the local Irish priest above whose
fireplace hung a crucifix and a rifle, mixed images of the frontier. Offered brandy, Elizur refused because of his temperance principles. After
an unproductive debate with the cleric over the nature of the true faith,
he concluded in standard evangelical fashion that "the whole [encounter]
made me wish I was as good a follower of Christ as he was of Antichrist."
His contact with the Hibernians only reinforced his Protestant prejudices
about their poverty, culture, and religion.[31]

Faced with the obstacles of a huge wilderness, a booming frontier city,
and destitute Irish Catholics, Elizur doggedly carried out his mission. He
rode some twelve miles on horseback on a cold winter day in order to
gather a dozen people into an auxiliary society. On another occasion, he
stopped at a community of Disciples of Christ, more popularly known as
Campbellites after the sect's founder, Alexander Campbell, who had settled in the region. They were theologically an offshoot of Scotch-Irish
Presbyterianism, which was just what evangelicals feared—that the frontier would splinter established denominations. Although observing that
"all around me is moral death," he handed out tracts as his horse
munched on oats, and he hoped the Campbellites would return to orthodoxy. He did not achieve his ambition of "putting at least one tract in ev-

ery home west of the Allegheny [River]." He calculated, however, that after some three months he had given away fifty thousand pages of tracts, formed twenty auxiliary societies, and ridden over fourteen hundred miles. "This work is far more pleasing to me," he wrote Susan, "than anything I have engaged in before. It promotes health of the soul and body."[32]

In order to render the tract work more effective, Elizur sought in December 1828 a license to preach from the Portage, Ohio presbytery, his home county. The clergymen, however, refused to examine him because he had not completed a course of systematic study in theology. Elizur later asserted that the presbytery's ostensible reason masked the real cause—his doctrinal dissent over the literal truth of the Book of Genesis—so as not to embarrass his sponsors, who included his father, John Todd, and the American Tract Society. He claimed even to have withheld from distribution tracts that were "quite contrary to justice and common sense and [that] founded their teaching on alleged facts without evidence or even probability." In January 1829, however, he rationalized his rebuff: "Though it would be an advantage to me in my present business, I do not mean to make preaching my business till I have studied the Bible more, and perhaps if they had licensed me I should lose that study." Despite his face-saving disclaimer, the presbytery's rebuke marked the end of his ministerial aspirations.[33]

Later that January Elizur learned that President Day had appointed him a tutor at Yale. His father highly recommended the tutorship, especially because of "the excellent advantages" for completing his "studies in Theology." The frustrated son confided to his fiancée that his father was "very firm in his notion to make a preacher of me." The Yale offer placed him in a very difficult position. The tutorship required that the holder abstain from marriage for the duration of the annually renewable contract. The acceptance of the Yale position meant he would have to break his promise to marry Susan that fall. He had to choose between marriage and the ministry, between his desires and his parents' hopes. Elizur promised to let President Day know of his final decision by April 15.[34]

Almost at the last moment, another opportunity arose. In early March a teaching vacancy opened at Western Reserve College in Hudson, Ohio. Elizur, Sr., was a founder and trustee of the college, and, not surprisingly, the board of trustees unanimously selected his well-qualified son to fill the $480-per-year post immediately. His father urged Elizur to accept for a variety of reasons. Since Elizur's peregrinations in western Pennsylvania delayed correspondence between him and Susan, he declined the Yale appointment and accepted the Western Reserve post without consulting her. He soon learned that his decision greatly pleased her, because it allowed their intended marriage to take place on September 12, 1829. "To think I shall have you with me always!" she happily wrote. "I shall be more than contented."[35]

After completing four months of his one-year contract with the American Tract Society, Elizur resigned his commission in March 1829 in order to become professor of mathematics and natural philosophy at Western Reserve College, a position more congenial to his interests than the ministry. A satisfying solution to many of his needs had been found. His parents were pleased that he would be living close by and that he still had the opportunity to prepare for the ministry, a course he no longer pursued, however. The religious orientation of the college permitted him to fulfill a Christian calling in lieu of the ministry—an alternative his disappointed parents gracefully accepted. As a professor he continued to evangelize and educate in the West, while developing the intellectual talents that he had displayed at Yale. In good conscience he followed his heart's desire in marrying Susan, and he enjoyed a salary three times greater than that of a colporteur. Soon the cause of abolitionism would provide even greater attractions to lure him away from an academic career.

Part Two

Abolitionist

Chapter 4

From Colonizationist
to Immediatist

Leonard Bacon probably expected the worst as he opened a letter from Elizur addressed from the New York headquarters of the American Anti-Slavery Society. Nevertheless, he still became infuriated as he read, "I put it to your inmost soul Bacon: you know you were wrong in that whole miserable humbug of colonization,...Now take my advice and come out like a man—a true Christian—and confess your sin." These young men who had been playmates on the Western Reserve were bitter ideological opponents in 1837. Both opposed slavery. But Bacon, already a prominent New Haven minister, was an influential supporter of the American Colonization Society, which advocated gradual emancipation. Elizur was an early advocate of immediate abolition, an allegiance that led Bacon to regard his former boyhood friend as a deluded zealot.[1]

Elizur's indictment of Bacon raises the perplexing question of motivation. Although most first-generation immediatists were evangelicals, most evangelicals were not immediatists, and some antislavery evangelicals such as Bacon were openly hostile. Recent scholarship suggests that the early, prominent immediatists differed from their peers not in their values per se but in the moral urgency with which they held them. The uncompromising fervor expressed in Elizur's letter is a case in point. More specifically, there was a close correspondence between the love-oriented childrearing practices of his family, especially the internalization of a strong sense of conscience and the great expectations that his parents had for him, and the psychology of his commitment to immediatism. Predisposed to perform good works, circumstances and the call of duty led him to renounce his support for colonization.[2]

Accompanied by Susan, his bride, Elizur moved to Hudson, Ohio, in the fall of 1829 to begin his academic appointment. He diligently prepared hundreds of pages of lecture notes on chemistry and geology for his popular science and mathematical courses. Although he had abandoned theological study, he retained an evangelical ethic worthy of any minister. His impassioned lecture against the "selfish indulgence" of smoking delivered in the college chapel aroused a student audience to request its publication. He continued his active support of the Protestant benevolent societies. A colleague described him as "a fast friend of the Bible, Missionary, Tract, Sunday School and Temperance associations." He was an officer of the Portage County Auxiliary Tract Society and labored to place a tract per month with each of the three thousand families in the region. He also endorsed colonization. A local paper characterized his address at the July 4 fundraiser for the American Colonization Society as "interesting and instructive." Elizur worried, however, that there was too little popular concern for "temperance or truth or the poor Africans."[3]

Like its sister organizations, the American Colonization Society sought to shape social change in the early Republic. Northern evangelicals and leading slaveholders from the Upper South agreed that an expanding black population, free and enslaved, posed a national problem. Organized in December 1816, the American Colonization Society promoted the voluntary expatriation of free blacks to a colony in Liberia which the society hoped would encourage gradual emancipation in America and would Christianize Africa. Slaveholders were particularly interested in removing free blacks whom they regarded as a destabilizing force in southern society. However much northern evangelicals deplored slavery, they saw white supremacy as inevitable and regarded colonization as an expedient solution to America's complex racial situation.[4]

The program of colonization reflected a heightened awareness of the paradox of slavery and freedom in the Republic. Fifty years after the Revolution, slavery was virtually extinguished in the North. In contrast, the southern cotton boom expanded the peculiar institution westward and further tied the entire nation's economy to slave labor. Regional antagonism, heightened by the War of 1812, dissolved into sectional discord over the next two decades. The divisive issue of slavery underlaid political confrontations over Missouri statehood, the Tariff of Abomination, and the Nullification Crisis, which artful compromise only temporarily quieted. African-Americans also protested the nation's racial double standard. In 1817 free blacks gathered in a Philadelphia convention to condemn the policy of racial expatriation through colonization, and in 1829 David Walker issued a ringing denouncement of slavery from Boston. More ominously, Denmark Vesey in 1822 plotted black insurrection in South Carolina, and in 1831 Nat Turner mounted a bloody rebellion in Virginia. In the British Caribbean, emancipation was declared on August 1, 1834 in the wake of a massive slave rebellion in Jamaica in 1831.[5]

Growing national attention on the intractable racial dilemma developed alongside the burgeoning religious revivals with their euphoric message of the immediate repentance of sin and the immediate restitution of grace. It was left to William Lloyd Garrison, a young Boston editor, to extend in 1831 the message of redemption to the national sin of slavery. The transgression was not only the brutalization of fellow human beings, but that enslavement prevented blacks from being free moral agents ultimately accountable to God, not to an interposed human master. Garrison's weekly newspaper, *The Liberator,* and an influential pamphlet, *Thoughts on African Colonization,* argued in a fusion of Puritan jeremiad and republican exhortation for a revolution in racial relations. A former colonizationist, he called for the dissolution of the benevolent society in a resounding polemic. He documented that the expatriation of hundreds of thousands of African-Americans was financially impractical, but the brunt of his indictment was moral. By not advocating that "all title of property in the slaves shall instantly cease," colonizationists were nothing but apologists for sin. He demanded that whites "recognize the people of color as brethren and countrymen who have been unjustly treated and covered with shame." Instead of exiling one-sixth of the American population, Garrison called for the elimination of racial prejudice and the implementation of the egalitarian ideals of the Christian republic.[6]

Garrison's message of racial brotherhood had special relevance for Ohio. Since 1804 its restrictive Black Laws were designed to bar free Negroes from the state. The legislature declared their presence an "unmixed evil" and endorsed their colonization outside the United States. Taking matters into its own hands, a white mob in Cincinnati attacked free blacks and drove them from the city during a bloody riot in 1829. Such violence in Cincinnati with its close southern ties represented an extreme, but throughout the state whites did not welcome blacks.[7]

In the northeastern corner of the Buckeye State antislavery evangelicals uniformly supported colonization. A leading citizen of Hudson typically praised the American Colonization Society as an "angel of mercy" for its humanitarian work to aid "the sixth part of our population in abject slavery." Elizur listened with approval as the new president of Western Reserve College, the Reverend Charles B. Storrs, in his inaugural address of 1831, praised British abolitionist William Wilberforce as a man "pervaded and controlled by moral principle." Later that same year Elizur and his father played an active role on behalf of the American Colonization Society in circulating a petition to Congress for the abolition of slavery in the District of Columbia.[8]

Antislavery sentiment on the Western Reserve was building during the early 1830s. Garrison's compelling arguments provided the catalyst to transform a vanguard of these New England emigrants from colonizationists to immediatists. In contrast, traditional and revisionist scholarship has promoted a polycentric thesis of immediatism. During the 1930s Gilbert H. Barnes and Dwight L. Dumond formulated a geographic distinction between the abolitionism of western evangelicals and eastern Garrisonians with a notable anti-Garrisonian bias in favor of Theodore Weld, "the greatest figure from [abolition's] earliest beginnings." A recent interpretation by Lawrence J. Friedman is more sophisticated but also posits a similar dichotomy between "temperate immediatists," such as Elizur, and "insurgent immediatists," such as Garrison.[9]

These distinctions obscure the ideological affinity and intemperate enthusiasm that immediatists in the Western Reserve had for Garrison's message in 1832 and 1833. Garrison's antislavery activities were common knowledge in Hudson as early as 1830. Copies of *The Liberator* first appeared on the Western Reserve College campus in February 1831, only one month after its premier issue, thanks to a student boarder in Elizur's home who had recently returned from Massachusetts. Rapid communication was not only a testament to the conflation of time and space wrought by the transportation revolution, but to the cultural linkage between New England and the Western Reserve.[10]

Elizur read *The Liberator* with increasing fascination. But it was *Thoughts on African Colonization,* which he saw shortly after its publication in 1832, that persuaded him to endorse Garrison's iconoclastic position wholeheartedly. With the fervor of a recent convert, he entreated "every man who values sound reasoning and loves his fellow men to get this work at whatever expense of money or trouble. It is worth its weight in gold merely as a curiosity. It is unanswerable if not convincing." He urged colonizationists to "read at least a dozen numbers of *The Liberator* and Mr. Garrison's 'Thoughts on African Colonization.'"[11]

The logic of Garrison's presentation overcame Elizur's initial uncertainty about the doctrine of immediatism. "Your 'Thoughts on African Colonization' have dispelled these doubts," he wrote to Garrison. "I find that I was misinformed as doubtless thousands are, in regard to your opinions." And Garrison warmly responded, "I do most heartily congratulate myself, the cause of bleeding humanity and all true abolitionists on the acquisition of so able and uncompromising [a] coadjutor as yourself." Years later, even after a bitter break with Garrison, Elizur still recalled, "It was early in 1832, I think, that Mr. Garrison struck the greatest blow of his life—or any man's life—by publishing in a thick pamphlet, with all the emphasis that a printer knows how to give with his types, his 'Thoughts on Colonization.'" By the late summer of 1832, Elizur was the preeminent immediatist in the West.[12]

Before his adoption of immediatism, Elizur went through a period of critical self-examination that was akin to a religious conversion. He recognized in Garrison's writing "the very principles of truth and righteousness," the standards by which a true Christian must judge himself. At once impressed with Garrison's compelling argument for human rights, he was taken aback by the vehement attack on colonization, which he had previously felt duty-bound to support. Not only had he publicly advocated colonization and donated money to the cause, but also he had hoped it would result in the eradication of slavery. However, as Elizur applied Garrison's logic to his own colonizationist position, "the more I was troubled with his great fundamental principles—the more sick was I of that flexible, convenient expediency on which I say my own cause was based. In short, I burnt up my colonizationism.... " Faced with the discrepancy between belief and practice, Elizur's conscience drove him "struggling at every step, till I was fenced up on both sides to the road of consistency and fairly compelled to go straight forward" to immediatism. As he explained to an unreceptive friend, the choice between immediatism and colonization was one between "religious sincerity and hypocrisy."[13]

The imperative of conscience is the key to understanding the psychology of Elizur's conversion to immediatism. His mentality derived from the revised Calvinism of the New Haven theology for which the love-oriented child nurture of his parents had well prepared him. Like his Yale professors, Elizur believed that God created man "to be able with certainty to distinguish between right and wrong." The existence of an absolute dichotomy between good and evil, grace and sin, was an ontological category. Conscience was the link between a sinful humanity and a virtuous deity. "If God has a moral government at all," he explained, "every subject of it must be so constituted as to feel, naturally, an approbation of that which is right and a disapprobation of that which is wrong. This feeling is conscience." It was God calling Adamic man to divine righteousness. Elizur had intuitively divinized conscience.[14]

Asserting an enhanced moral ability, Elizur argued that man was free to choose right or wrong. Sin could, however, silence conscience. An "inordinate sensual appetite," such as smoking or drinking, he told his students, stilled conscience and rendered man callous to virtue. The immanence of divine truth could not be entirely eradicated, even by wrong action. "It may be doubted whether any man's conscience is silenced or 'seared,'" he lectured, "as not to respond to the harmonious system of truth revealed in the word of God, when it is clearly explained."[15]

Evangelical reformers had the duty to awaken the unregenerate to divine mandates rather than human appetites. "Every man," Elizur instructed, "is under obligation, in all cases to do all in his power, short of employing deceptive or physical force, to bring his fellow men to think and do that which is right," an ethic that undergirded his entire reform career. The evocation of Christian truth would save lost souls by reconnecting them to the godhead via conscience. In his words, "In all our attempts to reform man, we should regard them, as having consciences, as being adapted, in the indestructible constituents of their souls, to the service of God, and accordingly, that we should depend upon an exhibition of plain truth for success."[16]

The evangelical conception of social change was accordingly personalized. Moral suasion would reestablish the primacy of each individual's conscience, reclaim the sinner, and render people faithful subjects of the kingdom of God. Elizur explained in a millennial vein that "conscience, when it speaks, is an infallible guide. Its voice, when uttered from a thousand hearts is perfect harmony. Would the world but yield itself to the guidance of conscience, such are the gracious arrangements of God, all would be order, peace, and happiness."[17]

Historian John Thomas has aptly termed the enthusiasm of early antebellum reformers for moral suasion "romantic reform." It has been little appreciated, however, that such a perception as Elizur's was in effect an enlarged family drama. Parents relied on moral dictates to guide their children's behavior from within. Ministers expected the divine voice of conscience to call the sinner to repentance. And immediatists believed that Christian truth would compel conscience-stricken masters to free their slaves. A childrearing technique based ultimately on the coercive power of parental love was unrealistically expected to redeem the world.[18]

Elizur turned from colonization to immediatism because of the compunction of his conscience and his will to act on his religious principles. He described his conversion as one marked by guilt, repentance, and finally faith in Christ as the remedy for sin. As a colonizationist, he had been lulled by a false consciousness. Colonization, he wrote, "reduces conscience to mere opinion based on what is called expediency—it may be right, it may be wrong—it does not necessarily respond its amen to the doctrine of God's word." Garrison's logic challenged his sense of evangelical duty. Elizur felt pangs of guilt over his failure to apply his Christian ideals in a consistent manner. "When I look a little backward and remember my own apathy," he reflected, "while my eye rested on scenes [of racial degradation] that were enough to move stones to pity, I am covered with shame." And in a telling phrase he recounted that his adoption of immediatism involved "an entire change of thought and feeling, a revolution of the soul." Morally embarrassed by his prior allegiance to colonization, Elizur resolved to practice his faith fully, to confess his sin, to embrace Garrisonianism.[19]

Elizur's "revolution of the soul" involved no less than a spiritual rebirth. "The effect of abolition truths . . . ," he testified, "is astonishing—showing their adaption to move the human soul with an evidence as full as that of miracles." In contrast to his earlier self-doubt about his intended clerical career, he adopted immediatism wholeheartedly. He had found what historian Donald M. Scott has called a "sacred vocation," not in the ministry, but in abolitionism. "I have great occasion to thank God," Elizur exalted, "that he has permitted me to engage in the support of a cause so evidently just and righteous, as that of the poor slaves." His renunciation of colonization originated from a sense of violated values; his commitment to immediatism was a means to achieve his ideal self-image. Conscience compelled change.[20]

For Elizur, immediatism was the culmination of evangelicalism. "I should rejoice to be deemed worthy to exert a more direct influence in favor of immediate, universal emancipation," he wrote to his friend Theodore Weld. "This is the doctrine of the Savior, and it must be preached from one end of the land to the other, tho' the very 'Stars of heaven' should be shaken by it." Slavery was not only a blatant affront to his ethical sensibilities, but to his theology with its antinomian orientation toward a direct communion to God through conscience. Weld put it just so, "God has committed to every moral agent the privilege, the right and the responsibility of personal ownership. This is God's plan. Slavery annihilates it. . . ." Driven by lust and power, the slave master, immediatists charged, had sacrilegiously interposed himself between man and God. Slavery was the negation of "free moral agency," a concept so important to Elizur who had been weaned on doctrines of self-reliance and individual accountability.[21]

Just as Elizur was for total abstinence from alcohol and tobacco, so too was he for unconditional emancipation. "It is a truth, obvious as the sun at cloudless noon," he believed, "that all gradual reformation in practice, which has blessed the world, has been the fruit of stern immediatism in doctrine. What, then, can the fruit of gradualism itself be but everlasting procrastination?" "Ultraism," as he called it, in reform was not only efficacious, it was morally incumbent on Christians. For colonizationists to advocate "the gradual abolition of sin" was, Elizur chided, "nothing better than to escape the righteous curse of God, in some other way than by a direct repentance, confession, and reparation of injury—the only way which He has appointed." The difference between colonization and immediatism, he told Weld, was that of "cringing EXPEDIENCY on the one side and ETERNAL TRUTH on the other."[22]

The moral imperative of Elizur's immediatism differentiated him from most of his evangelical peers and elders. Despite his appeals, his friend Leonard Bacon and Yale roommate Reuben Hitchcock remained colonizationists. To his dismay, "our beloved" Lyman Beecher, Nathaniel William Taylor, and Benjamin Silliman, so important in shaping his spiritual and scientific perspective, failed to embrace immediatism. Most of the clergy in the Western Reserve remained unpersuaded, as did the churchmen at Andover Seminary. Elizur scornfully noted that the Presbyterian church after 1818 had abandoned its condemnation of "the guilt of slaveholding." He might well have added that all of America's major institutions, sacred and profane, were inextricably linked with slavery and white supremacy.[23]

Elizur's conversion to immediatism also redefined his relationship to his family. As the first to renounce colonization, he assumed his father's role as moral leader. It was less an Oedipal rebellion than a new generation's application of revised evangelical values to slavery, the central moral dilemma of their time. Confident that entrenched social evils could be directly confronted and successfully eradicated, Elizur found the more restrained, often pessimistic doctrines that had attracted his father's generation unattractive. Less wedded to the religious status quo, the son was better able to divorce himself from institutional attachments and to apply his ideals to a new sectarian career. He had already spurned the ministry and would soon abandon pedagogy, the two occupations for which his father had groomed him. Instead, Elizur translated his evangelical values and missionary experience with the conservative benevolent societies into a fundamentally radical crusade. Immediatism affirmed his family's emphasis on the social gospel at the same time it served as his personal declaration of independence from their tutelage.[24]

Though the father cautioned his son to tone down his caustic attacks on colonization, he followed Elizur, Jr., into the cause of immediatism, becoming president of the Tallmadge Anti-Slavery Society. More moderate than his son, Elizur, Sr., nevertheless called for the unconditional end of "the sin of slavery" and denounced the "unchristian" character of colonization. Immediatism became a central concern of this remarkable family. "I am glad for more reasons than one that you have espoused the cause of injured humanity, and hope the Lord will direct you in your deliberations," Clarissa told her son. "You was [sic] among the pioneers in this noble cause," his father later wrote him, "and have fought so valiantly and even successfully on the side of truth." In addition, four of Elizur's siblings taught in black schools. His sister Lucy was secretary of the Portage County Female Anti-Slavery Society and a missionary to the Chippewa in the Wisconsin Territory. The proud family patriarch praised their efforts: "It is certainly a superlative favor to have so many of our children espouse the righteous cause."[25]

As historian David C. French has suggested, illness and death in Elizur's new family added an emotional tension that commitment to an altruistic cause may have eased. Susan was frequently sick and spent much time convalescing at her in-laws'. Out of sorts with rustic life in Ohio, she longed for her family and the more refined society of Groton. Elizur neglected her when he was busy with academic work and the immediatist crusade, although he took her East on an abolitionist speaking tour in the spring of 1833 and "cheerfully" stopped at health spas. Adding to the grief over the death of their first child, Susan Louisa, on January 6, 1832, their second child was chronically unhealthy. "Our little Johnny is a pale and tender boy," Elizur squeezed into a letter crowded with abolitionist news to Weld, "and has often seemed ready to bid us adieu." He may well have had his own paternal anxiety in mind when he angrily criticized slave masters for treating their abandoned mulatto children like "brutes." He would suffer a great deal of anguish before he achieved a harmonious balance among his often conflicting roles as husband, father, and reformer.[26]

Elizur's conception of Christian witness, unlike that of his childhood playmate Leonard Bacon, required him to testify not only against slavery but also against what he thought was the shameful temporizing of colonization. He shared a moral fervor with other early immediatists that distinguished them from their colonizationist peers and that made the abolitionist crusade into a secular version of a religious quest. These idealistic young evangelicals were doing the Lord's work, but largely outside the normal Christian institutions because most churchmen worshipped at the altar of white supremacy. When Ralph Waldo Emerson spoke of a generation born with "knives in their brains," he could have pointed to no better example than the first generation of immediatists with their penchant for passionate introspection. It was the shared abolitionist intensity that joined Elizur in a bond of immediatist fellowship at Western Reserve College.[27]

Chapter 5

The Western Reserve College Controversy

Although Elizur's adoption of immediatism involved a deeply personal commitment, it occurred within an influential social setting. Friendship and ideological affinity with his colleagues, the Reverend Charles B. Storrs, president of Western Reserve College, and the Reverend Beriah Green, professor of sacred literature, bound them together into an immediatist clique arrayed against the predominantly colonizationist college trustees. During 1832 and 1833 these factions confronted one another in the first major controversy over abolition in the West and the first such event in American higher education, a significant precedent for subsequent confrontations at the Lane Institute and Oberlin College. Both sides opposed slavery, but the question arises on the group level that was previously examined in terms of individual conversion: why did some evangelicals become immediatists, while others remained colonizationists? At least among the main protagonists of the faculty and the trustees, there were notable differences between them in age, in relationship to the community, in attachment to the college, and in enthusiasm for the revised Calvinist message of the immediate repentance of sin.[1]

The three faculty members were recent arrivals to the village of Hudson and were a generation younger than the trustees. As young evangelicals they had been caught up in the wave of revivals that swept the North during the 1820s. They were more concerned with right action, repentance, and regeneration than the college fathers, who as the well-established leaders of the community highly valued stability, harmony, and consensus. The faculty adopted immediatism because it reaffirmed their belief in man's moral ability to free himself at once from sin even at the price of social disruption. Their more cautious elders clung to colonization because of its stress on orderly social change, even if it meant tolerating sin. The professors believed their duty was to teach the moral imperative of immediatism, but the trustees were fearful that this controversial doctrine would alienate popular support and dry up financial contributions to the new school. The confrontation became even more acrimonious when the trustees sought to silence and then to oust the outspoken faculty.[2]

Elizur recalled years later that theological differences were at the heart of the dispute. Despite the combative anticlericalism of his old age, he was right that religious antagonism was a significant factor. Old-school Congregationalists and Presbyterians on the Western Reserve regarded the New Haven theology of Nathaniel William Taylor and the New Measures of Charles Grandison Finney with suspicion. The critical point of departure between the disputants was that the faculty extended the implications of the New Divinity beyond the limits that the more traditional trustees (and even Taylor and Finney) could tolerate. Elizur damned the evil of slavery with boundless passion: "Prudence is a virtue, and a most blessed virtue in its place, and so is meekness, but they have no business to go single and alone in the forefront of the great enterprise of reclaiming society from giant sins." In fact, most Christians, whether old school or new, condoned white supremacy and condemned the immediatist argument.[3]

Wright, Green, and Storrs preached a degree of personal piety that threatened to subvert traditional ideas of Christian community. Elizur's fervent essays on religious duty, many of which appeared in the columns of the local evangelical newspaper in the summer of 1832, directly foreshadowed his public advocacy of immediatism. His emphasis on the divine attributes of conscience carried an antinomian message of individual justification in opposition to the cohesion of social norms that alarmed more staid believers. An earlier series of newspaper articles that spring, he remembered, "scandalized" the local churchmen, because he sought to reconcile geology and Genesis in a manner that limited "the field of inspiration of the Bible." Elizur's extrapolation of the teachings of his Yale professors, particularly Taylor and Silliman, made clear to old-school evangelicals in Hudson the wisdom of the local Portage Presbytery in rejecting his request for a license to preach some years before.[4]

The mandate of Western Reserve College to provide intellectual and moral instruction to its students lent itself to discussion of the abolition of slavery. The establishment of the college in 1826 was a mark of the maturity of the original settlement which dated from the turn of the century. The overwhelming evangelical population of the Western Reserve considered educational institutions essential to Christianize and civilize the frontier. With an influx of settlers during 1810–20, parents faced the undesirable prospect of sending their young men back to New England for a college education. There was also a critical shortage of ministers in the Portage Presbytery. In 1820 there were thirty-three churches but only eight ministers. The demand for a college in the Western Reserve to educate local youth and to supply its pulpits resulted in competition among the area towns to be the site of such an institution. Hudson was selected not only because of its favorable location but because its generous residents subscribed over seven thousand dollars, two thousand of which was pledged by David Hudson (the town's founder) toward the institution. For the pioneering generation who had founded a new Connecticut in Ohio, Western Reserve College was intended to be the Yale of the West.[5]

Because of the emphasis on Christian education, it was imperative that professors of exemplary merit be selected. President Storrs, Massachusetts-born and Andover-educated, was descended from a family of distinguished Congregationalist ministers. He had evangelized in South Carolina, gaining firsthand experience with slavery before settling in Ohio. In 1828 he accepted the first professorship (that of theology) at the fledgling college. In his inaugural presidential address of February 9, 1831, he set high goals for Western Reserve College. "The glory of God requires us to make," he told his audience, "the elevation of our moral nature our constant aim—our unwearied endeavor in the work of education." Elizur's other two colleagues, Beriah Green and Rufus Nutting, were also ministers. Born in Connecticut and educated at Middlebury College, Green had been a contemporary of Storrs's at Andover. Green had arrived in 1830, a year after Elizur, to take charge of biblical studies and act as campus chaplain. Rufus Nutting, a Vermont native and Dartmouth graduate, taught languages and served as librarian. Perhaps, because of what Elizur, Sr., described as his "peaceable disposition," Nutting remained a colonizationist and did not take an active role in the controversy.[6]

Tranquility prevailed until the late summer of 1832 when Wright, Storrs, and Green became convinced that Garrison's ideas were morally incumbent on all Christians. Acting as a catalyst, Elizur had persuaded his two friends to accept "all of" immediatism, as he excitedly put it. He also initiated public advocacy of the provocative cause with an indictment of a case of racism at Yale. At first reluctant to publicize the embarrassing event at his alma mater, he felt an obligation to make the circumstances known after learning more of the outrageous details. He wrote to *The Liberator* a caustic letter titled "The Victim of Prejudice," but diffidently masked his identity with the nom de plume "Friend of Light."[7]

Elizur angrily described what had happened to a former student of his from Groton Academy whom he had recommended for enrollment at Yale. Although not a gifted scholar, the young man's studiousness and piety would, his former teacher thought, serve him well enough. The problem was, however, not the student's academic ability, but his swarthy complexion and dark, bushy hair. Some at Yale mistakenly identified him as a black man. Soon after the start of the first term, a student from a prominent South Carolina family refused to eat at the same table with the supposed Negro. Instead of instructing the southerner on the obligation of Christian fraternity, the Yale tutor attempted to prove that the putative Negro was in reality a Caucasian. Tension mounted as southerners demanded barring him from the refectory, while some students opposed that position. The dark-skinned student was actively harrassed: he was openly insulted and the windows of his room were broken. Stoically bearing the ordeal as long as he could, he finally withdrew from Yale after failing to get a commitment from the faculty to protect his rights.[8]

The acquiescence to racism at Yale outraged Elizur. If such behavior were tolerated against "a rather dark-skinned but full blooded Anglo-American," he pointedly asked, "what would have been done to an acknowledged African?" He saw blatant hypocrisy in the college's position: Yale preached Christian brotherhood but practiced racial bigotry. The way to resolve the contradiction, he proposed, was for Yale to inculcate in its students the ideal of human solidarity. He demanded of the Yale administration "whether such facts should have occurred in an Institution where all was done that could be to break down distinctions of rank not founded in moral character, and to plant the conviction in the minds of youth that no man has a right to hold in slavery his fellow man of whatever color?" In Elizur's view, Yale was remiss in its Christian stewardship by not bearing witness to the doctrine of immediatism.[9]

The Yale incident illustrated Elizur's sensitivity to the degradation of racism. During his own undergraduate years in New Haven, he too had encountered the arrogance of the haughty planter class. It was only a short, emotional distance from his own experience and that of his Groton

student's to the cause of the ultimate "victim of prejudice," the slave. Elizur's first abolitionist polemic, though anonymous, characterized what
psychologist Silvan S. Tomkins has described as "the radical magnifica-
tion of negative feeling toward the oppressor and of positive feeling toward the oppressed," which is so important in the evolution of a reform
commitment. Moreover, as Elizur took a more forceful stand for immediatism, Storrs and Green were prompted to declare their own positions. A
student boarding at Elizur's house recalled how his landlord, "his face all
aglow with joy," announced that his two friends had embraced "abolitionist doctrines." Through the fellowship of their missionary project on
behalf of the slave, this Garrisonian triumvir—and its supporters—
provided each other with the resiliency needed to persevere in the face of
determined colonizationist opposition. In words of common purpose,
Green asked, "[We] are now making the inquiry with unwonted solici-
tude, 'Lord, what wilt thou have us do?' "[10]

By September Elizur's answer was to write a column in the *Hudson Observer and Telegraph* on behalf of immediatism. The editor, Warren
Isham, was a colonizationist, but quite willing at first to allow an outstanding young man in the community, who had already written on religious themes, continued access to the local evangelical paper. Elizur's
weekly essay was, however, more than Isham had anticipated. A fluent
stylist with a gift for biting satire and moral indictment, Elizur soon
gained notoriety as a zealous immediatist. Oliver Johnson, a close associate of Garrison's in Boston, remembered that Elizur "wielded a pen as
keen as a Damascus blade." His analytical mind excelled in reducing arguments for slavery and colonization to their presuppositions, where-
upon he pointed out their glaring contradictions in terms of religious and
republican principles. He demanded no less than the consistent application of the evangelical precept of immediate repentance to the sin of slavery.[11]

What Elizur accomplished in his essays during the fall of 1832 was to
disseminate Garrison's radical views throughout the Western Reserve. He
damned the policy of colonization for its accommodation to white racism. "If we should, as a community, treat the black people with the kindness which the Gospel enjoins," he predicted, "that [American
Colonization] Society would die and be forgotten." Unnerved by Elizur's
truculent attack on the highly regarded benevolent organization, Isham
observed that " 'E.W.' appears to be getting quite bold of late." The editor
weakly rebutted that the evils of colonization "exist only in the fervid

imaginations of the Abolitionists." "We do not know," he added, trying to calm troubled waters, "that the two projects necessarily interfere with one another." Unwilling to compromise, Elizur charged that colonization and immediatism were incompatible. "The tendency of the plan [of colonization] is," he countered, "to rivet the chains of the slave" by draining off free blacks to Liberia. In contrast, immediatism challenged Christians to "give up prejudices, and conquer antipathies, and sacrifice wealth so as to abolish slavery, and live on terms of social amity and good neighborhood with the free blacks among us. . . ."[12]

As Elizur's castigation of colonization continued, opposition mounted. Oliver Clark, a local businessman, provided the major defense of colonization in the pages of the *Observer and Telegraph*. He agreed with Elizur that slavery was wrong, but argued that colonization was the only realistic way to encourage emancipation. Since blacks had "scarcely more intelligent notions of right and wrong than the cattle on their plantation," he predicted that Garrisonianism would result in "a scene of destruction and bloodshed" far worse than all the horrors of slavery. He challenged Elizur to prove his principles by "making a negro [*sic*] his intimate companion and friend and unequivocally aver[ing] his willingness to have a sister or daughter marry one."[13]

Elizur cited the Bible to justify immediatism and the oneness of mankind in response to Clark's blatant Negrophobia. Unmasking the bogeyman of miscegenation, he declared, "I, for one, am not so absurdly arrogant as to tell full-grown men and women within what boundaries of complexion they shall restrict choice, in a matter which can affect the rights of no other living person." He explained that immediatists did not plan for the emancipated slaves to run amuck, but rather to become diligent, free laborers under the equitable restraint of the law in a Christian republic.[14]

Despite Isham's maxim that "it ill befits an age of free inquiry to foreclose discussion upon a subject of such moment," by December he had closed the newspaper to Elizur's commentary. The editor explained that the discussion had reached its natural conclusion, but Elizur charged that clerical opponents had threatened the cancellation of five hundred subscriptions. He condemned the censorship as "exactly of a piece with the great machinations of Satan to keep the population of this world from ever seeing the light." Isham denied that economic coercion forced the termination of Elizur's column. He was, however, under considerable pressure from influential community leaders, including David Hudson,

who resented that the local paper had inadvertently become an immediatist organ.[15]

Elizur was not without abolitionist allies in Hudson. At the time of the
newspaper crisis, Green, Elizur's close friend, turned his rhetoric class
into a debate over colonization versus immediatism. The final decision
was ostensibly left to the students who were to weigh the moral issues and
then vote in a campuswide election. One class member complained privately that Professors Green and Wright used "their learning and station"
to gain unfair advantage. The opportunities were, he continued, "unfa-
vorable" for "the remaining friends of Colonization to defend their case
and parry off the attacks of the foes." The debate started a process on
campus by which a majority of students, undoubtedly swayed by their
zealous instructors, soon became immediatists.[16]

Chaplin Green, with Elizur's support, next used the college pulpit to
preach on the subject of immediatism. His four sermons delivered on
successive weeks in November and December 1832 were a thinly veiled de-
nunciation of colonization. Addressing the colonizationists in the congregation, he boldly invoked the style of the jeremiad: "Urge upon them the
hateful nature and damning tendency of their cherished sins, till their un-
derstandings shall condemn them, and their consciences upbraid them,
and their wicked hearts sicken within them." Some town fathers stalked
out; others refused to attend the remaining sermons. David Hudson, the
Reverend Caleb Pitkin, and the Reverend Harvey Coe, college trustees
and outspoken colonizationists, were in high dudgeon over Green's clerical excess. They viewed Garrison's doctrine as a dangerous chimera: "We
see it both naturally and morally impossible, in a moment or a year, to set
all blacks in our land free and raise them to an equality of intellectual
power and privilege with the whites." They were furious that Green's indictment of colonization had emanated from an institution they had established and that it had disturbed the tranquility of the community they
had founded. They declared that a majority of the trustees opposed the
sermons and that the parents of students and patrons of the college were
upset by the emergence of immediatism on campus.[17]

Practical patriarchs, the colonizationist trustees wished to keep evangelical enthusiasm within what they considered reasonable bounds and to
avoid public controversy lest the existence of the college be jeopardized.
The *Observer and Telegraph,* which was largely owned by the college and
its trustees, refused to print Green's sermons. Censorship of Wright and
Green, however, did not prevent the spread of their ideas among the stu-

dents. During the winter of 1832, a committee of Western Reserve colonizationists reported to Ralph Gurley, national secretary of the American Colonization Society, that a "revolution of sentiment" had occurred at the college. "A large portion of the students...have become," they warned, " 'all of a sudden,' thorough-going Abolitionists." The committee characterized Wright and Green, who worked closely with one another, as "bold and warring advocates of this new-fangled theory."[18]

Opposition to Green's sermons rallied immediatist support. "Our prayer is that [the sermons] may awaken extensively the spirit of inquiry, in reference to the principles on which, and measures by which, we should seek, the salvation of our colored brethren," Wright and Storrs wrote in endorsing Green's position. Owen Brown, father of the legendary John Brown and also a college trustee, backed the abolitionist academics. Elizur, Sr., a trustee who had followed his son into immediatism, came to Green's defense. Deacon Wright concluded, "The subject of the abolition of slavery [is] a suitable one to be introduced into the sacred desk on the Sabbath." The father was, however, a moderating force in the controversy, even cautioning his son to tone down his caustic condemnation of colonization.[19]

By December 1832 Elizur, Jr., had joined other immediatists in founding an abolitionist society at Western Reserve College. The society's constitution declared, "Every person of sane mind has a right to immediate freedom from personal bondage of whatever kind, unless imposed by the sentence of the law, for the commission of some crime." Dedicated to the elevation of the African-American, the society urged moral suasion, not violent means, as the desired path to emancipation. It charged colonization with being "wrong, unscriptural, and ill-adapted to effect the abolition of slavery."[20]

A further incident underlined the growing impasse between the Hudson evangelicals. Alexander R. Plumley, an agent of the American Colonization Society, had arrived in town to revitalize the flagging colonization cause. According to Elizur, Plumley had agreed to respond to a list of objections to colonization that Green had drafted. Yet, in his speech at the local Congregational church, Plumley refused to respond to Green's sharply worded indictment and refused to yield the floor to his opponents. Instead he merely refuted a concoction of innocuous criticisms that he had put together for the occasion. Indignant, Elizur and others wrote an exposé for the *Observer and Telegraph,* but Isham refused to publish it.[21]

The contention continued during the winter of 1832–33. Six trustees, including Elizur, Sr., formed a committee to report on the confrontation. Hoping to calm the controversy, they evenhandedly deplored the "unyielding, self-justifying disposition on both sides." They refused to censure the faculty, but warned they might take such action in the future, if necessary. Dissatisfied with these moderate recommendations, Hudson, Coe, and Pitkin held a clandestine meeting with some of the trustees in which they demanded the ouster of Green from the college pulpit. Neither the college president nor the faculty had been invited. Storrs learned, however, of the conclave and made a surprise appearance in which he ardently defended the faculty's right to free speech. Green also defied the colonizationists by publicly declaring that it was his moral duty to address the issue of slavery. Unable to rally sufficient support, the colonizationist trustees waited for a more propitious moment to purge the faculty.[22]

From Boston, William Lloyd Garrison provided moral support and open access to the pages of The Liberator to Hudson's beleaguered immediatists. "It now is palpable as the sun in heaven," he observed about the confrontation, "that the slaveholders and the colonization party are united together to suppress the freedom of speech and of the press and even to exclude from the pulpits of our land those who plead for an immediate abolition of slavery." Garrison was pleased indeed to have found in Elizur's newspaper column an ardent and articulate advocacy of abolitionism. "I have pursued your masterly essays in the Observer and Telegraph," he wrote to his Ohio disciple, "with a delight bordering on enthusiasm." When Isham closed the local paper to Elizur, Garrison printed his essays in The Liberator.[23]

During the first part of 1833 Elizur continued in The Liberator his attack on the American Colonization Society and also on its influential clerical supporters. In a series of essays, he rebutted what he titled "The Christian Spectator's Defense of 'Slavery and Colonization' against Abolition Pamphlets." An orthodox religious publication, The Christian Spectator epitomized what Elizur denounced as "the false ethics of Northern divines...and the cruel apathy and prejudice of Northern Christians." He sharply rebuked ministers who backed colonization as false prophets. Christian duty was to make clear the sin of slavery, not to be "forever plastering over the gap between right and wrong." Elizur's perception of moral hypocrisy among leading churchmen marked a growing—and momentous—disaffection with the religious establishment.[24]

Elizur's polemic in *The Liberator* gained him a national reputation among immediatists. Garrison hailed him as "the Charles Stuart of the West," a reference to the revered British abolitionist. With the support of abolitionists in the Northeast, he traveled to Boston and New York City during April and May of 1833 to debate Robert S. Finley, a leading representative of the American Colonization Society. He proved to be Finley's match. At Boylston Hall and in Boston's leading churches, he frankly told large audiences that "we must preach the naked truth, plainly and pointedly" about slavery and colonization. He met with the Garrisonian circle in Boston and reported that he was pleased at "the progress of Anti-Slavery sentiment in New England."[25]

Acclaimed by immediatists for having "made many converts to the abolition cause" during his Boston tour, Elizur's next stop was New Haven. He had come at the request of Simeon S. Jocelyn, a white minister of a black congregation who had been frustrated in his effort to establish a black school because of strong Negrophobia. Although some Yale faculty supported Jocelyn, much to Elizur's dismay his former professors, Nathaniel William Taylor and Benjamin Silliman, and his boyhood friend, Leonard Bacon, pastor of New Haven's leading Congregational church, remained staunch colonizationists. Elizur sardonically noted that Taylor, the innovative theologian, "did violence to his own dashing 'heresy' in his attempts to defend the Colonization Society." Elizur savored the personal triumph of reviling slavery as "perpetual theft" at his alma mater's North Church, which prompted southern students—his former antagonists—to walk out of his lecture. His tour continued to New York City. At dramatic moments in the ongoing debate with Finley, "colored friends," who were crowded into the galleries, hissed the colonizationist and applauded the abolitionist. Summing up his tour, an antislavery newspaper regretted only that all opponents of immediatism had not "seen how a good man may make his honest convictions known, in relation to a great subject of national reform, without being unjustly charged with fanaticism, or incendiary designs." And Elizur himself was pleased with his missionary work: "I trust many that love the Savior have been brought to think and feel and act on this subject as they never did before."[26]

During the summer of 1833, Elizur's tract, *The Sin of Slavery and Its Remedy,* appeared in print. Garrison praised it as a "valuable pamphlet." In effect a sequel to Garrison's seminal *Thoughts on African Coloniza-*

tion, the pamphlet was intended neither for the slaveholder nor the slave but for evangelicals who had not embraced immediatism. Elizur indicted colonization with fostering "a sympathy with the slave-holders, and a prejudice against the slave, which shows itself in palliating the crime of slave-holding, and in most unrighteously disregarding the rights, and vilifying the characters of free colored men." He espoused an ethical corrective to colonization. In his words, "Under the government of God, as exhibited in this world, there is but one remedy for sin, and that is available only by a repentance, evidenced by reformation." He romantically believed that moral suasion would convert Christians to immediatism until "we expect to see, at length, the full tide of public sympathy setting in favor of the slave."[27]

Having written and spoken extensively on immediatism for over a year, Elizur's abolitionist activity came into critical conflict with his professorial role at Western Reserve College. He had hoped to aid "the cause of our persecuted colored brethren," while teaching at his "beloved college." His brother-in-law, the Reverend John Seward, a colonizationist and college trustee, however, berated him: "May I not ask you to consent, just to go on in attending to the appropriate duties of your office without meddling with subjects which are not necessarily connected with the faithful discharge of those duties?" He viewed Elizur's abolitionism with "regret and grief." The well-publicized East Coast lectures, Seward maintained, had embarrassed the college with a radical reputation that had led patrons to cancel much-needed financial donations. With the exception of Elizur, Sr., and President Storrs, the remaining trustees, Seward threatened, "would feel themselves solemnly bound to pass a vote of disapprobation; unless they can have some reason to expect that a different course will be pursued hereafter."[28]

Despite the possibility of being censured or fired, Elizur boldly pursued a course of agitation. He was instrumental in organizing the Western Reserve Anti-Slavery Society during the late summer of 1833. When colonizationists disrupted their meeting at the Congregational church, immediatists withdrew to his house to complete their business. Elizur blamed clergymen "who cannot give up their grudge against Garrison" with fomenting the opposition to immediatism. In contrast to the rival Western Reserve Anti-Slavery and Colonization Society, the preamble of the Western Reserve Anti-Slavery Society declared that the "slaves should be immediately freed, and that all persons of whatever color, should be placed on a perfect equality, in regard to the operation of the law." The schism between evangelicals over the explosive issue of slavery had taken an institutional form.[29]

The solemn commencement exercises of the college on August 28, 1833, provided the occasion for Elizur's most provocative attack on racist attitudes. With honored guests and dignitaries assembled in the audience, students under his guidance staged a skit that satirized colonization. Warren Isham denounced the presentation as a crude caricature. Elizur defiantly rebutted that "if the faculty of a college are bound to exclude from their commencement exercises every truth which does not accord with public sentiment, or which may be impalatable to some part of the audience, [it] is a position which we were never willing to admit." In addition, Elizur walked arm-in-arm in the academic procession with J. B. Vashon, a black "gentleman" and fellow immediatist visiting from Pittsburgh. "A certain renowned lawyer, when he saw us approaching the meeting house," Elizur recalled, "threatened to 'break down the d——d door' and not to wait and go in 'behind a d——d nigger.'" He "regarded as much as the way the weathercock happened to stand" the outrage from the college trustees, town fathers, and local clergy over his behavior. For Elizur, conventional bigotry prevailed over Christian principles.[30]

A staid academic career was incompatible with Elizur's desire for full-time abolitionist activity. "For one," he told an associate, "I am resolved not to remain in any station which requires silence with regard to human rights." Moreover, his two close friends had departed. Beriah Green had resigned on June 26, 1833 to accept the presidency of Oneida Institute at Whitesboro, New York, where he pioneered a program of biracial education. With Green gone, their joint plan to publish immediatist literature for the Western Reserve collapsed. Elizur pledged "not to stay long where I cannot have the free use of a press." After overtaxing himself with the delivery of a three-hour antislavery address on a rainy May day, Charles Storrs fell critically ill with tuberculosis, a disease that had long plagued him. He took a six-month leave of absence in July and died at his brother's Massachusetts home that September. In addition, Susan, who was frequently ill herself, longed to return to the Northeast. Then, with propitious timing, the philanthropic merchant Arthur Tappan offered Elizur an executive position in the immediatist camp in New York City. A number of factors thus converged to influence him to leave Ohio. As he put it, "Some time before Commencement, I had resolved to resign my place and throw myself wholly upon the cause of the oppressed slave." Prudently, he resigned on August 29, one day after the controversial gradua-tion ceremony, his defiant farewell to Hudson's colonizationists.[31]

Colonizationists proclaimed that the attempt to turn Western Reserve College into a "Seminary for Educating Abolition Missionaries" had failed. "The promptitude [sic] with which the Trustees have accepted the resignation of the late Professor Wright," a letter-writer to the *Observer and Telegraph* noted, "may, under the existing circumstances, be regarded as a doubtful expression of their views in relation to the past, and their determination respecting the future." Elizur publicly denied that he had resigned in order not to be fired. "My resignation was produced," he countered, "not by any attitude the Board had assumed or was likely to assume, but simply by an invitation to another field of labor; and that ev-ery member of the Board probably perceived that a refusal to accept it would be unavailing." He added that any attempt to censor the faculty or limit discussion would cause most of the students to "leave the moment that any restriction should be laid upon them." He concluded that imme-diatism was in a "safe state" at the college.[32]

Elizur was not, however, entirely correct in his assessment. With Storrs mortally ill in Massachusetts and Green at a new post in New York, the trustees were able to contain but not extinguish immediatism on campus. As Elizur privately confided about his resignation, "It was perfectly ob-vious that a majority of the trustees would otherwise have voted for the resolutions against free discussion and they would have probably disci-plined me formally." Sixty-three students signed a petition supporting the right to discuss abolitionism, which helped to prevent the trustees from imposing censorship. Immediatist sentiment and organizations survived Elizur's departure. Nevertheless, without the energetic leadership of Wright, Storrs, and Green, the confrontation at Western Reserve College quickly subsided. Yet their immediatist example provided the precedent for a similar event that occurred at Lane Seminary in January 1834, which convulsed that Cincinnati institution and led to the founding of Oberlin College. Theodore Weld, the inspirational leader of the Lane rebels, had visited Hudson in October 1832 during which time Elizur had helped sway him to immediatism.[33]

The four years at Hudson were a formative period in Elizur's reform career. Immediatism provided him with a holy cause which superseded his former evangelical interests as an aspirant to the ministry, a tract agent, and a professor. It also afforded him a wider scope for exercising his considerable talents as a writer and debater. Outraged that Christians, especially leading churchmen, tolerated slavery through their support of the American Colonization Society, he made common cause with those evangelical dissenters who demanded the immediate renunciation of that most heinous sin, slavery. The courage of his actions and the persuasiveness of his argument earned him widespread recognition beyond Ohio. Now he had the opportunity to assume a major role in the national anti-slavery movement in America's largest city.

Chapter 6

Secretary of the American Anti-Slavery Society

"You know we have organized—that is, put together the mere bones of a national Society," Elizur wrote to his fellow immediatist Amos Phelps shortly after the formation of the American Anti-Slavery Society on December 4, 1833. "It remains to put on the muscles and transfuse the warm blood and breathe into it the breath of life." As secretary of domestic correspondence of the American Anti-Slavery Society for the next six years, Elizur was a central figure in creating a viable abolitionist movement on a national level. His regular activities included supervision of field agents, correspondence with the auxiliary societies, solicitation of funds, editing of publications, circulation of literature, authorship of the annual reports, and formation of policy with other members of the executive committee. On a day-to-day basis, he was in effect the office manager of the New York headquarters. By the end of the decade, the American Anti-Slavery Society had over one thousand affiliates and a yearly budget of nearly fifty thousand dollars. Much of the nation was flooded with over two million pages of abolitionist literature. Elizur's exceptional administrative talents greatly contributed to making the society the central immediatist organization of the 1830s.[1]

The daily experience of coordinating a national organization taught him the utility of what he described as the "plain, common sense view." Yet, the lessons of practicality and efficiency, which he valued as an administrator, were combined with his characteristic moral fervor and outspoken individualism that increasingly alienated his more restrained New York colleagues. Although he highly valued the bonds of comradeship forged by long hours and common dedication to an unpopular cause, he soon chafed at the cautious financial practices and lack of passionate commitment exhibited by Arthur Tappan and his business associates on the executive board. In addition, Elizur's earlier estrangement from organized religion escalated. He refused to join a church, and he rivaled Garrison as one of the most caustic critics of Christian tolerance for slavery. Despite a shared anticlericalism with Garrison, he found the Boston abolitionist too domineering and self-righteous for his taste. In New York the church-oriented leadership exemplified by Arthur's brother Lewis and a clique of former Lane Seminary immediatists headed by Theodore Weld reacted with alarm to Elizur's emerging secularism. Weld even maneuvered behind the scenes to restrict Elizur's influence. Despite his managerial talents, the erosion of Elizur's adherence to formal religious standards undercut his affinity with New York's evangelical leadership.[2]

All began auspiciously enough in late September 1833 when Elizur arrived from Ohio to "more directly plead the case of the slave" at an annual salary of five hundred dollars subsidized by silk merchant Arthur Tappan. His colleagues, most of whom he had met during his spring speaking tour, were new-school evangelicals centered around philanthropic businessmen such as the Tappans, with a sizable clerical contingent including several black ministers. "The design of the friends of the cause at the east...," he explained to Theodore Weld, then at the Lane Seminary in Cincinnati, "is to have a number of sectional societies formed, which may form a national Society by delegates." Elizur's duties involved the coordination of regional meetings in Boston, Providence, New York, and Philadelphia in preparation for the formation of a national society. On October 2 prominent colonizationists and their sympathizers incited a mob of some fifteen hundred Negrophobes to disrupt the scheduled meeting at Clinton Hall to form the New York City Anti-Slavery Society. The abolitionists secretly changed the convention to the Chatham Street Chapel and none too quickly formed the new society before "a genuine drunken, infuriated mob" discovered the ruse. "Who would have thought," Elizur asked incredulously, "that a benevolent society of the nineteenth century would endorse the 'Clinton Hall' mob?" Far from being intimidated by the violence, he predicted that "some thousands" would now see through the "delusions of the Colonization Society."[3]

During their hasty meeting, twenty-eight abolitionists managed to elect officers and ratify a constitution. Arthur Tappan was chosen president, and Elizur officially became corresponding secretary with his salary raised to eight hundred dollars per year. "Slavery is," the delegates resolved, "contrary to the principles of natural justice of our representative form of government, and of the Christian religion." In contrast to the mob's violence, they affirmed their commitment to peaceful emancipation through moral suasion. They also declared their adamant opposition to the temporizing policy of colonization and pledged themselves to obtain for "our colored fellow citizens an equality with the whites of civil and religious privileges."[4]

The threat of anti-abolitionist violence accelerated plans for organizing the national society. William Lloyd Garrison and Lewis Tappan persuaded a hesitant Arthur, as Elizur put it, that "after the Clinton Hall mob the enemy might triumph too much and some friends be disheartened if we should seem to dally on that account." Because the secretary bore much of the burden of preparation for the convention, Elizur would have preferred more time. He nevertheless accepted the "necessity" of "organizing a Society for the nation this season," though "it might have been better to wait." Working closely with Arthur and the Reverend Joshua Leavitt, editor of *The New York Evangelist* and a prominent abolitionist, Elizur mailed out "scores" of letters to selected "friends of immediate abolition." They were invited to attend a convention on December 4 in Philadelphia, an effort to add antislavery Quakers in that important city to the New York–Boston abolitionist axis. He instructed that the time and place of the gathering be kept "confidential" in order to "avoid interruption" by mobs. "Let abolitionists show that they are in earnest, rally from one end of the land to the other, take counsel together, lay their plan of operation, and go forward," he wrote Weld, unsuccessfully trying to entice him from Ohio to the meeting. If the National Anti-Slavery Society of Great Britain and the American Temperance Society could arise from "feeble and obscure" origins to "great influence," so, too, the New York committee reasoned that immediatists could soon "act with irresistible power."[5]

Despite the hurried preparations, nearly sixty abolitionists met at the appointed day in Philadelphia. Elizur attended not only as an officer of the New York City Anti-Slavery Society but also as a representative of the Western Reserve Anti-Slavery Society and his father's own Tallmadge Anti-Slavery Society. Anticipating more violence, he warned ominously, "The demands of the Revolutionary struggle were not half so great." The police restrained a milling mob, and the delegates proceeded to found the American Anti-Slavery Society. Patterned after the Protestant benevolent societies, the new organization had a distinctive evangelical character. In impassioned prose, "The Declaration of Sentiments," which Garrison stayed up all night to complete, called for "the abolition of slavery by the spirit of repentance." "There are, at the present time," he enjoined, "the highest obligations resting on the people of the free states to remove slavery by moral and political action, as prescribed in the Constitution of the United States." He urged creation of auxiliary societies, use of agents, circulation of antislavery literature, and enlistment of "the pulpit and the press" in the holy cause. Similarly, the society's constitution invoked "Christian religion," "our republican form of government," "the prosperity of the country," and "appeals to conscience" against the system of slavery, all shibboleths for entry into the immediatist camp.[6]

The significant difference between the American Anti-Slavery Society and conventional Protestant stewardship was in their goals. The Philadelphia delegates advocated nothing less than a revolution in racial relations. They called for "the entire abolition of slavery in the United States" and damned slaveholding as "a heinous crime in the sight of God." Slavery was a dynamic aspect of the antebellum economy, and immediatism held profound implications for the North as well as the South. The society's constitution also declared that blacks, "according to their intellectual and moral worth, share an equality with whites of civil and religious privileges," an egalitarianism at complete loggerheads with the well-entrenched racial caste system of Jacksonian society. Consciously couched in the language of Christian conscience and American republicanism, renouncing violent means and affirming the rule of law, the abolitionists confronted the country's most serious problem within the context of the nation's founding ideals.[7]

In keeping with the emotionally charged drama of the moment, Elizur intently oversaw the convention, which his friend Beriah Green chaired and the New York contingent directed. "The young professor...," Quaker poet John Greenleaf Whittier recalled of Wright, "with a look of sharp concentration in keeping with an intellect keen as a Damascus blade, closely watched the proceedings through his spectacles, opening his mouth only to speak to the purpose." With the exception of Garrison, who was chosen foreign secretary, the New York abolitionists took over the leadership of the American Anti-Slavery Society. The delegates elected Arthur Tappan its president and Elizur its domestic secretary. Along with the other participants, including three black men and four Quaker women, Elizur signed Garrison's statement of principles on December 7. In emulation of the Founding Fathers who had met in Philadelphia over a half century ago, the American Anti-Slavery Society had set its program "before our country and the world." A new generation, he later reflected, had assumed "the cause which had warmed the hearts and kindled the eloquence of Franklin, Rush, and Jay."[8]

As a full-time administrator at the New York headquarters, Elizur's challenge was, as he wrote Weld, that "the national society is organized, the question is whether it shall live." He was a permanent member of the agency committee along with Joshua Leavitt and Arthur Tappan, the chairman. The former colporteur was responsible for the recruitment of agents who would give lectures, facilitate the formation of auxiliaries, distribute literature, and spur fundraising. Paid at the rate of eight dollars per week plus traveling expenses, the agents were assigned specific territories. The executive committee instructed them to stress the society's "great fundamental principle of IMMEDIATE ABOLITION" and "to insist principally on the SIN OF SLAVERY, because our main hope is the consciences of men." The church-oriented strategy of the New York abolitionists was forthrightly stated in their directions to "especially stir up ministers," for they were "the hinges of the community," and, if possible, "to obtain a house of worship" for antislavery lectures. Agents were also expected to "write frequently" to Elizur, who supervised their operations.[9]

By February 1834 Elizur had sent out "about a dozen commissions" to "sterling abolitionists [in] different parts of the country." "We must have men," he emphasized, "who will electrify the mass wherever they move—and they must move on no small scale." Unsuccessful in recruiting the much sought-after Weld to "buckle on the whole armor" for Ohio, Elizur sent him a partial commission to do whatever he could in the "immediate vicinity" of Cincinnati, where he was leading the immediatist insurgency at the Lane Seminary. Elizur was successful in securing the Reverend Amos A. Phelps, "a first rate man," as the society's first permanent agent. "It will be enough for you to know," he peremptorily told his former Yale classmate, who on April 1 undertook his assignment to canvass New England, "that Jesus Christ has a right to any man whom he pleases to call—and we trust that you will regard this as His call." Six months after the formation of the society, some seven agents were in the field and more than sixty auxiliaries had been established.[10]

During the formative period of the American Anti-Slavery Society, shared opposition to the American Colonization Society united regionally based immediatists from the Lane rebels in Cincinnati to the New York evangelicals and Boston Garrisonians. "The victory is ours!" Elizur exclaimed on learning from Leavitt that the colonizationists, lagging in critical support, had reported more than forty thousand dollars in debts at their January 1834 convention in Washington. "Even the rubbish of the Colonization Society will," he predicted to Weld, "not long lie between us and the monster's den." As a result, he informed Phelps, "The whole South is in a ferment—deep and effectual." Despite the exhilarating news that the colonizationists were "found to be bankrupt in funds as well as moral principles," and despite Elizur's own strong words, he lectured Garrison not to gloat. "Let us show ourselves worthy," he cautioned his sharp-tongued colleague, "to retain the field that truth has now won for us." Elizur had earlier confided to Beriah Green that Garrison's failure to "economize his epithets" alienated "some good men, who do not discern the whole cause, [and] totally misapprehend his spirit." " 'The wrath of the Lamb,' " as Elizur described Garrison's abrasive style and self-righteous personality, was at odds with his more constrained organizational concerns.[11]

Moreover, Elizur soon grew restive with what he regarded as the overly cautious leadership of Arthur Tappan in New York. Both worried about the negative effects of Garrison's belligerency. And Elizur had originally endorsed Arthur's prudent plan "not to start the National Car till we had got our team harnessed." Ten months after the hasty formation of the national society, he still bemoaned to Beriah Green that "Garrison and the New Englanders prevailed, and the Car was set a-going by hand and now we are trying to 'tackle' while it is in motion—no easy matter." He valued sound organization and financial stability, but Arthur's policies were too conservative for him. Arthur's goal was to make the American Anti-Slavery Society an attractive successor to the American Colonization Society for morally discerning evangelical gentlemen and clerics who would guide the nation to repentance. In addition to businessmen John Rankin and William Green, Jr., Arthur garnered support from William Jay, son of the former chief justice of the Supreme Court, physician Abraham Cox, and wealthy landowner Gerrit Smith. Elizur's desire to combine rapid expansion of the society with a sharp indictment of slavery came into increasing conflict with this group's concern for respectability and restraint.[12]

One of Elizur's major efforts was to broaden the financial base of the society to the grass-roots membership. Initially Arthur and his wealthy friends had generously capitalized the society as they had also come to the financial relief of an impecunious Garrison. At the society's second annual meeting on May 9, 1835, treasurer John Rankin's report revealed that more than one-half of the society's income of a meager $9,831.29 for the fiscal year had come from contributions of the wealthy members of the executive committee. The dependency of the abolitionist cause on a few rich men held it hostage to their pocketbooks and priorities. "Indeed, the idea that friend Tappan," Elizur realized, "will do all the giving must be broken up, or our society is a nullity." In frustration he complained to Phelps that "want of funds" postponed publication of the *Anti-Slavery Reporter* and the appointment of "more first rate agents." The fluctuating cycle of the national economy during the Jackson and Van Buren administrations of the 1830s compounded the society's problems. "The business pressure upon the country...," Elizur explained to Weld in the summer of 1834, "curtails the means which would be at our disposal for the advancement of the cause."[13]

Elizur solicited "the friends of abolition scattered up and down for the funds we need." "It needs only to organize," he told his sister, "so as to have each have his share of the burden to carry all before us." Arthur and his associates were reluctant to "give more liberally," Elizur explained to Weld, until "they see the friends of the cause cheerfully and systematically coming up to their help." In addition, he worried about the "critical state" of the financially ailing *Liberator* in 1834. He made a ten-dollar contribution and suggested Garrison turn the newspaper's editorship over to David Lee Childs so he could spend his full time fund raising.[14]

The national society strongly encouraged abolitionists, as Elizur put it, to "give their immediatism a practical shape." The last Monday of each month was a time of prayer for the oppressed slaves and a time for donations. On the Fourth of July, abolitionists held sober, nonalcoholic rallies and contributed to the crusade as they did on August 1, the anniversary of emancipation in the British West Indies. "Let it be understood," Elizur exhorted, "that a single cent will put in existence a tract which may gain a powerful friend to our cause." Such appeals inspired his mother and her friends to contribute three dollars raised from the sale of their knitting, an example multiplied many times over by other committed women. By the end of 1835, Elizur hoped to publish fifty thousand copies of the *Anti-Slavery Record,* which generated income through monthly sales at 12.5 cents per issue. He also hectored the society's agents to have the auxiliaries forward locally generated money to New York.[15]

Grass-roots appeals succeeded in almost tripling the society's annual income to $25,866.30 in 1835 compared to a year earlier. "A much larger proportion of the donations than in former years consists of small sums among the mass of people," Elizur and his colleagues happily reported in 1838. Yet, the circumspect businessmen on the executive committee imposed a restraint on expenditures that galled Elizur. "Our friend A.T. [Arthur Tappan] should be disabused of the idea," he complained to Weld, "that if he and G. Smith and two or three others should fail to pay their notes at three o'clock some day, the cause of God's oppressed would fall through!" Along with Arthur Tappan and Gerrit Smith, Elizur was at odds with John Rankin and William Green, Jr., whom he charged fell into "a fit of practical 'expediency' " and put "prudence against faith" in the crusade. The national economic depression of the late 1830s placed additional constraints on what Elizur had hoped would become an expansive fiscal policy. The society's annual income slowed from an increase of almost $5,800 between 1837 and 1838 to only $3,100 in the next comparable period, a decline of 47 percent. The Panic of 1837 took with it the firm of Arthur Tappan and Company, bankrupt with a staggering debt of more than one million dollars. The society's budget was stretched so thin that Elizur, though strapped himself for money, vowed not to draw his salary "till necessity" made him. The rapid growth of funding up to 1837 leveled off during the depression and forced cutbacks in the aggressive national campaign Elizur sponsored.[16]

Latent differences between Elizur and Arthur's faction of the executive committee were also made manifest over their reactions to the July 1834 race riot in New York City. "Daily presses with few exceptions," Elizur accurately reported, aroused "a series of the most frenzied and ungovernable mobs" with the inflammatory accusation that abolitionists promoted "intermarriage of blacks and whites" and plotted "the destruction of their country." Working-class whites methodically attacked the homes and businesses of prominent abolitionists such as the Tappan brothers and John Rankin. The worst violence was committed on July 10–11 as the mob rampaged through black neighborhoods in lower Manhattan, demolishing the home and church of black Episcopalian minister Peter Williams, a member of the society's executive committee. Though threatened by two knife-wielding men, Elizur escaped the brunt of the violence. He convinced Mayor Cornelius W. Lawrence to suspend the East River ferry to bar the Manhattan mob from crossing to his Brooklyn home. Susan was ailing after having recently given birth, and neither mother nor infant could be safely moved. Nevertheless, Elizur barricaded their home and stood ready at the door with an ax to defend his family.[17]

With order finally restored on July 12 by a military show of force, Arthur Tappan and John Rankin, whose businesses had been endangered by the mob, quickly distributed a "Disclaimer" on behalf of the American Anti-Slavery Society. They disavowed any desire "to encourage intermarriages between white and colored persons" or "to violate the constitution and laws of the country." Specifically they disapproved of "a handbill recently circulated in this city, the tendency of which is thought to excite resistance to the laws." That July 8 handbill titled "Lookout for Kidnappers!!!" told of the plight of Jock Lockley and his family who were being tried as fugitive slaves, and concluded with the ringing injunction, "Opposition to Tyrants is Obedience to God." Elizur wrote the handbill, but, he asserted, as a private individual, not as a representative of the national society. William L. Stone, the anti-abolitionist editor of the *Commercial Advertiser,* denounced such ideas for encouraging "forcible resistance to the laws" and provoking the riots. Tappan's and Rankin's law and order disclaimer was in clear contrast to Elizur's opposition to the "villainy perpetrated by the law" on the hapless Lockley.[18]

On July 17 seven members of the executive committee, including Tappan, Rankin, and Wright, signed a letter to Mayor Lawrence and the common council. The statement elaborated on the disclaimer of July 12 and also expressed the abolitionists' determination as "free American citizens to live and die" by their principles. Nevertheless, Elizur complained privately to Beriah Green, "Disclaimers are too negative while millions are held in unrelenting bondage—besides 'amalgamation' is too small a crime to be worth a disclaimer." Unlike some of his colleagues, he saw the July riots as a boon to organizing. "The violence of our enemies," he wrote Garrison, "has in a few days accomplished for us the work of years." He informed his sister, "Since the riots there has been a much greater demand for our publications." And he reassured his parents that "I never felt more safe and happy or more confident of success than now." The week of anti-abolitionist violence also tempered his romantic radicalism, giving his world view a more realistic cast while hardening his resolve. "[Some] talk of abolishing slavery in five years—but I have put on the harness for life—," he confided to his sister, "and expect to see worse times—It may be I shall live long and still die before the happy jubilee comes—but come it will."[19] He now recognized the depth of opposition, but he remained confident of final victory.

Despite his differences with Arthur Tappan and John Rankin, Elizur thought it "astonishing" that "our wealthiest members," given "their

LOOK OUT FOR
KIDNAPPERS!!!

Last March, Dr. RUFUS HAYWOOD seized and imprisoned his *cousin*, John Lockley of this city, and his family, AS SLAVES. He *swore* that they left Raleigh in Dec. 1832. Lockley *proved* that he was in this city before that time. The Recorder allowed HAYWOOD, on account of his respectability, more time to prove his *property*. He went to the South, came back with a full pack of *slave holders*, and undertook to prove that Lockley absconded in Dec. 1831. Lockley issued his writ, as allowed by our laws, and the *common law* of England, for a *jury trial*. Haywood endeavored by his "learned counsel" to overthrow the law granting a jury trial, as *unconstitutional*. The Judges were slow to decide. In the mean time Haywood gets a requisition from the Governor of North Carolina, and on the top of it a warrant from Gov. Marcy, to the Sheriff, to give up Lockley and his wife as *fugitives from justice*,

For Stealing!

And the kidnapper is now waiting, with the warrant in his pocket, to hear the decision of the Court, which will be given in Utica to-day. If it be in his favor, he will take off *all three*, by a certificate from the Recorder! If in favor of *justice*, he will take the *man* and *wife*, by virtue of his warrant, and leave the *child!!*

Will men who love LIBERTY, and believe that all *innocent men* have a right to it, tamely see such villany perpetrated *by law* in this city?----A man would be *hung* for it, if committed on the Coast of Africa!

OPPOSITION TO TYRANTS IS OBEDIENCE TO GOD.

New York, June 8th, 1831.

(Reprinted from University Microfilms International, *American Periodical Series*, II, reel 391.)

business habits," had come through the riots "so well." While the gentlemen on the executive committee escaped the city with their families during the heat of August, Elizur was impatient "to take advantage of the crisis." James G. Birney, a prominent colonizationist and former slaveholder, had recently converted to immediatism largely through Weld's influence. "Mr. Birney is ready to devote his whole energy to the cause," Elizur rejoiced. "He must be supported." But Arthur did not share Elizur's urgency about enlisting Birney's services. "But we must not consent to this," Elizur wrote Weld in "strict confidence." Left virtually alone in the empty New York headquarters, Elizur personally wrote two hundred letters to "auxiliaries and friends" to distribute Birney's celebrated *Letter on Colonization*. "It will be our fault," he averred to his father, "if it does not pierce slavery through all its brazen shields." Elizur planned to print one hundred thousand copies of Birney's *Letter* by which "time Mr. A. T. according to the laws of his mind, which are anomalous, will be ready to afford any part of the expense that may be requisite." On August 19 Wright, Leavitt, and Lewis Tappan prevailed on Arthur to fund Birney for a three-month agency in Kentucky with the understanding that other contributions would be used to extend the appointment for a full year.[20]

The conservative faction frustrated Elizur, but the New York headquarters was an exciting, challenging place. "Our hearts are wonderfully knit together," he rejoiced in good fellowship after the July riots. Even in 1842 after Arthur and Elizur had gone their separate ways, he named a son after his former patron. Elizur also thrived on the myriad responsibilities of his catch-all job. "I have but one regret," he told his parents after a few months at his post. "I have to see a thousand things on every side of me which need to be done, but which remain undone." On one typically busy day in March 1834, he was answering correspondence, mailing *Anti-Slavery Reporters*, soliciting charity for the imprisoned Lockley family, preparing for a lecture at the Chatham St. Chapel, and compiling an account of an escaped slave. By the fall of 1834, he was overwhelmed. "I am ready to confess," he wrote Beriah Green, "that the physical part of my labors has been permitted to assume a most absurd preponderance." There was not time for "moral and intellectual life." Part of the problem was that he had to learn "the job of business doing" on the spot. With his eye for efficiency, he quickly saw that his work could be divided into specialized tasks with "Lewis Tappan for a financial secretary, a good clerk to conduct the details of the office, and I should be left free to the use of my pen." Arthur and his business friends, as Elizur grouched, "could be convinced by no logic of mine that *economy* required them to allow me any more physical assistance than could be hired for ten or twelve shillings per week."[21]

The harried secretary was grateful for Lewis Tappan's volunteer assistance. A central figure on the executive committee, the older man regularly lent an experienced hand with finances, publications, and office management after finishing a long day's work at the Tappan brothers' store. Unlike Arthur, Rankin, Green, and Jay, Lewis during the mid-1830s formed a close working relationship with Elizur. Both shared a concern with expeditious procedures. "Brother L. is a most wonderful man for the dispatch of business and truer than the needle to the pole," Elizur wrote Weld. Nevertheless, Elizur still bore the responsibility of keeping the office functioning on a day-to-day basis. "My future is shingled over with mortgages to every minute," he sighed in 1835. And a year later, he still found "our poor self has too many irons in the fire."[22]

New York was hectic, but stimulating—a pleasing contrast to backwoods Ohio. The Manhattan headquarters was the nerve center of the abolitionist movement. In addition to the Tappans, Elizur worked side by side with such immediatist stalwarts as Joshua Leavitt, William Goodell, Amos Phelps, John Greenleaf Whittier, Henry B. Stanton, James G. Birney, and Theodore Weld, all of whom served some time at the national office during the 1830s. Their strong sense of solidarity was reflected in their evangelical form of address. Other holy warriors were "brothers" and "sisters"; or, as Elizur affectionately put it, "[I] should be glad to see Dear Stuart" in welcome to visiting English abolitionist Charles Stuart. Even subcommittee meetings in the office opened with a prayer, bonding blacks and whites, purse-conscious merchants and aggressive reformers. "There was not want of talk," Elizur reported to his sister, referring to the evening he and Susan entertained the popular author and immediatist Lydia Maria Child along with house guest George Thompson, an English abolitionist who was an agent of the society.[23]

The Wrights shared half of a two-story frame house with Elizur's colleague William Goodell on the residential edge of Brooklyn. Elizur walked a mile to the Fulton Ferry, where he took a five-minute steamship ride across the East River that brought him to within a half mile of his 130 Nassau Street office on lower Manhattan. Like modern commuters, he sheltered his family from the commercial district "agog with all kinds of chariots and horses" and "tremendous high stores." "We have a pleasant little yard, a woodhouse and a little stable in which we keep a red cow to give milk for the babies," he observed of his modest home. Unlike some wives of abolitionists, Susan remained apart from her husband's crusade. She kept the house and reared the children, freeing her husband to work long hours at the office. Some nights he arrived home at 10:00 P.M. after a sixteen-hour day, finding Susan waiting for him "quite lonely."[24]

A growing family did create demands on a busy reform career. Apparently avoiding birth control techniques, Elizur and Susan were a very fertile couple. She bore four children in little more than five years of their stay in Brooklyn. Infant diseases killed two of their children and plagued three others. "The little one had become exceeding dear," he sadly remembered of his daughter Clara, who had died "after a long agony of suffering" from whooping cough. "Her affectionate little ways we cannot think of without opening the fountain of tears afresh." He emotionally endured "this great affliction" by rededicating himself to the cause of the oppressed African-Americans, with whose suffering he empathized. Yet, the busy schedule and erratic pay of the reformer took its toll on family life. "My wife quite sick—worn out with a sick child for some days past and I am all in hurry, bustle and sweat—but in good hope!" he scrawled on the margins of a letter to Weld crammed with abolitionist news.[25]

With the groundwork of the society in place, Elizur was eager to proceed on all fronts. He and other immediatists were dismayed, however, at Arthur's attraction in early 1835 to the Union for the Relief and Improvement of the Colored Race. The Boston-based union was a recently created halfway house for prominent evangelicals such as Lyman Beecher who were alienated from immediatism but unhappy with colonization. "The news from New England is highly encouraging," Elizur learned firsthand from Lydia Maria Child in March. "The cause has over-powered all opposition—colonization and prejudices and the new vamped 'Union.'" Arthur was soon "convinced that the favor which he began to bestow on it was misplaced," Elizur gladly reported. Embarrassed by his near apostacy, Arthur yielded to the imperative of his colleagues, as Elizur put it, that "the truth must be preached."[26]

The executive committee prepared to use the 1835 convention to gain support for an all-out national campaign. "We are striving," Elizur informed Weld, "to secure a full delegation from all parts of the country to that meeting." In a reassuring display of unity and determination, immediatists gathered on May 9 in New York for what was to be a pivotal meeting. Disavowing Arthur's conservatism, delegates approved a strongly worded series of resolutions by William Lloyd Garrison, James G. Birney, and George Thompson that reaffirmed their allegiance to immediate abolition. Proposals by Arnold Bufum, Amos Phelps, and Lewis Tappan to petition Congress against slavery in the District of Columbia and the territories, to expand the auxiliaries, and, in Elizur's words, "to use the press on a large scale" gave concrete direction to the society. In his annual report for 1834, Elizur stressed the rising tide of abolitionism. He noted that two hundred new auxiliaries had been formed since the last meeting and that through the work of such dynamic agents as Amos Phelps, Charles Stuart, George Thompson, Theodore Weld, and Samuel J. May, "thousands have been brought to see in our growing cause the dawn of a brighter day for our dishonored country, and her millions of enslaved children." He was very pleased that the convention embodied his concern for "a plain common sense view of how emancipation and abolition are to be brought about by the correction of public sentiment."[27]

With the mandate of the convention, the New York headquarters was, as Elizur said in June, "making arrangements with all possible expedition to use the press on a larger scale—shall issue gratuitously from 20,000 to 50,000 of some publication or other every week." Lewis Tappan, head of the publications committee, and Elizur bore the daily responsibility for what became known as "the great postal campaign," an effort to flood the nation with abolitionist literature. The former tract agent marveled at the technological efficiency of the new steam-driven press, "one of the most powerful engines of reform." He edited the *Anti-Slavery Record* (which replaced the *Anti-Slavery Reporter* after 1835), *Human Rights, Quarterly Anti-Slavery Magazine,* and occasionally filled in at *The Emancipator,* the society's official organ. Elizur designed the *Anti-Slavery Record,* which sold at the reasonable price of 12.5 cents and had attractive woodcuts, to draw a general audience. "It is well known that no publications are more effective than well prepared and beautifully printed tracts," he noted. *Human Rights,* or, as Elizur punned "Human Wrights," was a popular, four-page monthly selling for 25 cents. He intended the *Quarterly Anti-Slavery Magazine* to "tell with overwhelming force upon our Seminaries and upon our reading and thinking men," an abolitionist counterpart to the intellectual *North American Review.* "I am in agonies," he complained, short of time and copy, "at the responsibility of such a thing as the *Quarterly* ought to be." Despite the rush of dashing off a "sheet or two overnight" for the printer's deadline, Elizur was a skilled editor, whom Garrison hailed as "a thorough logician, dextrous, transparent, straight-forward."[28]

One of the publishing committee's challenges was to enliven *The Emancipator,* which Elizur lamented "has thus far rested." William Goodell left the editorship in 1836 to run the Utica-based *Friend of Man,* much to Elizur's relief. Instead of Goodell's "interminable 'House that Jack built' style," he wanted a replacement "whose sinews are of brass and his blood of electricity." "After a thorough search we could find none," Elizur noted in the spring of 1836, "except Brother Phelps." The illness of Phelps's wife soon forced his return to Boston, and Joshua Leavitt, who had to sell his financially troubled newspaper *The Evangelist,* took charge. Leavitt, who had abandoned the pulpit for immediatism, was not only the best editor *The Emancipator* had, but he became a close ally of Elizur's at the New York headquarters.[29]

"The great postal campaign" was an impressive success. The total number of pages of books, pamphlets, papers, and tracts the society issued for the year ending in May 1836 was well over a million, a dramatic ninefold increase over the previous year. "What seems now the greatest difficulty," Elizur complained in June 1835, "is to get the names of *inquiring, candid, reading* men who are not abolitionists." He singled out ministers, public houses, and lycea for distribution of *The Emancipator.* "Immense good," he believed, "may be done in this way." In addition, the society started publishing in 1835 the *Slave's Friend,* a juvenile monthly whose moral tales captured Elizur's dictum that "children are all abolitionists." Despite the publication bonanza, the eager editor wanted to *"expend ten times as much."*[30]

A violent anti-abolitionist backlash throughout the nation, however, greeted the society's publication campaign. On July 30, 1835 a mob of three thousand burned bundles of antislavery literature looted from the Charleston, South Carolina post office. Major riots followed that October in Utica and Boston. Local disturbances broke out from New England to Illinois and only waned after 1837. Supported by President Andrew Jackson and outraged southerners, the New York City postmaster barred abolitionist literature bound for the South. Northern politicians added their approval to the censorship of the mails. The New York committee was clearly surprised by the widespread, hostile reaction. "Anti-Abolition mobs appear to have had their day," Elizur misjudged in March 1835. "I doubt whether they can be brought into fashion so easily as before." Another casualty of the persistent riots was romantic reform. Elizur's utopian sentiment expressed in 1833 that "the sympathy of Christians will mingle and bear down in one still, deep rapid current" appeared naive at best only a few years later.[31]

Yet Elizur remained convinced during 1835 and 1836 that the society's appeals to Christian conscience and republican principle were the correct strategy. "Notwithstanding the southern storm," he observed after his own literature fueled the Charleston bonfire, "we are frequently applied to by southerners who are in a state of serious and anxious inquiry for papers!" After a year of turmoil, he pointed out that "these anti-abolition meetings and mobs have done more than could have been done by the arguments of a thousand lecturers to convince the sober and disinterested that slavery is a crime." Indeed, by May 1836 the number of new auxiliaries more than doubled and total membership swelled to fifty thousand, while annual income climbed to twenty-six thousand dollars and publication output exceeded a million pages. "I do believe God is pouring out a medicine," he still believed, "that will cure the church if not the nation of 'gradualism' and 'expedience.'"[32]

But by 1836 abolitionists began to reassess in significantly different ways the original course of the movement in the face of endemic hostility. At the third annual convention of the society in New York, Garrison, himself the victim of a Boston mob, damned American society as a "land of religious despotism and home of republican injustice." In little more than a year he extended the logic of his sweeping condemnation to conclude that only a fundamental moral transformation could redeem a thoroughly corrupted nation.[33]

At the same May 10, 1836 meeting, Elizur offered a contrasting analysis. In part, he explained the anti-abolitionist reaction in social and economic terms, an important departure from the usual moralistic mentality characteristic of most abolitionists. "Let it be understood," he instructed in a suggestive but hesitant class analysis, "we do not say [rioting] was the answer of the North—it was the answer of those who set themselves up as the organs of the North—the merchants, and politicians, and aristocrats of our principal cities, who are most corrupted by southern trade and companionship, and their humble imitators in our more inland towns." In order to defend their southern "interests," "purse proud aristocrats" in the North had inflamed mobs of "penniless profligates" against the abolitionists. But the vast majority of the American people, he continued, the "mass of uncorrupt yeomanry in the land" and "the clear-headed, free laborers and mechanics of the North" were the natural ene-mies of slavery. It was this Jeffersonian "bone and muscle of the nation" that the abolitionists would arouse. Lapsing back into evangelical rheto-ric, Elizur predicted that they would "lay slaveholders under an embargo, surround them, as the moral invalids of the universe with a cordon sani-taire." "Though the great men of the city dare not be with us," he had concluded after the 1834 New York riots, "hundreds of small ones are coming up to the standard."[34]

In contrast to Garrison, Elizur argued that American institutions were not intrinsically degenerate. Although he was the sharpest clerical critic in the New York headquarters, he still concurred with the 1836 statement of Henry B. Stanton, a former Lane seminarian, that "we rely mainly for the removal of slavery upon the faithful testimony of the Christian Church against it." "But to suppose the church will not yield to truth," Elizur added, "is to suppose her radically corrupt." Along with his New York colleagues, he believed that "the church will come out purified as gold." The South had barred "professedly Abolition papers," but, he told Birney, "she cannot shut out the influence of our renovated churches." In the spring of 1836 he still worried about "a tendency in some parts to build hope too much on political measures. We ought all to understand each other on this point, and be made to feel that our busi-ness lies with the heart of the nation, not its fingers and toes." Neverthe-less, he strongly supported "our excellent form of government" and bemoaned that "slavery makes our republic a laughing stock."[35]

Despite its avowed church-oriented strategy, the executive committee initiated in 1836 what would become a growing political agenda. "The postal controversy" had given the issues of abolition, slavery, and censor-ship unprecedented national attention. The society now sought to seize this opportunity in order to mobilize a broad, antislavery constituency through a greatly expanded petition and agency campaign. Petitions to Congress against slavery in federally supervised areas, notably the Dis-trict of Columbia and the territories, was a standard abolitionist tactic. But such a deluge of antislavery memorials reached the House of Repre-sentatives by 1836 that a bipartisan coalition of Democrats and Whigs voted to "gag" or table these petitions in order to block the sensitive issue of abolition from entering the national political dialogue and disrupting the sectional alliances of the two-party system. The society responded by calling John Greenleaf Whittier to New York that May to coordinate the enlarged petition campaign in which he was subsequently joined by Theodore Weld and Henry B. Stanton.[36]

Although Elizur did not devote full time to the petition campaign, he was an enthusiastic supporter. While the congressional debate on a gag rule was under way in the winter of 1835–36, he instructed agents to forward petitions to Abner Hazeltine, a New York delegate to the House of Representatives. Hazeltine, a "firm friend of the oppressed," pledged to "present, cordially, all that are committed to him." The congressional protocol of automatically tabling antislavery petitions became a means, Elizur explained, to educate the public that "a right guarded expressedly by the Constitution has become a dead and buried right." The society commended "the upright and manly course" of former President John Quincy Adams, then a Whig congressman from Massachusetts, in his principled defense of "the periled right of petition." Representatives William Slade of Vermont, Seth Gates of western New York, and Joshua Giddings of the Western Reserve joined "old Man Eloquent" in defying the House ban. Excited by the political agitation, Elizur exhorted the May 1837 convention, "Let us year by year send up increasing floods of petitions till our object is gained or a satisfactory reason given for refusing it." The same convention instructed him to supervise an ambitious campaign with each county antislavery society that would distribute petitions to "active individuals in each town" in the free states. A year later he happily reported that petitions "poured into Congress without precedent." By the spring of 1839 an astonishing two million people had signed antislavery petitions.[37]

In addition to the expanded publications and petition campaign, the executive committee embarked in the summer of 1836 on an effort to increase the number of the society's agents in the field. Elizur reported that as a result of the agency system, "Prejudice has been removed, light has been shed, love has been kindled, and thousands have been brought to see in our growing cause the dawn of a brighter day for the dishonored country and her millions of enslaved children." Weld's phenomenal success since the fall of 1834 in converting hostile audiences in Ohio, western Pennsylvania, and upstate New York made him the logical choice to head the society's revamped agency program. After conferring with the New York committee in July, he agreed to recruit the "Seventy," a biblical reference to the number of missionaries who had assisted Moses and Jesus. Elizur emphasized that these agents "have the destinies of millions in their hands." With abolitionist publications excluded from the South and riots sweeping northern cities, he exhorted, "Let us take hold of the country—the yeomanry of the *country towns,* leaving the cities to themselves for the present, and we shall soon carry the question."[38]

Elizur was the central liaison person in New York with the "Seventy" while Weld was active in the field. He was a permanent member of the agency committee, which Arthur chaired, to which Weld submitted the names of his recruits for final approval, commissioning, and payment of salaries. "The success of Bro. Weld has been more cheering...," Elizur wrote to Birney in the fall of 1836. "We hope to have 50 lecturers in the field in October and thence forward that their number and success will go on increasing." Much to his frustration, however, the "Wall St. fever" postponed appointment of twelve prospective agents from Oberlin College whose names Weld had submitted to the committee on October 25. "A. Tappan especially was afraid," Elizur informed Weld, "to go ahead any more till he could see where the funds were to come from." While Elizur and Joshua Leavitt pressured Arthur "to go on again with full faith and steam," Elizur cajoled a reluctant Weld to chair an agents' convention in New York that November. Elizur's concern with effective organization and esprit de corps conflicted with the solitary Weld's sense of pietistic autonomy and desire for anonymity. "It must be folly for fifty agents just about to rush upon the 'hydras, gorgons and chimeras' dire of prejudice and slavery, [not] to sit down *together* for a fortnight, make common stock of experience, and settle understandingly the *principles of their measures,*" he pleaded with Weld. "When our band of worthies come to pray together and feel together," he felt the spirit of unity would put the "silly fears" of Arthur's business circle to "a shameful rout."[39]

Despite these difficulties, Elizur reported to the fourth annual convention on May 12, 1837 that "upwards of seventy agents" were at work. The number of auxiliaries increased to 1,006, of which 484 were created in that record year. These measures of tangible success were, however, undermined by the Panic of 1837 and a tendency toward decentralization of abolitionism from New York's control that cut into the society's funds and forced a sharp retrenchment in the agency system.[40]

The achievements of the society by the mid-1830s, even in garnering some cooperation from national politicians, contrasted glaringly with the failure of all the major denominations, the benevolent empire, and most clergymen to embrace immediatism. The American Bible Society turned down the abolitionists' offer of five thousand dollars, which Elizur initiated, "to see to it that every colored family in the United States be furnished with a copy of the Bible." He was the first at the New York headquarters to point out the failure of the society's church-oriented abolitionism, an indictment that Garrison was making simultaneously in Boston. Since childhood, Elizur's deeply held sense of Christian ethics conflicted with what he ridiculed as the "fogland" of theology that lost "sight of the most precious beacons of faith." "Christ was a 'Radical'—see his sermon on the Mount. So were his Apostles," he wrote in denouncement of religious "conservatism" in December 1835. "Our soul is sick of the everlasting hypocrisy of this nation," he thundered in an 1836 essay titled "Slavery and Its Ecclesiastical Defenders." He shocked the pietistic Weld by dismissing a "very orthodox cavil" with the recollection that "I was once refused a license to preach. . . because I had not studied *systematic* theology, and I confess I have never been very chary of the technics thereof." He vowed "to speak English, the whole English and nothing but English, whatever may become of creeds and shorter catechisms."[41]

The anti-abolitionism of leading ministers drew forth Elizur's spleen. "O! the matchless wisdom of reverend apes" was his sarcastic dismissal of the proslavery apologia of the eminent Andover professor Moses Stuart. "I beseech you," he wrote the Reverend Leonard Bacon, "to make common cause with humanity against brute force and ecclesiastical chicanery." He lambasted his former Yale teacher Nathaniel William Taylor and his one-time idol Lyman Beecher for their retreat before the "human flesh trade." He reviled "our reverend Doctors of Divinity" who "in one breath preach from the Bible that it's 'a mortal sin to steal a pin' and, in the next, appeal to the same Bible to show that stealing a man or woman is no sin at all!" His blunt response to Charles Grandison Finney, then president of Oberlin College, that abolition should be "an appendage of a general revival of religion" was that revivals "left much good undone," unless a convert was willing to "sit beside a poor despised 'nigger.' "[42]

In a typically provocative manner, Elizur used the fourth annual report to reassess the society's priorities. "The most effective opposition we have met has been from the professed ministers of Christ," he declared on May 12, 1837. The ministry was "a fashionable conscience-soother for the exclusive use of genteel worshippers of mammon, doing their weekly penance to God in cushioned pews." He denounced the "leading lights of New England theology" who endorsed the "prejudice and oppression" of colonization. "The most extensive denominations of Christians," he continued, used their moral influence "to the utmost against the doctrines of equality and immediate abolition." He singled out the Methodists and Congregationalists for blame. And in a graphic alliterative allusion, he compared the lack of antislavery resolve on the part of the General Assembly of the Presbyterian church to "the stagnant sea over the slime of Sodom." Never before had the inefficacy of the society's church-oriented abolitionism been so thoroughly castigated in such inflammatory language by one of its executive officers.[43]

"The question of questions," Elizur had posed earlier that year, was if the abolitionists were correctly interpreting Scripture, which was "at war with every manner and form of slavery," then "the visible church, to a great extent, must fall in with Satan." "Real Christianity must—and she will be disenthralled," he argued, "from the putrid carcass [of slavery] to which she has been bound." In order to honor the high ethical imperatives he associated with "real Christianity," he could no longer in good conscience belong to a corrupted church, a position similar to Garrison's in 1836 and 1837. But unlike his former mentor, there was a practical as well as moral side to Elizur's "come-outerism." With Finney, and even the Tappan brothers in mind, he pointed out that some argue "exclusively" for an "appeal to the religious feelings to end slavery" by which "the mass of men are made speculatively and professedly religious." He no longer could accept such evangelical utopianism, of which he had been an eloquent advocate, in the face of the overwhelming inertia of the church and ministry. "Our immediatism," he concluded, "has led us to appeal to that religion which will go immediately to work...through all lawful and right means."[44]

What Elizur suggested was that in order to be effective, church-oriented abolitionism must be politically engaged, albeit to a limited extent. "The religion we appeal to is no more out of place in politics than salt in the ocean," he maintained. Slavery was the result of spiritual error, but it was "politically created," "politically sustained," and "can only be politically broken." "What needs to be done," he instructed in the 1837 annual report, "is to excite sympathy for the oppressed which shall make itself felt through the law-making and law-executing powers." The success of the petition campaign especially convinced him that Christian ethics could in some cases be translated into a political context. But, like most other abolitionists at the time, he condemned Jacksonian politics as the clubhouse of "base and selfish men, rising into power by the generalship of a party." He therefore warned abolitionists against "setting up candidates of their own, but told them they were duty bound "firmly [to] refuse to vote for a man who will not support abolition measures." Elizur's new secular awareness made him uncomfortable with the strategy of New York's church-oriented abolitionists and also with Boston's Garrisonian come-outers, who shared in their differences a belief in the primacy of moral reformation, not political action. Disillusioned with sectarianism of whatever stripe, Elizur pledged his opposition to "that religion which makes a man shrink from his political responsibilities."[45]

By the spring of 1837 Elizur's blunt personality and castigation of the church made him suspect to other members of the executive committee. On one level, the solidarity and harmony he valued still existed. "Weld, Whittier, Stanton, Wright—what a pestilent, dangerous clump of fanatics all in our little room plotting freedom for slaves!" he wrote in mock alarm about his new co-workers who had joined the expanded staff of the Nassau Street office. He liked to describe abolitionists as "one great family," united in "the spirit of the cause." Yet, the conservatism of Arthur Tappan and his business circle, whom Elizur felt "have never more than half conceived the magnitude and urgency of the work," had soured the association between them. He complained of the religiously devout William Green, who had resigned in 1835 as the society's treasurer in order to work for the benevolent societies, that "he makes too much of conversion in the abstract." And Elizur's vocal anticlericalism now troubled Lewis Tappan and Amos Phelps, devoted but church-oriented abolitionists who were already upset with Garrison's come-outerism. Elizur's disaffection with religion even extended to his family, who unsuccessfully sought to reclaim him to the faith. "I rejoice," he told his unsympathetic younger brother James in failing to dissuade him from divinity studies, "that I have been kept out of the ministry, for I know that I am not adapted to it." Such impiety, which clouded his relationship with Lewis, in Weld's confidential opinion had become "personally and strongly obnoxious" by the summer of 1837.[46]

A worried Weld conspired with his friends Henry B. Stanton and James G. Birney to contain Elizur's provocations. Different personal styles had already created friction between Weld and Wright, diminishing what had been an early attraction when they had first met during the Western Reserve College controversy. Elizur had little patience for what he regarded as the cloying quest for personal holiness that Weld and his intimate English friend Charles Stuart cultivated. He chided Theodore for his "egotism" and "vanity" in not allowing his own letters, which described the power of his spellbinding oratory, to be published in the abolitionist press. He unsuccessfully prodded the nongregarious Theodore to attend the important annual conventions, but did finally convince him to direct the agents' rally in November 1836. Elizur, who was not a vegetarian, chided Weld, who was, that "every southern slave I ever saw complained bitterly about the prevention of meat." Nor did the practical-minded Elizur find Stuart's plan for a boycott of all slave-produced products feasible. Unlike Elizur, a family man with home and hearth, Theodore lived as a self-styled "hermit" in the bleak Manhattan attic of a black abolitionist. He was unable to find "the congeniality and incorporation of spirit in indissolvable identity" at the society's headquarters which Elizur did. Indeed, the "buzz, buzz" of "Wright, Stanton, and Leavitt jabbering all the time" got on his nerves. The latent tension between the two was captured in Theodore's remark to Birney, then contemplating a new job at the New York antislavery office, "Would such close contact with Wright be *disagreeable* to you?"[47]

After the critical May 1837 convention, Theodore maneuvered behind the scenes in New York to reorganize the national staff, in part to lessen Elizur's influence. He urged that Leavitt, "the most important member of the Executive Committee," edit almost all the society's publications, which had mostly been Elizur's responsibility. Leavitt was not only a talented editor, but Theodore stressed that this clergyman had "more actual influence over the giving, doing, daring, praying and accomplishing part of the Church than any other man. . . . Besides—he will be a far safer helmsman than our brother Wright in the difficult and hazardous navigation upon which we are just launching." Theodore also pressured Birney to leave the editorship of *The Philanthropist* in Ohio and accept appointment as one of three corresponding secretaries created at the spring business meeting. Birney would join Stanton, one of the society's best agents, in dividing up the burdensome duties for which Elizur had previously been responsible. But whereas Birney and Stanton were to spend half their time in missionary work throughout the Northeast, Elizur, Theodore envisioned, was "to be on the ground all the time." It was a sensible division of labor, but premised on confining Elizur, along with his provocative ideas and brusque personality, to the office.[48]

Theodore complained privately of Elizur's "asperity and undignified snappishness." "It is *indispensable* absolutely," he pleaded with Birney, that the new secretaries reclaim "the confidence of those who are real Christians in the Church and in the ministry." Stanton warned that Elizur "is not popular with a certain class of men [churchmen], does not desire to be; has not their confidence, does not wish it and hence is taking no pains to get either their applause or their confidence, he will never have either." He concluded, "Brother Wright never will have the hearty confidence" of influential clerics, "a class of men which must be *won not driven* over to our ranks." Charles Stuart wondered, "Is beloved E. Wright as wicked and as inconsistent as ever, or has he opened his eyes?" For the New York evangelical circle gathered about Lewis Tappan and Theodore Weld, Elizur's anticlericalism and outspoken style had by the summer of 1837 become a liability for their church-oriented abolitionism.[49]

Yet, Elizur's castigation of the church was only part of his evolving secular perspective. The rapid organizational expansion of the American Anti-Slavery Society convinced him that most Americans—particularly the independent yeomen, artisans, and mechanics—could be won to the abolitionist ranks. The success of the postal campaign, petition drive, and the Seventy persuaded him that there was a morally attainable majority of citizens independent of the church. With typical intellectual acumen, he developed legal and economic indictments of slavery intended for this constituency. During the 1830s he was in the vanguard in formulating the accusation that slavery was a threat to free men and free labor. As secretary of the national society, he was not only an able administrator, but also a creative thinker who helped to expand the purview of the abolitionist argument beyond religious assumptions.

Chapter 7

Free Men, Free Labor

Screams in the night startled Elizur and Susan from their sleep. They hurried to comfort their house guest, a seven-year-old Negro boy, whose nightmares of enslavement awakened him with cries of alarm. Earlier that spring of 1834 the New York police had seized the young Henry Scott in his classroom, and the judge had incarcerated him as an alleged fugitive slave belonging to the Haxall family of Virginia. Elizur believed that the Haxall's claim that they only wished to return Henry to his slave mother masked a scheme to flush out his father, who had fled the South and brought Henry with him. Through the efforts of free blacks, including his classmates, and white abolitionists, Henry was freed on bail. Elizur took the traumatized child home to care for him. For Henry's safety, Elizur later placed him with an abolitionist family upstate. In 1842 father and son were reunited: the father had established himself in New Bedford, Massachusetts, but the mother apparently remained in bondage.[1]

This personal experience with the plight of harrassed blacks in New York, many of whom did not share the even bittersweet fate of Henry Scott, galvanized Elizur. For his efforts on behalf of the child, the Haxalls threatened him with violence. "A vile and despicable outrage upon justice and humanity," he concluded about a law that permitted the imprisonment of children. He was appalled and angered, reactions that strengthened his abolitionist determination. He was also provoked to develop new arguments against slavery and racism in addition to the standard evangelical charge that slavery was sin, and beyond the conventional reliance on Christian stewardship to convert the nation. During the decade of the 1830s he elaborated on the ideals of free men and free labor, inherent but only embryonic in early immediatist thought, in order to contrast them with the lack of freedom that slavery engendered. His intellectual affinity for the legal and economic aspects of antislavery thought further distanced him from the church-oriented abolitionism of the Tappan-Weld clique at the New York headquarters.[2]

Elizur's active involvement with the issue of civil rights began shortly after his arrival in New York City in an effort to protect the freedom of African-Americans. The Fugitive Slave Law, passed by Congress in 1793, provided that escaped slaves must be returned to their legal owners. Slaveholders had initiated the legislation in order to clarify that part of the Constitution which sanctioned the rendition of "fugitives from labor," but they had not specified the mechanism by which such fugitives were to be reclaimed. The 1793 law stated that a claimant had to establish through oral or written evidence his ownership of the alleged "fugitive from labor" before a magistrate in the state where the accused was apprehended. After a hearing to evaluate the evidence, the presiding magistrate would decide the case either by issuing a certificate to the claimant for the repossession of his chattel or by freeing the defendant. A five-hundred-dollar fine could be levied on anyone aiding or abetting an escaped slave.[3]

The national Fugitive Slave Law did not end the legal ambiguities and practical difficulties over the enforcement of the federal law in the North. A slaveholder or his legal agent could utilize the assistance of the local police in the capture of suspected fugitive slaves, and they could employ the services of professional bounty hunters, an especially hardened group of men. After being arrested and jailed, the supposed fugitive was provided a hearing before a local magistrate who had sole authority to dispose of the suit. In New York City during the 1830s the judicial process was routinely prejudiced against the defendant because of the currying of southern favor, pervasive racism, and outright bribery.[4]

In order to prevent blacks from being extradicted to the South, Elizur worked with a committee of vigilance. The nation's largest metropolis with its bustling seaport and well-established Negro neighborhoods provided the escaped slave with a similar sanctuary to the runaway serf in the medieval town. But the Fugitive Slave Law acted to contravene the maxim that city air meant freedom for the escaped bondsman, and even the legitimately free black might be perversely enslaved. The committee vowed "to protect unoffending, defenseless and endangered persons of color, securing their rights as far as possible, and obtaining for them when arrested under the pretext of being fugitive slaves such protection as the law affords." Elizur and his associates were a moral and intellectual vanguard who established a precedent of systematic opposition to the Fugitive Slave Law as early as 1834. In addition to a petition campaign directed at the New York legislature, Elizur, William Jay, Gerrit Smith, and Henry B. Stanton had started during 1837 to question politicians about their position on a jury trial statute for fugitive slaves. They demanded that abolitionists vote accordingly. Their efforts largely succeeded with the passage of such legislation in 1840 which brought New York in line with similar guarantees in Pennsylvania and New Jersey. Their activity also foreshadowed the widespread public concern that occurred in the North after the passage of a new Fugitive Slave Law in 1850.[5]

Elizur's involvement with the desperate circumstances of persecuted fugitives personalized the abstract evil of slavery. His strong sense of family ties provided an emotional impetus to his commitment. Such was the heartbreaking case of a father, mother, and child who were seized as fugitives and imprisoned while awaiting probable enslavement. "They have begged me," Elizur wrote his parents, "in the most moving manner to do something for them." Their plan was to secure bail for the mother and child, so, if the court decision went as expected against the father, they could forfeit bail and flee to freedom. Although the slaveholders were likely to exact revenge on the father, the painful decision hoped to save at least two members of the harried family. In addition, he and Susan opened their home to Matilda, a girl who had been illegally held as a slave in New York, and to Mary Gordon, an elderly laundress, whose son had been executed in Cuba for possession of antislavery literature. Elizur also helped Damon Jones, a former slave, to secure lodgings, and he had a "colored lad," whom he taught Latin, assist him in the antislavery office.[6]

In order to publicize the plight of other blacks subjected to abuse under the Fugitive Slave Law, Elizur wrote a column, "Chronicles of Kidnapping in New York," in *The Emancipator* and *Anti-Slavery Record*. His descriptions emphasized not only the poignant human story but also the willing collusion of northern officials in supporting the slave system. His essays represented the first systematic indictment of the federal law among immediatists and further documented his emerging concern with tangible legal issues, especially the goal of equality under the law regardless of race.

Elizur told how the local police staged a midnight raid on the residence of Jock Lockley. Lockley, his wife, and two-year-old son were imprisoned as the purported slaves of Dr. Rufus Haywood of Raleigh, North Carolina, reportedly the black man's white first cousin. Haywood convinced the New York court that the Lockleys were thieves, and was allowed to proceed home with his charges. In another case, Peter Martin was sent to enslavement in Virginia after weeks of imprisonment in a "coffin-like cell" and unsuccessful litigation. As punishment, his master sold him to an owner in the Deep South. "Here is a man, whose extorted labor has paid for him many times over," Elizur bemoaned, "and yet he is claimed as a beast—and the system of slavery, makes an example of him, by selling him to the south." Martin's resourceful wife, with the assistance of her husband's employer in New York, was able to purchase him through a ruse. A month after his involuntary bondage, Martin was, Elizur happily reported, back at home and at work in New York.[7]

Not all people were as fortunate as Peter Martin. Stephen Downing was held eighteen months in jail despite the efforts of the vigilance committee to free him. Just before a sympathetic superior court was to hear his case, the local judge awarded Downing to his southern claimant. Elizur damned the uncooperative judge to his face, but sadly concluded that "the liberty of an honest man was lost." One April day, Elizur found aboard a New Orleans–bound schooner four mulatto children, the offspring of a Dr. Mairs, a slaveholder from New Bern, North Carolina. On investigation Elizur learned the shocking information that "there can be no doubt that the father intends to sell his children as slaves; and that he took the route by this city to avoid the odium which even in New Bern must fall upon such a fiendish transaction." And one Francis Smith, who had fled slavery in Virginia, was captured shortly before he was to marry and move to safer regions. Manacled and confined in a small, stifling cell, the despairing man suffered a mental breakdown.[8]

The miserable prison conditions fueled Elizur's outrage. Alleged fugitive slaves were locked up in the Bridewell, an old city prison where confinement was in single cells 7 by 3$\frac{1}{2}$ feet. The only ventilation was through a grate, and the heat in summer was oppressive. Prisoners were in irons and allowed neither to leave their cells nor to receive visitors. Five suspected slaves spent two months in what Elizur described as "the most horrible solitary confinement," until one man consented to go South. The only crime they were accused of, Elizur defiantly observed, was that "they were suspected of loving liberty so well as to have taken it without waiting for the consent of other people." Some years later he met one of the men he had helped free from the Bridewell. Antonio, who had embodied "raggedness and misery" while in prison, was now a "well dressed and substantial looking man."[9]

As Elizur well realized, public sentiment condoned harsh treatment of suspected fugitive slaves. He correctly foresaw, however, that the issue of "legalized kidnapping" was an effective pivot on which to move northern opinion. "It has been my aim," he declared in his essays, "by the exhibition of FACTS, in their naked ugliness, to arouse my fellow citizens to the necessity of reformation." During the 1830s abolitionists such as Elizur began to shape an alternative viewpoint that by the 1850s would garner popular support for the fugitive slave. In 1834 white citizens assisted in the capture of Peter Martin and Francis Smith in New York City; twenty years later a company of marines was needed in Boston to restrain an unruly crowd from blocking the return to the South of Anthony Burns, a runaway. Even by 1841, Elizur noted with some pride: "My old colored friends...are all quite sensible of the benefits of our labors in their behalf, and a more grateful people there could not be. When I compare their condition now with what it was in 1833, I do not feel as though my antislavery labors have been in vain."[10]

In an effort to delegitimize the Fugitive Slave Law, Elizur argued that it clashed with the standards of jurisprudence and threatened the civil rights of all citizens, even whites. "It was enough for me to know," he explained, "that in the city of New York men, women and children had been arrested and thrown into miserable dungeons, for no offense—but merely because they were claimed as property. If I understand my mother tongue, this act, under whatever forms of law, or by whatsoever honorable agents it may be performed, is essentially kidnapping." He maintained that contrary to judicial procedure during the 1830s a jury trial was legally mandated in order to establish whether the defendant was an escaped slave or a free man. If the precedent was created that a magistrate's decision superseded a jury's in such momentous cases, then, he averred, "are the free citizens of New York deprived of a right which is the pride of the English Common Law—we are all carried back, for the convenience of slave owners, to the usages of feudal despotism." State legislation in 1840 concurred—a defendant in the case of a "fugitive from labor" must have a jury trial.[11]

Elizur's aggressive stand against the Fugitive Slave Law drew fire not only from public officials and prominent citizens, but also from the executive committee of the American Anti-Slavery Society. William Green, John Rankin, and William Jay, conservative members of the executive committee, found Elizur's essays intemperate and his fraternization with blacks unseemly. Green and Arthur Tappan disconnected themselves and the national society from Elizur's handbill on behalf of Jock Lockley, which castigated the Fugitive Slave Law as "villainy." Newspaper editors denounced him for advocating disobedience to the law. The wealthy upstate landowner Gerrit Smith, who later supported John Brown's raid on Harper's Ferry, blamed Elizur's essays for provoking the July 1834 riots. "Let him remember his own persevering efforts in his 'Chronicles of Kidnapping in New York,'" Smith admonished, "to obstruct the administration of the laws, and to kindle an irregular and factious opposition against them; and let him pause to consider, whether the sin of these mobs does not, in some measure, lie at his own doorstep."[12]

In response to his critics, Elizur took the moral high ground. The handbill, he explained, urged opposition only to "tyrannical laws" and to politicians such as Governor William Marcy who endorsed legalized "kidnapping." Virtuous citizens were obligated to disobey "bad laws" that enjoined "actions contrary to divine law." "God has devolved upon every individual," he instructed in the enduring American tradition of legal disobedience, "a certain responsibility towards making civil government what it should be." He justified his actions during the 1830s with reference to a "higher law" doctrine. As he put it, there was "an older and nobler Constitution," God's commandments, to which people must ultimately submit. By the 1850s invocation of a "higher law," such as in William Henry Seward's celebrated speech, would become a standard part of the opposition to the Fugitive Slave Law. In prophetic words, Elizur stated in 1840 that the fugitive slave issue lay bare "the irreconcilable enmity of slaveholding and free principles."[13]

Although an antinomian in sentiment, Elizur did not embrace a form of Christian anarchism as William Lloyd Garrison and his Boston circle would by the end of the 1830s. He supported the Constitution as the codification of republican and Christian principles, which rational, enlightened men had bound "to the throne of God." The nation's founding document, he maintained, established that "no person shall be deprived of liberty without due process of law," including accused fugitive slaves. It was a "solemn oath" that secured freedom under the law. The masthead of his publication, *Human Rights,* declared, "Our object is liberty for all; gained by moral power, and regulated by impartial laws."[14]

Among immediatists, Elizur was an early interpreter of the Constitution as an antislavery document. He contended in 1836 that the nation's fundamental law was not meant to sanction slavery permanently but represented only a temporary quid pro quo between southerners and northerners. "The obvious understanding with which [northerners] consented to the compromise was," he argued, "that the South should of its own accord, at no distant date, abate the monstrous evil which they had so dexterously contrived to avoid mention of." "Slavery is unknown to the Constitution," he wrote in 1837, "which declares that no person shall be deprived of liberty without due process of law." His self-serving and historically inaccurate reading of the antislavery resolve of the Philadelphia convention of 1787 and existing legal opinion nevertheless appropriated the Constitution for the abolitionists. Historian William M. Wiecek rightly calls Elizur's declarations "the starting point of radical constitutionalism." By the 1850s the perception of the Constitution as an antislavery statement would have an increasing appeal in the North, unlike Garrison's inflammatory indictment that it was "a covenant with death and an agreement with hell."[15]

The anti-abolitionist backlash of middecade broadened the issue of civil rights beyond the specific case of the Fugitive Slave Law. President Andrew Jackson's support for a ban on abolitionist literature to the South provoked Elizur to comment, "The broadest and highest bulwark of our liberties lies prostrate to make room for the grasping monster." In response to the 1836 congressional gag rule, he warned, "Our great charter of self-government was, in fact, permitted to give way, and we now live under the dominion of a tyranny which makes our humanity a crime, and tramples in the mire the humblest of our rights." In his annual reports to the national society he recited a litany of infractions against the civil rights of abolitionists: Amos Dresser whipped in Nashville; Reuben Crandall imprisoned in the nation's capital; Garrison mobbed in Boston; and Elijah Lovejoy shot to death while defending his antislavery press in Alton, Illinois. As southerners warmed to the abolitionist challenge, Governor Wilson Lumpkin of Georgia offered a five-thousand-dollar bounty for the delivery of ten leading abolitionists, including Elizur, to his state to stand trial for fomenting emancipation. "It is slavery, and not the Constitution," Elizur alerted, "which governs the United States at the present time."[16]

Ironically the suppression of the rights of white abolitionists rather than the denial of freedom to blacks produced greater awareness over the issue of civil liberties. "The abolitionists have seized hold," Henry Clay, "the Great Compromiser" and Kentucky planter, warned, "of the fact of the treatment which their petitions have received in Congress, and made injurious impressions upon the minds of a large portion of the community." The executive committee of the American Anti-Slavery Society reminded the public, "Let no one think for a moment, that because he is not an abolitionist, his liberties are not and will not be invaded. We have no rights distinct from the rights of the whole people." They concluded their 1836 statement with words Republican politicians would echo twenty years later: "We must be all free, or all slaves together." As Elizur and his colleagues came to realize, it was not only the rights of fugitive slaves that were in question but the very survival of constitutionally guaranteed civil rights. "Only think," he remarked, "of a democratic republic suppressing free discussion." In part, Elizur's actions during the 1830s established a tradition of opposition to the encroachment on liberty that opponents of slavery would amplify during the next two decades. With the help of his pioneering arguments, the linkage of abolitionism with the rallying cry of free men gained the antislavery cause a more sympathetic hearing in the North.[17]

Elizur's interest in the legal issue of free men was complemented by an attraction for the ideology of free labor. He was one of few immediatists during the 1830s who elaborated on what would become a standard economic indictment of slavery. The intellectual distance between the Second Great Awakening's credo of free will and the economic analogue of free labor was easily bridged by evangelical abolitionists. Although the idea of free labor was explicit in immediatist thought from the beginning, the overwhelming stress on Christian stewardship and the sin of slavery retarded its systematic development during the first decade of the abolitionist crusade. Most immediatists agreed with Theodore Weld's 1836 dictum, "The business of abolitionists is with the heart of the nation rather than with its purse strings." Elizur's affinity for practical arguments and disaffection for the church, however, led him to explore the subject unlike most of his colleagues during the 1830s. His economic analysis advanced what historian Louis S. Gerteis calls the conflation of "morality and utility" in antislavery thought—that is, the growing acceptance in the North by midcentury of a liberal bourgeois agenda which posited that slavery was not only a moral abomination but that free labor with its emphasis on individual autonomy and liberty in the marketplace was the proper relationship between capital and labor. Free labor negated slavery, and, as English utilitarians of the day put it, would secure "the greatest good for the greatest number," the ideal of nineteenth-century middle-class democracy.[18]

William Lloyd Garrison had initially broached the free labor argument in the first issue of *The Liberator* and added further comments in his 1832 *Thoughts on African Colonization*. Echoing his immediatist mentor, Elizur sought to counter the prevailing white fear that the slaves were too lazy and too dangerous to free. "Emancipate the slaves at once," he told the readers of the *Hudson Observer and Telegraph*. "Settle them as free-holders on the land which they have watered with their sweat, if not with their tears and blood." He assured colonizationists that as "free laborers under the equitable control of the law," blacks would be as worthy citizens as whites.[19]

For immediatists, slave labor was the antithesis of free labor. Economic freedom meant self-ownership, the ability to work, as Elizur put it, as "voluntary laborers on equitable wages." Like his colleagues, Elizur did not advocate liquidation of the southern gentry nor redistribution of the land to the tiller (as do Marxist-inspired revolutionaries in the Third World today). Their liberal ideology stressed the harmony between capital and labor, and the virtues of private ownership of wealth, social mobility, and individual initiative. What was radical about their ideas was that they demanded, in Elizur's words, that the South "open her doors to the actual introduction of a new system of labor." In effect, they wanted to extend to blacks equality of opportunity in the marketplace, a racial egalitarianism that was completely at odds with the white supremacist values of the Age of Jackson.[20]

Elizur pointed to emancipation in the West Indies as proof of the success of the conversion from slave to free labor. "Hayti stands forth," he wrote in praise of their new labor system, "a monument of strenuous and well directed enterprise, honorable alike to herself and to human nature." The abolition of slavery in the British colonies on August 1, 1834, varied between outright emancipation and a gradual apprentice system. "In Antigua, where emancipation was immediate and entire," he reported about the ex-slaves, "they work better than anywhere else." For Elizur, the Caribbean example vindicated the ethical and economic premises of immediatism. The implication was clear: "If emancipation was safe in St. Domingo, if it is safe in the British colonies, if it has been safe whenever it has been tried, why should it not be safe in the United States?"[21]

The crusade of immediate abolition itself had emerged at a time of unprecedented business expansion and fundamental structural transformation in the way people lived and worked in the North. By 1840 a dynamic capitalism had effected a transition from household manufacturing to factory production. The free-labor ideology of the immediatists reflected a buoyant confidence in the nascent industrialization and the liberal middle-class values that accompanied it. Evangelical abolitionists with their predominant moral inclination exemplified what Max Weber termed "the Protestant ethic and the spirit of capitalism." They extolled those who worked hard, overcame adversity, practiced frugality, amassed property, but also observed Christian pieties. In contrast, they perceived the system of slave labor as degrading the work ethic. "Our blessed Savior was not a slaveholder, nor the son of a slaveholder, but of a carpenter," Elizur pointed out. "He honored manual labor, upon which slaveholders throw all manner of contempt, by laboring with his own hands."[22]

More from their own moral intuition than close study of *The Wealth of Nations,* immediatists repeated Adam Smith's postulate that the self-interest of the free laborer encouraged greater efficiency than that found in slave production. "The profit of his master is made the end of his being," Elizur explained, "and he is a mere means to that end, a means to an end of which he is no part—a mere instrument for the accomplishment of an object into which his interests do not enter, of which they constitute no portion." Slavery was not a just or accurate measure of the black work ethic, he argued in an effort to refute the stereotype of the lazy Sambo. "The fruits of all their toil [are] appropriated by the other race to their own use and aggrandizement." Like the Scottish professor and unlike the analysis of some modern historians, he believed that "the work done by free men comes cheaper in the end than that performed by slaves." "Abolitionists attempt to prove by facts," Elizur instructed, "not only that slavery is unjust and cruel, but that its immediate abolition would be safe and profitable to every state in the Union." Free labor was not only morally just, it was the economic wave of the future.[23]

Elizur included free black workers in his vision of an economically dynamic nation. "Fellow citizens, the wealth of the nation lies chiefly in its free citizens," he announced. "The colored portion is a mine which we shall throw away or fail to explore, only if we are fools." Although he supported training for black youth, white immediatists (with some exceptions, such as the Oneida Institute during Beriah Green's tenure) made little effort to employ or train blacks. Instead Elizur emphasized that hard work brought its own rewards, such as a former Georgia slave who became a successful farmer, and a washerwoman whose earnings purchased her family's freedom. He did demand that the "abominable sin and self-destructive folly" of white racism be eliminated, so blacks could compete equally in the marketplace. In his scheme of social mobility, "one man shall have as good a right to acquire wealth as another," regardless of race.[24]

Rather than apologists for the northern economic elite, immediatists saw themselves as victims of the "gentlemen of property and standing" who instigated the anti-abolitionist mobs. "It is from these men," Elizur charged, "entrenched in offices of church and state, or wielding the power of old establishment presses that we have the bitterest opposition to expect." The economic expansion of the North hinged on the southern cotton trade, an alliance between the "lords of the lash"—the slaveholders—and the "lords of the loom"—textile manufacturers—as the immediatists phrased it. "The North will not," Elizur exclaimed, "assert the rights of the slaves because that would injure her trade!"[25]

With the Panic of 1837 and subsequent years of depression, Elizur's free-labor attack on slavery took on increased importance. He blamed the hard times on the unsound economic connection between the slaveholders and the northern business class. Northern bankers and merchants, he explained, had loaned capital to the South for the westward expansion of slavery in order to reap large profits from the rising price of cotton. Credit, however, had been dangerously overextended. In his words, "The price of cotton, had it kept up, could not have borne the enormous extravagance and mad speculation that have grown out of the slave system. ... No scale of profit can permanently enrich a slaveholding country." And, "the thriftless and speculating monopolizers of labor" in the South had squandered northern investments. The speculative bubble burst; the panic resulted.[26]

Elizur predicted that profits from the cotton trade would drop, while the planter's penchant for "violence and arbitrary will" would hinder debt collection. An agriculture dependent on cotton and cane was vulnerable to competition from India and the cultivation of the sugar beet. Because the South needed economic credit, "the great stream of enterprise and capital which has heretofore flowed to the southern states from the northern, and given value to men as beasts, will then be cut off," once northerners equated slavery with injustice. In any case, the slave system could not consume enough of northern production to relieve the glut on the market. But with abolition, three million freedmen, Elizur indicated, would "well nigh double the consumption of northern goods." Ethics and economics encouraged emancipation.[27]

Besides a general business recovery, other economic benefits, Elizur believed, would accrue to the nation through abolition. The end of slavery meant more equitable forms of taxation and a better expenditure of public funds. No longer would the issue of the national bank be confused by slaveholders who wished a Bank of the United States when they needed credit and argued against it when they had overborrowed. The national bank would not be a conduit "by which the capital of the free North shall flow into the bankrupt South." The troublesome tariff question would also be simplified: the duty on foreign sugar, which provided an excessive two-million-dollar profit to Louisiana planters, could in part be returned to the workers in the form of higher wages.[28]

The villains of free labor were clearly the slaveholders, but its heroes were not the northern manufacturers, merchants, and bankers. Instead, the future of abolition was with "the honest hard-handed, clear-headed free laborers and mechanics of the North," whom Elizur believed could "be made to see and feel that their brotherhood is rather with the honest but oppressed laborer of the South than with the lordling who lives at ease upon his unrequited toil." In Elizur's labor theory of value, "The moral influence of the nation...does not come forth from the merchants, those who handle the produce of other people's toil, but from the original producer." He anticipated that "the middling ground of society"—the yeomanry, artisans, and mechanics—would "identify their interests with those of the slave. They will throw away political and sectarian predilections, and stand forth on the broad ground of human rights."[29]

But, paradoxically, the very labor solidarity of the "producing classes" that Elizur sought to forge into an antislavery coalition was subverted by his evangelical abolitionism and its free labor ideology. He warned "working men" that slavery "turns all laboring men into objects of property—objects to be owned, bought and sold," but ignored the exploitation of workers in northern capitalism. The independent craftsmen's fear of "wage slavery"—low pay, long hours, little control over the work place, the degradation of skilled trades—was not his concern. For immediatists economic freedom was self-ownership: the ability to sell freely one's labor on the marketplace in return for equitable wages. Elizur was oblivious to the structural transformation occurring before his eyes in New York City that threatened to turn proud artisans and mechanics into dependent factory operatives. He, like virtually all his colleagues, expressed no interest in the Working Men's party, the trade union movement, or the ideas of labor reformers Thomas Skidmore and Robert Dale Owen.[30]

Elizur was correct that northern labor formed a natural antislavery constituency. Yeomen throughout the North joined the American Anti-Slavery Society. Artisans and small shopkeepers were the major signatories of antislavery petitions in New York City, and factory operatives in Lynn, Massachusetts formed an antislavery society in 1837. But in their enthusiasm to praise free labor in order to damn slave labor, evangelical abolitionists in general and Elizur in particular could not relate to the pressing concerns of the urban working class during the 1830s. Their romantic assessment of the marketplace as a sphere of personal freedom conflicted with the artisan concept of craft independence. Evangelical abolitionism arising out of the Second Great Awakening was unable to connect during the 1830s with the artisan antislavery tradition, which, inherited from Thomas Paine, included a religious tradition of deism. That union, coalescing about the antislavery slogan of "Free Soil, Free Labor, Free Men," would occur in the Republican party two decades later in a triumph of liberal middle-class ideology. In the meantime, Elizur found himself at the center of a shattering crisis within the abolitionist ranks.[31]

Part Three

Transitions

Chapter 8

Tripartite Schism

William Lloyd Garrison was shocked and dismayed. He confided to his brother-in-law that he found it "difficult to believe that [Elizur] wrote" the letter that he had received in mid-September 1837. He had expected support in a controversy with clerical abolitionists in eastern Massachusetts, but instead Elizur thoroughly castigated his former mentor in some of the most bitter prose he ever wrote. "As you well know, I am comparatively no bigot to any creed, political or theological," Garrison read; "yet, to tell the plain truth, I look upon your notions of government and religious perfection as downright fanaticism—as harmless as they are absurd." The letter continued, "It is not in the human mind (except in a peculiar and, as I think, diseased state), to believe them. . . ." Frustration with the abolitionist fratricide in New England prompted Elizur to point an angry finger at the churchmen as well as at Garrison. "I cannot but regard," he concluded," the Boston controversy as wrong, wrong, wrong, *on both sides.* If strict military justice were done, I am thinking both parties would be cashiered!"[1]

The contention that provoked Elizur's caustic comments erupted that August with clerical abolitionists centered around Boston in outspoken opposition to Garrison's expanded social agenda and radical pietism. They impugned Garrison's recent espousal of nonresistance, a type of Christian anarchism which embraced pacifism, human spiritual perfection, and renounced civil government for ultimate allegiance to the moral government of God. His breach of sexual decorum in encouraging the antislavery sisters Sarah and Angelina Grimké to lecture to mixed audiences of men and women that summer further offended the socially conservative and religiously orthodox among the abolitionist fold. One riled minister, James T. Woodbury, an agent for the American Anti-Slavery Society, declared in one of several clerical appeals, "I never swallowed William Lloyd Garrison, and I never tried to swallow him." Garrison's heterodox ideas and polemic style were too much for the churchmen.[2]

In New York the executive committee of the American Anti-Slavery Society anxiously followed the controversy, prominently featured week after week in the pages of *The Liberator*, with the ill-founded belief that the dispute would be short-lived. Hoping not to inflame the heated quarrel, they maintained what Garrison denounced as a "studied silence" in his dispute with "the scribes and pharisees." As the schism evolved, Elizur, however, became a leading opponent of Garrisonian nonresistance and what he regarded as its advocacy of issues extraneous to the abolitionist cause. But he did not prove to be a compatible ally with the clerical faction whose patriarchal obsession against an expanded abolitionist role for women also seemed a wasteful diversion from the antislavery goal. He faulted both sides for disrupting the tenuous solidarity that he had labored to create as an officer of the national society. During the next two years he was attracted to a third faction of political abolitionists who by 1839 endorsed the formation of an antislavery party. Unlike the Garrisonians and the rival churchmen, political abolitionists backed a "human rights" party, dismissed the "woman issue" as irrelevant to the antislavery agenda, and increasingly distanced themselves from church-oriented abolitionism, not to mention nonresistance.[3]

Elizur could barely contain his anger over Garrison's advocacy of nonresistance, "a downright fanaticism," which he blamed for sparking the controversy. In mid-August 1837 he warned James G. Birney, who was preparing to join the staff at the New York headquarters, that "the very absurd doctrines broached by our good, but not very strong brother, Henry C. Wright," a close associate of Garrison's, "show us the importance of our having here the strongest center of confidence and attraction we can get." "It is downright nonsense," he complained shortly thereafter to Amos Phelps, then an agent for the Massachusetts Anti-Slavery Society, "to suppose that the Anti-Slavery cause can be carried forward with forty incongruous things tacked on to it. You can't drive a three tined fork through a hay mow, though turn it t'other end to, and you can drive in the handle."[4]

By mid-September Elizur had lost all patience. In a series of letters to Garrison he denounced him for creating "the boundless gulf of distress between you and the abolitionists" with his "notions of government and religious perfection." It was folly, he maintained, to provoke the clergy over issues of "theoretic theology" rather than confronting the churches' opposition to abolition. "You exalt yourself too much," he charged, recognizing a syndrome of self-righteousness in Garrison that would repeatedly surface in bitter disputes with dissenting abolitionists, most notably Frederick Douglass. Elizur demanded that Garrison admit that he had "left the old track" and had "started on a new one—or, rather, two or three new ones at once." The American Anti-Slavery Society had no inclination to defend an "antislavery sect," or what Elizur would later disparage as "Garrison's Anti-Slavery Church." In effect, Elizur sought to purge nonresistance and issues not directly related to emancipation from the abolitionist crusade.[5]

Although both men still adhered to immediatist principles, their differences were profound, rancorous, and enduring. The rift that grew between them in 1837 was never bridged. In response to the anti-abolitionism backlash of the mid-1830s, Garrison believed that only a sweeping moral transformation could remake the nation's fundamentally flawed institutions and redeem a sinful people. Elizur held that the Republic was basically sound, except for slavery which he thought political abolitionism could eliminate. They disagreed over the very nature of human nature itself. Rejecting the doctrine of human perfection, Elizur countered that "men are not completely freed from sin by the grace of God." He ridiculed as a charlatan the leading spokesman of perfectionism, John Humphrey Noyes, who had influenced Garrison earlier that spring and would later gain notoriety as the founder of the Oneida community. He gossiped to Phelps that rumor had it that Noyes came to believe that he had achieved "the perfection of the flesh" after having had been "dead drunk" for several days.[6]

For the former professor of mathematics and natural science, perfectionism defied reason and logic. "I cannot receive a revelation," Elizur chided Garrison, "which asserts that which my senses pronounce to be false, nor one which visibly fails to accomplish its object." As he later put it in some lines of sarcastic doggerel:

> The men who preach this hopeful plan
> Of righting all that's wrong in man
> Quote Scripture with great confidence,
> Not heeling in their folly dense,

That Scripture, in its scope immense,
Must leave some work for common sense.

"The wind of perfectionism has blown off the roof of his judgment," he confided to his old friend Beriah Green. "I have no more hope from him in the future than I have from the inmates of Bedlam in general." And he wrote his father, "I greatly fear Garrison will make shipwreck of himself. He has got into his head some of the foolishest religious whims which ever disturbed a mortal brain."[7]

What Elizur feared most was that Garrison would steer the immediatist ship onto the nonresistant shoals. The "no human government" doctrine, he told Phelps, meant that Garrison had "finished his course for the slave." He added that the "plan of rescuing the slave by the destruction of human laws [is] fatally conflictive with ours." He pointed to Garrison's current attack on the legitimacy of civil government as a contradiction of his own "Declaration of Sentiments" of 1833 that stressed the obligation of political action against slavery. He confronted Garrison with the question, "You impeach my christianity because I 'cannot cease looking to man for protection and redress'; how can it consist with your christianity to demand for others, 'the protection of the law'?" The problem was that Elizur's republicanism and Garrison's antinomianism sought to guide abolitionism in different directions. For Garrison, man was perfectible, but only divine government could be just; for Elizur, man was imperfectible, but human government could be just.[8]

Like John Greenleaf Whittier and Theodore Weld, his colleagues at the New York headquarters, Elizur regarded the "woman question" as "a false issue" diverting attention away from freeing the slave. His position put him in between the feminist Garrisonians and the patriarchal churchmen. "The day this American Anti-Slavery Society refuses," he wrote on behalf of the Grimké sisters, "to employ well qualified agents to address all who will hear, because they are women, I for one shall leave it. If the sects can't bear women's preaching, let them stay away. . . ." He pointed to the active role of abolitionist women, including the Quaker Lucretia Mott who participated in the formation of the national society in 1833. Yet, without the Garrisonian agitation, he believed that the "blessed modesty" of women would "prevent them from making any considerable use of their constitutional rights." Personally he admitted to being most comfortable with the conventional pattern of sexual segregation. "I think the tom turkeys ought to do the gobbling," he reassured the conservative

Phelps. "I am opposed to hens crowing and surely as a general rule to female preaching." Elizur was in effect ambivalent, if not confused, about changing gender roles. His major frustration with the "woman question," however, was that it "belittles us—it is tying a tin kettle to the tail of our enterprise."[9]

While Garrison and his Boston circle remained committed to what their critics disparaged as the "no human government" doctrine, Elizur was attracted to the various possibilities of political abolition. "I believe God has devolved upon every individual," he stated in an 1835 affirmation of his Christian republicanism, "a certain responsibility towards making civil government what it should be." He kept the faith that the common people would "identify their interests with those of the slave. They will throw away political and sectarian predilections, and stand forth on the broad ground of human rights." He concurred in 1837 with the church-oriented leadership in New York that "the ballot box is not an abolition argument" and that "abolitionism knows nothing of parties." Nevertheless he exhorted every abolitionist that May to "follow the leading of his own political principles so long as he can do it without sacrificing the paramount claims of the slave."[10]

By 1838 the evolving political tactics of the national society included the questioning or "interrogation" of candidates on a variety of antislavery issues. That September Elizur and his co-secretaries, James G. Birney and Henry B. Stanton, issued a pre-election statement on behalf of the executive committee: "We deprecate the organization of any Abolition political party; but that we recommend to abolitionists throughout the country to interrogate candidates for office, with reference to their opinions on subjects connected with the abolition of Slavery; and to vote irrespective of party, for those only who will advocate the principles of Universal Liberty." They explained that a distinct antislavery party would morally taint itself with the crass electioneering of the Jacksonian Era. The interrogation of candidates would, however, pressure politicians to recognize that the antislavery vote held the balance of power at least in some congressional districts. The plan was to "scatter" the antislavery vote among the best candidates of either the Whigs or Democrats, but to withhold votes in protest if no acceptable candidate was forthcoming. The slogan of political abolition in 1838 was "form alliances with no political party but enstamp our principles upon all."[11]

Yet, the national society's concentrated effort to forge a united abolitionist position for the November elections was at odds with Garrison's boycott of the ballot box. A perennial problem between the parent organization and the Garrisonian-dominated Massachusetts Anti-Slavery Society over the distribution of funds between the two added to the tension. The executive committee feared that if abolitionism was not completely disassociated from nonresistance, the movement, already financially hard-pressed by the depression, would flounder. By the winter of 1838–39 the franchise had become for political abolitionists the moral test of commitment to the cause. That meant Garrison and *The Liberator,* symbols in the public mind of immediatism, had to be purged from the ranks.[12]

The confrontation occurred on January 23, 1839 at the annual convention of the Massachusetts Anti-Slavery Society in Boston. The New York headquarters had sent Henry B. Stanton to aid the anti-Garrisonians who hoped to wrest the organization from the nonresistants by passing a resolution endorsing the antislavery ballot as incumbent on all abolitionists. Forewarned, Garrison had filled the meeting hall with his raucous partisans. When challenged on stage by Stanton's blunt question, "Do you or do you not believe it a sin to go to the polls?" Garrison shot back, "Sin for me!" to the applause of his supporters. His clever but evasive rejoinder meant that suffrage should be left to each individual's conscience, but implied that nonresistants were better men for not voting. Such ambiguity did not satisfy political abolitionists. "Proclaiming on one page that all human attempts to protect the innocent and punish the guilty by physical force are of the devil," Elizur later complained, "he preaches on another that those whose *consciences approve* of government are bound *to vote.*" "Conscience seems to be a chameleon-like thing with these men," he concluded in disgust. Nevertheless Garrison's resolution that suffrage not be required of all abolitionists carried the day.[13]

The schism widened as anti-Garrisonian insurgents abandoned the Massachusetts Anti-Slavery Society. On February 7, 1839 the first issue of *The Massachusetts Abolitionist,* a weekly rival to *The Liberator,* appeared with an editorial proclaiming a return to the principles of political action. In May, after further frustration with the old organization, they founded the competing Massachusetts Abolition Society. The publishers of *The Massachusetts Abolitionist* chose Elizur to edit their paper and to serve as an officer of the new society. "All reflecting men say," Stanton persuasively cajoled, "that the *isms* must be expelled or it is ruined and all agree that you are the man to expatriate them." Elizur formally notified the executive committee of the national society in early February that he had accepted. Although he wrote some unsigned essays for the paper, he did not assume the editorship until May 23, after his work for the annual spring convention of the American Anti-Slavery Society was completed.[14]

In many ways, Elizur was well suited for the new job. A number of factors influenced his move to Boston among which was the attractive salary of fifteen hundred dollars per year and the benefit that his wife would be near her relatives. His polemical style, which unnerved his New York colleagues, matched Garrison's. No one could accuse him of being a lackey of a clerical faction. Garrison recognized in his opponent that "in securing his services, they have 'caught a Tartar,' we have very little doubt. He is an able, ready and caustic writer and will not spare any political dough-face or clerical dumb dog in the Commonwealth of Massachusetts or elsewhere." Elizur's newspaper experience and outstanding immediatist record were, as Stanton put it, "worth [their] weight in gold" to the Massachusetts dissidents. He was also eager to leave behind the office politics of the national headquarters, in which his own anticlericalism had made him suspect, and enter the thick of the fray. "With all respect to G[arrison]," he wrote to an unsympathetic Maria Weston Chapman, "I consider his 'nonresistance' sheer lunacy—and sadly ill timed, as it cuts the hamstrings of abolitionism just at the crisis of battle—so far as it has any edge at all." As he confided to Beriah Green, "My plan is not to enter the field to cut up the weeds—the isms—but to hoe the corn and till it well, and let the weeds look out for themselves."[15]

But as editor, Elizur chopped the weeds as well as tended the corn. In his first official statement at the paper, he declared, "As to the practical and vital matter of applying antislavery moral power to the thing to be done, Mr. Garrison is not where he was, therefore we are where we are." In contrast to nonresistance he asserted that political effort had increased abolitionist influence "tenfold." Throughout his tenure he affirmed "the duty of exercising our political power in behalf of the slave." He unsuccessfully sought to win over Boston's black community which remained loyal to Garrison, a proven friend. "Can our colored friends," he queried after pointing out that Garrison had chided them in 1834 for not voting for an antislavery candidate, "allow us the liberty of differing from him as much as he differs from himself?"[16]

Unsympathetic to Garrisonian agitation for women's rights, Elizur sought to divorce abolitionism from that "vexatious question." He protested against "pack-saddling our cause with an innovation upon received customs—a 'reform' which has no more to do with slavery than it has with the banks." He wondered aloud at Garrison's "discovery in morals" that barred physical resistance against a woman's "ravisher." A barbed poem he wrote some years later captured his incredulity at perfectionism:

> All institutions built on striking,
> Must be abolished to its liking.
> The slave whip and pedant's birch
> The government, and the church...
> This sweeping, to perfection brought,
> The world will equal heaven, 'tis thought....

In defense of Cinque, the African mutineer who seized a Portuguese slave ship in June, he argued, "We dare not say that the instinct of physical self-defense is never to be exercised."[17]

Thanks in part to Elizur's energetic promotion of political action and indictment of nonresistance, *The Massachusetts Abolitionist* outstripped *The Liberator* in circulation. Yet, despite some notable victories in the November 1838 elections, the policy of scattering antislavery votes among the most attractive candidates appeared to have little significant influence on the two major parties. A closely watched gubernatorial race in New York and another critical contest in the Bay State's fourth district demonstrated the general unwillingness of party loyalists to cross political lines and vote for an antislavery candidate. The defeat of Senator Thomas Morris of Ohio, whom the Democrats had purged from the party for his abolitionism, was a further setback. Elizur added that the Atherton gag rule on antislavery petitions in the House of Representatives and Henry Clay's "infamous speech" of February 7, 1839 against abolitionism in the Senate were conclusive proof that Democrats and Whigs were firmly committed to the defense of slavery. The "plan was to operate on the existing parties by influencing them to put up antislavery candidates," he later remembered. "Some years' trial of this plan convinced us of its futility."[18]

Frustration with the two-party strategy provoked Alvan Stewart and Myron Holley in early 1839 to lead a group of New York abolitionists toward the formation of a third party. Stewart's arguments persuaded Elizur that summer, only shortly after he took over the editorship of *The Massachusetts Abolitionist,* of the necessity of creating an abolitionist party. Elizur enthusiastically supported Holley's organizational efforts in western New York, and later credited the Rochester abolitionist in a glowing biography with doing "more than any other man to start the political movement." At a tumultuous gathering of five hundred abolitionists in Albany on July 31, 1839, delegates overrode Garrisonian objections and affirmed the antislavery franchise, but stopped short of endorsing a third party.[19]

Undaunted, Holley prepared to lobby a special convention of the American Anti-Slavery Society in Cleveland on October 23 to make its own distinct nominations for president and vice-president in the forthcoming national elections. Elizur judged the success of Holley's effort essential in order to redirect the fragmented abolitionist movement. "There will," Lewis Tappan lamented to an English friend, "probably be an abolition political party—religious association—a Garrison party, etc., etc." Tappan was right; a tripartite schism had emerged. Anti-Garrisonians split between church-oriented abolitionism, which included Tappan's evangelical circle in New York and the clerically dominated Massachusetts Abolition Society, and the partisans of an abolitionist party. The church-oriented abolitionists endorsed the antislavery ballot but drew back in religious reproach at the corrupting process of party politics. They shared with the rival Garrisonians the belief that abolitionism was fundamentally a moral endeavor that depended on the spiritual regeneration of the American people. As the conservative William Jay complained, the third-party movement was an ill-advised attempt "to change the antislavery enterprise from a religious to a political one."[20]

By endorsing Holley's position, Elizur was not only breaking with many of his colleagues at the New York headquarters of the American Anti-Slavery Society, but also confronting his clerically dominated publishing committee in Boston. Nevertheless, in his first major editorial on the subject in *The Massachusetts Abolitionist* on October 17, 1839, he declared his full support for a "human rights party." "We have long anticipated," he wrote, "a state of things which would make it the duty of abolitionists to nominate separate candidates for the President and Vice-President of the United States. We believe it is now almost inevitable. . . . If it is the duty of abolitionists to vote, it is their duty to make the most of their vote." He claimed that "both politics and religion will be humanized," but the churchmen were not persuaded.[21]

Privately Elizur worried that the Massachusetts Abolition Society stood at the brink of ruin and the national society faced its "Rubicon" at the Cleveland convention. His criticism hinged on the prescient assessment that if abolitionism was to succeed it must ideologically advance beyond the confines of a church-oriented strategy into the political realm.

In a highly confidential letter to a wavering Stanton on October 12, 1839, he argued that the delegates must nominate an abolitionist ticket, possibly ex-Senator Thomas Morris or philanthropist Gerrit Smith, to oppose the proslavery candidates of the Whigs and Democrats, probably Henry Clay and Martin Van Buren, respectively. "We must have," he demanded, "a free northern nucleus—a standard flung to the breeze—something around which to rally." In sum, the benefits of separate nominations would, he argued, unite the anti-Garrisonians, outflank the nonresistants, and strike terror "to the heart of the South from Clay downwards."[22]

In the "streak letter" (so named because that word appeared in the first line), Elizur explained that without the rallying point of distinct nominations the "shockingly mismanaged" Massachusetts Abolition Society would flounder. "Everything has been made to turn upon the *woman question*," he moaned. "The political has been left to fall out of sight." Without "something practical for every man to do," the new organization would waste its energy in a futile debate with the Garrisonians over "the *confounded* woman question." Stanton was not persuaded. Nor was the Cleveland convention, which tabled Holley's proposal as premature because the Whigs and Democrats had not yet officially named their standard-bearers.[23]

Making matters worse, the controversial "streak letter" mysteriously fell into the wrong hands and was sensationally featured on the front page of *The Liberator* for several successive weeks. Garrison proclaimed a "plot" by Elizur and the third-party faction against nonresistants. Adding to the woe, the executive committee of the Massachusetts Abolition Society repudiated their editor and fellow officer. They denied any knowledge of a plot and charged that Elizur took the woman question too lightly. They also denied supporting an abolitionist party and rejected Elizur's prognostication of the imminent demise of the society.[24]

The exposé put Elizur uncomfortably between the anvil of the old organization and the hammer of the new. He acknowledged authorship of the letter, but divorced himself from any plot. He pointed out that his views on politics, the woman question, and nonresistance were already well known from the columns of *The Massachusetts Abolitionist*. The plot, he countered, was a creation of the conspiratorial fantasies of the Garrisonians, who he sarcastically noted had the "honor of receiving and divulging secrets from a stolen letter." Garrison claimed to have "accidentally" gained the letter apparently after Stanton misplaced it. In response to the charges of his own society, Elizur reiterated that "without a third party, we have no doubt the new organization would continue to live as the old one does, passing resolutions but making no converts and acting with no efficiency on politics." The pertinacious editor told his employers that he would continue to advocate a third party in the newspaper, and they could fire him if they wanted. For the moment, they grudgingly retained their capable but intractable employee.[25]

Elizur's remaining tenure with *The Massachusetts Abolitionist* was devoted to arguing for a human rights party. He endorsed the formation of an abolitionist party at a convention held at Warsaw, New York, on November 13 and 14, 1839, under Holley's sponsorship. The delegates nominated a presidential ticket of James G. Birney and Francis J. LeMoyne; both, however, declined their nominations as premature. But, with the subsequent nomination of the Democratic and Whig tickets, Elizur joined Myron Holley, Alvan Stewart, Joshua Leavitt, Gerrit Smith, William Goodell, Charles Torrey, and Beriah Green in demanding abolitionist standard-bearers for the 1840 elections. "There is certainly a large and fast increasing portion of abolitionists in this state," Elizur claimed, "who will rally for a true party." He was a member of the business committee at an Albany convention chaired by Stewart on April 1, 1840, that met to reconsider the selection of independent abolitionist candidates. A close vote of 44 to 33 with many abstentions approved a third party, and the delegates selected James G. Birney and Thomas G. Earle as their front-runners.[26]

Ridiculed by the Garrisonians as the April Fools' convention and rejected by church-oriented abolitionists as unrepresentative, the third-party movement launched at Albany began inauspiciously. In a poem titled "Liberty Party, 1840," Elizur recalled his hope that:

> ...so shall wax the party
> Now feeble at its birth,
> Till Liberty shall cover
> This tyrant-ridden earth.

He hailed Birney "OUR CHOSEN MAN." "We hope within twelve years," he confidently predicted, "to see the executive power of this government wielded by James G. Birney, or some kindred spirit, to the utter overthrow of slavery, and the liberation of the millions, white and black which it now tramples in the mire." The only alternative to a human rights party, he warned, was "antislavery suicide."[27]

One-half the readers of *The Massachusetts Abolitionist* were not convinced and cancelled their subscriptions to protest the editor's political stance. The support from within the Massachusetts Abolition Society for the Whig presidential candidate William Henry Harrison, a northerner who had beaten Henry Clay, a Kentucky slaveholder, for the party's nod, worked against the third-party movement. "The Whig, new organization abolitionists plainly tell us," Elizur lamented, "if we don't go against the distinct nomination [of a third-party presidential candidate] they will go back to Garrison."[28]

By early May the publishers of *The Massachusetts Abolitionist* had enough of Elizur's "inopportune" editorials and fired him. He wryly recalled that his advocacy of a third party resulted in "offending the clergy, losing about 1,000 subscribers, and finally our bread and butter." In his final column he mused that "the expectations we indulged seven years ago are certainly in some measure disappointed." He blamed the reluctance of too many abolitionists to back a third party with retarding the crusade. And he again damned the Garrisonians who "on the pretense of securing a heaven hereafter or making one here" retreated from the contest of "checking the brutal propensities of a physical and brutal world." The new party, he predicted, would eventually make "antislavery principles a living and practical matter." Even though that November Birney garnered only a meager 7,000 votes, including 1,618 in the Bay State, Elizur thought that the electoral struggle would "gather strength."[29]

Out of a job, he momentarily found himself without full-time abolitionist employment. His support for what became known as the Liberty party had cut his ties to the Massachusetts Abolition Society and the American Anti-Slavery Society. The national organization had been captured by the resourceful Garrisonians at the May 1840 convention, and the rival church-oriented American and Foreign Anti-Slavery Society led by Lewis Tappan remained opposed to a third party until 1843.

During the spring of 1841 *The Free American* began publishing in Boston as the organ of the Liberty party in response to a changing political climate which attracted alienated antislavery Whigs to the new party. President Harrison's death after only a month in office elevated to the White House the Virginia slaveholder John Tyler, who opposed most of the Whig's 1840 platform. Elizur called the April succession a "salutary lesson." In a play of words on the party campaign slogan, he observed that "multitudes" of Massachusetts Whigs had enough of "Tyler too" now that "Tippecanoe" was dead. The publishers of *The Free American* hired Elizur to run the paper on June 24. In the wake of events, his argument that the Liberty party could "compel the other parties to give heed to the voice of justice and humanity" gained new attention. He pointed out the growing strength of the Liberty party in New England where even a small third-party vote had great significance because a victorious candidate needed by law a majority of all votes cast. The idea that the Liberty party could act as an electoral spoiler by forcing the two major parties to appeal to the antislavery constituency showed a growing level of political sophistication.[30]

The religious critics of the Liberty party, however, drew renewed fire from Elizur's imprudent editorials. The scruple of "backing out" of politics, he blasphemed, had originated with the "holier than thou clergy" whose "religion [was] too pure for any day but the Sabbath." "You back out of all responsibilities and for aught we know, back into heaven," he continued in an attack that included the Garrisonian nonresistants. "For our own part we had rather take our chance of getting there, face foremost, going through our full share of all social and political responsibilities which are necessary to the existence of society among men constituted as we find them." His abrasive point was that those who claimed religious or nonresistant principles for not endorsing the Liberty party were in effect apologists for slavery.[31]

Boston's churchmen and pious antislavery Whigs who opposed the third party bridled at Elizur's vitriolic attack on the church. Despite his desire to "live, breathe, and vote" for the Liberty party, he left the paper on October 21, 1841, under unpleasant circumstances. He claimed somewhat misleadingly that "private affairs," his low salary, and impoverished family forced him to resign. Editing a third-party paper can be a "starving business," he complained to Beriah Green. But as Wendell Phillips observed to fellow Garrisonian Elizabeth Pease, "He's an able man and strange to say his honesty on the church question obliges them to turn him out of the editorship of *The Free American* and put in someone who would pander to sectarianism." The Reverend Charles A. Torrey, a Congregationalist and leading opponent of Garrison during the "clerical controversy" of 1837, was more acceptable to the paper's readership and became the new editor. "Thus, having lost all popularity out of the Anti-

Slavery Society," Elizur remembered, "I soon lost consideration in it, and was left in fact to cut my own fodder in my own way, looked upon by ecclesiastical people as an infidel, by political people as an ultra, and by the abolitionists, so called, as a renegade." At thirty-seven years old with a growing family, he was faced with how to cut that fodder.[32]

The Sisterhood of Reforms

The sunny days of August 1843 and scenic views of western New York afforded from the deck of the Erie Canal barge did not cheer one of its passengers. Elizur's efforts to raise desperately needed funds by selling his translation of La Fontaine's *Fables* seemed futile. These business trips took him away for weeks at a time from his impoverished family whom he blamed himself for failing. "But my hope is dead," he wrote to Susan at their Dorchester home outside Boston. "My plans all fail. The world does not seem to have much need of my services anyway. I cannot understand this at all. It seems to me that I can do some things as well as anybody." He wiped away the tears, which came quickly when he thought about their plight. That night he sank into a melancholic sleep on some soft bags of black pepper in the hold of the barge.[1]

The cruel depression that gripped America after 1837 had put a severe strain on abolitionist budgets. While still with *The Massachusetts Abolitionist*, Elizur's salary was reduced by the austerity to one-half of the fifteen hundred dollars he had been promised. He resorted to farming six acres of land at his rented Dorchester home outside Boston in order to feed his wife and four children. The end of his brief tenure with *The Free American* in October 1841 had made his situation desperate. For the first time in eight years he was not on an abolitionist payroll, and he turned to other endeavors to gain a livelihood. Garrison mocked that his ideological antagonist "once a flame of fire...[is] absorbed in selling some French fable which he has translated into English." His old friend Beriah Green admonished, "Elizur Wright—in the name of God and bleeding humanity, I ask—Where art thou?" Lewis Tappan chided, "Your pen was wanted for the anti-slavery cause and we could not afford to relinquish it to write fables."[2]

Elizur Wright, Jr., 1841. (Reprinted from Philip Green Wright and Elizabeth Q. Wright, *Elizur Wright: Father of Life Insurance* [Chicago: The University of Chicago Press, 1937]. © 1937 by The University of Chicago Press. Reprinted by permission.)

During the two decades before the Civil War, Elizur did not abandon abolitionism, but he did revise the terms of his engagement. The combination of the abolitionist schism and his family's destitution served to widen the distance between himself and other first-generation immediatists. His anticlericalism cut him off from the church-oriented abolitionism of Lewis Tappan, and his intolerance for nonresistance kept him apart from the Garrisonians. His evangelical faith that moral suasion alone would transform the world gave way to support for the fusion politics of the Free-Soil and Republican parties. In addition to abolitionism, he endorsed a "sisterhood of reforms," including land redistribution, justice for the laborer, the end of war, public education, and even women's rights. "These reforms are all so connected," he declared in 1846, "that we defy any man to advance one of them sincerely without advancing others." His expanded social agenda was, however, more provocative than systematic; he was a gadfly, not a philosopher. Although he abandoned pietistic, sectarian movements for more practical, instrumental means of social change, he retained the individualistic, passionate style that made him suspect to every stripe of activist. In the rough-and-tumble world of the reformer in which he was now a relatively isolated figure, he increasingly drew the emotional nurture to persevere from his beleaguered but loving family rather than his colleagues.[3]

The survival of his growing family was Elizur's primary concern during the early 1840s. "You who know our circumstances," he wrote Beriah Green, "will understand why I do no more in the *Free American*—others, I suppose may think I have lost my first love for the good cause." By 1841 he and Susan had five children, including two invalids. The toddler Charles Storrs, named after Elizur's deceased colleague at Western Reserve College, was congenitally crippled on the right side of his body. Unable to walk except by holding on to chairs, he got about in a "go-cart" his father made. Harriet Amelia, nicknamed "wee-wee" for her small size, suffered from an incurable spinal ailment that left her "feeble and helpless," with her head dangling downward "like a dead chicken's." "We don't know what to do for her," Elizur lamented. He built his daughter a swing, whose rocking motion soothed her pain.[4]

Death was a frequent caller to the Wright home. Elizur dedicated a New Year's sonnet in 1840 to his wife that included the sad refrain: "...our tender offspring number—seven—/Divided, four on earth and three in heaven." Three children had died in infancy during the 1830s, and two more youngsters, including Harriet Amelia, joined them within the next four years. A despondent father cried out: "The want of bread is sore indeed/Worse is the want of mouths to feed." His conversion to the "daily matutinal baptism" of cold water, part of the fad of hydrotherapy, was an effort to improve the health of his children. But ducking a squealing, sixteen-month-old baby into a tub of cold water may have had the opposite effect. Susan "suffered terribly" from repeated pregnancies, including having nearly died in labor in the fall of 1838. Contrary to growing middle-class practice, Elizur and Susan apparently avoided birth control techniques that would have relieved the mother's ordeal and eased their poverty. Death and destitution did have the positive effect of bonding the family closely together.[5]

The family budget had never been secure, but money matters worsened during the hard times of the early 1840s. "I am terribly sick of salaries— especially, such as are not paid," he complained to Beriah Green about abolitionist employment. Since moving to Dorchester, he grew hay, potatoes, and vegetables, and kept a milk cow and chickens in order to feed his family and supplement his spasmodic salary. The depression had dried up contributions to the factious Massachusetts Abolition Society and forced Elizur to return to the yeomanry skills of his rural youth. "The only way I see to prevent the banks from starving us all," he believed, "is to take our places next to Mother Earth and take her givings first hand." Despite Susan's making all their clothes, household help from her sister, and homemade goods from his mother and sisters in Ohio, Elizur was "absolutely penniless" by the spring of 1841. In the midst of their woes, his frequent household poems, such as an 1842 "thanksgiving" offering, sought to lift their spirits:

> ...though we own no deeded acres,
> Nor any stock in banks,
> We own whatever is our Makers,
> And we will give him thanks.

His basic trust in the benevolence of providence helped to sustain them.[6]

The abolitionist schism had complicated his relationship to the abolitionist crusade, but it was his family's poverty that forced him to limit efforts on behalf of the slave. "With such a household and housefull as mine," he explained, "it is my resolute duty to provide for them first, by the most feasible and most effectual among honest methods. To find that is the problem." He embarked on several plans. He proposed to his friend

Beriah Green that he serve as a "worldwide agent" for the Oneida Institute, the biracial and manual labor school in central New York of which Green was president. Because the financially strapped school could not fund such a position, Green offered Elizur a professorship. But he declined because Susan's health had improved since they had moved near the coast. The issue soon became moot because the institute itself fell victim to the economic hard times and competition for antislavery students from Oberlin.[7]

Dire circumstances led Elizur to turn his inclination for poetry and affinity for French into what he hoped would be a money-making venture. In 1837 he had made a present of Jean de La Fontaine's *Fables,* which he had picked up at a Broadway bookstore, to his five-year-old son John because of the intriguing illustrations that accompanied the French text. La Fontaine, a seventeenth-century poet and friend of Racine and Molière, had given a number of the world's fables his own witty rendition. Although the grace and simplicity of his style had made his work a staple of French culture, no English version existed. John's incessant requests for an explanation of the story spurred his father to translate the irregular rhyme scheme, which he did early in the morning before he left for the antislavery headquarters. Favorable critical response to his initial efforts led him to publish in September 1841 with Boston's Tappan and Dennet a deluxe, two-volume, ten-dollar edition of 585 pages with 240 illustrations by the noted French engraver J. J. Granville. The Gallic verse appeared next to Elizur's English translation. Henry Wadsworth Longfellow, George Ticknor, William H. Prescott, and other leading literati lauded the translation. "He is kith and kin with La Fontaine," a review in the prestigious *North American Review* praised. "He has the same good-natured way of looking upon the world and the doings of man, and something of the same humorous expression." Elizur needed to sell 450 advance subscriptions in order to pay for publishing costs, but he hoped to place 1,000 orders and gain a substantial profit.[8]

But the *Fables* were not a financial success, despite the successful translation. The *New York Observer,* a staid religious newspaper, denounced the whimsical tales as "licentious" and ill-suited for children. La Fontaine imparted the worldly wise morality of Bourbon France to his anecdotes, which the reviewer found unwholesome. For example, in the well-known Aesopian fable of the industrious ant and frivolous grasshopper, La Fontaine suggests a self-righteous cruelty to the ant in the grasshopper's hour of need, a revision of the original. Elizur was incensed at the sanctimonious criticism of the newspaper. "So you have not turned good-natured old Jean [de La Fontaine] and me out of doors on account of the awful discovery of the *New York Observer!*" he wrote in mock sarcasm to Beriah Green, himself a dissident Congregationalist minister. "Nor felt your cloth insulted by the story of the Rev. John Cabbagepate (Jean Chouart)," one of the light-hearted fables. But Elizur reported that the "pious article" about "the corrupting book" had depressed sales and made his publishers "shake in their shoes a good deal." He found the clerical accusation galling and absurd since the stories were part of his family's practice of reading aloud. Such prudish criticism further alienated him from the church. The real difficulty of the publishing venture was, however, that the depression had reduced demand for a ten-dollar book no matter what its merit. Elizur's literary talent clearly outshone his business acumen.[9]

In his first effort in the new year of 1841 at soliciting subscribers to the nearly completed *Fables,* the "hatchet-faced, spectacled, threadbare" translator, as he described himself, spent seven weeks on the road in the major cities of the Northeast. The work was time-consuming and fatiguing. A typical sales day was thirteen hours and involved contacting customers with whom he would leave a copy of the book, a prospectus, and then call back within a few days. Among his buyers were notables such as jurist Chancellor Kent, Professor Benjamin Silliman of Yale, poet Henry Wadsworth Longfellow, publisher George Ticknor, and President Martin Van Buren. He sold 350 subscriptions by early March and was optimistic that the *Fables* would support his family. "Every day confirms my opinion that my book will succeed," he enthused after a good day in Brooklyn. Once he was back on his financial feet he hoped to return to abolitionism, "the cause of the downtrodden." "My heart," he confided to his wife, "is surely there."[10]

By December 1841 the first flush of enthusiasm had waned. Sales slowed substantially. Elizur noted with frustration that "bankruptcy has fallen upon almost everybody." The "fearful obligation of debt" and the "threat of starvation" drove him on from city to city. The precarious business of bookselling remained his chief source of income for the next two years. In the nation's capital, he even tried to sell a copy of *The Fables* to the arch spokesman for slavery, John C. Calhoun. The senator from South Carolina recognized his abolitionist antagonist but steered away from that "delicate subject," Elizur mused to Beriah Green. To compensate for declining sales he did French translations at a dollar per page for the publishing house of Haskell.[11]

The lonely life of a traveling salesman wore especially hard on Elizur. The separation from his family was emotionally gruelling. "I long to see you and clasp you in my arms—I do—I do," he wrote to Susan from Albany, "and to hug and kiss those dear, dear babies that God has given us." The frequent month-long stretches away from his troubled home from 1841–43 drove him at times to despair, an emotion so different from his usual sense of trust and hope in the world. "In short, how do you get along—dear, dear woman," he wrote Susan, again pregnant, "and how much do you have to suffer? To think you are my wife and have to bear such a load, makes me about frantic. The tears start in good round drops." "I should either go crazy or go home if I sat down to think five minutes," he lamented. "O may God help you—my help is nothing." Because of his itinerant schedule, he was not able to receive regular correspondence from Susan. Only after his arrival home from a trip to Pittsburgh did he learn the heartbreaking news that their previously healthy eight-month-old son was dead. Arthur Tappan, named in honor of Elizur's former patron, had died two weeks earlier in his mother's arms after suffering from smallpox.[12]

For a while Elizur contemplated abandoning the ill-fated *Fables* and returning to Ohio to farm and perhaps teach in a district school. In 1843, in addition to peddling books, Elizur became a salesman of a rotary knitting machine, the creation of a Springfield, Massachusetts, inventor. The device was touted to restore the competitive edge to home production of textiles over factory production. The effort to market an invention that would putatively reverse the trend toward industrialization was not unexpectedly a failure. Elizur canvassed prospective buyers from Massachusetts to Ohio for a month, before abandoning the quixotic project. Besides the desperation of finding a way to make money, his lack of a critical sense of economic trends also was his undoing.[13]

The opportunity to take a three-month business trip to England, however, dissuaded him from returning to the Buckeye State. Boston booksellers Tappan and Dennet offered him five hundred dollars with paid passage and a liberal commission on his sales of their books plus the right to sell the *Fables*. He also acted as a fiduciary for English contributors to the debt-ridden Massachusetts Abolition Society. In addition, a Massachusetts life insurance company engaged Elizur, a talented mathematician like his father, to investigate English actuarial practices, an assignment that would eventually develop for him into a distinguished career in life insurance reform. The "horror of leaving home" held him back, but economic necessity drove him forward. He sadly realized that "my poor little ones can better do without me than without bread."[14]

With his family waving a sad farewell from the Boston wharf, Elizur sailed for Liverpool on March 1, 1844. The trip was a failure, at least, in its intended goals. Despite connections with English abolitionists and introductions to writers such as Thomas Carlyle, Charles Dickens, and Robert Browning, he was unable to defeat the "Demon of debt." Rooming in a London garret and spending twenty-five cents a day on food, the impoverished salesman found it difficult to gain entry into the fashionable society that contained his most likely clientele. The painful separation from home dragged on until October. Nevertheless the seven months he spent in England and Scotland were to have a profound influence in broadening his reform agenda well beyond abolitionism, a development for which ironically he had castigated Garrison only a few years before. The "sisterhood of reforms" that he would so enthusiastically advocate after his return was prompted by a frustrating but stimulating trans-Atlantic trip.[15]

Imperial England—urbanized, industrialized, and class-bound—was an education for an open-minded American with strong humanitarian concerns. Parliament had recently freed the slaves, removed disabilities against Catholics, passed factory regulation, and expanded suffrage. But social agitation remained unabated in 1844. The abject poverty of the slums, working-class protest, especially the Chartist crusade, the arrogance of the aristocracy, Irish nationalism, and the anti–Corn Law movement made a strong impression on Elizur. Notes he made of what he saw became the sources for "Gropings in Great Britain," which he later published in his newspaper *The Chronotype*. Though intended as an entertaining travelogue for his readership, "Gropings" contain revealing social observations amidst the florid prose describing picturesque castles and sweeping greenswards.[16]

The Dickensian poverty throughout England strongly affected the struggling book salesman. At St. Mary's in Coventry he heard Daniel O'Connell, the charismatic Irish nationalist, address "the sweltering mass of the great unwashed." As the irresistible O'Connell described "the poverty and honest toil of the poor Irish laborers," a tearful Elizur, like most in the crowd, "felt the brine overflowing my own eyelids." Learning that Elizur was an abolitionist, O'Connell warmly greeted the American at the end of the speech. The Irish poor, including a mother and child he encountered at Eton begging for bread, were a common sight, a plight soon to be made catastrophic by the potato blight. Moved by such experiences, Elizur later denounced nativist bigotry against Irish immigrants in America, something which he had been guilty of as a tract agent in Pennsylvania.[17]

Elizur maintained, however, an ambivalent attitude toward the poor, which included a combination of heartfelt sympathy, evangelical pietism, and bourgeois disdain. "There are," he wrote to his wife, "many sights to make one's heart ache." He likened London's alleys to "human rat-holes, almost choked up with children." In the desperate Houndsditch neighborhood of the East End, he found "as much as you can bear of London's vice, poverty and human rubbish," a living replication of a William Hogarth painting. Yet, he still could sermonize, "How much happier they would be in their poverty, if they only *knew how* to live!" Too much tobacco, too much liquor, too much poverty remained his equation. Suspicion of working-class agitation for electoral reforms, he referred disparagingly to "the beer drinking Chartists."[18]

In the republican tradition of Thomas Paine, Elizur had a democratic loathing for the hereditary privilege of England's aristocracy. He inveighed: "To the great mass of the aristocracy, whose titles and wealth are their all, there is no employment apparently, but attending these midnight orgies and sleeping off their effects. To enable them to do this, every British laborer's loaf has heretofore been cut down at least one-third; India has been ransacked with disciplined bands of robbers, and the Celestial Empire itself invaded." Poet William Wordsworth told him during a visit to the Lake District that a leisure class removed from the mundane concerns of the world was needed to invigorate a nation's culture. Elizur responded bluntly, "The longer I staid in England, the more this class of independent, hereditary gentlemen seemed to me like a perpetual devouring curse of locusts." He found after conversation with Thomas Carlyle in Chelsea that the famous writer was egotistical, authoritarian, and "profoundly ignorant" about American slaves whose condition he deemed "about as well as their nature admits of." Elizur was appalled at how the gentry abused their landless tenants, the sterile academic conformity of Oxford University, and the corruption in Parliament. In England, he wrote to his wife, the laws make "the rich richer and the poor poorer."[19]

Sympathetic but suspicious of the downtrodden, and disdainful of England's elite, Elizur clearly revealed his affinity for bourgeois liberalism. "Between great poverty and extreme wealth the middle class is kept safe and steady...," he believed. "In the middle class there is permanence," an accurate assessment for Anglo-American society that contrasted with Karl Marx's and Frederick Engels's contemporaneous prediction of widespread destitution and proletariat revolution in the heartland of industrial capitalism. He attended meetings of the Anti–Corn Law League, and praised free-trade advocate Richard Cobden. He generally endorsed their goals of laissez-faire, natural economic laws and individual liberty for manufacturer and operative. After an exciting rally in Carlisle he enthused that "the right of the producing man in every nation to the markets of the world was vindicated." Elizur cheered the attack on a protective tariff on grains which benefited the landed gentry and raised the price of bread for the masses. He failed, however, to grasp the point—which Marx and Engels well recognized—that when Parliament repealed the Corn Laws in 1846, power in England passed from "the proud aristocracy" to the ascendant manufacturing class of Manchester and other textile centers, in the guise of a genuine popular reform. Elizur's economic individualism blocked his understanding of class formation during the Industrial Revolution.[20]

The beauty of Hyde Park and Kensington Gardens and the wonders of the British Museum momentarily distracted him from the thought that he was "An exile! an outcast! hard toiling in vain!" But the sight of women and children begging in the squalid streets of London's East Side conjured up visions of his own family's plight. Letters from America brought sad and frightening news. On March 26 the frail Harriet Amelia died from her congenital ailment. "Wee [sic] miss her very much," his eleven-year-old son John wrote the next day. Later that spring Susan saved the children from their burning house which a conflagration in their Dorchester neighborhood suddenly engulfed. "I took both the babies in my arms and ran with them," she recalled, careworn with domestic problems made worse by an absent husband. The homeless family found refuge with Susan's parents in nearby Groton.[21]

Death and devastation beckoned Elizur home. "I think you had better come home at the time you meant to," his son pleaded, "so as to be here when the children are sick." The struggle to make money, however, kept him in England for seven long months, making him extremely forlorn. "Job could not have cursed the hour he was born more sincerely and thoroughly than I do that in which I published La Fontaine," he wrote his wife from Liverpool. His anxiety was heightened after not having received a letter from Susan since the first of July. On board the ship that returned him to America on October 9, he captured his excitement at returning home to his wife:

> O for her sake let our prow
> Rejoicing dash the foam,
> Till I may kiss her careworn brow
> And I will never roam.

Although the English trip would eventually spark a successful career in life insurance, for the moment it was a business failure. Debts of some thirteen hundred dollars remained unpaid.[22]

During his family's travail, Elizur's old immediatist colleagues, excluding the still antagonistic Garrisonians, rallied to help. Beriah Green and Gerrit Smith sent money. Lewis Tappan and Amos Phelps assisted Susan and the children after their house burnt down. "E. W., Jr. and his family are poor and miserably off," Tappan reported to Theodore Weld. "They have thrown themselves out of all their social relations and the children are growing up non-descripts," a critical reference to Elizur's refusal to join a church. Tappan offered Elizur a six-hundred-dollar-a-year post in his New York office, and the Reverend Joshua Leavitt sought to engage him for *The Emancipator.*[23]

Elizur turned down their job offers. His anticlericalism had reached sufficient proportions not only to break irrevocably with church-oriented immediatists, but also to confront his parents and siblings in Ohio over his apostasy. "I am sick, sick unto death," he wrote them in the winter of 1839, "of the eternal parade of outside Christianity—church-going and psalm-singing and revivaling—on the part of men who will not lift one sliver of a cross to finish the work for which Christ died." He still believed in the teachings of Christ. The "husks" and "idols" of religion, "the art of seeming to be wise and pious," however, forced him, not unlike the Garrisonians, to "come out" of a hypocritical church. "I drifted into the anti-slavery struggle with full faith in the church as an organization of conscientious men, not afraid to follow the truth, lead where it would," he later remembered. "This faith perished, of course."[24]

The Ohio family was confused and appalled at Elizur's heterodoxy. James rejected his older brother's advice to find a career more worthy than the ministry. "Sometimes I have thought perhaps if I had encouraged you more," his mother lamented, "that now you would have been a preacher of righteousness." Her deathbed wish in June 1843 was that "her dear boy" recite daily Psalm 100, which includes the refrain, "Serve the Lord with gladness!" "Can you not select a church in your vicinity," his aged father implored, "with which you can unite and feel at home? Certainly the time is near at hand when we hope to make one grand family in heaven." Elizur honored his father, who died in 1845, as a thoroughly good man, and remembered his mother as "infinitely better than her creed." But he remained forever apart from their religion.[25]

During the personal and professional transitions in Elizur's life at early middle age, the Liberty party served as a way station between the personal piety of early immediatism and the practical politics of the Free-Soil and Republican parties. He remained a staunch supporter of the Liberty party and refused to be drawn back into church-oriented abolitionism. Between efforts to support his family, he engaged in some limited political activity. He was cheered by the presence of even a small number of antislavery men in Congress, where, he wrote Beriah Green in July 1842, the "little lump of abolition leaven has established itself." In the Bay State elections that November, the third party ran a spirited race against the Democrats and Whigs. "They must look for the young giant hereafter," Elizur reported to Gerrit Smith. He worked part-time for the general committee of the Massachusetts Liberty party in the fall of 1843, wrote three campaign tracts and sent thousands more throughout the state, arranged for James Birney and Henry Stanton to speak at Faneuil Hall, and planned a western business trip so he could attend the Liberty party convention at Buffalo in 1843. He was Suffolk County head of the Liberty Party and responsible for organizing party structure in the local towns surrounding Boston.[26]

The early Liberty party was for Elizur a form of evangelized politics. "A party ruling its members by *truth* and the *fear of God*" was how he described the party to Gerrit Smith. He wrote his father, also a political abolitionist, "God was there [at the Buffalo Convention] and was offering the Liberty party a great work to do." "The Almighty God wants a man to stand up for Him," he congratulated Birney, again the presidential nominee in 1844, "and be shown to the people as a sample of the manhood which he requires and loves; and you are the man." He finagled to give a Sabbath speech at the Groton church where he had been a devout member some fifteen years earlier. The minister opposed the Liberty party because politics offended his piety. Elizur, however, "preached politics as well as I knew how" to a full congregation. "I tried at any rate," he explained to Beriah Green, "to make them ashamed of their religion, who were inclined to vote with pro-slavery parties." He also edified an 1845 meeting of the Phi Beta Kappa society at Yale with the lines:

> Each good man has a part to act,
> And cannot flee, afraid to mix
> Religion with his politics.[27]

By middecade, Elizur concluded that most abolitionists, excluding the nonresistants, were casting a Liberty party vote. He argued that Henry Clay and Martin Van Buren, leaders of the two major parties, had been forced by the swing vote of the antislavery party to oppose the annexation of Texas, a proslavery region. "The fear of the Liberty party," he claimed, "has made more abolitionism in this nation than all other causes put together. By it other parties are driven to profess abolitionism, to discuss it and, in the end, possess it." He pointed to the reality of a growing Liberty party vote, which had totaled fifty-seven-thousand in 1843. During the presidential election of 1844, the financially strapped book salesman profited from his principled partisanship. He wagered with Massachusetts Senator Daniel Webster, Whig spokesman for the prosouthern textile industry, that the "Garland letter," which revealed that Birney (a Liberty party stalwart) had sold out to the Democrats for a seat in the Michigan legislature, was a forgery. The letter was bogus, and Webster paid off his losing bet.[28]

In the spring of 1843, Elizur sought to establish in Boston his own reform newspaper with a Liberty party orientation. He needed capitalization of twenty-five hundred dollars to see the paper through its first year, but by the winter he had only five hundred dollars in pledges. After his return from England and with mounting popular opposition to the question of Texas's statehood, he secured the financial backing of John A. Andrew, Henry Wilson, Samuel G. Howe, and especially Francis W. Bird, who contributed several thousand dollars. Mostly dissident conscience Whigs, these well-established, reform-minded men organized the antislavery political movement that soon led to the formation of the Free-Soil and Republican parties in Massachusetts. They had found in Elizur a talented editor with impeccable antislavery credentials who would make an energetic case of third-party politics. His attraction for the practical politics of a second generation of abolitionists marked his disenchantment with the reliance on moral suasion cultivated by religious abolitionists and Garrisonians alike.[29]

The Chronotype, dedicated to "all new ideas, without waiting to ask leave of priests, politicians or monopolists," first appeared on February 2, 1846. For the first run Elizur bought a bundle of paper, lugged it on his back to the printer, and then delivered the copy. "The newspaper," he declared in lingering evangelical tones, "is a divine institution" stirring mankind to good deeds. The four-page Boston daily featured political abolitionism, but also contained articles on a variety of reforms, business news, general information, and human interest stories. "The thinking, active, faithful editor," he preached, "picks up a thought here and there in haste, throws the varied gathering before his readers, irritates their curiosity, and leaves them to think and act." A visitor to his small office found a wiry man of less-than-average height hunched over a desk busily writing. Graying black hair barely covered a bald spot, and beneath gold-bowed spectacles hazel-blue eyes intently followed the flowing script. Or the editor might be napping on newspapers in a corner, a respite from long hours and his own nervous energy.[30]

Irreverent, intemperate, and unwilling to suffer fools gladly, the paper was an independent forum for Elizur's expanded social views—"The Sisterhood of Reforms," as he called it in September 1846. "Racy and caustic political writing" was how *The Nation* praised his provocative journalism. "That vile little *Chronotype*" was the opinion of Anne Warren Weston, a Garrisonian who differed over abolitionist strategy with the outspoken editor. His four-year editorship began an intellectual odyssey in search of a program of social justice that transcended the dogma of the church and the pietism of early immediatism. "One can not have had the experience which I have had in this world," he wrote his brother, "without learning some things and unlearning others, and if honesty *is* the best policy, it is but to confess what one has learned." In addition to political abolitionism, he defended Irish immigrants, deplored the tariff, demanded cheap postal rates, and denounced capital punishment. He commended Dorothea Dix's work on behalf of the mentally ill and advocated a phonetic orthography of his own devising. He endorsed rights for women, including suffrage, and praised the bloomer costume, a feminist dress reform, as "neat, graceful, modest and bewitching."[31]

Self-criticism broadened not only his social views but his personal life as well. He educated his own children at home because the schools were

THE SISTERHOOD OF REFORMS

too regimented, and encouraged his daughters to dance and act in his own amateur plays. "I regard the stage," he later wrote his prudish sister, "as a necessity of city life as much as the church is." The exhibition of Hiram Power's controversial sculpture, "The Greek Slave," provoked a clerical call to ban the statue of the bare-breasted maiden in Boston. Elizur rejoined, "The very essence of Christianity would seem to lie in our clothes." He enjoyed painting (praise for Titian's *Venus*), the opera (bravos for *Norma* and *The Barber of Seville*), and musical virtuosity (an accolade for violinist Camillo Seviro). The one-time critic of Unitarian urbanity had become a connoisseur of the beaux arts. Yet, city life had not transformed the former farm boy into the complete cosmopolite. Neither cigars, cognac, nor coffee ever crossed his still pious lips.[32]

To the dismay of the devout Lewis Tappan, Elizur was an infidel. In the pages of *The Chronotype,* he opposed Sabbatarianism, denied biblical inerrancy, and rejected the idea of eternal punishment. He challenged Lewis's faith with the charge that a "vast machinery of priestcraft...has usurped the place of the free, prison breaking spirit of Christianity." The silence of the pulpit before the outrage of the Mexican War, he told his readers, meant an atheist might be a "far better Christian than many in regular standing with the church." "There are many very excellent and pious infidels, my brother," he wrote James, "whom Christ loves better than he does many that pass by his name." Unlike his siblings, he had at midcentury broken free of "bondage to the terrible doctrines of our traditional theology."[33]

The religious equivalent to Elizur's affinity for practical politics was his substitution of reason and experience for faith and theology. "I find before me two pictures of God and his character," he wrote his sister, "one in the Bible and the theology founded on it, the other in the nature of men and things as illustrated by everything I know, or as I love to call it, the universal revelation." Most theology was "untrue and impossible." What mattered was doing "earthly good." He asked, "Whosover does a right thing is not God manifest in his flesh?" " Christianity itself is a total failure, "he wrote in *The Chronotype,* "so far as it is a plan of saving souls for a future life without saving souls and bodies for this." The challenge confronting Elizur was how to translate his secularized, evangelical ethic into meaningful social reform.[34]

In economic terms the transition took the form of various plans to restructure the social relations of production about which he speculated, notably in a series of columns titled "The Philosophy of Labor" in *The*

Chronotype. Elizur had earlier identified free labor—"self-ownership," or the personal autonomy in the marketplace to sell one's labor, in contrast to slavery—as a sufficient condition for honest, hard-working citizens to improve their material conditions in life. Like other first-generation immediatists, he had blamed poverty on individual immorality and personal profligacy. Indeed, he never lost the pietist inclination to fault the poor for drinking themselves into penury. But his own plight sensitized him to the widespread maldistribution of wealth, so visible in England's slums and in the urban North itself, of industrializing societies. He concluded, "There is fault somewhere in the machinery of society." Although he did not develop a comprehensive critique of capitalism, he did recognize to an extent unusual for abolitionists of the day that structural factors caused economic hardship and inequality in the antebellum North.[35]

The fortunate Appletons and Astors, the Lawrences and Lowells had accumulated extensive wealth during a time of rapid economic expansion, while many diligent people were crushed by the burden of debt. Elizur was shocked to report in his paper that one-tenth of the population owned one-half of the nation's property. "There are many things wrong in this world," he observed about the new class structure, "but none more so than the relations between capital and labor." The inequity of class relations violated his labor theory of value. "When capital gets into large masses, immense sums are inverted for purposes of personal luxury and grandeur," he explained, "other sums go into war loans and perish in idle or useless speculations and laborers wholly lose the benefit of what is really their own accumulated labor." Fault was not only with the wantonness of the masses but with the decadence of the rich.[36]

New York seamstresses were paid "a starvation wage" of four cents per shirt while frivolous Newport socialites cavorted at fancy dress balls. "This is what makes us so radical," Elizur told his readers. "This is what makes us want to see rich men hoeing corn, and rich ladies at the wash tub." He denounced John Jacob Astor and his ilk as "greedy." Astor became wealthy "not by his own industry but by the industry of others." In a proposal remarkably different from the pietism of evangelical and Garrisonian abolitionists alike, he recommended that Astor's estate of one million dollars be taxed at the rate of 50 to 75 percent. His goal was to reconcile capital and labor by creating a reasonable balance in the distribution of wealth. Unlike his European contemporaries Karl Marx and

Frederick Engels, Elizur sought to avoid revolution through reform that established a just mutuality between capitalists and workers.[37]

In *The Chronotype,* Elizur declared war on poverty. "There is capital enough in the community," he suggested, "to give all employment, and food and clothing enough to make all perfectly comfortable." He supported reform of debtor laws, an eight-hour day in the textile industry, safety precautions for lead workers, and a homestead act that would make 160 acres of public land available to settlers. "In a country where the means of living are so exuberant, we contend that the government can so arrange that no honest, well doing person shall suffer from destitution."[38]

Elizur's concern with "the machinery of society" attracted him to "associationism," a form of utopian socialism that substituted rational, secular planning for formal religious thought in addressing economic ills. Albert Brisbane, who had studied in France with Charles Fourier, popularized the idea in America after 1840 that the creation of ideal, cooperative communities would produce the good society. *The Chronotype* devoted three columns to "association" and expressed admiration for the Fourier "phalanx." In place of class struggle, Elizur called for "associations of capitalists and operatives, on strictly just principles, and guaranteeing to every person out of the common gains the exact product of his capital, his labor, or his skill." He urged workers themselves or philanthropists to establish model factories such as Robert Owen's at New Lanark, Scotland. He even proposed his own variant of a Fourieristic commune for his readers that would create an "independent man" freed from social and economic inequities. "It is just such an arrangement as this," he wrote in the non-Marxist fashion of the utopians, "making every workman his own employer, putting an end to all grinding oppression on the one hand and all hostility on the other, that we mean by the Organization of Labor [association]."[39]

Abolition, however, remained at the center of his sisterhood of reforms that he publicized in *The Chronotype.* "A man must be either a knave or a blockhead to pass about or stay anywhere in this District and not be a radical abolitionist," Elizur observed after a business trip to the nation's capital, where slavery was still legal. After a tour of a model plantation at the invitation of a Virginia congressman, he found slavery was "much worse than I expected." It was a "curse" that made him "sick, sick at heart." The press of national events and his expanded social program altered his allegiance to the Liberty party. The party had proved itself an electoral spoiler in Massachusetts, where James G. Birney, in 1844 again the Liberty candidate for president, increased his popular vote to 10,830, nearly seven times more than his 1840 total in the Commonwealth. And in New York, enough antislavery Whigs deserted their party for Birney (who captured 3 percent of the popular vote in the Empire State), that Henry Clay lost the state by a mere percentage point and ultimately the presidency to the Democrat James K. Polk. The election of Polk, a Tennessee slaveholder, provoked a crisis in the second-party system that political abolitionists artfully exploited.[40]

The cry of a slave-power conspiracy greeted President Polk's support for statehood for Texas in December 1845 and his declaration of war on Mexico in May 1846. *The Chronotype* damned "King Polk's war" as aggression "waged for the benefit of slaveholders who want an increased market for their human flesh, more power in Congress and the absolute control of all the labor of the country." "In such a dastardly, knavish, thievish, lying war as this against Mexico it is quite enough to ask," Elizur protested, "of any rational man not to take up arms on the side of Mexico." Democratic partisans encouraged army enlistees, who brandished their unsheathed bayonets, to harry Elizur and other speakers during an antiwar rally at Faneuil Hall. Undaunted, Elizur damned Caleb Cushing, a prominent Massachusetts Democrat and commissioned army officer, as leading a band of "drunken men and thoughtless boys...to cut throats and to ravish women" in Mexico. He called General Zachary Taylor, a war hero, Louisiana slaveholder, and Whig presidential nominee in 1848, a "devil." Popular opposition to the Mexican War opened the door of electoral opportunity for political abolitionists. On its masthead, *The Chronotype* emblazoned, "NO SLAVEHOLDER, NO INSTRUMENT OF THE SLAVEHOLDERS' WAR FOR THE PRESIDENCY."[41]

The debate over the extension of slavery into the western territories, which the Mexican War had raised to a fever pitch, reoriented party loyalty and allowed broad antislavery coalitions to form. In the 1846 congressional race, Elizur cast his vote for John Palfrey, a conscience Whig, instead of for the Liberty candidate. Beriah Green and Joshua Leavitt, Liberty party stalwarts, castigated his defection. "We have little more faith in the maxim that there is no honesty out of the Liberty party," Elizur rejoined, "than we have that there is no salvation out of the church." His practical point was that the most viable antislavery candidates should be supported regardless of party. Palfrey's victory with 51 percent of the vote not only put an antislavery man in Congress, but it further divided the conscience and cotton factions of the Whig party.[42]

Elizur was enthusiastic about the possibilities for fusion among Liberty men, conscience Whigs, and antislavery Democrats. By the summer of 1847 he was aware that the Liberty party's single issue of abolition was too narrow a platform to attract a broad constituency and to build an enduring movement. "To talk of abolishing negro slavery," he argued, "in a country where a few whites own all the land and can make what terms they please with the landless laborer is talking of a very temporary and partial and superficial improvement." A sisterhood of reforms—"equal rights, equal protection, equal privileges for all, and no monopoly or slavery for anybody"—was necessary to secure universal justice. He supported the Liberty League, which organized in June 1847 at Macedonian Locks, New York, and broke with the "one idea" of the Liberty party. He backed its leaders, Gerrit Smith and William Goodell, in their expanded program of abolition and land reform. In addition, Elizur formulated his own wide-ranging manifesto that included tax reform, temperance, antimilitarism, woman suffrage, just distribution of wealth, free trade, and the end of capital punishment. "We have no faith in abolishing slavery or doing any other political thing as it ought to be done," he explained, "till we can establish government on the one idea of equal rights for all."[43]

The presidential election of 1848 marked a political turning point. The Democratic nomination of Lewis Cass, whom Elizur derided as a "doughface," and the Whig candidate Zachary Taylor, who opposed the Wilmot Proviso's ban on slavery in the territories acquired from Mexico, were clearly unacceptable to him. Nor could he back the Liberty party's choice, John Hale, formerly an antislavery Democrat from New Hampshire. Unlike Elizur, Hale argued that the Constitution protected slavery in the states, and, besides, the narrow party platform did not seek "the overthrow of all monopoly." Elizur attended the Liberty League's Buffalo convention on June 14–15, 1848, and endorsed its standard-bearer Gerrit Smith. He hoped, however, that former president Martin Van Buren, now leader of the antislavery Barnburner faction whom southern partisans repudiated at the recent Democratic convention in Baltimore, might head a fusion ticket. "A fig for party creeds and tests," Elizur declared. What he wanted was the combination of a broad party platform coupled with an antislavery nominee who had the best chance to win. Politics was the art of the possible.[44]

At Buffalo on August 9, 1848, another convention made up, as Elizur put it, "of the honest Whigs and Democrats and the Liberty men," created the Free-Soil party. He deserted Smith and the Liberty League for the coalition ticket of the antislavery Democrat Van Buren and Charles Francis Adams, a Bay State conscience Whig. Smith and Goodell refused to support the diluted abolitionism of the Free-Soilers, which was limited to opposing the spread of slavery in the territories. In contrast to most other first-generation immediatists, Elizur thought that the Free-Soil party had the only realistic chance to counter "the very absurdity, mendacity, and general rascality of the Cass and Taylor factions." The party captured two of ten congressional seats and amassed 300,000 votes in Massachusetts after only three months of existence. Though Taylor was elected president, Van Buren gained 120,510 votes in New York, compared to Smith's paltry 2,545. For Elizur, the role of the small, morally cohesive antislavery party was over. The future of abolitionism was with what was feasible and expedient—coalition politics.[45]

The need for a single Free-Soil newspaper in Boston, especially to promote Charles Sumner's bid for the Senate, meant the end of *The Chronotype*. Fourteen-hour days and provocative writing had boosted circulation to six thousand, but Elizur was never able to put *The Chronotype* on a firm, financial footing. Free-Soilers Samuel G. Howe, Francis Bird, William Jackson, and John Jewell purchased *The Chronotype* in December 1850 and first published its successor, *The Commonwealth,* in January 1851. They offered Elizur twenty-five hundred dollars in cash, the same amount in stock of *The Commonwealth,* and thirteen hundred dollars salary as a subeditor. In order to create a disciplined party organ, Howe made clear that the outspoken Elizur was "to do the office work, news, etc., to have a bit in his mouth and say nothing editorially that the Chief does not approve." He accepted the position even though his style and wide-ranging views ran counter to the moderated tone and narrow party politics of the publishers.[46]

The subsequent problems of *The Commonwealth,* however, stemmed from the unstable Free-Soil coalition in the deceptive calm after the Compromise of 1850 in which lingering party loyalty resurfaced as well as the perennial financial problems of reform newspapers. For the first three months, the publishers ran *The Commonwealth* in place of the designated editor, John G. Palfrey, the former conscience Whig. He had inopportunely come out against the Free-Soil alliance with the Democrats in Sumner's Senate race. After March, the newspaper was given greater stability with Elizur as general editor and Bird as political editor. On June 16, 1851, after the persistence of Elizur's impassioned writing, Palfrey became contributing editor and the incorrigible general editor was shifted from news commentary to the restricted confines of the business department. "A paper belonging to so many with so many tastes to please," Elizur complained, "is a botheration."[47]

A good example of Elizur's immediatist exuberance which disturbed the equanimity of his Free-Soil associates was his vehement attack on the strengthened Fugitive Slave Law of 1850. That national legislation denied the right of jury trial to defendants, suspended the writ of habeas corpus, negated state liberty laws, and empowered the federal government to use all necessary force to return fugitives to slavery. Elizur denounced it as "the meanest and most cruel of crimes" and denied that "the Constitution sanctions or can sanction a crime." His poem, "The Fugitive," dramatized the ordeal of the runaway:

> I seek a home where man is man
> If such there be upon this earth,
> To draw my kindred, if I can,
> Around its free, though humble hearth.
> The hounds are baying on my track.
> O Christian! will you send me back?

In effect, he called for civil disobedience to an unjust law.[48]

Life imitated art in February 1851. The police arrested Elizur under the Fugitive Slave Law for assisting in the daring escape from police custody of Shadrack (Frederick Wilkins), a waiter in the Cornhill Coffee House close to the offices of Garrison's *Liberator*. In accordance with the law, marshalls had arrested Shadrack at the behest of his alleged slavemaster from Norfolk, Virginia. After defense lawyers gained a postponement in his hearing and the Boston courtroom was being cleared, a milling group of blacks suddenly engulfed the defendant and in the confusion spirited him away to freedom in Montreal. Although Elizur openly admitted he was not part of the rescue, his well-known opposition to the Fugitive Slave Law and his presence in the courthouse provided circumstantial evidence for complicity in the escape, which soon drew national attention for its defiance of federal law. "The prosecution of Wright," Samuel G. Howe confided to Horace Mann, "is all gammon, of course." It was an effort, Howe thought, to fix blame on *The Commonwealth*'s provocative editor in order to damage Charles Sumner's Free-Soil bid for the U.S. Senate which the newspaper strongly endorsed. Howe complained, "Wright has, however, much damaged Sumner without doing any good by what he has written." After three months of contention in the state senate, Sumner was nevertheless elected.[49]

Acting as his own attorney, Elizur turned his trial, which did not begin until June 4, 1852, into a harangue against the Fugitive Slave Law. His fifty-page plea, much of which he had printed earlier in *The Commonwealth,* concluded with an address to the jury "to contradict and rebuke that horrible delusion by which this Christian republic persuades itself that it can perpetrate the meanest cruelty that ever disgraced God's universe, under the sanction of our venerable Constitution." Antislavery philanthropist Gerrit Smith, who had criticized Elizur twenty years earlier for his aggressive actions on behalf of fugitive slaves in New York City, contributed five hundred dollars to his defense fund, which helped to meet his two-thousand-dollar bail. One juror, who later admitted to being one of Shadrack's rescuers, blocked the guilty verdict of his eleven peers. In a retrial that October with the skillful Richard Henry Dana representing him, Elizur was acquitted.[50]

The Free-Soil vote declined in 1851, and *The Commonwealth* floundered. Elizur and two associates bought the newspaper, and on November 25, 1851, he returned as editor and publisher. He broadened *The Commonwealth*'s columns beyond its limited Free-Soil focus. Charles List, the assistant editor, grew irritated at what he regarded as Elizur's extreme views, which would alienate the largely Free-Soil readership. List blamed Elizur for the newspaper's continuing financial woes and succeeded in ousting him in May 1852. Elizur rebutted vaguely that List's "perverse and unreasonable conduct" was at fault, but he left the newspaper for good.[51]

Two decades after he first espoused immediatism at Western Reserve College, Elizur found himself estranged from his evangelical colleagues of the 1830s and not quite at home with the new generation of political abolitionists. His distance from the pietism of his former associates was epitomized in his support for the Republican party and Abraham Lincoln in the election of 1860. "You, Elizur Wright, who would, I think, in better days have seen him [Lincoln] damned first!" Beriah Green thundered in echoes of early immediatism. "Expediency in opposition to simple justice has long seemed to me equally devilish and destructive, but never more so, than in thinking of the strange attitude to which it has reduced my dear old friend." In turn, Elizur explained to Green, "I have ceased to expect or look for any outward representative of my sense of justice in church, party, or government. I have begun to learn that such a thing is not possible and never will be."[52]

Unlike Green who still thought in terms of moral absolutes, Elizur acted in a circumscribed world of limited options. Although the Republicans included "sapheads, poltroons, and Pecksniffs," he pointed out that the Democrats represented "cut-throats, women whippers, and baby stealers." The Republican platform was inadequate in redressing slavery, but it contained "some just and right things" worthy of support. In contrast to the church-oriented abolitionism of his former colleagues, he added, "I don't believe in the God of books, I don't believe in anything but facts appreciated by some degree of evidence."[53]

Elizur remained associated, however, with the Free-Soil and later Republican partisans in Massachusetts who had subsidized *The Chronotype*. He was an early member of the Bird Club, which Francis Bird, a well-to-do paper manufacturer, had organized to promote political abolitionism and other reform. He regularly attended their Saturday afternoon dinners which included a number of influential politicians and prominent Bostonians. Yet, Elizur remained too outspoken, too moralistic, too individualistic to be fully accepted in the coalition politics he supported. He complained in good evangelical fashion about the stench of their cigars, a latter-day version of the sermon he had given against the sin of smoking three decades earlier at Western Reserve College. One Bird Club participant, Henry Wilson, a senator, vice-president, and chronicler of abolitionism, recalled, "If his words were sometimes curt and caustic, they were always vigorous and effective; and if he was sometimes impulsive and impractical, there was always an air of refreshing boldness and honesty in what he said and did." Wilson's ambivalence reflected the difference between the passionate style of the older immediatists and the moderated tone of second-generation abolitionists.[54]

In 1854, Elizur, who had turned fifty, observed in his typically blunt manner: "The only interest of my life—to the world or to myself—attaches to my humble efforts as an agitator against human slavery. My contempt for slaveholding and the miserable flunkies who govern this country in its behalf and all other schemes of money without labor is as great as any man's." But his commitment to political abolitionism was not the only reason Elizur enjoyed the camaraderie of the Bird Club, despite distrust about his intense manner. Since becoming editor of *The Chrono-*

type, he had interested other members in the social beneficence of life insurance. These powerful men, including three governors, two senators, and one vice-president, provided the political backing that helped Elizur become the century's most important life insurance reformer.[55]

Part Four

Actuary

Chapter 10

Commissioner of Life Insurance

"*Life insurance,* it's the greatest humbug in Christendom," English songwriter B. F. Proctor declared in disgust to the American book salesman seated next to him. Visibly unnerved, his breakfast companion managed to say, "You surprise me, Mr. Proctor. If I had not taken a policy from a life company just started in Boston, I should not have dared to cross the water, leaving a wife and five children on the other side." "Go to the Royal Exchange Thursday afternoon at three o'clock," Proctor continued, "and you will see what I mean." At that London center of trade, Elizur watched the sale to speculators of policies on aged men who no longer could pay the premiums. "I had seen slave auctions at home," he remarked in disbelief. "I could hardly see more justice in this British practice."[1]

The analogy was apt. Slavery and life insurance reified human beings by placing a cash value on their existence but presumably for different social purposes. Yet, the sale of lapsed policies to the highest bidder at the Royal Exchange involved a dehumanizing process similar to the slave auctions that Elizur had observed in Washington, D.C. "If I should ever become old myself, I thought, I should not like to have a policy on my life in the hands of a man with the slightest pecuniary motive to wish me dead," he reflected. In addition, the elderly Englishmen had no legal recourse to any equity accrued in their policies. The comparison of an outrage in the life insurance business with slavery showed the link in Elizur's mind between insurance reform and abolition and eased his transition between the two endeavors. Both ultimately involved similar humanitarian concerns—freedom for the slave and justice for the policyholder. Life insurance was a continuation of his antebellum reform impulse, a type of actuarial "associationism."[2]

Elizur Wright, 1865. (Reprinted from Philip Green Wright and Elizabeth Q. Wright, *Elizur Wright: Father of Life Insurance* [Chicago: The University of Chicago Press, 1937]. © 1937 by The University of Chicago Press. Reprinted by permission.)

The incident of the Royal Exchange in 1844 was a significant event in prompting Elizur, as historian R. Carlyle Buley rightly put it, to become "one of the most famous, if not one of the most important, figures in the history of American life insurance." "I resolved, if I ever returned to America," Elizur remembered, "it should be otherwise here, if my voice could avail." Beyond the outrageous abuses of policyholders' rights that existed, there was a fundamental personal motivation to his forty-year crusade in life insurance. It was not fortuitous or clever public relations when he typically advocated that life insurance must provide "a sufficient fund to sustain the widow and orphan," must provide "a perennial providence for the widow and orphan," and must prevent "the plunder of the widow and orphan." The repeated reference to a fatherless family recalled the potential tragedy that he had feared might befall his impoverished family if he had died during the English trip, and they had been mulcted on his life insurance policy. His wife and children would have been reduced to the pitiful circumstances of the abandoned old men in London. He was able to merge private feelings with public activities in a constructive relationship that provided him with psychological wholeness while he struggled for progressive social change.[3]

The beginning of Elizur's forty years in life insurance reform developed out of one of his efforts during the early 1840s to support his hard-pressed family. The Massachusetts Hospital Life Insurance Company had commissioned him, based on his mathematical expertise, to procure information on English actuarial practices during his bookselling trip in 1844. Before he set sail that spring, he took out a life insurance policy on himself which he left with an executor, Samuel Sewall, a friend and attorney. His perceived need for a life insurance policy was representative of many residents of northeastern cities who increasingly turned to extrafamilial institutions at this time in order to cope with the social transformation wrought by the Industrial Revolution.[4]

Rapid urbanization, the erosion of the lineal family, and a bourgeois sense of self-reliance made life insurance an attractive, if not essential, method of protecting a family against the loss of the principal breadwinner. Elizur did not expect kith or kin to bear the burden of his fatherless family, and he would not abrogate what he thought was his role as provider and protector. Nor would he, like his devout acquaintance F. Julius Le Moyne, not take out a life insurance policy because it was an immoral act, a presumption against God's control over human destiny. For Elizur the attraction of life insurance indicated a growing secularization of his religious background. Right living in this world was becoming an end in itself rather than a preparation for an afterlife. The boom of the life insurance business at midcentury reflected not only the surge of a dynamic economy but also the voluntarism of the age. The ethical imperative was for the individual to take charge of his life and to provide for his dependents in event of his death. Life insurance was a new, rational method to manage death through the application of the predictable, uniform rules of actuarial science.[5]

During the months Elizur spent abroad, he had a firsthand opportunity to examine the booming life insurance business in England. Since the beginning of modern life insurance there during the mid-eighteenth century, hundreds of firms had started but many had failed. Financial practices in this capital-intensive endeavor were not yet exactly established, causing numerous bankruptcies and wreaking untold hardship on policyholders. The fledgling American counterpart was poised for its own rapid increase and concomitant confusion in the decades spanning the Civil War. After 1840 in the United States, the amount of life insurance held in force expanded exponentially throughout the century, doubling in the decade 1850–60 alone to two hundred million dollars. Elizur conferred with the English actuary Joshua Milne, author of the widely used "Carlisle Table of Mortality" and head of the Sun Life and Fire Insurance Company. His initiation at the Royal Exchange into the rampant malpractice of life insurance sparked the effort to rectify what another critic, Charles Dickens, caricatured in the unsavory figure of Montague Tigg and his fraudulent Anglo-Bengalee Disinterested Loan and Life Assurance Company in *The Life and Adventures of Martin Chuzzlewit*. In brief, Elizur's contribution to the development of the industry was to reform, rationalize, and regulate its practices, laying the foundation for safe and secure life insurance. He was, simply, the premier life insurance reformer of the century.[6]

The establishment of *The Chronotype* in Boston during the winter of 1846 provided a forum to publicize what he had learned in England. His first attempt at a systematic innovation, temperance life insurance, sought to combine life insurance with evangelical piety. Encouraged with the success of an English firm that operated on a temperance policy, he made an arrangement on August 12, 1845, with the New England Mutual Life Insurance Company of Boston to provide an alternative for American teetotalers. Hard actuarial data did not exist, but Elizur assumed that nondrinkers were less a risk than imbibers, and that it would be to their financial advantage to form an exclusive association. The taking of an intoxicating beverage would void the policy. He foresaw that through a monetary reward for morality the temperate would "at last enjoy the precise value of their total abstinence."[7]

Despite a favorable agreement with the New England Mutual, the temperance plan was unsuccessful. It was technically sound, but the prescription for right living approached a secular religion of the body that discouraged all but the most zealous. Elizur preached a regimen of physical culture for the insured that barred all stimulating drinks, eschewed overeating, required frequent exercise, and demanded at least one cold water bath daily. He exhorted the insured "to approach [physical] perfection as fast as we can" out of fair play for their fellow policyholders who were presumably immersing themselves in tubs of cold water.[8]

Although Elizur's pet project failed, his critique of other life insurance practices in *The Chronotype* put him in the mainstream of reform. The prevalence of the Montague Tiggs, the abridgement of policyholders' rights, and the insolvency of many companies had persuaded him that "life insurance was the most availably convenient and permanent nidus for rogues that civilizations had ever presented." In contrast, he envisioned life insurance as mathematically determined altruism, a more precise counterpart to his interest in Fourieristic association. Life insurance could provide in a changing society what Christian charity could not— the protection of a family from the financial destitution caused by death. It minimized the pecuniary risk of mortality through rational control over the future. "While nothing is more uncertain than the duration of a single life," he explained, "nothing is more certain than the average duration of a thousand lives." In other words, a "risk factor" could be placed on the unpredictability of individual longevity because the life span of a person's age cohort was based on a constant decrement over time that was derived from actuarial tables. Life insurance was also a happy medium between collectivity and individualism. In his words, it resolved "the great problem—how to secure independence by means of general dependence." Mutual life insurance, which gave each policyholder the benefit of shares in the company, presented the possibility of a socially beneficent capitalism in which the pursuit of private profit would be used for the general good. For liberal thought that extolled the virtue of voluntarism and the laws of the free market, it did no less than to link organically the one and the many in an indivisible whole.[9]

The harmony between the individual and the group that Elizur foresaw rested on the sound financial practices of the life insurance companies. "A company which adopts proper rates and manages honestly," he stressed, "is just as sure to meet its engagements as the general structure of society is to last." In Elizur's rational mind, the steam engine—a physical exemplar of Enlightenment thought and nineteenth-century concepts of progress—and life insurance were in effect the same because both operated according to fixed, scientific principles. Consequently, he strongly criticized the excessive use of premium notes, employed during the 1840s by the insurance companies to increase their sales, as a threat to solvency. Some companies required only a quarter of the premium in cash, after which they would loan their customer the remaining amount in interest-bearing notes. He denounced the credit system as "financial quackery" which jeopardized the company's ability to meet future obligations when losses were heavier, and forced the policyholder or survivor (most likely a widow) to assume the burden of paying off the notes. The siphoning of the company's surplus to reduce premiums in order to expand business could lead to bankruptcy and to default on the policies. His indictment of "moonshine life insurance" persuaded the Mutual Benefit Life Insurance Company of New York to undertake a partial reform of their premium note system.[10]

The perils of the premium note system pointed to the need for stability in the rapidly expanding but financially troubled life insurance business. There was no standard procedure for calculating the net premium reserve or other factors necessary for maintaining solvency. The English practice of gross valuation of policies deceptively omitted expenses, and American firms, such as the Mutual Benefit Life Insurance Company of New York, imprecisely figured liability as the sum of the amount insured upon lives plus debts due on other accounts. As early as 1844, Willard Phillips, president of the New England Mutual Life Insurance Company, asked Elizur to apply his mathematical expertise to the problem of solvency. Nearly a decade later, shortly after his departure from *The Commonwealth,* the New England Mutual and five other companies subscribed a total of $2,196 for what became the landmark publication of Elizur's *Valuation Tables* in 1853. Aided by his older children, he spent nearly a year completing the laborious project that required tens of thousands of calculations and remains one of the most prodigious feats in actuarial history.[11]

Valuation Tables was a milestone in the search for order in the life insurance business. Taking into account a percentage of the company's probable expenses, an average rate of interest on investment, and contemporary mortality statistics, the almost one hundred pages of tables gave the net value of each policy on a single life to any assignable month or day. The tables showed that the amounts deducted from each premium for reserve purposes could be exactly fixed, and thus the aggregate capital a company must maintain in order to ensure solvency need no longer be an estimate. *Valuation Tables* provided a data bank which even a clerk could reliably consult in a fraction of the time it would take a well-paid actuary to calculate the proportion of the premium to be charged against the reserve.[12]

Elizur's highly praised efforts to bring financial stability to the insurance business did not at once cure his own money problems. He had hoped for a "tolerable living" from the sale of the *Tables*. As late as December 1856, he complained that several of the "soulless corporations," which had subscribed for his work, were holding back purchase of the *Tables* until he got "hungrier." The publication, however, gained him prominence as an actuary and soon led to employment with the state of Massachusetts and with the major insurance companies that provided him with a comfortable living during the last three decades of his life.[13]

Valuation Tables provided the basis for financial order in the insurance business, but Elizur perceptively argued as early as 1852 that state regulation was necessary to protect the consumer. He believed that insurance companies should be required to make a public annual statement of their assets and liabilities. Although in many ways a typical nineteenth-century liberal, he had no qualms in demanding governmental intervention when justice was at stake, whether on behalf of the slaves or policyholders. In 1854 he launched a vigorous lobbying campaign in the Massachusetts legislature to secure a law mandating that all insurance companies doing business in the state submit a yearly valuation of their policies. The next year Massachusetts established the first state insurance department in the nation with three commissioners paid on a per diem rate, but without what Elizur regarded as sufficient regulatory power over the one hundred million dollars' worth of insurance underwritten in the Commonwealth.[14]

Elizur's own proposal, designed to strengthen the state supervision (for which he would be implicitly a prime job candidate), was repeatedly rejected in the legislature. In 1858 Julius Rockwell, the Speaker of the House, successfully saw Elizur's bill through that chamber. During a rump session of the upper house, Senator William Fabens seized an opportune moment when the bill's opponents were absent in order to have the rules suspended. Elizur's bill was reconsidered, and "An Act for the Better Establishment of the Board of Insurance Commissioners" was approved. According to one dramatic account, the reformer rushed to Governor Nathaniel P. Bank's office with the bill in hand and badgered the chief executive until he signed the measure into law.[15]

The new statute provided for more extensive state supervision of life insurance. The governor was empowered to appoint two commissioners for three-year terms at a yearly salary of fifteen hundred dollars. Their job was to assess the value of all the policies of companies doing business in the Bay State, for which the companies were taxed one cent per thousand dollars of insurance in force. Because of the highly technical function of the position and the enormous amount of work involved, Governor Banks appointed Elizur a commissioner after political favorites sensibly refused the demanding post. The other commissioner, George W. Sargent, congenially retired to the background, allowing his more energetic colleague a free hand in creating the role of active state supervision on behalf of the public, a first in insurance regulation.[16]

During his tenure as commissioner from 1858 to 1867, Elizur put his mathematical skill, organizational talents, and literary ability to good use on behalf of insurance reform. His annual reports to the legislature remain a model of lucidity and forceful exposition that bureaucrats of any age might well emulate. Unlike the nonresistant Garrisonians who conscientiously refused to participate in civil government, Elizur's support for political action had culminated in state employment. He believed that state supervision of the powerful life insurance business was the public's right of self-defense against corporate abuses. Since the state chartered corporations, he argued that they must conform to the legislated expression of the people's will. He saw the commissioner's role as that of an active referee who had "a sentiment of satisfaction and pride in the insurance companies," but was ready to cry foul the moment a fair bargain was not struck between the companies and the policyholders.[17]

The task of valuating the policies of the rapidly expanding life insurance enterprise on an annual basis was immense. Working in a cramped office, Elizur compiled the figures necessary to determine the solvency of the companies. In 1858 fourteen life insurance firms in Massachusetts issued 42,000 policies with insurance worth $116 million and had net premium reserves of $13 million. By 1864 the same indices had expanded to twenty-eight companies, 93,000 policies, $263 million insured, and reserves of $32 million. During the same period, death claims rose from

$1,197,582 to $13,281,470. He estimated that the 1862 report required 72,000 distinct computations, which by 1866 had mounted to a staggering 250,000.[18]

Necessity was the mother of invention. Elizur, who held an 1853 patent on a self-acting water valve and served in 1855 as secretary of the New England Inventors' and Mechanics' Association, turned his mechanical talents to the practical problem of expediting computations. In 1869 he patented the arithmeter, a cylindrical calculating device—in effect, a crude computer—that was widely adopted in the insurance field. The arithmeter was comparable to the typewriter in mechanizing office work during the late nineteenth century. The ability to ascertain accurately companies' assets provided the foundation for discontinuing about a dozen unstable firms from "taking risks" in Massachusetts.[19]

As commissioner, Elizur not only acted as an independent check on corporate behavior, but he also attempted to educate the public about the theory and practice of life insurance, especially in the absence of popular writing on the subject. His annual reports were intended for the layman as well as the professional. He consequently relegated the algebraic basis of his conclusions to the appendix where the actuary could ponder the equations. The reports were "the most vivid and popular exposition of the doctrine of insurance that has yet appeared," one trade journal extolled of the bound works that sold for $1.25 in 1868. He went beyond the letter of the law to perform the public service of compiling a life insurance registry, which contained a serial listing of every policy issued in the Bay State. Policyholders were invited to his Boston office where he would show them their share in the reserve fund, the loss for forfeiture because of nonpayment of premiums, and what the equity in surrender value of the policy should be. He undertook the burden of popular education because he understood that a well-informed public was the foundation for sound life insurance practice.[20]

When Elizur uncovered dishonest or unsound activities, he relentlessly sought their correction, often through public condemnation in his *annual reports*. His zeal for justice and mathematical ability led to the punning proverb among life insurance men that "Elizur Wright was always right." He urged criminal prosecution of the State Fire Insurance Company of New Haven for falsifying its 1861 reports, and he refused president Henry B. Hyde's inducement to promote the Equitable Life Assurance Society of New York in the annual report of 1862. He waged a four-year struggle against the fraudulent activities of the American Mutual Insurance Company of New Haven nominally headed by his former Yale science professor Benjamin Silliman but managed by his unscrupulous son-in-law Benjamin Noyes. "Men of science may misplace their confidence," Elizur chided, "in the science of others." Excessive expenses and an inadequate reserve caused the company's collapse and led to Noyes's imprisonment.[21]

Elizur's indictment of the International Life Assurance Society of London developed into a major confrontation. The International was ostensibly a flourishing company with a board of directors which included nobles and an actuary who held membership in a royal society. Elizur charged in 1859 that the International was $160,177 in debt, that it had mismanaged millions of dollars, and that its officers were inordinately overpaid. In order to make this transnational corporation accountable, he recommended to the Massachusetts legislature that it require foreign companies with questionable financial practices to deposit with the state treasurer the net value of all policies held by Massachusetts citizens. By November 1860 the International's operations in the Bay State were suspended because it failed to submit financial data required by the law of 1858. The International retaliated by hiring, among others, Benjamin Pierce, a distinguished Harvard professor of mathematics and astronomy, to refute the charges. Other actuaries chose sides, and newspapers reported the fray. The effort to discredit Elizur became a full-blown affair whose implications extended beyond the credibility of one man to the viability of state supervision itself. Pierce attacked Elizur's assessment of the International as "directly opposed to established experience and the sound deductions of science." Elizur stood by his calculations and a decade later was vindicated when the International declared bankruptcy.[22]

Elizur's crusade was not a vendetta against life insurance corporations but against incompetence and malpractice. In fact, his efforts brought stability, security, and success to an industry which was in the midst of convulsive growth and more prone to seek quick profits than employ sound business practices. On occasion the companies were all too eager to utilize his services. After November 15 of each year, when the annual reports were completed, the press of company agents checking how they fared against the competition disrupted his office. He continually hectored the companies to maintain an adequate reserve, a careful balance between an overaccumulation of reserves and excessive dividends. In the very competitive marketing of life insurance, he warned that large dividends could dangerously shrink the reserve and risk the assets of current subscribers to attract new ones. He also urged the itemization of working expenses, an area where the reporting of a lump sum figure could conceal dubious expenditures. In addition, he updated the actuarial tables based on information supplied by the companies. During the Civil War, he found the mortality rate among men of combatant age went up only slightly and that the withdrawal of southern policyholders from northern companies had not deterred the rapid growth of life insurance. For Elizur, the evidence of the "safe and successful operation" of the life insurance companies demonstrated the strength of the Union itself.[23]

While insurance commissioner, Elizur remained an outspoken abolitionist. His commitment to insurance reform, however, greatly abbreviated his antislavery activity. Though he maintained a cordial connection with members of Boston's Bird Club—the operative center of Massachusetts Republicanism—he retained a largely independent position, penning provocative letters to a variety of newspapers and publishing his own occasional pamphlets. His reform style was a mix of persistent passion combined with an appreciation for political practicality that prevented him from being an organization man, whether with his old colleagues of the 1830s or the new generation of Bay State Republicans.

Elizur expressed an "intense" sympathy with the program of the Republicans even though his position was more radical. He argued, unlike the new party, that the Constitution permitted the eradication of slavery in the states by the federal government and invalidated the legitimacy of the Fugitive Slave Law. He also hailed John Brown's 1859 raid on the federal arsenal at Harper's Ferry, Virginia, as "grand and glorious." To the irritation of some Massachusetts legislators, the crusading commissioner inserted in an insurance report a gratuitous eulogy that praised the executed insurrectionary as an "honored patriot whose soul is now marching on." "The chances seem so great," he accurately predicted after Lincoln's election in 1860, "that slavery piqued beyond its moderate endurance will strike the first blow, and thus make the Republican party as good an Abolition party as could be wished." Forced into a defensive war, the Lincoln administration, he explained, would have to liberate the slaves in order to vanquish the rebellious planter class, a foreshadowing of the wartime strategy inherent in the Emancipation Proclamation.[24]

With the rebel sentiment for secession gaining momentum after the November presidential election, Elizur warned that southern fire-eaters might try to block Lincoln's inauguration through mob action in Washington. Actual hostilities, however, began on April 12, 1861, with the South Carolina cannonade of Fort Sumter, the vulnerable federal bastion in Charleston harbor, after which Elizur adopted a militant stand against the Confederacy. Unlike the pacificist Garrisonians who had to choose either peace or war, he had maintained ever since the abolitionist schism of 1837–40 the right of self-defense, which he now applied to the Union cause. He called the young men of Massachusetts to arms in order "to make the human Magna Charta of '76 the living law of this whole land." His preliminary plan for the conduct of the war involved declaring martial law throughout the Confederacy. Then, in order to divide the rebels, the federal government should offer compensated emancipation to Unionist slaveholders. Disloyal southerners would have their slaves confiscated without any remuneration.[25]

Although his agenda differed significantly from Lincoln's call for compensation and colonization during 1861 and much of 1862, both were notable for their political expediency. During the 1830s the fervent young immediatist had railed against the immorality of compensation—an integral part of the American Colonization Society's program—because it economically validated the planter's exploitation of the slave. The opportunism of the middle-aged man three decades later measured his increased attraction for what was practical and workable, though he continued to denounce the expatriation of blacks as a solution to America's racial problem.

Shortly after the shelling of Fort Sumter, Elizur urged the reluctant Republican administration to arm blacks to fight for the Union. He rejected the stereotype that blacks were naturally servile and pointed to their military distinction in the Continental Army and in the Haitian Revolution. He noted that actuarial data showed that they had a lower mortality rate from tropical fevers (an actual genetic difference between the races) and would therefore make better soldiers than whites in the lowland South. The conscription of African-Americans, he predicted, "would by its moral force more than half finish the war and would be easily pardoned by the most proslavery at the north on the decree of necessity." He criticized Lincoln for a lack of "political gumption" for not recruiting blacks early in the war. Then, after their mobilization in 1863 during which some two hundred thousand blacks served in the Union ranks, he protested unsuccessfully against the inequitable pay differential of black soldiers that was one-half the rate of whites, a blatant example of northern racism.[26]

Elizur was among the radical critics of the Union government who demanded the complete eradication of slavery, equality under the law, and land to the tiller. Voices like his acted to prod the Republican administration, which hoped to cultivate pro-Union sentiment in the South, especially in the critical Border States, and also sought not to alienate white voters in the North who might support a war to preserve the Union but not one to secure black rights. In 1862 he denounced Lincoln's cautious countermand of Generals John Frémont's and David Hunter's emancipation decrees in the war-torn areas of Missouri and South Carolina under their respective military occupation. "The destruction of slavery and the very foundation on which it stands," Elizur countered, "has become a necessity, whatever damage may come from it." Early in the conflict, he lectured Secretary of the Treasury Salmon P. Chase, "There is no practical way of ending this war but to single out the real foes & rebels[,] the slave-holding class[,] and let them and the world understand that not only their slaves are to be free, but their lands are to be divided among those who help conquer them." He pointed out that the Emancipation Proclamation of January 1, 1863, which only freed slaves in the rebel states not under Union control, was a halfway measure, and he opposed those who talked of peace without total abolition. "By the abolition of slavery," he announced in 1865, "we mean full citizenship, the right of suffrage, and a homestead, irrespective of origin or color."[27]

His program for Reconstruction went beyond that of most to include land redistribution. He envisioned a postwar South dominated by yeoman farmers, black and white, who owned their own homesteads of some 120 acres. The utility of free labor in the South would, he wrote Chase in 1861, increase "the aggregate wealth of the country." The land is opened to the capital and skill of the civilized world," he explained, "with all its natives placed in a position to enjoy the benefit of such capital and skill. The curse [of slavery] is wholly, instead of partially, lifted off." He foresaw a political coalition of loyal whites and enfranchised blacks governing the reconstructed states. He assumed that a combination of free labor and free men would be the foundation for a new South.[28]

The "boneless, kidglove Republicanism of the North" failed to remake the South along his recommendations. "The thing is," Elizur urged, "not to eradicate the landholders, but to radicate [root] the landless. . . ." He estimated that 75 percent of the South was loyal but lacked the economic resources to sustain its independence from the planter class, which rendered the ballot a mockery. "Suffrage is a lever to move the world," he observed critically about the Thirteenth Amendment, "but not without something to stand on." How could blacks vote for the Union, he asked, when the freedmen had "not land to raise a turnip on?" Their former masters had the power to force the ex-slaves to vote Democratic or starve. Elizur wanted the federal government to supervise the South as a conquered territory with a "vigilant army" until an equitable land policy was established and the secessionist states were transformed into working "republics" with equality under the law. Although he idealized the productivity of free labor and the Jeffersonian capacity of the yeoman to maintain his freedom, his equation linking civil liberties with the necessity of land reform was exceptional for nineteenth-century liberal thought.[29]

The failure of President Andrew Johnson and the Supreme Court to prevent the rebels from reestablishing themselves in power in the southern states was what Elizur called "the second rebellion." He categorized Johnson's failure to protect the civil rights of freedmen a "mountainous" crime that demanded impeachment. He was outraged at the "seething hell of injustice" the "redeemer" governments were inflicting on the African-American. "Do you see," he challenged now Chief Justice Chase, "any chance of our country's escaping another more terrible civil war than the last, if the question of suffrage is left wholly to the states?" His experience as insurance commissioner convinced him that active governmental regulation was necessary to secure justice, whether for the freedmen or the policyholders.[30]

Insurance reform, not Civil War and Reconstruction legislation, was where Elizur exerted significant influence on public policy. He was distressed at the common business practice of either voiding a policy or returning only a small fraction of its equity because of the policyholder's failure to pay a premium. He pointed out that forfeiture was undesirable for the companies: it alienated the public and deterred sales; it constituted only 3 percent of all insurance income in 1860; and it allowed unsound companies to use these funds to conceal fraud or insolvency. For a company to rely on forfeitures for its profits was to reduce life insurance income to gambling, violating its mathematically precise nature. His rebuttal to the usual charge that it was not feasible to determine the amount of money due on lapsed policies was in the form of eleven pages of tables showing that such a value could be readily assigned to any pecuniary risk. He argued that on principle alone the insured was entitled to a fair and fixed return on his equity. In his view, the law of 1858 had made life insurance safe but not just for the policyholder.[31]

Many life insurance companies were not convinced, and they opposed Elizur's sequel to the reserve law of 1858. Nevertheless, "An Act to Regulate the Forfeitures of Life Insurance" had enough support in the Massachusetts legislature (with no small thanks to his association with the Bird Club) to become law on April 10, 1861. "The modern reader," Professor of Insurance J. David Cummins observed in 1973, "can scarcely appreciate the radical nature of Wright's 1861 law, embodying as it did many profound implications for the life insurance industry and for public policy in general." The nonforfeiture law was restricted to companies chartered in the Commonwealth and consisted of two parts. The first provided that the nonpayment of premiums did not terminate the policy, but that it continued in effect with four-fifths of its net value used to extend the coverage as temporary insurance. Second, if the insured died during the period of temporary insurance, the company had to meet its obligations as on any legitimate policy. In other words, the company could no longer confiscate the reserve on lapsed policies as a windfall but must apply 80 percent of the insured's equity toward the extension of full protection. The act of 1861 established several important precedents for life insurance. Nonforfeiture was a right, not a privilege. The idea of an individual reserve was a meaningful actuarial concept, and the state had the power to regulate a private contract. Even out-of-state companies soon adopted the nonforfeiture practice because it was an attractive selling point for the customer.[32]

Not all opposition was so successfully overcome. Elizur contended that his role in exposing fraud among the receivers of the Eagle Mutual Fire Insurance Company cost him his job as state commissioner. More accurately, his aggressive and exuberant style made him a vulnerable target from the powerful insurance lobby. An 1864 Massachusetts law empowered the state life insurance commissioners to monitor companies, such as the Eagle Mutual, which had been placed in receivership because of financial difficulties. Elizur reported to the chief justice of the Massachusetts Supreme Court that the receivers, Joshua Webster and Isaac S. Morse, were mulcting the company's creditors. Webster's son-in-law had bought claims against the Eagle Mutual at thirty cents on the dollar but received a tidy fifty cents on the dollar from the receivers. The court removed the receivers from their position on April 25, 1865. Morse was, however, subsequently elected to the state legislature where he used his influence against Elizur.[33]

A year later the legislature began a probe into the income of the insurance commissioners. Elizur accused Representative James Pierce of initiating the inquiry at the behest of Joshua Webster in retaliation for the

Eagle Mutual exposé. Another representative charged that Elizur received ten thousand dollars in fees beyond that of his fifteen-hundred-dollar-a-year salary as a civil servant. He implied that Elizur's income included bribes from foreign companies for the privilege of operating in Massachusetts and that Elizur in effect used the insurance laws of 1858 and 1861 to enrich himself.[34]

Elizur countered that his income as commissioner had been legal and honorable. He had drawn his mandated $1,500-a-year salary and done outside consulting worth $3,500. In addition, he paid five members of his family a total of $5,633.96 for clerical assistance according to an 1860 law that allowed up to $1,000 annually for clerical assistance. The special joint legislative committee on salaries did not level the charge of nepotism at Elizur. His children, especially Lucy Jane and Walter, were well-known actuaries in their own right. The committee did find Elizur engaged in a conflict of interest, though they could not find any evidence of corruption or legal violation. The problem was that Elizur did private consultation with the same insurance firms whose policies he valuated as commissioner. He saw no temptation in such a dual posture, because he regarded his calculations as a self-evident, technical exercise. What he did not appreciate, however, was that others less steadfast than himself might accept graft in order to compensate for the low pay and enormous amount of work that the job entailed. The legislative committee declared that the insurance commissioners "should not be tempted to grant such certificates [to companies to do business in Massachusetts] by the payment of money." They did not propose, however, to discourage malfeasance by making the position more remunerative.[35]

Elizur charged the whole investigation was an effort to drive him from office and thereby weaken forceful state regulation. "The zeal with which they entered the work of demolishing my reputation for integrity as well as of protecting the treasury of the Commonwealth," he retorted, "should have been a brilliant credit to humanity, if their premises had been sound." The committee denied his repeated requests to testify, and he resorted to a war of words in the newspapers and in pamphlets to defend himself.[36]

At the same time, Elizur and his co-commissioner George Sargent lobbied against a legislative proposal to weaken their office. In Elizur's words: "The present bill, which reduces the board to one commissioner and a clerk to an aggregate salary of $3,000 only, cannot save anything to the state, for it cannot make the valuation of life insurance policies in addition to its other duties, and could not probably do it for that sum, if it had no other duties." He pointed out that the increased work load of the commissioners went from the valuation of 42,802 policies worth $116,484,000 in 1858 to 211,537 policies worth $563,396,000 in 1865, and thus retrenchment was not in order. Two acts, however, passed the legislature on May 23–24, 1866, that overrode his objections. The old board of insurance commissioners was voted out of existence, and, in Elizur's view, insufficient funding was mandated for effective monitoring of the insurance companies. Despite the personal affront and the emasculation of the office, he offered Governor Alexander H. Bullock his candidacy for the new position in the hope that the next legislature would rescind the new laws. He also wished to be allowed to supplement the inadequate state salary with private actuarial work. The governor did not appoint him, and on July 1, 1867, the crusading commissioner was involuntarily retired.[37]

The legislature refused Elizur's demand for an inquiry into the charges of corruption against him, which he denounced as "wholly feigned and unfounded." What he regarded as a conspiracy in the legislature was an outgrowth of the energetic and outspoken role he played as insurance commissioner, which even today in the age of consumer protection would be unusual. In addition to Morse and Webster of the Eagle Mutual, he had made many powerful enemies. He had driven fourteen insurance companies out of Massachusetts, and vengeful officials, such as Benjamin Noyes of the New Haven Mutual, lobbied legislators to oust him. Although state supervision benefited the insurance business, powerful corporate presidents jealously guarded their prerogatives. Nor did Elizur's blunt style and moral intensity fit well into the political machinations of the Boston statehouse or the profit-making concerns of the business world. His well-known, radical views on the Civil War and Reconstruction and his irreverent criticism of religion also left him vulnerable to attack.[38]

Personal correspondence between Governor Bullock and the new insurance commissioner, J. E. Sanford, made clear that the accusations of impropriety against Elizur had no substance. Elizur had, however, at first regarded the governor's failure to select him as endorsement of the charges. Bullock privately wrote Sanford that Elizur's "vindication was complete," but he had not appointed him because of "political pressure," a euphemism referring to the effectiveness of the insurance lobby. Bullock allowed Sanford to forward a copy of his letter to Elizur with the stipulation that it remain confidential. A number of prominent officials in the insurance world sent letters of support to Elizur that denounced the "corruption" of the legislature and expressed "outrage" at his removal.[39]

Elizur remained indignant at the appearance of scandal that surrounded the close of his pioneering career as insurance commissioner. "My enemies, personal, political, and religious, may comfort themselves," he defiantly vowed, "that the deader they kill me, the more I shall live after I am dead." Nevertheless, the unsavory incident bothered him for the rest of his life. In 1882 he published a glowing biography of abolitionist Myron Holley that staunchly defended Holley against the charge of malfeasance that had led to his dismissal as a state official supervising the Erie Canal. The biography seems in part a case of psychological displacement in which Elizur vicariously sought his own vindication through the defense of the impugned Holley. Ironically, after leaving the commissionership, his income as a private actuary was reportedly twelve thousand dollars per year, eight times greater than his official state salary had been, undercutting the insinuation that he had sought public office to enrich himself. His new income gave him the means to continue his quest for life insurance reform.[40]

Chapter 11

Independent Life Insurance Reformer

The innovative 1861 nonforfeiture law was intended to correct the abuses that Elizur had witnessed at London's Royal Exchange in 1844. He had flattered himself that he had provided a "solution of this mystery [of life insurance], so that honest businessmen can conduct this business as safely as any other, without a priesthood of algebraists." By 1868 he made the alarming discovery that the legislation was technically deficient. "It was the greatest mortification of my life," he lamented, "to discover, after it was passed, that its surrender charge of 20 percent on the reserve was a stupid blunder." The 1861 act provided for extended life insurance based on 80 percent of what the reserve of the policy would cover after debts were deducted. He subsequently calculated, however, that a stipulated cash surrender value and a surrender charge based on the insurance value of the policy were far more equitable.[1]

The concept of a surrender charge based on the insurance value rather than the reserve was of critical significance. Elizur treated the standard-level premium as consisting of two parts, the insurance and self-insurance. The insurance met the claims and expenses of other policies, and the insurance value measured the present cost of meeting those obligations until the policy matured. The self-insurance or reserve was the investment component of the premium which the company held in trust for the policyholder until the claim on his contract occurred. The insurance value showed the financial stake to the company of a specific policy, while the accumulation of the reserve over time—in essence, a trust fund—belonged to the insured.

His insight was that a surrender charge based on the reserve unfairly taxed the policyholder on his own money, especially in the later years of the policy when the reserve was large. In the early years of a policy when the reserve was small, the company in turn was shortchanged by a surrender charge on the reserve. Therefore he argued that the determination of a surrender charge on the insurance value, which he fixed at 6 percent to cover the expense of procuring a replacement policy, would accurately reflect the company's actual financial needs and justly deal with all policyholders. He urged that the self-insurance or reserve be returned to the insured after the deduction of the surrender fee. His encouragement led the Brooklyn Life Insurance Company in 1869 to adopt the practice of a cash surrender after at least two annual premiums had been paid.[2]

Elizur submitted an "Act to Fix the Surrender Value of Policies of Life Insurance" in 1871 to the Massachusetts legislature. The act guaranteed a cash surrender value, fixed a 6 percent surrender charge based on the insurance value, and abrogated the 1861 nonforfeiture law. He hailed the proposed law as a means to eliminate the "swindling" of retiring policyholders. The bill passed the House but was defeated in the Senate, where an amendment to make it apply to companies chartered in other states caused its defeat. The large New York City corporations led by Frederick Winston, president of the Mutual Life, successfully lobbied against the extension of stipulated cash surrender values to their policies. Elizur correctly charged the Mutual with making millions of dollars by not paying equitable surrender values on thousands of lapsed policies. Of 6,340 policies terminated with the Mutual in 1870, only 564 were by death. He identified Richard A. McCurdy, a vice-president of the Mutual, with directing a well-financed campaign against the bill at the statehouse. He bitterly blamed the Mutual's "treachery" with sabotaging the reform.[3]

The legislative rebuke began a nine-year crusade before the 1871 reform became law. Elizur challenged his adversaries to political combat. "I will put them down," he pledged "or they must put me down." He turned to "enlightening the public mind"—an updated reliance on moral suasion from his evangelical days—through the press, public addresses, and legislative testimony to promote the cause. The former tract agent published polemical pamphlets such as *The Politics and Mysteries of Life Insurance* (1873), *Life Insurance: The Way to Make It a Public Benefit with the Least Injury to Individuals* (1874?), *Traps Baited with Orphans, or What is the Matter with Life Insurance* (1877), and *The Necessity of Reform in Life Insurance* (n.d.). He inundated newspapers in the Northeast with letters to the editor, and wrote regularly for trade journals, such as *The Insurance Times, The Insurance Monitor, The Insurance World,* and *The Baltimore*

Underwriter. It was a war of words against "the surrender value swindle."[4]

Elizur launched his own political campaign on behalf of the stymied 1871 legislation. He ran in 1875 for state senator from the second Middlesex district on an independent ticket of life insurance reform. He lambasted the Mutual's opposition to the reform and denounced Massachusetts Governor Alexander H. Rice, who was a trustee of the Mutual, as the insurance firm's toady. Although Rice was an influential Republican, Elizur had grown increasingly alienated from the party during the Gilded Age and did not spare a fellow Bird Club member from his wrath. Some Boston newspapers refused to print his acerbic attack on the governor, but the *Boston Herald* endorsed Elizur as the "best authority" on life insurance in the United States. His campaign flyers contained the nostalgic message from his former antislavery colleague, John Greenleaf Whittier, that "I confess I should like to see one of the old abolition leaders in the Senate of Massachusetts." Not unexpectedly, Elizur lost the election, which he had based on a single issue.[5]

Progress was made at the federal and state level on behalf of equitable surrender laws. The Supreme Court review of the *New York Life Insurance Company v. Statham et al.* in 1876 decided the case of policyholders living in the Confederacy who stopped payment on their premiums with northern insurance companies. The Court ruled that nonpayment of premiums voided the policy, but that the insured was entitled to the equitable value of the policy arising from the premiums actually paid up to the time of the forfeiture. The decision on lapsed southern policies gave legal validation to Elizur's argument that the reserve on self-insurance belonged to the policyholder. He was so buoyed by the decision that he proposed in 1877 a class action suit of some five thousand policyholders be undertaken to establish the right to the reserve. He volunteered to figure the self-insurance and insurance value of each policy and to assist the claimants in the litigation. Although the mass suit was never initiated, California enacted a progressive law in 1878 modeled after the defeated 1871 Massachusetts bill.[6]

The most ambitious effort Elizur made on behalf of guaranteed surrender values was the creation of an alternative insurance institution, the Massachusetts Family Bank. Disgusted with the malpractice of the giant corporations and frustrated with their opposition to his reform legislation, he sought to establish a model of what life insurance could be. The policyholder's premium was divided into three parts: two financial components covered the company's working expenses plus the annual insurance risk. The Family Bank treated the third part of the premium, the self-insurance or reserve that belonged to the client, as a deposit available for withdrawal. Therefore the savings aspect of a bank was combined with the protection of life insurance. The argument for a surrender value had been extended to include a banking function, a cash reserve on demand. Though the general idea of savings bank life insurance was not original with him, he gave it his own distinct interpretation. In the pamphlet *Savings Bank Life Insurance* (1872), he computed the annual insurance value, self-insurance, and surrender value on the premiums of 268 policies based on one thousand dollars' worth of insurance in order to demonstrate the technical feasibility of the plan and to enlighten the public. The division of the premium into three parts not only informed the policyholder exactly how his payments were used, but also facilitated the determination of a company surplus and the amount of dividends. With a fixed surrender charge, the surrender value for any policy could be readily known by consulting a series of tables in the pamphlet. He taunted his opponents by offering a one-thousand-dollar prize to anyone who could prove that the conventional form of life insurance was superior to savings bank life insurance. The prize was never collected.[7]

Some newspapers endorsed savings bank life insurance. Most encouraging was its adoption in 1872 by the Knickerbocker Life Insurance Company of New York. The number of such policies sold by the Knickerbocker, however, was modest. The lure of tontine insurance (a type of speculative life annuity that went to survivors usually after twenty years), opposition by other companies, and lower agents' commissions held sales to three thousand policies after four years. As Charles M. Hibbard, the Knickerbocker's actuary, aptly remarked in 1876, "Reformations are never successful from the beginning—Savings Bank Life Insurance is no exception."[8]

Elizur used a committee appointment in 1874 by the Boston Board of Trade and his connections with liberal Republicans (to which members of the Bird Club had defected en masse in 1872 over dissatisfaction with corruption and other issues involving President Ulysses S. Grant's administration) to gain support for savings bank life insurance. The committee's task was to suggest the best way to promote thrift, an object of civic concern and also moralistic hectoring of the poor at a time of nationwide depression, a periodic phenomenon of America's expansive capitalistic economy in the last quarter of the century. Under Elizur's prodding the committee recommended the creation of a family bank. The board endorsed the plan, and, with the added support of such prominent citizens and businessmen as Amos A. Lawrence, William Claflin, Samuel G. Howe, Francis W. Bird, and Samuel E. Sewall, the legislature incorporated the Massachusetts Family Bank on April 17, 1876.[9]

The Family Bank was an amalgam of a savings bank and a life insurance company. The charter provided for capitalization at five hundred thousand dollars in fifty-dollar shares. In order to prevent a wealthy few from dominating the stock, one vote was permitted per share but no person could have more than thirty votes. The self-insurance or reserve was to be kept distinct from the insurance value, and a surrender value of 6 percent on the insurance value was set for each year of the policy. Home loans to low-income people were favored in order to encourage stable family life among the urban working class. All transactions were based on gold which Elizur thought the least variable standard during a period of monetary fluctuation. Policies were only permitted when an insurable interest existed, such as the principal wage earner of a family, and no insurance was offered after age seventy-five at which time the accumulated reserve was returned as a retirement fund. Any surplus would be distributed annually, unlike the practice of some companies whose less regular return of dividends penalized those who retired their policies. Because he believed that agents' commissions had grown excessively large and that people were capable of coming to the Family Bank to subscribe on their own, he dispensed with salesmen entirely. The Family Bank was put on a sound financial structure that provided income protection in case of death, security after retirement, and the right to borrow from the reserve.[10]

There was a utopian quality to the Family Bank not unlike Elizur's antebellum fascination with Fourierism. In his words, life insurance was "capable of so much wider application and so thoroughly in unison with the spirit of our republican society, that it cannot fail, by-and-by, to be understood by everybody and enjoyed by everybody who needs it, as universally as the various arrangements by which steam and lightning are utilized." He saw life insurance as a necessary component to the transformation that the Industrial Revolution, powered by the energy of steam and electricity, had wrought in all aspects of society. Urban family life was particularly vulnerable to financial hardship and probable destitution if the principal wage earner died. The Family Bank offered institutionalized security, especially to the hard-pressed working class, in an era of changing conditions.[11]

Elizur proclaimed that the Family Bank represented no less than "a long step taken towards the solution of the great labor questions" which convulsed the nation during the 1870s in a series of violent strikes. In testimony before the legislature in opposition to a tax on savings banks, he warned, "If the capitalists and large property holders of Massachusetts do not wish to be harassed into insane asylums or suicide by clamors for eight hour laws and rise of wages from men who spend every additional dollar on rum and tobacco, they will by all means encourage all sorts of savings." The Family Bank provided the means for the worker to save money, buy a house, and protect his family. In evangelical tones, he exhorted workers to emulate the frugality of Benjamin Franklin and to renounce the expensive evils of alcohol and tobacco. "You don't need to rob anybody but yourself," he claimed, "to make yourself a capitalist."[12]

The Family Bank was the structural embodiment of a secularized Protestant ethic in which right living was equated with financial success and social mobility, the formula for success of late nineteenth-century American liberalism. It secured "at the same time," Elizur believed, "the benefit of association and the independence of mankind." Actuarial science allowed the pooling of collective capital which individuals could use without compromising their independence. The panacea of the Family Bank further estranged him from the struggle for labor solidarity and union organization during the 1870s. In fact, since the 1830s he had denounced unions as a "monopoly" that upset the supposedly free bargain struck between capital and labor in the marketplace. As a member of what amounted to an anti-union committee appointed in 1866 by Republican Governor John Andrew to examine the labor question in the Bay State, Elizur, like other Bird Club members, opposed the movement of an eight-hour day and any state restraints on the rights of private property. It seems Elizur had forgotten that during his own time of woes in the mid-1840s he had endorsed the eight-hour day in the textile industry, though not unions. Instead, the committee preached the pious phrases that through "temperate industrious habits" and "co-operative labor securing to each work man a share of the profits of his work," workers may "become their own capitalists."[13]

Elizur lectured Boston wage earners on the anti-union theme that "individualism is the formation of American liberty, and its true type is not a trade-union but trade unit, as, for example, the young [Benjamin] Franklin seeking employment in a strange city [Philadelphia] with two ridiculous loaves of bread." Franklin, the archetype of the American success story, had made it without the contemporary equivalent of the Knights of Labor. Whatever inequities existed in the free market, Elizur believed that the Family Bank rectified, making unionization, the subjection of the individual to the group, even more undesirable. He had been nurtured on the Arminianized evangelicalism of the Great Awakening, and the transition from free will to religion to free labor in economics was much more a part of his mentality than a call for the workers of the world to unite. His earlier indictment of slave labor, attraction to "associationism," and now the Family Bank were not rejections of capitalism per se but attempts to improve the position of labor in the free market. Similarly he had pioneered state regulation of the life insurance companies to ensure that big business operated with mutual regard for their profits and the welfare of their policyholders. An individualist at heart, he was oblivious to the plight of labor in an age of concentrated corporate power, a trait that he shared with most other evangelical abolitionists, not to mention Republicans and other Americans.[14]

The opposition to the Family Bank was overwhelming. It was, after all, a potential challenge to business as usual. Frederick Winston of the Mutual was again in the forefront of critics from the insurance industry. An 1871 cartoon in *The Chronicle*, a New York insurance publication, depicted Elizur as a persistent but eccentric reformer confronting a determined Winston. The depiction of the two characters is illustrative of their antagonist roles. The younger insurance executive is clean shaven, shorthaired, and well dressed, the very model of a modern businessman. He stands erect, staring straight forward, as he clutches possessively a replica of his corporate citadel to his bosom. Winston knows what he wants—profit and power. In contrast, a white-maned and long-bearded Elizur looks like the biblical patriarch that his Old Testament name suggests. The wily old man with an algebraic equation written on the tail of his smock completes his last reform, savings bank life insurance, presumably a birdhouse fit only for birds. His other "toys"—the beneficial ark of "net evaluation," the stubborn ass of "state supervision," and the "dead beat" drum of "nonforfeiture"—gather cobwebs in his workshop.[15]

"Baseless theory," "Wright's hobby," "sham reform," "complex impracticality," and "Wright's hallucination" were some of the harsh characterizations that damned savings bank life insurance. *The Insurance*

Times, a leading New York trade journal, ran a series of articles discrediting Elizur's concept as detrimental to the interests of life insurance. "Elizur Wright is wasting his old age," one columnist scolded, "in the vain attempt to destroy the edifice of benign beauty and practical beneficence built in his prime." Stephen English, editor of *The Insurance Times,* and Elizur exchanged insults that an earlier age would have seen settled by code duello. Even friends, such as Emory McClintock, actuary of the Northwest Mutual of Milwaukee, cautioned, "You were our pope. I dislike to see your great influence over the companies abandoned...."[16]

Elizur's adversaries were less concerned with the viability of the Family Bank as a rival institution than that the argument for savings bank life insurance challenged established practices. The Family Bank, in fact, never even opened its doors. Capitalization was never achieved despite an amendment of April 26, 1877 that reduced the required funds to two hundred thousand dollars. The dominance of existing firms, systematic opposition, the popularity of tontine insurance, and the lack of agents contributed to the stillbirth of the Family Bank. A new impetus of reform, the Progressive Era at the turn of the century, revived the idea of savings bank life insurance, twenty years after Elizur's death. In the Bay State, Louis D. Brandeis, best known as the brilliant jurist, led the successful drive for the establishment of an alternative form of life insurance after the insurance scandals of 1905. "Massachusetts established for the world," Brandeis wrote in 1906, "the scientific practice of life insurance by the work of its great insurance commissioner Elizur Wright."[17]

Persistence had its reward. On April 23, 1880, "An Act Limiting the Forfeiture of Policies in Life Insurance Corporations," which repealed the defective 1861 statute, became Massachusetts law. But the contest in the legislature had been hard fought. The insurance commissioner had sponsored a rival bill that continued the surrender charge as a percentage of the reserve in opposition to Elizur's proposal based on the insurance value. Both bills became deadlocked; after legislative maneuvering Elizur's reform passed. The new law gave the policyholder two options in claiming the reserve. One allowed for automatic paid-up insurance by converting the present reserve into future premiums. The other was a guaranteed cash surrender value, if not detrimental to the beneficiaries, which prevented irresponsible voiding of protection for families. Eligibility occurred after two annual premiums were met and applied only to policies issued by Bay State companies. The actuarial precedent of calculating the surrender charge based on the insurance value was established, and in effect a version of savings bank life insurance had been instituted.[18]

The sophistication of the 1880 Massachusetts law is evident in comparison to the industry-sponsored legislation in New York in 1879. The New York law was highly favorable to corporate interests. It provided for a high $33\frac{1}{3}$ percent surrender charge based on the reserve and allowed no cash surrender. Equity was forfeited if not requested within six months of the payment of the last premium, a stricture the companies rigorously enforced. The surrender proviso could be voided if such a waiver were printed in red ink on the policy. In keeping with the legalized chicanery of the Gilded Age, the Equitable printed its whole policy in red! The New York law, rather than the Massachusetts statute, became the model for the insurance business until the major revisions of the 1940s, which were more in keeping with the protection of the policyholder that Elizur advocated.[19]

In addition to other insurance activities, Elizur was an active consulting actuary until the end of his life. By 1877 he estimated that he had served as an actuary for five or six companies or the equivalent in the aggregate to more than twenty years with one company. From an office in Boston's business district, he made a good living advising individuals, associations, and corporations. A ten-dollar fee gained one client the advice not to insure with the Equitable because Elizur had "no faith whatever in [its] stability or soundness." Other individuals hired him to determine the equity of their policies. He also advised the Policyholder's Association of America to take legal action in order to secure a fair surrender value.[20]

Corporations often sought his counsel. The actuary of the Asbury Life Insurance Company of New York pleaded for him to straighten out their books; the Knickerbocker Life Insurance Company of New York paid him over thirty-seven hundred dollars for valuating their policies; and a two-year contract with the Economical Mutual Life Insurance Company of Providence gained him one thousand dollars. He put the dividend policy of the Northwest Mutual Life Insurance Company of Milwaukee and the Aetna Life Insurance Company of Hartford on a sound basis. He resigned, however, on principle as an actuary for the John Hancock Mutual Life Insurance Company of Boston when they denied him full access to their records. He urged policyholders to challenge the Hancock's financial statement at its forthcoming annual meeting on the suspicion that all was not in order. He defended the financial integrity of the Hartford Life and Annuity Company and the Mutual Benefit Life Insurance Company of Hartford against the charge of malpractice by the Travellers' Life Insurance Company, their local rival. General approbation greeted the arithmeter, which his son Walter, an actuary with the New England Mutual from 1866 until 1900, helped to market. Elizur must have taken some entrepreneurial pride in selling his invention at the price of five hundred dollars to companies, such as the Mutual, whose practices he vociferously opposed.[21]

Elizur's idealistic goals for life insurance, however, brought him into conflict with the growing consolidation of the insurance business after 1860. He favored mutual companies because management rested in theory with the policyholders. But he observed, "The government of these institutions in which so much of the country is wrapped up...is simply autocratic, de facto." He estimated in 1877 that 50 percent of the insurance business was done by five companies, with one doing 20 percent of the total. He decried the concentration of wealth and power of what he termed the life insurance "autocracy." Management frequently shaped public legislation, corrupted the press, disregarded policyholders' rights, and used proxies to perpetuate itself. Abusive corporate power cut Elizur to the quick: it violated his sense of republican civic virtue, his secularized Christian ethics, and his liberal faith in a socially beneficent capitalism.[22]

The successful promotion of tontine life insurance by the giant corporations was indicative of abuses in the proliferating life insurance industry. The American version of the European tontine—created by seventeenth-century Neapolitan financier Lorenzo Tonti who delighted the court of Versailles with his scheme—was a modified or deferred dividend plan of usually twenty years, though shorter schedules of five and ten years existed. The policyholder paid for life insurance, but all dividends were placed into a common pool that were to be apportioned among surviving subscribers at the end of a stipulated period. In an age without social security or pension plans, the highly popular tontine met the twin needs of life insurance plus retirement income for survivors. It was a high-yield life annuity on the installment plan. According to a recent evaluation by economic historians Roger L. Ransom and Richard Sutch, the tontine was in purely financial terms "actuarially sound" and an "excellent investment." The gamble was, of course, that one would live to divide the accumulated dividends of the deceased. The seduction of the tontine was that it mingled present security with the lure of substantial future gain. It was a pecuniary variation of social Darwinism in which the fittest were rewarded for their survival.[23]

Tontine life insurance galled Elizur. The argument by historian Morton Keller that Elizur's criticism of the tontine was muted because of retainers from powerful companies engaged in the practice needs reconsideration. He accepted employment from the Equitable Life Assurance Society and the New York Life Insurance Company, two of the nation's largest insurance corporations. If they succeeded in deflecting any condemnation from themselves, they failed to stop his strong attack on the tontine system. In fact, Elizur, along with Jacob L. Greene, president of the Connecticut Mutual Life Insurance Company, and Amzi Dodd, president of the Mutual Benefit Life Insurance Company of New Jersey, were the only leaders in the insurance world who consistently denounced the tontine as inherently unsound and dishonest. Elizur began his criticism of the tontine from its introduction in 1868 by Henry Hyde, president of the Equitable, despite Hyde's efforts to quiet him.[24]

Tontine insurance contradicted Elizur's efforts to transform life insurance from speculation into mathematical certainty. It was the antithesis of his ideal, the Family Bank. In the press and pamphlets, he pilloried the tontine as an "absurdity," "life insurance cannibalism," and "superfluous and unnecessary." He denounced the Equitable's tontine policy as "regulated gambling," and, though he noted that the computations of the New York Life's tontine system were accurate, he refused to endorse it. Another liability of the tontine, besides an early death, was that all rights to the reserve and dividends were denied for nonpayment of the premium. Elizur pointed out therefore that the tontine favored the rich since the wealthy were less likely to default on their policies. In addition, he argued that the tontine violated state laws against gaming, and he called for a legislative investigation of the practice. His son Walter published a statistical analysis that showed that a majority of tontine subscribers lost money, and concluded that the tontine was "a real disgrace to the institution of life insurance." The Wrights' arguments were prescient because they anticipated the famous Armstrong Insurance Investigation of 1905 in the New York State Senate that uncovered flagrant corruption in the administration of the tontine system, among other things, and that resulted in 1906 in an outright ban on the practice. In the minds of progressive Senator William W. Armstrong and committee counsel Charles Evans Hughes, later chief justice of the United States Supreme Court, the tontine epitomized the problems of a scandal-ridden industry.[25]

The development of the lucrative tontine was part of the New York insurance wars of the late 1860s and early 1870s in which the New York Life, the Equitable, and the Mutual Life battled for corporate dominance. The competition between the Equitable and the Mutual was especially ruthless. Henry Hyde, president of the Equitable, had formed his own company in 1859 after leaving the Mutual. Frederick Winston, president of the Mutual, had maintained his well-entrenched position as the industry's leader with the popular attraction of frequent dividends, which became annual in 1863. Lacking the financial resources to fund an annual dividend, Hyde developed the tontine as a rival sales tactic that would attract new subscribers while it allowed the Equitable to amass capital by deferring dividends. It was a stroke of entrepreneurial genius. Hyde's marketing of the tontine was so successful that the Equitable surpassed the Mutual and the New York Life as the largest insurance corporation by 1884. Even though almost all insurance companies were forced to offer the tontine to survive, Hyde's hard-driving style was difficult to match. Hyde was to life insurance what Rockefeller was to oil, Carnegie to steel, and Morgan to finance. With the surplus created by the tontine, Hyde raised agents' commissions, attracted aggressive agents, lobbied the legislature, and prudently kept Elizur on retainer from 1868 to 1885 (the negative consequences of which will be discussed later).[26]

Hyde was not successful in quieting Elizur's criticism of tontine insurance. He was, however, fortunate in having much of the indictment of the "New York Ring" directed against the Mutual. Elizur was nevertheless capable, as H. P. Duclos of the Hartford Life put it, of delivering "sledgehammer blows" against Hyde and the Equitable. In part, Hyde's achievement was a result of the Equitable's skillful solicitation, but he also had good luck on his side.[27]

Winston had unwittingly made Elizur an enemy. What had previous been a cordial working relationship between the two quickly soured during the insurance wars. In 1869, when Elizur had reached the age of sixty-five, Winston used Stephen English, editor of *The Insurance Times,* as a spokesman to offer a retirement annuity worth one hundred thousand dollars for Elizur and his wife. Instead of a generous act of friendship, Elizur concluded the offer was a blatant attempt "to silence" his advocacy of equitable surrender values, especially reform of the 1861 Massachusetts nonforfeiture law. He absolved English of any devious designs but damned Winston with deceit. Elizur sarcastically said he would accept the annuity provided the money came out of Winston's own pocket instead of being stolen from the Mutual's policyholders. English later admitted that Winston had duped him and had hoped to gain Elizur's support in blocking an investigation of the Mutual. Elizur "demolished the entire arrangement at one fell swoop," English revealed, "by declaring that it must be stopped at once and forever."[28]

Having clumsily failed with the proposed annuity, Winston again antagonized Elizur. In 1870 some twenty actuaries met in the boardroom of the Mutual's New York office to consider Elizur's revision of the current accounting practice of loading the premium. He wished to use the insurance value of the policy, not a percentage of the gross premium, as the standard for weighting the agents' commission and for assessing the company's working expenses. He claimed Winston broke a pledge made at the meeting to call a convention of the insurance companies to consider the changes. It was not, however, in the Mutual's narrow self-interest to do so. Insurance agents uniformly opposed Elizur's recommendation because of the significant reduction in their commissions, which reached as high as 75 percent of the first year's premium. Insurance companies used the incentive of high agents' commissions as the principal means to expand their businesses, and Winston was not about to weaken the Mutual at the height of its rivalry with the Equitable.[29]

The retirement annuity and premium revision episodes were the prelude to the Mutual's lobbying against the nonforfeiture bill, opposition to savings bank life insurance, and a sustained effort to discredit Elizur's criticism of their corporate practices. The revised nonforfeiture bill threatened the Mutual's lucrative windfall from a surrender charge on the reserve of at least 50 percent. The Mutual consequently became the focus of Elizur's attack on the life insurance "autocracy." "My quarrel with Winston has arisen," Elizur explained, "wholly from his unreasonable and persistent opposition to paying an equitable cash surrender value and to his publishing, year after year, a defective financial statement."[30]

Elizur attacked the Mutual on their proposed premium rate reduction of 1872 and 1878. Unable to compete with the Equitable's aggressive marketing of tontine insurance, the Mutual abandoned the tontine on November 20, 1872, and in turn proposed a bold rate reduction in order to attract new policyholders. In a joint statement with his fellow actuaries, Sheppard Homans and David Parks Fackler, Elizur called the proposed reduction of 1872 "unwise, deficient in security, unjust to existing policy-holders, and prejudiced to their rights and interests and deserving our unqualified disapproval." They explained that the equity of older policy-holders would be exploited to subsidize new subscribers and thereby increase company profits. The general outcry of some twenty insurance companies against the Mutual's plan, which would have undercut the rest of the industry, stopped the 1872 reduction.[31]

At the same time, Elizur defended his colleague, Sheppard Homans, in the press against Winston's displeasure. The Mutual had fired Homans as its chief actuary because he refused to audit what he termed its president's "false accounts" of the firm's 1872 finances. "I think you and I and all honest friends of reform in life insurance," Homans wrote to Elizur, "are now in the same boat and are enlisted for the war."[32]

In 1878 the Mutual again attempted to establish a 30 percent rebate for new policyholders. Elizur testified before the judiciary committee of the New York legislature that "this inequitable rebate, coolly proposes to throw the mathematical laws of the game overboard entirely, and convert American life insurance by one coup de grace from a semblance of mutuality into an undisguised and unmitigated autocracy." Protest scuttled the planned reduction, but the wrangling between Elizur and Winston continued.[33]

During the New York wars the influence of the large insurance companies over the press amounted to censorship. The Mutual's harassment of Stephen English not only closed *The Insurance Times* to Elizur's reform essays but also deflected Elizur's and English's attacks from the Mutual to one another. English was imprisoned in 1873 for seven months in New York's Ludlow Street jail on the charge of fraud brought by the Mutual because of his exposé of the company's financial malpractices. The Mutual's persecution broke his independent spirit. English told Elizur that the Mutual's harassment had weakened his health, ruined his business, and depleted his wealth.[34]

English had previously been a warm admirer of Elizur and had actively solicited his reform essays. After his incarceration, *The Insurance Times* became another organ defaming Elizur and discrediting savings bank life insurance. The observation of *The Insurance World* that "Elizur Wright had received more wholesale abuse than any insurance writer on the continent" was not something that English helped to invalidate. *The Insurance Times* carried articles entitled "Elizur Wright on the Rampage," "Follies and Blunders of Elizur Wright," and "The Vagaries of Elizur

Wright." English accused him of charging "exorbitant" consulting fees, of "frequently making actuarial errors," and of being motivated by "revengeful malevolence." Elizur rejoined that he was attacking real abuses and that *The Insurance Times* had joined the score of trade publications that the "New York Ring" controlled.[35]

Elizur was not, however, immune from corporate pressure. The influence of the Equitable was subtle and covert compared to the Mutual's firing of Homans and persecution of English. During most of his relationship with the Equitable, Elizur took their money but continued an independent line. He received $250 in 1873 for fulfilling Hyde's request that "an article from your pen would do good" in exposing the Mutual's financial manipulations. Hyde praised his writing and solicited his good will, even though Elizur continued to attack the tontine. Moreover, he still intractably declared, "I have no faith whatever in the stability or soundness of the Equitable, and still less in its equity," and he warned of a "terrible crash" coming in the company.[36]

Hyde finally, however, did gain Elizur's support for the Equitable. Hyde was angered in 1882 by what he regarded as Elizur's gratuitous attack on some of the company's promotional literature. "He has got [no] more than ten years longer," the president of the Equitable coldly told an associate, "in which to do this kind of thing, as he is about seventy-five now." Actually Elizur was seventy-eight. But Hyde was correct that the time was right to buy the old man's acquiescence, if not approval. In return for a minimal amount of work and for public support of the company, the Equitable promptly paid Elizur five hundred dollars on each quarter of the year after 1882. Through the guise of a retainer, Hyde had achieved what Winston had failed to do in 1869. In historian R. Carlyle Buley's apt phrase, Elizur was a "virtual pensioner" of the Equitable during the last several years of his life. His antagonist Stephen English less euphemistically called Elizur a "lackey dog." "I must confess," English gloated, "that you are a much cuter man than I imagined, but far from being so high toned as I fondly believed."[37]

The lure of two thousand dollars per year virtually gratis marked the first time in Elizur's long career that he violated principle in return for pay. James W. Alexander, the vice-president of the Equitable, even requested Elizur's support to prevent the Massachusetts nonforfeiture law of 1881 from applying to the New York companies and urged him to work against his former ally, E. D. Williams, the president of the Policyholders' Association of America. Although Elizur's response remains unclear, in

1885, the year of his death, he went so far as to endorse a misleadingly worded circular that extolled the Equitable's management and financial practices, including the tontine. Elizur's colleagues were incredulous. The explanation for his failing is not clear. But he apparently used at least some of the money in preserving the Middlesex Fells, an expensive conservation effort that was dear to his heart during his last years. The blandishments of a rich corporation, however, had taken their toll on the octogenarian and reduced him to a well-paid sycophant.[38]

The extraordinary aspect of Elizur's forty-year crusade for life insurance reform was not that he was co-opted, but that it took so long. In the two decades after the Civil War, the consolidation of the huge life insurance corporations gave them pervasive control over wealth and ideas. With millions of dollars of other people's money at their disposal, the life insurance moguls established business practices, wrote legislation, censored the press, and silenced critics. The Hydes and Winstons ran their companies autocratically, as Elizur said. The Equitable and the Mutual were not as their names suggest but more akin to personal fiefdoms. A few corporate officials made policy that affected countless people but with a minimum of public accountability.

Certainly Elizur's personal struggle, even given the lapse of his last years, was exemplary. The valor of one reformer, however, was not enough to make life insurance just. He knew that. He believed that public influence over the powerful corporations was essential to achieve policyholders' rights. From 1858 to 1867 he pioneered the role of active state supervision in order to make the life insurance business accountable. His rationale for governmental regulation was that "corporations are not individuals. They are creatures without consciences and created by legislatures of finite wisdom. When they make promises only to break them, breaking the hearts thereby of many innocent people, it is time for the legislature to put down the brakes."[39]

Yet state legislation alone was inadequate to police the national scope of the burgeoning life insurance business. Elizur advocated a national bureau, the Chamber of Life Insurance, "a grand union of all the companies of America, for objects promotive of the common welfare." He hoped that the chamber would standardize actuarial practices, procure uniform legislation, and supervise the companies, including the mandate to bring legal action against those executives who knowingly misrepresented their financial statements. There was some support for making him the director of such an organization. The large corporations, however, opposed national regulations, especially with Elizur as a crusading commissioner. Winston, for example, did not wish to lose the Mutual's powerful lobby in the New York legislature. A convention in Hartford on September 26, 1866, sponsored by Connecticut firms did lead to the creation of the Chamber of Life Insurance in that year. Although the chamber did attempt to act as a national umbrella group, it was not given the mandate for action that Elizur had wanted. With the withdrawal of the Mutual in 1877, the chamber collapsed, having been inactive for nearly half of its eleven-year existence. The passing popularity of national authority in the wake of the Civil War was not sufficient to overcome the countervailing pressure for laissez-faire and states' rights.[40]

The Supreme Court in 1868 further undermined national life insurance regulation in the decision of *Paul v. Virginia*. The ruling contradicted Elizur's contention that the transaction of life insurance constituted interstate commerce which Congress had the authority to regulate. The Court decreed that a policy of life insurance was a personal contract for indemnity governed by local law, not commerce between the states. He called the decision "ruinous" and urged the friends of national legislation to bestir themselves. There was, however, not enough support for national regulation.[41]

Elizur even urged the governmental sponsorship of life insurance as the British had done. In his most radical proposal, he argued: "It would be even better for the federal government, like the British, to enter the field as a life insurer itself, than not to prevent it. What are regarded by capitalists as the profits of the business had better go to pay the national debt than to support a class of unscrupulous parasites and plunderers, frightening honest and busy people with the fear of death, merely to fill their own pockets." Despite the rhetoric, he was not advocating nationalization. He was supporting a governmental alternative, similar to the Tennessee Valley Authority of the New Deal, that would provide a yardstick to measure the performance of private corporations. But government-sponsored life insurance had fewer partisans than the Chamber of Life Insurance.[42]

The efficacy of reform finally depended on how advantageous the large corporations thought it for maintaining their hegemony. Elizur's opposition to the tontine and his advocacy of a cash surrender law, savings bank life insurance, and national regulation were firmly opposed by the corporate powers because they feared an emphasis on policyholders' rights would lessen their huge profits and diminish their power. In 1959

David Houston, then a doctoral student at the Wharton School, completed a mathematical analysis of Elizur's reforms and found them fundamentally in accord with present actuarial knowledge. "Generally, the rejection of Wright's proposals," he concluded, "was based on grounds of expediency rather than on a logical refutation of his position."[43]

Elizur's crusade for life insurance reform points to a persistent dilemma in the political and economic structure of the United States. Corporations chartered by the legislature and engaged in a vital social function were able to frustrate efforts for effective public accountability despite the overwhelming evidence of inequity and malpractice. The contradiction that Elizur realized and strove to resolve was that an economic autocracy existed within a political democracy. He assumed that capitalism could be made socially just, but corporate self-enforcement was an obvious failure, state regulation was only locally operative, and national regulation was declared unconstitutional in 1868. He still had faith, however, that the force of popular opinion could eventually be brought to bear on the corporations. "What is wanted," he wrote, "is that the schoolhouse and the press—the universal educators—shall take up the matter, not in the interest of the companies or their agents, but in that of the public and its coming generations." Widespread outrage over corporate abuses did lead to the Armstrong Insurance Investigations of 1905 in New York and partly vindicated his struggle for public accountability through increased governmental regulation.[44]

His forty-year life insurance career demonstrates the essential continuity of his thought. The conventional concept of the Civil War as an intellectual watershed or the familiar rubric of antebellum reform does not neatly divide or contain his activities. Concern for justice, evangelical zeal, praise for free labor, and support for political action were characteristics of his abolitionism from the late 1830s that combined with his mathematical expertise to make him America's premier life insurance reformer during the nineteenth century. Another major consistency was his passion for individual freedom and personal independence. The actuarial wonder of life insurance was, as he put it, that it realized "fraternity without the destruction of independence and individuality." The concern for individualism coupled with his long-standing anticlericalism led during the late 1870s to his leadership in the free thought movement of the National Liberal League.[45]

Part Five

Atheist

Chapter 12

President of the National Liberal League

On August 1, 1878, the forty-fifth anniversary of the emancipation of the slaves in the British West Indies, a familiar figure strode to the stage of Boston's Faneuil Hall, the scene of numerous abolitionist meetings. The fringe of long white hair surrounding his balding head and full uncut beard gave the spry old man the appearance of a biblical patriarch. "Nobody would have come here," Elizur told the crowded assembly in a voice shrill with indignation, "if loose and careless Federal legislation had not been used to prosecute, proscribe and punish honest freedom of opinion." The subject was no longer abolition, but the conviction of Ezra Heywood to two years' imprisonment for publishing *Cupid's Yokes,* a tract advocating sexual reform that the U.S. Circuit Court deemed obscene under the 1873 Comstock Law. The speaker warned the receptive audience that "the old bull dog of religious persecution" threatened to undermine liberty of the press and the Constitution itself. By a voice vote, the assembly approved resolutions upholding "free thought, free speech, and free press." They also demanded a presidential pardon for Heywood and repeal of the Comstock Law.[1]

An irony lost on most of the large audience was that a half century earlier the irreverent chairman of their protest meeting had been a pious aspirant for the ministry. Stephen English, editor of *The Insurance Times,* described the elder Elizur as a "firm and uncompromising atheist," terms he would not have disagreed with. During the 1870s, he joined a small but vocal assortment of unbelievers who in historian James Turner's phrase were "without God, without creed." Certainly the astounding progress of industrialization, urbanization, and the achievements of science provided the broad context for the rise of secular thought, a phenomenon that

British commentator Lord Bryce observed in his visit to America in the late nineteenth century. Yet, Elizur did not embrace infidelity solely because he was a practical Bostonian with a keen, mathematical mind and an appreciation for what he called the "facts."[2]

The event that had led Elizur and other immediatists to come out of the church during the mid-1830s was the moral issue of clerical antiabolitionism. "The pulpit everywhere—with a very few exceptions—either justified slavery from the scriptures," he recalled in 1882, "or denounced abolitionism as a pestilent sin." His friend, Robert G. Ingersoll, the best-known infidel of the day, accurately described Elizur's transition from anticlerical abolitionism to free thought. "He found that a majority of Christians were willing to enslave men and women for whom they said Christ had died...," Ingersoll wrote in an 1885 eulogy. "Elizur Wright said to himself, why should we take chains from bodies and enslave minds—why fight to free the cage and leave the bird a prisoner? He became an enemy of orthodox religion—that is to say, a friend of intellectual liberty."[3]

For the young Elizur, the essence of religion was ethical, especially the imperative to do good works, a theme his parents thoroughly inculcated in him. The failure of the church to embrace these high standards in the abolitionist crusade led him to seek his "sense of justice" through doing "earthly good" in his varied and persistent reform career. "Christianity itself is a total failure," he wrote in 1847, "so far as it is a plan of saving souls for a future life without saving souls and bodies for this." He discarded the "husks" and "idols" of theology, but retained the secularized morality of evangelicalism. The delegitimation of the church as a moral authority set the stage for a rational, analytical refutation of the "myth and fancies" of religion. "I don't believe in the God of books," he wrote Beriah Green in 1860. "I don't believe in anything but facts appreciated by some degree of evidence." Religious skepticism and a type of scientific positivism evolved from his disenchantment with "a hypocritical church and age."[4]

The stagnation of party politics in the mire of narrow partisanship and repeated scandals during the "Great Barbecue" of the 1870s and 1880s cleared the way for Elizur's involvement in free thought activities. During the late 1860s a preoccupation with public corruption began to overshadow concern among reformers with Reconstruction itself. What little enthusiasm Elizur had for the Republican party evaporated during the inept administration of Ulysses S. Grant. Elizur told "colored voters" in the election of 1872 that the party of Lincoln had only freed the slaves as a wartime "expedient." "It is you[r] obvious policy not to wed yourselves for better or worse to either party," he lectured the black electorate, "but to go for that which best deserves and most needs your help." Like other members of the Bird Club, Elizur endorsed the Liberal Republican insurgency in that presidential year against the Stalwart Republicans who remained loyal to Grant. As a member of the Liberal Republican central committee of Massachusetts, he backed the insurgent Horace Greeley, influential editor of the New York *Herald Tribune,* for president. "The great question now before the Republican party, and all the rest of us," he declared during the 1872 election, "is whether after our bloody cutting out of cancer [slavery], we are to rot by the cancer of our corruption."[5]

A partisan of coalition politics since the days of Liberty and Free-Soil parties, Elizur even advocated fusion with the Democrats. "The Democratic party has changed," he announced in conjunction with other Bay State insurgents. The Democrats, besmirched by their association with slavery and secession, had in their opinion turned over a new leaf with their support for the Reconstruction amendments to the Constitution and adoption at their Baltimore convention of the Liberal Republican platform along with its standard-bearer, Horace Greeley. Although Elizur supported Grant's dispatch of federal troops to combat Ku Klux Klan terror in the South, he complained, "What is the use of keeping people's throats from being cut, if they are to be perpetually robbed?" The troubled Grant administration had done nothing to stop the "rings and robbery" in the former Confederate states from exploiting black and white alike. In contrast, the Liberal Republicans offered "honorable and manly terms of reconciliation with the South," including the protection of black rights. Greeley's defeat at the polls, however, dashed his hope for a redirected Republican party.[6]

Elizur voted for Republican loyalist Rutherford B. Hayes in 1876, but only because he feared that the Democratic party, despite earlier hopes, was unwilling to embrace a reform platform. During the next quadrennial contest he urged the formation of a free thought ticket with Robert G. Ingersoll as standard-bearer, but this quixotic project came to nought. And in the election of 1884, "Mugwumps" or Republicans disaffected with their party's nomination of Senator James G. Blaine of Maine, who was tarnished with railroad graft, bolted for Democratic candidate Grover Cleveland, governor of New York. Though identifying himself as a "Mugwump," a contentious Elizur even quarreled with the dissidents.

His alienation from the two major parties and support for diverse interests—life insurance reform, the end of the patronage system, the gold standard, free trade, railroad regulation, and especially the emerging free thought movement—characterized, as historian Louis S. Gerteis put it, "the restlessness and uncertainty of liberal reformers in the Gilded Age."[7]

Among other free thought newspapers that he read, Elizur was attracted to *The Index,* a weekly that began publication on January 1, 1870 in Toledo, Ohio. Its editor, Francis E. Abbot, an apostate Unitarian clergyman, espoused "faith in the human race and the sufficiency of secular law for a secular world." A leading patron of *The Index,* Elizur bought five shares of stock in 1872 and encouraged Abbot to move the newspaper to Boston the next year. By 1878 he became a regular editorial contributor. He pronounced Abbot's efforts at disestablishing the vestiges of religion from the state a "noble fight."[8]

Abbot codified his goals for a completely secular government in "The Nine Demands of Liberalism" in 1872 and "The Religious Freedom Amendment" in 1874. These manifestos provided the guiding principles for the creation of the National Liberal League, which organized at Philadelphia during July 1-4, 1876, the centennial of the Declaration of Independence. The league declared that its object was "the total separation of church and state: to the end that equal rights in religion, genuine morality in politics, and freedom, virtue, and brotherhood in all human life, may be established, protected, and perpetuated." Although unable to attend the centennial convention, Elizur at Abbot's bequest joined James Parton, Samuel Sewall, Robert Dale Owen, Rabbi Isaac Wise, and Robert G. Ingersoll, among others, as a vice-president of the league. He endorsed the resolution that "a guarantee of the rights of conscience" must be added to the Constitution in order to counteract Christian attempts to add a theistic statement.[9]

Liberals were a disparate but articulate group. They celebrated black emancipation, bemoaned women's degradation, but above all they identified themselves as individualists threatened by the imposition of state-enforced Christian dogma. "The platform of the coming millions is the individual," Elizur enthused. In addition to Elizur, other prominent, first-generation immediatists, including William Lloyd Garrison, Wendell Phillips, and Parker Pillsbury gave at least nominal support to the league. Except for Pillsbury, these Garrisonians, from whom Elizur had distanced himself since 1837, played little role in the organization, which muted the problem of their previous ill relations. It was a logical step from the abolitionist argument that slaves, like all people, were autonomous moral agents with the right of self-ownership, to the league's stress on personal rights and freedom of thought. "Christianity," Abbot observed in an antislavery analogy, "is essentially an organized slavery of the mind." Feminists Lucretia Mott and Lucy N. Colman, abolitionist Thomas Wentworth Higginson, sexual reformers Ezra Heywood, Edward Bond Foote, and Edward Bliss Foote, atheistic editor D. M. Bennett, lawyer Thaddeus B. Wakeman, and a host of other unbelievers made up the league's constituency, which was concentrated in the cosmopolitan centers of the nation where religious skepticism thrived.[10]

Abbot's success in organizing the league was temporary. Liberals quickly divided over their policy toward the Comstock Law. The eponymous Anthony Comstock was initially the agent of the Young Men's Christian Association and then in 1874 of its independent offshoot, the New York Society for the Suppression of Vice. A large, rotund man whose bull-dog tenacity was mirrored in his muttonchop whiskers, he claimed to have destroyed more than five tons of obscene publications, 180,000 lewd photographs, and 30,000 assorted contraceptives during one year alone in the Empire State. Dissatisfied with the nominal national legislation on obscenity, his successful lobby of Congress included a special exhibit of offensive material in the capital office of the vice-president. With only cursory deliberation, Congress overwhelmingly passed the legislation.[11]

Comstock's timing could not have been better. Congress was seeking to cast blame for the Credit Mobilier scandal (a particularly flagrant example of graft even for the Gilded Age) and was reluctant to oppose a bill designed to restore the nation's violated virtue. The law made the manufacture, possession, or distribution of obscene publications, contraceptives, or abortifacients a misdemeanor with punishment not to exceed five years imprisonment at hard labor for each offense and total fines of two thousand dollars. The postal laws were amended to allow prosecution for the mailing of such material, and Comstock secured appointment as a federal postal inspector. His achievement was no less than to enforce the legislation he wrote.[12]

The Comstock Law was the first comprehensive effort to police the nation's morals through federal supervision. In a Gilded Age of ubiquitous political corruption and unsettling social change, obscenity in Victorian America was a catch-all term for moral deviance from conventional mores. The original bill and subsequent amendment in 1876 failed, as only a few senators and congressmen tentatively acknowledged, to define obscenity with any precision or to clarify the enforcement procedures. The Senate voted unanimously for the bill; thirty-three representatives cast negative votes, but none spoke against it on the House floor. Cautious politicians did not want to be identified with opposition to an anti-obscenity statute however loosely worded it was.[13]

The vagueness of the law also gave the religiously devout Comstock broad enforcement power. The former dry goods clerk, who had left rural Connecticut for bustling New York City, defined obscenity in an open-ended way that included erotic literature, anatomical illustrations, birth control devices, and atheistic tracts. Appointed a special agent of the United States Postal Service, he censored the mails and personally arrested hundreds of people. His vigorous prosecution of religious infidels and sexual reformers raised serious constitutional questions about guarantees of freedom of speech and of the press. The postal censors enforced the law without recourse to policy decisions by the attorney general or federal district attorneys. Comstock himself employed the questionable practice of legal entrapment. He solicited suspected material in a "test" letter signed with an alias and then arrested the perpetrator if he judged the mailed literature obscene. Comstock's genius was to translate his personal obsession with sexuality, disorder, and infidelity into the publicly sanctioned role of censor.[14]

The Victorian vice crusaders were Christian soldiers marching in the army of evangelical Protestantism. They successfully appealed to the very real fears of people whose lives had been disordered by the Civil War, rapid technological change, urbanization, and fluctuating economic cycles. "That old time religion," which the Reverend Dwight L. Moody preached in urban revivals, provided the continuity, certainty, and comfort for many people to face the disruption, alienation, and apparent meaninglessness of the new industrial age. Obscenity was a conservative barometer for the erosion of conventional values. It suggested a dangerous loosening of sexual control and the breakdown of social order. "Unless the restraining forces of religion and morality keep ahead of all other considerations," Comstock warned, "the ship of state will soon be dashed to pieces upon the boulders and quicksands of immorality."[15]

With little faith in voluntary constraint or moral suasion, the purity movement opted, as most antebellum reformers had also eventually done, for legal coercion to produce desired behavior. Censorship of the mails was nationalized, a sign of the increasing role of the federal government as the institution of last resort in ordering the society, whether in Reconstruction policies, supplying troops to break strikes, or regulating the railroads. "Religion and morality are," Comstock postulated, "the only safe foundations for a nation's future prosperity and security." The prima facie intent of the 1873 censorship law was to ban obscene literature and materials from the mail. In effect, the legislation was also a blasphemy statute.[16]

The Comstock Law was not on the agenda of the National Liberal League's Philadelphia meeting. Delegates, however, raised the critical issue from the floor. They agreed that the postal law was being abused in order to censor religious liberalism under the guise of protecting public morality. Some delegates argued that the law ought to be repealed entirely, but others responded that a more discerning form of censorship was a worthy goal. Just before the convention adjourned, a compromise resolution was adopted that urged that the Comstock Law be precisely defined so not to allow the prosecution of "honest and conscientious men" for presenting views that did not violate "the acknowledged rules of decency." The resolution was, however, an ambiguously worded expedient that only postponed the hard decision on what the league's specific course of action should be.[17]

While the league temporized, Comstock acted. He was particularly offended by a "most obscene and loathsome book," *Cupid's Yokes*. The author, Ezra Heywood, an eclectic reformer and radical individualist residing in Princeton, Massachusetts, reviled marriage as legalized prostitution that permitted a libidinous husband a "tyranny of lust" over his victimized wife. "Is coition pure," he asked, "only when sanctioned by priest or magistrate?" An emphatic yes was Comstock's answer. He arrested Heywood on November 2, 1877 just as the reformer finished addressing a Boston audience of 250 people. Elizur, who had been faithfully married to the same woman for almost half a century, did not share Heywood's free love views, which in effect left the decision to engage in sex to mutually consenting adults. Nevertheless, he posted Heywood's bail of fifteen hundred dollars the next day in order to protest what he regarded as a gross violation of freedom of thought. Elizur further demanded total repeal of the offensive Comstock Law. The U.S. Circuit Court, however, sentenced the defendant on June 25, 1878 to two years at hard labor in the Dedham jail.[18]

Ten days after Heywood's arrest Comstock apprehended D. M. Bennett in his New York office for, among other things, mailing a copy of the infamous *Cupid's Yokes*. Bennett was editor of *The Truthseeker*, a provocative anticlerical newspaper, and, like Elizur, a vice-president of the league. Comstock characterized the atheistic Bennett as "everything vile in blasphemy and infidelism." "I am a prominent advocate of heterodox opinions," the combative editor responded in explaining his arrest, "and have made myself obnoxious to the theological powers that be and am considered a belligerent enemy to the system of Christianity." Colonel Ingersoll was, however, able to exert his considerable political influence in the Republican party in order to have the postmaster general drop the charges.[19]

The prosecution of Heywood and Bennett focused attention on the Comstock Law as the league's paramount concern during its second annual congress at Syracuse during October 26–27, 1878. The announcement for the convention asked that delegates be prepared to take a stand either for the total repeal or partial reform of the 1873 censorship law. Abbot, who remained president, had so firmly committed himself to the reform position that a majority vote for repeal would amount to a vote of no confidence in his leadership. He maintained that a meaningful distinction could be made between publications that appealed to the intellect and those that pandered to the passions. Unless the league came out forcefully against obscenity, he warned that churchmen would seize the opportunity to discredit free thought as a bedfellow of free love. He therefore conspicuously avoided support for the beleaguered Heywood and Bennett. Abbot went so far as to declare, "Anthony Comstock has done a great deal of dirty but most necessary work." Ingersoll, a vice-president of the league, supported Abbot's position. "Let them spend their time examining each other's sexual organs," he quipped about free lovers, "and in letting ours alone." Above all, the colonel and the former clergyman sought respectability for the league.[20]

At the highly charged Syracuse convention, most delegates favored repeal. A tangle of conflicting resolutions and contentious debate led to an agreement to postpone a vote on the divisive issue of the Comstock Law until the 1879 meeting. The majority, however, prevailed indirectly by voting Abbot and his reform slate out of office. They elected Elizur, who had remained in Boston hard at his insurance work, president, and placed other advocates of repeal in the remaining positions. The unsolicited election of the old abolitionist and distinguished actuary, well known for his impeccable personal morality, gave prestige to the repeal faction. "There are many wrongs among mankind," he had observed earlier of postal censorship, "with which law cannot meddle without making them worse." Unable to abide the repeal position, Abbot and his faction withdrew from the league and formed an ephemeral, splinter organization. Ingersoll remained in the league during Elizur's tenure until he finally left in 1880 over frustration with "this infernal question of obscenity."[21]

The schism was rooted in different perceptions of the league which the contention over the Comstock Law brought to the fore. The Abbot faction saw the league as a prototype for a secular religion, a type of scientific theism. Elizur accused Abbot of moving "in the direction of forming a church." Their interest in developing a respectable alternative to Christianity meant they had to disassociate themselves from the taint of free love and repeal of the Comstock Law. Abbot therefore declared that secession from the league was "a great moral victory," for it separated those Liberals pure in thought from the supposed libertines. He saw himself as a victim of the licentious forces who had taken over the Syracuse convention. "The real object of the repeal party," he confided to his diary, "was to wreak *personal revenge on me* for my fearless course in opposing their measures."[22]

After the Syracuse convention, Abbot launched a vituperative attack on the league and its new officers. He was resourceful enough to uncover evidence of embarrassing sexual behavior on the part of Albert L. Rawson and D. M. Bennett, two officers of the league, and vindictive enough to make it public. Although Rawson denied Abbot's charge that he was a bigamist, he acknowledged fathering a child by another woman while he was separated from his wife. He declared, however, that his past liaison had no bearing on his conduct as secretary of the league. Bennett forthrightly admitted the authorship of amorous letters to a woman other than his wife, but added that his spouse had long since forgiven him. Nevertheless Abbot charged that the league was "corrupted by the poison of free love." He called Elizur a dupe of profligates and demanded his resignation.[23]

Elizur's initial response to the schism was an effort at rapproachement. He explained that his election had not officially committed the league to the repeal position, because it had been agreed at Syracuse that the issue would be formally voted on at the next convention. Abbot's attacks, however, ended any attempt at reconciliation. He accused Abbot of wanting the league to be "a sort of watch-over-my brother church" responsible for every member's morals. The Comstockian argument for postal inspection, he charged, had made Abbot myopic on the peril of censorship, which could even affect *The Index*. Comstock and Abbot had in fact arrived at a similar assessment of the league during Elizur's presidency. Comstock identified two types of freethinkers: Abbot's reform faction was made up of "the strong, pure, and clean men," but their opponents were "the howling, ranting, blaspheming mob of repealers." Abbot could not have agreed more.[24]

In contrast, Elizur claimed for "the great body of the Liberal League a moral aim as high as that of the church." It genuinely sought the eradication of vice but not through censorship of the mail. Personally he believed that the dissemination of scientific knowledge about human sexuality was the best way to eliminate a market for prurient material. State legislation against obscenity was, however, necessary and sufficient in the interim. For sexually descriptive material without redeeming social value, he supported local legislation that dealt harshly with the perpetrators. He demanded the repeal of the Comstock Law because it was an arbitrary restriction of First Amendment freedoms. "I hold a law," he wrote the postmaster general, "which excludes from the mails a publication of my own or any other man, for the production of which no court has convicted me or him as a criminal, to be an utterly unconstitutional invasion of my rights as a man and a citizen."[25]

The Syracuse schism ended what had been a cordial relationship between Elizur and Abbot. Asserting that cooperation between them was "practically impossible," Abbot revoked Elizur's position as an editorial contributor to *The Index*. Elizur, who nevertheless remained a director of the newspaper, retaliated by seeking Abbot's ouster as editor at the November 17, 1879 board of directors' meeting. Abbot was not removed, and Elizur resigned from the board, completely severing his association with Abbot.[26]

During his three-year presidency of the league, Elizur took a strong stand on behalf of Rawson, Heywood, Bennett, and civil liberties in general. Despite the advice of influential Liberals, he refused to accept Rawson's resignation as secretary of the league. Elizur asserted with sarcastic wit that Rawson was not the enemy, because he was "too much married fifteen years ago." "The enemies of justice and the republic," he reminded the secretary's critics, were the "ecclesiastical corporations" that paid no taxes and taught "theological superstitions" in the public schools.[27]

The league adopted Ezra Heywood as a virtual prisoner of conscience after his indictment under the Comstock Law. Elizur continued his efforts on Heywood's behalf by petitioning President Rutherford B. Hayes for a pardon. He argued that there had been no violation of public morality, for *Cupid's Yokes* was no more obscene than the Bible, which, as freethinkers liked to point out, had its share of racy stories. He added that the federal government should not have jurisdiction over what people thought or over censorship of the mails. The Comstock Law, he reminded Hayes, was akin to the mentality that had led the Jackson administration to censor abolitionist literature posted to the South. In a politically courageous act, Hayes freed Heywood on December 20, 1878. Comstock exclaimed in high dudgeon that the president had succumbed to the persuasion of "infidels and liberals, free lovers and smut dealers." Hayes agreed, however, with Elizur that Heywood's views opposing religion and marriage did not constitute a crime, even though he found them repugnant.[28]

Bennett had escaped prosecution in 1877 for mailing *Cupid's Yokes,* but the determined Comstock soon arrested him again on a similar infraction. On May 31, 1879, Bennett was fined three hundred dollars and sentenced to thirteen months at hard labor. Comstock dubbed the editor of *The Truthseeker* the "apostle of Nastiness" and described his writings as "so blasphemous that they almost make one's blood run cold." After his first arrest under the 1873 statute, the pugnacious atheist had further antagonized his nemesis by publishing the muckraking biography, *Anthony Comstock: His Career of Cruelty and Crime.* Bennett's declaration that his object in repeatedly mailing *Cupid's Yokes* was "to vindicate the liberty of thought and of the press and of the mails" made his conviction a preeminent issue for the league.[29]

After the courts refused to review Bennett's case on appeal, the league asked President Hayes to pardon him. Elizur wrote the president that the Comstock Law was unconstitutional, and Ingersoll presented his fellow Republican a petition on Bennett's behalf signed by sixty thousand people. Hayes declined to override the courts even though he was not satisfied that their rulings were correct. The political liability of granting clemency to another infidel was too great. In order to publicize Bennett's plight, Elizur chaired a protest meeting on August 8, 1879, at the Astor

House in New York City. He told the gathering that the "great crisis" raised by Bennett's incarceration was that "under the sanction of the United States courts an American citizen is deprived of his freedom simply because he exercised a constitutional privilege of mailing certain sentiments expressed in decent language." The point was that regardless of Bennett's views he was the victim of an unjust law that suppressed fundamental rights.[30]

Bennett nevertheless served out his prison term. Upon his release, he was honored at a reception chaired by Elizur in New York City and attended by prominent league members. As Heywood dramatically embraced Bennett on stage, Elizur told the audience that not since the Dred Scott decision had there been a greater legal outrage than the Comstock Law. He denounced the statute for allowing "ecclesiastical trials" and "the murder of freedom of thought." Bennett, an ailing man in his sixties, wept openly as he acknowledged the cheers of the crowd and clutched a bouquet of flowers. *The New York Times,* a guardian of Victorian morality, damned the meeting as rife with "blasphemy and filth."[31]

The major administrative role for Elizur as president of the league was to chair its conventions. The announcement that "Free Thought, Free Speech, Free Ballot, and Free Mails Must be Secured by a Secular Republic Emancipated from Church Domination" invited Liberals to the third annual convention of September 13–14, 1879, in Cincinnati. In his opening address to delegates representing some 162 chapters, Elizur indicted the tax exemption for the church as an "unjust privilege." If religious doctrines were persuasive, he argued, let the church support itself. He assailed the Comstock Law as "an engine of religious persecution" and a dangerous violation of civil rights. He expressed his gratitude to Heywood and Bennett for their principled defiance of a repressive law. Finally, he summed up the overarching ideal of the league as a "profound reverence for the rights of the individual."[32]

The resolutions passed at the Cincinnati convention were numerous and diverse, expressing the league's support for a multitude of social reforms. In addition to the standard call for complete secularization of the state, the delegates officially called for the repeal of the Comstock Law. Linking the past with the present, Elizur recalled for a new generation that *Human Rights,* an immediatist publication that he once edited, had been burned in the anti-abolitionist sack of the Charleston post office in 1835. The platform also included opposition to child labor and endorsed equal rights for women, land reform, and government regulation of large corporations. An effort to establish a National Liberal party with Ingersoll as its nominee failed to gain momentum. Nevertheless, Elizur thought it proper and essential to work through the established political process to secure what he termed the right of "personal mental liberty."[33]

Despite the schism of 1878, the number of the league's affiliates tripled to 212 by 1880. The Chicago convention of 1880 elected Elizur to a third term, but he declined to run the next year because of his advanced years. "Let the young do the fighting," the septuagenerian urged. In December 1882, he nevertheless posted bail for the tenacious Heywood, who once again was arrested for mailing *Cupid's Yokes* and other literature that Comstock deemed obscene. The league, however, was never able to reach a satisfactory resolution on the difficult issue of obscenity and censorship. The question was too divisive and continued to polarize the membership. At the eighth convention of the league in 1884 president Thaddeus B. Wakeman, who supported total repeal of the Comstock Law, urged a return to first principles—"The Nine Demands of Liberalism"—and the creation of a united front. Delegates dissolved the old organization in favor of a new society, the American Secular Union. In the spirit of reconciliation, the eloquent Robert Ingersoll, an opponent of total repeal, was elected president.[34]

Although after 1880 Elizur's main reform interest had turned toward the preservation of the Middlesex Fells, he was elected president of the National Defense Association in October 1885 at age eighty-one. Founded in 1878 the National Defense Association continued to aid the victims of the Comstock Law, a cause that was no longer a central concern of the American Secular Union. The association foreshadowed the American Civil Liberties Union by almost fifty years in its commitment to defendants who were prosecuted for "no other crime than exercising the natural right of an American citizen to think his thought and express it orally or in print." Shortly after accepting the office, Elizur died. In tribute to his long career on behalf of individual rights, the association retained his name as president.[35]

Despite its brief existence, the National Liberal League and its kindred offshoots represented the coming of age of religious infidelity in postbellum America. Liberals differed on what individualism meant, but they agreed that the collusion between church and state must end. Like slavery, they stigmatized Christianity as an unsavory relic of the benighted past, a medieval bondage of the mind unbefitting the scientific age. Some, like Ezra Heywood, embraced a type of personal anarchism, which led him to declare "the Natural Right and Necessity of Sexual Self-Government." Or, as one Josephine S. Tilton wrote to Elizur, "I will be mistress of my person and therein lies the right to private judgment in morals." Elizur fought for their right to express such sentiments without being gagged by a censorious Comstock. But, as in his opposition to the Christian anarchism of the Garrisonian abolitionists during the antebellum period, this devoted second-generation republican politically grounded individual liberty in the Constitution and the Bill of Rights. The league's initial opposition to the Comstock Law has continued in various permutations over the last century as to where the balance ought to be set between individual rights and state censorship. Underlaying the debate was, as the former aspirant to the ministry emphasized, the fact that a long era of unquestioned Christian hegemony over cultural values had come to an end.[36]

Elizur did not attempt to construct a systematic philosophy of free thought as Abbot did. He had, however, developed a set of coherent, personal beliefs. He rejected the creed and theology of institutionalized Christianity as "incredible" and "inconceivable." His opposition to what he regarded as organized religion's "war against the freedom of the human mind" made him an active proponent of a secular state and a staunch supporter of civil liberties. His own credo was the ethical obligation for the individual to "judge for himself what is right and what is wrong." "Among mental slaves," he professed, "there can never be that manhood and womanhood without which morality is an unmeaning word." Government was instituted to secure individual rights, not "to dictate, coerce or suppress opinion." Until "the individual by an overt act of hostility wages war on others," he explained in the quintessential liberal tones of John Stuart Mill, "outside government has nothing to do with him." The crucial importance of individual choice and enhanced moral ability was a secular echo of the evangelical theology and revivals of the 1820s that had so impressed the young Wright. The old man, however, discarded conventional theistic views while maintaining an anthropocentric vision.[37]

By the 1880s Elizur variously described himself as an "infidel," an "atheist," and a "pagan." Rejecting supernatural explanations, he proclaimed that he was a "materialist" in the tradition of Spinoza, Paine, Darwin, and Huxley. "I suppose that I must fall into the category of 'Materialists' or 'Atheists,'" he reflected, "because I do not profess to know or believe that mind was the first cause of matter or that I can or shall consciously exist without a material body, any more than I know or believe that I did exist before I had one." His thought was highly rationalistic, partial to scientific empiricism, and influenced to some degree by Comtean ideas. He termed "positivism" the religion of humanity with the individual at its center and ethical behavior as its goal. "The degradation of the human soul can only be prevented or cured," he maintained, "by pure scientific thought." All he could reliably verify was what reason and experience taught him. The course of life was "afloat in an ocean of time and space," but it was not rudderless. The abandonment of religious superstition, he argued, gave hope "in the efforts of human reason to diminish the evil and increase the good, as the boundless current rolls on." For Elizur, the meaning of human existence was in the imperative, which his pious parents had originally instilled in him, to establish a "sense of justice" in the world.[38]

Chapter 13

The Family, Death, and Nature

"Since 1856 death has been a frequent visitor at my home," Elizur wrote to his Yale class of 1826 on its fiftieth anniversary, "removing three sons and three daughters, and at last mother and wife in March, 1875. I am left with four daughters and two sons. The grandchildren are eight." In 1879 another of his eighteen children, Mary Vashon, died at her St. Paul, Minnesota, home. In sum, the aged patriarch had outlived thirteen of his children and his wife. The effort to cope with the staggering loss of so many of his large family spurred him to his last reform, the crusade to save the Middlesex Fells.[1]

The Fells are a wooded plateau in and around Medford, Massachusetts, that the glaciers of the last ice age cut into rugged hills, dotted with ponds. Unsuited for agriculture, it remained a wooded region six miles north of Boston. Elizur had bought land in the Pine Hill area on the edge of the Fells in 1864 and became in 1870 a permanent resident there in a gracious Victorian home complete with an octagonal tower and large front porch. After the passage of the nonforfeiture legislation in 1880, he curtailed his life insurance work and his activities with the National Liberal League in order to devote himself to the preservation of the Fells.[2]

The Fells had a special significance for the old man. In the face of numerous family deaths and his own advanced years, the survival of the natural environment with which he strongly identified represented continuity with life itself. The untamed land of the Fells recaptured earlier experiences: growing up in the Berkshires and in frontier Ohio, climbing Mount Taghkannuc near his childhood home in South Canaan, and colportage in the wilds of western Pennsylvania. At Pine Hill he supervised a small farming operation much as his father had done on the Western Reserve.

WRIGHT FAMILY NECROLOGY

Birth Order

1. Susan Louisa
   b. Oct. 1831
   d. Jan. 1832

2. John Seward*
   b. 1833

3. Clara Richards
   b. Apr. 1834
   d. 1835

4. Josiah Elizur
   b. Jan. 1836
   d. Sept. 1836

5. Charles Storrs
   b. July 1837
   d. Apr. 1858

6. Mary Vashon
   b. Sept. 1838
   d. 1879

7. Ellen Martha*
   b. Sept. 1839

8. Harriet Amelia
   b. Sept. 1840
   d. Mar. 1844

9. Lucy Jane
   b. Jan. 1842
   d. May 1867

10. Arthur Tappan
    b. Dec. 1842
    d. Aug. 1843

11. Kathleen*
    b. Feb. 1844

12. Winifred
    d. 1873

13. Walter Channing*
    b. July 1846

11. Ida Russell*

15. Rosalind
    (died before five years old)

16. Anne Carroll
    b. 1852
    d. 1870

17. Edward Kittredge
    d. 1860

18. Richard Hildreth
    d. 1860

Susan Clark Wright
    b. 1810
    d. 1875

Elizur Wright
    b. Feb. 12, 1804
    d. Nov. 21, 1885

*Indicates the five children who survived their father.

It was also the location of the family's vivacious domestic life in which botanical walks, bird-watching, and sleigh rides provided happy memories. Through nature Elizur recovered the past while he sought transcendence over death.[3]

The family played an important role in his reform career, even though this very private man purposely kept it apart from the contentious public arena in which he operated. It was his retreat, his refuge from the strife-torn world. In his poem "Home" he wrote:

> Holds it the wife or child
> Who on his toil has smiled,
> No matter what its trim,
> It is heaven to him.

His intense temperament, what Thomas Wentworth Higginson described as a "mixture of fire and bonhomie," made him a difficult person to work with, which even his immediatist colleagues—evangelical and Garrisonian alike—attested to during the 1830s. Beyond a rather formal relationship with the Bird Club, he was, after the abolitionist schism of 1840, a very independent, if not cantankerous, reformer. It was the counterpoint of his warm family life that provided the emotional sustenance for him to persevere. As Robert G. Ingersoll observed, the outspoken, passionate agitator was "loving and gentle in his family."[4]

Elizur regarded the family as constituting a little commonwealth, a training ground for responsible citizenship. "Well-ordered, loving families are the only stuff," he maintained, "that a real republic can be made of." Love and harmony, order and justice cultivated among parents and children constituted the values for the good society. In contrast, strife and tyranny in the family were the prototype for despotic government. His abolitionist concern for the well-being of black families preyed upon by fugitive slave bounty hunters mirrored his latter efforts for the Family Bank that sought to provide a better standard of living for the northern working class.[5]

His romantic affection for Susan, which had helped to entice him from the dreary prospect of Andover Seminary and into marriage, did not wane. He recalled in verse:

> When first thy face I saw,
> Dear Susan, in thy prime of youth,

> To tell the simple truth,
> I felt thy beauty draw.

"The worship of each other by two human beings of the opposite sex," he asserted, was the foundation of civilization itself. Longing for her on one of his business trips during the early 1840s, he wrote suggestively (in tones that would have embarrassed his prudish colleague Theodore Weld) that she was *"well put together . . .* everybody says so; *I* know so. I see plenty of women—nay, even *ladies* daily—but they are all flatter than pancakes." One of the mysteries of their relationship was why they went against the nineteenth-century trend toward smaller families in such an exceptional way by having eighteen children. The untimely deaths of a number of their sons and daughters probably encouraged their procreation. Certainly they did not practice sexual abstinence as a means of birth control.[6]

Susan played a conventional role as a homemaker. She was not a social reformer nor very well lettered, despite the fact that her husband had been her teacher. She remained apart from the public sphere in which her husband was so energetically engaged. Nevertheless, her full-time role as mother (she was pregnant for a total of nearly ten years of her life) and wife sustained her spouse's reform career. Stephen English perceptively noted, "She was the gentle and efficient mistress of his home, which she always rendered a source of solace and comfort to him giving him strength and fortitude to combat and conquer the difficulties of the world from which he has never shrank." On the death of his companion of nearly a half century, her widower remembered with deep emotion, "She was as good a woman as God ever gave to earth."[7]

Elizur and Susan purposefully constructed a child-oriented home. "Make home more attractive than any place out of it," Elizur advised parents. "Fill its evenings with instruction, amusement, fun. Take the lead in it yourselves. Get up plays and concerts at home and play yourselves. . . ." A reading aloud of *Martin Chuzzlewit* marked a typical evening at their house. He encouraged his sons and daughters to play the piano, compose poetry, draw, and act. He wrote short verses to celebrate their birthdays and plays for them to perform in. He taught his children at home because of his dislike for the regimentation of public schools. The older siblings instructed the younger on the model of the Lancaster system that his father had employed. In contrast to his use of corporal punishment at the Groton Academy, he abandoned the birch with his own children. The Wright family epitomized the nineteenth-century trend among the middle class in which parents placed a high value on child nurture, although their eighteen children were far from a typical number.[8]

The experience of poverty, suffering, and death acted to unify the family. In order to supplement their income, John, the eldest child, gave piano lessons. Several children assisted their father with the laborious mathematics involved in composing the actuarial tables. Lucy Jane and Walter became respected actuaries in their own right. Lucy Jane's budding career was, however, cut short by death in the spring of 1867. The family also rallied to help physically impaired members such as Charles Storrs, Harriet Amelia, and Rosalind. In Elizur's inspirational words about his congenitally crippled son:

> We'll all help honest Charley,
> For he can fairly talk,
> We'll help him late and early.
> In his learning to,
> learning to walk.

The ravages of death left the survivors closer together. Six children died in infancy. By 1880 Elizur had survived his wife and all but two sons (John and Walter) and three daughters (Ellen Martha, Kathleen, and Ida Russell). Disease and the tragic drowning of Charles Storrs took a heavy toll.[9]

The death of family members arouses intense emotion among survivors. Parents whose children die suffer not only a painful loss but a disappointment in self-realization. Their hopes, the sense of vicarious living through their offspring, are cruelly rebuffed. Parents may blame themselves for the premature death of their young, often in an unrealistic way. The normal process of grief may lead to guilt; mourning may turn to melancholia. When Elizur was in England in 1844, his three-year-old daughter, Harriet Amelia, was slowly dying from a spinal deformity. In anguish over her daughter's sufferings, Susan wrote to her absent husband, "Oh, if you were only with us, how can I get through them without you." The despondent reply from London was "my heart aches to be home." His perception of failure as a husband and father, of abandonment of his family during a period of hardship, came close to overwhelming Elizur.[10]

Psychiatrists speak of the importance of "ego strength" in understanding the way that survivors deal with death. Elizur had a strong sense of self, a feeling of basic trust in the world. After the deaths within the preceding five years of Susan Louisa, Clara Richards, and Josiah Elizur, he thankfully remarked in 1837 about John's survival during a smallpox epidemic, "How good is God in sparing him." In 1862 after the deaths of Charles Storrs, Harriet Amelia, Arthur Tappan, Rosalind, Edward Kittredge, and Richard Hildreth, he observed, "God orders everything for the best on the whole." By 1879 Mary Vashon, Lucy Jane, Winifred, Annie Carroll, and Susan had died. "It makes me sad always," he reflected, "to see my children go before me. But of Jane, and Mary especially, I feel that they have lived more in one year than I have in two."[11]

The successful resolution of grief also lies in the ability to communicate inner feelings that otherwise might become debilitating. Elizur was able to cope constructively with his grief in additional ways that gave his life renewed meaning and that at the same time comforted his family. Through his literary talents, he was able to express anguish and to externalize emotions. The death of a child invariably produced a memorial poem, which was kept in a family album and facilitated a collective lamentation among the survivors. He also wrote relatives and friends about deaths, which was a particular emotional necessity in managing the shock over the drowning of Charles Storrs.[12]

The context of family deaths contributed to Elizur's imperative for reform. The death of the first born, Susan Louisa, during infancy, in 1832 preceded his adoption of immediate abolition. The death of Harriet Amelia in 1844 took place when he learned that his life insurance policy was possibly worthless. These traumatic events added an increased sense of tension during a period when he was already very anxious about making a critical moral decision about slavery and with the survival of his impoverished family. The evangelical ethic to do good works predisposed him to translate inner anxiety into meaningful social action such as immediate abolition and life insurance reform. The ability to direct emotional energy into constructive social channels explains the longevity of his manifold reform career. In actively pursuing a "sense of justice" in society, he maintained personal integrity and also psychological stability.

People seek to blunt the finality of death through the creation of metaphoric representations of continuity. What psychiatrist Robert Jay Lifton calls "symbolic immortality" may take different expressions. The devout Elizur, Sr., looked to eternity "when we hope to make one grand family in heaven." The death of his daughter, Clara Richards, from whooping cough in 1835 provoked Elizur, Jr., to comment, "It has pleased a good and wise Providence to take our dear babe Clara. She has joined her older sister [Susan Louisa]. Thus have two of our little flock, as we trust, been taken to the bosom of the good shepherd." The death of his sister, Martha, a student at Oberlin College in 1836, made her abolitionist brother aware that it was "a loud call to me to follow more closely that Savior who is our only hope—our life—our immortality."[13]

By the 1870s a skeptical Elizur could not accept the palliatives of conventional eschatology. "I have stood over the death beds of three daughters, two adult and one adolescent, who had no other or better [religious] faith," he wrote in 1878, "than that of their mother and me, and who died in perfect peace, as did their mother, and as I hope to." In lieu of Christian consolation, he could take comfort that his good works as a reformer would live after him, and he could take solace in the survival of at least some of his family. But above all it was with the continuity of nature that he identified. The preservation of the Middlesex Fells, the single-minded reform effort to which he devoted himself after 1880, was in effect a living shrine to his family.[14]

The late nineteenth century marked the emergence of a national conservation effort in the wake of America's relentless exploitation of its abundant natural resources. With the close of the western frontier, the wonders of Yosemite and Yellowstone were given federal protection. In the East the Adirondack Preserve and Central Park were created. Elizur's conception of the Fells was a meeting point between John Muir's celebration of wilderness and Frederick Law Olmsted's city park. During his 1844 trip to England, Elizur had noted the contrast between the pleasant London parks and the dingy, urban squalor of the East End. A green oasis in the metropolis, he wrote, suggested "considerations that are of the utmost importance to the destiny of cities."[15]

Unlike the Boston Common and Garden, the Fells was of greater size and more primitive in character. Elizur envisioned the sanctuary stretching over four thousand acres with superfluous structures excluded and the wildness of the land left intact. An avid bird-watcher, he protested "the murder of the woods and their winged inhabitants" in anticipation of the Audubon Society. He wanted part of the Fells designated a nature center for public instruction. In addition to its aesthetic, recreational, and educational aspects, he pointed out that the Fells provided a vital water reservoir for the Boston area.[16]

Public officials, however, failed to pass a park bill. Consequently, in October 1880 Elizur helped to organize the Middlesex Fells Association with himself as president in order to protect the area from encroaching real estate pressures. The old reformer wrote letters to newspapers, lectured before clubs, and lobbied influential politicians. "Already a movement is on foot," the former Ohio pioneer warned, "to erect buildings and make avenues which will introduce a population inconsistent with the preservation of the forests or the purity of the water." With the help of naturalists Wilson Flagg and John Owen, the association held "forest festivals" to raise public awareness. The governor of Massachusetts, the mayor of Boston, Edward Everett Hale, Thomas Wentworth Higginson, and other luminaries attended a rally in January 1881 that featured a sleigh ride through the Fells followed by speeches at the Medford Town Hall.[17]

On May 25, 1882, the Massachusetts legislature passed a forestry act. The law provided that municipalities might designate forest preserves as part of the public domain under state management. In honor of the occasion the association held a forest festival in the Fells which a number of dignitaries attended. Elizur read his poem, "The Legend of Cheese Rock," that traced the history of the Fells back to the Puritan explorers who had "dined on simple cheese" on the very spot where the celebration was held. His former abolitionist colleagues John Greenleaf Whittier and Theodore Weld sent their congratulations. "In a few years Boston and the suburbs," the Quaker poet predicted, "will need such a breathing place as the Middlesex Fells." "Blessings on your Middlesex Fells Association—the first to cry aloud," Weld wrote in echoes of earlier evangelical enthusiasm, "in preaching the gospel of this *national salvation*."[18]

The problem remained, however, to gain the stipulated two-thirds of the electorate spread over the five towns involved to approve the appropriations necessary to acquire the land, which Elizur estimated at an expensive three hundred thousand dollars. He organized local, public-domain clubs, much in the spirit of today's Nature Conservancy, which solicited donations of money and land to preserve the Fells. He pledged five thousand dollars to the cause, and his son Walter offered one hundred. In an unsuccessful attempt to prevent the cutting of a roadside stand of virgin hemlocks and white pines Elizur offered to pay as much as one thousand dollars per tree. He pleaded:

> But Nature still asserts her rights
> Against all vulgar spells,
> And cries aloud, "Restore the pines
> To these my favorite Fells...."

The financial demands of saving the Fells and his emotional intensity on the subject suggest the motive during the last years of his life for his uncharacteristic willingness to accept a sinecure with the Equitable Life Assurance Society.[19]

Elizur was also an articulate advocate for the protection of Minnesota wilderness. His daughter Mary Vashon had moved with her husband to St. Paul, and Elizur had purchased a sizable amount of land in the Gull Lake region during one of his visits. When his daughter Winifred died of tuberculosis after a visit to St. Paul, her father renamed Gull Lake in her memory, another act linking his family to the survival of the natural world. He indicted the exploitative lumbering practices that failed to replant the forests and kindled devastating fires. In 1884 he was appointed to a federal commission that recommended against the building of dams on the headwaters of the Mississippi River. At the age of eighty he joined the other commissioners in personally investigating the Minnesota lake district, traveling much of the time in a birchbark canoe paddled by Indians. Any benefit to navigation was outweighed, the commission concluded, by the destruction of the surrounding forests and wild rice meadows of the Chippewas. Elizur denounced the dam construction as a plan that would benefit only the "timber thieves" who would use the reservoirs to float logs downstream to the sawmills.[20]

The preservation of the Fells was not achieved in Elizur's lifetime. On the morning of November 21, 1885, he suffered a stroke while working at his desk on the Fells project. He died several hours later at the age of eighty-one. In 1894, as part of legislation that provided for the incorporation of metropolitan Boston, two thousand acres of the Fells were designated a park. His children, Ellen and Walter, arranged for the donation of the Pine Hill estate to the Metropolitan Park Commission. His namesakes in the Fells, Wrights Pond and Wrights Boulder, are reminders of his devotion to conservation, the last reform project of a remarkable career.[21]

The Evolution of
an Evangelical

"He has for two generations been a familiar name and figure in Boston, and his death removes one of a great and heroic breed of New England men," *The Nation* eulogized on November 26, 1885, shortly after Elizur died at his desk in his Pine Hill home. In the phrase "a great and heroic breed of New England men" reverberates a half-century echo of Ralph Waldo Emerson's musings on the social ferment of the day in his 1840 essay "New England Reformers." The Concord sage astutely linked the "fertility of projects to save the world" during the antebellum period with "a falling from the Church nominal." Elizur was one of the spirited sons and daughters of New England for whom the declension of Congregationalism had profound implications during the turbulent nineteenth century, an era whose thought and institutions increasingly distanced themselves from their eighteenth-century predecessors.[1]

Against the backdrop of fundamental social transformation, a boy born in the Berkshires of Connecticut to a pious family came to embody the nineteenth-century phenomenon of the professional reformer—one whose entire career was devoted to promoting change. The sources of his commitment to reform were varied and interwoven. Three broad factors, however, describe his personal connection with time and place: he was a second-generation republican, a child of the Enlightenment, and an enthusiastic evangelical. His life spanning nine decades was bracketed by the belief that through equality of the law and through representative government the citizenry had the intelligence and virtue to construct a just polity. He abandoned the Congregationalism of his youth for atheism in old age; under the secular impact of his era he had reduced religion to its moral principles without reference to a higher being. He nevertheless retained a faith in the enhanced moral ability of the individual, in an ethic of the golden rule, and in an imperative to promote what he conscientiously thought was right. Unchurched though he became, his devout Puritan forebears would have recognized a kindred soul, one driven by moral intensity and evangelical zeal.

Among the personal qualities that made Elizur a reformer were an emotional willingness and intellectual ability to confront cultural contradictions. His exacting but loving parents inculcated in their favored son a conscientious obligation to act forthrightly on ethical principles. Circumstances and youthful ambivalence conspired to bar him from his intended career in the ministry. He found his calling instead in a lifetime devoted to reform, a progressively profane version of his original sacred quest. He came to terms with the national paradox of slavery and freedom first through colonization but soon abandoned it for immediate abolition, a more perfect embodiment of his Christian and republican ideals. A pious young man imbued with the millennial fervor of the Second Great Awakening, he was initially the quintessential romantic reformer. He naively believed that moral suasion, the redeeming power of God's word, would readily convert the unregenerated, stay the hand of the rum tippler, and transform slaveholders into abolitionists.

The impassioned arguments of William Lloyd Garrison persuaded Elizur that the gradual emancipation program of the American Colonization Society was a moral fraud. In a consistent extension of the evangelical belief that sin must readily be abandoned, he embraced the holy crusade of immediate abolitionism. Responsibility during 1833–39 for the daily operation and many publications of the American Anti-Slavery Society tempered his youthful euphoria that the millennium was at hand. The inefficacy of voluntary change in abolishing slavery and eradicating racism convinced him that political action and legislative mandates were essential to compel right conduct. The extraordinary failure of so many Christians, especially the ministry, to bear witness against the sin of slavery estranged him from organized religion as early as the mid-1830s and set him on a gradual but steady course toward free thought.

The significant turning point in Elizur's reform career occurred during the 1840s, belying the conventional interpretation of the Civil War as the critical watershed for antebellum reform. Differences over tactics and strategy during the abolitionist schism alienated him from antislavery churchmen and their Garrisonian opponents. Most of his evangelical colleagues in the New York headquarters of the American Anti-Slavery Society were initially reluctant to endorse an abolitionist third party, which Elizur advocated as early as 1839. He remained a major opponent of the Garrisonian nonresistants after 1837. Declaring himself a maverick among abolitionists, Elizur was increasingly isolated after 1840 from an influential organizational role in a crusade in which he had been a pioneer. In the wake of the schism, he was without secure employment, debt-ridden, and responsible for a growing family.

After a period of hardship and self-doubt during which he marketed his translation of La Fontaine's *Fables* in England, he secured financial backing from Liberty men and conscience Whigs to publish his own Boston newspaper, *The Chronotype*. He was an outspoken and irreverent journalist who editorialized for a sisterhood of reforms. Antislavery politics were an essential but not exclusive concern of his expanded agenda, which sought to address the myriad of social issues engendered by the rise of northern manufacturing and urbanization. Pressure to create a disciplined Free-Soil organ, however, forced him to sell the financially ailing newspaper in 1850. His evangelical fervor and independent style ran counter to the moderated tone and coalition building of the Free-Soil and Republican parties. At midcentury, he was estranged from his former immediatist colleagues, but only superficially accepted by a second generation of pragmatic antislavery politicians grouped about Boston's Bird Club, the center of Free-Soil and Republican politics in the Commonwealth.

Without a major role in the abolitionist crusade and desperate for a stable income, Elizur applied his mathematical talents to consulting work with life insurance companies after the mid-1840s. His consumer-oriented effort on behalf of the policyholder represented a continuity with his earlier abolitionist commitment in the quest for social justice. Unlike the early abolitionist crusade, his life insurance career was without overt religious overtones, a mark of his growing secularization and concern for rational solutions to social problems engendered by a dynamic capitalist economy. His actuarial innovations, sponsorship of landmark legislation, and tenure as Massachusetts commissioner of life insurance during 1858–67 were directed at placing the burgeoning business on a financially precise basis while making it safe and secure, as he put it, for "the widow and orphans." At a time when changing conditions made large numbers of families dependent on life insurance, his achievement was no less than the economic rationalization of death. His leadership in the governmental regulation of powerful corporations anticipated the efforts of twentieth-century Progressives, such as the Bay State's Louis Brandeis, to make corporate capitalism publicly accountable. His advocacy of national supervision of life insurance corporations was intellectually akin to his support for an active role of the federal government during the Civil War and Reconstruction on behalf of the slaves and freedmen.

No other asset of his long reform career presents so seeming a disparity as his defiant embrace of atheism. The distance between the dark-haired, would-be seminarian of the 1820s and the blasphemous white-bearded patriarch of the 1870s measured the enormous change possible in one life during the course of the nineteenth century. Moral indignation over organized religion's opposition to immediatism drove him out of the church; scientific skepticism led him to reject conventional theistic assumptions. Unrelenting opposition to state sponsorship of religion and the repressive Comstock Law of 1873 marked the culmination of his defense of First Amendment freedoms that stretched from the Jacksonian Era to the Gilded Age. His controversial election to the presidency of the National Liberal League in 1878 highlighted a schism among the nation's prominent freethinkers, including Francis E. Abbot and Robert G. Ingersoll, over the contentious issue of obscenity and free speech. Unlike Abbot and Ingersoll, Elizur called for the total repeal of the Comstock Law based on the belief that the federal government did not have the right to suppress unpopular opinions through censorship of the mail.

Though he was without God or creed, he retained a persistent commitment to the fundamentally sacred ideal of good works that characterized his social engagement. A decidedly evangelical bent also pervaded his personal style: no tobacco, no rum, no philandering; only moral intensity, frequent jeremiads, and a cantankerous individualism. Perhaps only the acerbic William Lloyd Garrison among his contemporaries rivaled his inclination for biting sarcasm and cutting invective. Even his early immediatist colleagues, such as Lewis Tappan and Theodore Weld, found his outspoken nature too much to bear at times. Yet, this determined, hatchet-faced man, filled with Old Testament righteousness and the will to do good, was kind and caring, especially in his important family circle. His devoted wife and numerous children drew out the gentleness of this holy warrior and provided him with a beloved refuge from the wrongs of the world.

After 1880 the old man dedicated his remaining few years to the preservation of the Middlesex Fells, the wooded hills and glacial ponds bordering his family home. Having rejected Christian eschatology and outlived most of his large family, his last crusade was in effect an effort to achieve a metaphoric triumph over death through identification with the survival of the natural world. Today the Middlesex Fells Reservation in metropolitan Boston provides water resources (including Wrights Pond), recreational opportunities, and wild land, a living testament to the early conservation movement of which Elizur was a part.

His pursuit of what he termed his "sense of justice" shared similar values with the classical liberalism of the age. Much less a philosopher than a practitioner of social change, there is little evidence that he read to any significant extent the work of Adam Smith, Jeremy Bentham, or the Mills, father and son. Rather his espousal of individualistic values was largely an indigenous product, though washed over by Anglo-American abolitionism and other waves of the English experience that he observed firsthand in his overseas journey of 1844.

On the scales of individual freedom and social cohesion, Elizur moved the balance between various points. He generally advocated limited government; he was a faithful friend of free trade, free labor, and the free market. But, in order to emancipate the slave, to safeguard the freedman, and to protect the policyholder, he demanded active governmental intervention. Much like John Stuart Mill's support for factory regulation, woman suffrage, and child labor laws, Elizur too believed that when individual rights were threatened government had to act as a referee, ensuring equality under the law and equality of opportunity. Then, so he assumed, the race for life began with a fair start in which healthy competition would yield the greatest good for the greatest number based on the talent, will, and morality of the contestants.

Republican government, representative of and responsive to its virtuous citizens, was his guarantor of liberty. He therefore vigorously opposed legislation that infringed on civil rights and freedom of conscience, whether injustice to the fugitive slave during the 1830s or censorship of the mails during the 1870s. In Fourieristic schemes of the 1840s and in the Massachusetts Family Bank of the 1870s, he sought to create a structural harmony between capital and labor. He came closest to finding a corrective to the imbalance of wealth and power in a capitalist economy in the state supervision of life insurance. His advocacy of public regulation of powerful corporations foreshadowed the reformist thinking of the Progressive and New Deal eras.

Though he confronted some of the major cultural contradictions of the century, Elizur's liberalism contained its own inherent ironies, notably in the areas of race, class, and corporate power. Religious principles, republican egalitarianism, and adherence to free labor made him an early opponent of slavery and racial prejudice. Much to his credit when most abolitionists and Radical Republicans thought that the Reconstruction amendments had finished their course for the slave, Elizur championed land redistribution. Despite his important recognition of the interconnection between political rights and economic wherewithal, he had by 1872 joined the Liberal Republican insurgency. Currency issues, free trade, graft in government, and civil service reform carried the day while the Liberals abandoned the freedman to southern Redeemers, Black Codes, and peonage. The contrast between his acute abolitionist vision of the 1830s and his myopia on race in the 1870s is stark. Partly it was the fascination with new issues, especially ubiquitous political corruption and the nationalistic desire to reunite the North and South. But it also reflected the limits of his individualistic ideology: Negroes had the same legal rights as the whites; let them compete.

Elizur espoused the doctrine of free labor twenty years before the Republican party emblazoned it on their campaign penants. His championship of the individual's right to sell one's labor for a fair wage in the marketplace was an effective intellectual weapon with which to batter proslavery apologists. Elizur's defense of liberal capitalism, however, blinded him to the plight of labor, whether the beleaguered artisans of New York City during the 1830s or Boston laborers during the 1870s. He consistently opposed unionization as a limitation on personal liberty, whether for workers to chart their own course or management to act unimpeded from group coercion. His moralism that the poor in London drank themselves into poverty was especially gratuitous, though thoroughly evangelical. His liberalism was based on the premise that individuals were independent economic units; he did not think in terms of class, trade solidarity, or the relationship to the means of production. He did not perceive the imbalance between worker and employer that a changing economy, particularly the rise of large scale manufacturing, had wrought. Thus like most first-generation abolitionists he formed no constructive connections with the labor movement before or after the Civil War.

His effort to make corporate power in the life insurance business publicly accountable pointed to some of the principle policy issues of the twentieth century. Despite his notable successes, his setbacks were instructive. The insurance lobby not only opposed much of his consumer-oriented legislation but was instrumental in ousting him as

Massachusetts' crusading insurance commissioner. Large corporations learned quickly how to emasculate reform and co-opt regulators. Indeed, by the early 1880s he accepted, completely out of character, a sinecure from Henry Hyde's Equitable, part of the insurance "autocracy" that he had damned. Wright was weary, and the Equitable's money could be used, among other things, to protect virgin white pines at one thousand dollars per tree from the logger's axe. His preoccupation with the preservation of the Middlesex Fells during his last years met personal needs in a way that the endless battles over insurance reform and against the Comstock Law no longer could.

The nineteenth century wore well on Wright. If he had been a man of his grandparents' generation, when God was in heaven and all was right with the world (as a nostalgic Henry Adams would have it), he might well have been a minister to a Connecticut congregation. But there were many transformations in his life: he moved West; left the Ohio farm for Yale; married before his parents met his bride; lived in Brooklyn and Boston; was a professor and poet, inventor and editor; and sought the improvement of the world through a variety of endeavors. And he had become an atheist, the culmination of a long history of religious declension in New England. The modification of the grim Puritan doctrine, the influence of Enlightenment rationalism, and the American experiment in republican government had a decided effect on the way he understood the monumental changes of his transitional century.

Abbreviations Used in Notes

AASS   American Anti-Slavery Society

Birney Letters   *Letters of James Gillespie Birney, 1831–1857,* ed. Dwight L. Dumond, 2 vols. (New York: Appleton-Century, 1938)

EW   Elizur Wright, Jr.; after 1845, he dropped "Jr." from his name

EW, Sr.   Elizur Wright, Sr. (1762–1845)

EWP, BL   Elizur Wright (Jr.) Papers, Baker Library, Harvard University

EWP, LC   Elizur Wright (Jr.) Papers, Library of Congress

HOT   *Hudson Observer and Telegraph*

Weld Letters   *Letters of Theodore Dwight Weld, Angelina Grimké Weld, and Sarah Grimké, 1822–1844,* ed. Gilbert H. Barnes and Dwight L. Dumond, 2 vols. (New York: Appleton-Century, 1934)

Notes

Preface and Acknowledgments

1. Ralph Waldo Emerson, *Selected Writings of Emerson,* ed. Brooks Atkinson (New York: Random House, 1950), 449-50.
2. David Brion Davis, "Some Recent Directions in Cultural History," *American Historical Review* 73 (1968): 705.

Part I THE MAKING OF AN EVANGELICAL

1. The Wright Family

1. EW, Sr., to EW, Oct. 13, 1825, EWP, LC.
2. Philip J. Greven, *The Protestant Temperament: Patterns of Childrearing, Religious Experience and the Self in Early America* (New York: Knopf, 1977), is a pathbreaking work, but his typology of evangelical, moderate, and genteel styles of childrearing is too rigid. The following works indicate an evolution toward an affectionate style of child nurture after the mid-eighteenth century: John Walzer, "A Period of Ambivalence: Eighteenth-Century American Childhood," in *The History of Childhood,* ed. Lloyd DeMause (New York: Psychohistory Press, 1974), 351-82; Carl N. Degler, *At Odds: Women and the Family in America from the Revolution to the Present* (New York: Oxford Univ. Press, 1980), 86-110; Mary Beth Norton, *Liberty's Daughter: The Revolutionary Experience of American Women, 1750-1800* (Boston: Little, Brown, 1980), 71-109; Daniel B. Smith, *Inside the Great House: Planter Family Life in Eighteenth-Century Chesapeake Society* (Ithaca: Cornell Univ. Press, 1980), 25-54; Bertram Wyatt-Brown, "Conscience and Career: Young Abolitionists

and Missionaries," in *Antislavery Religion and Reform: Essays in Memory of Roger Anstey,* ed. Christine Bolt and Seymour Drescher (Folkestone, Eng.: W. Dawson, 1980), 183–203; Jay Fliegelman, *Prodigals and Prophets: The American Revolution against Patriarchal Authority* (Cambridge: Harvard Univ. Press, 1982), 1–35; Nancy F. Cott, "Notes toward an Explanation of Antebellum Childrearing," *Psychohistory Review* 6 (1978): 4–20; Lawrence B. Goodheart, "Childrearing, Conscience, and Conversion to Abolitionism: The Example of Elizur Wright, Jr.," *Psychohistory Review* 12 (1984): 24–33.

3. For an overview of changing social conditions and thought, see Richard L. Bushman, *From Puritan to Yankee: Character and the Social Order in Connecticut, 1690–1765* (New York: Norton, 1967); James A. Henretta, *The Evolution of American Society, 1700–1815: An Interdisciplinary Analysis* (Lexington: Heath, 1973), 119–226; Richard D. Brown, *Modernization: The Transformation of American Life, 1600–1865* (New York: Hill and Wang, 1976), 74–158; Gordon S. Wood, "The Democratization of Mind in the American Revolution," *Library of Congress Symposia on the American Revolution: Leadership in the American Revolution* (Washington, D.C.: Library of Congress, 1974), 63–89; Bernard Bailyn, *The Ideological Origins of the American Revolution* (Cambridge: Harvard Univ. Press, 1967), 160–319.

4. Bertram Wyatt-Brown first pointed out for the antebellum period that a family's emphasis on the moral and career success for a particular child encouraged the development of what psychologist Kenneth Keniston has called "a sense of specialness." See Wyatt-Brown, "New Leftists and Abolitionists: A Comparison of American Radical Styles," *Wisconsin Magazine of History* 53 (1970): 256–68; and Keniston, *Young Radicals: Notes on Committed Youth* (New York: Harcourt, Brace and World, 1968), 44–51, 55–60. David C. French, "The Conversion of an American Radical: Elizur Wright, Jr. and the Abolitionist Commitment" (Ph.D. diss., Case Western Reserve University, 1970), applied Keniston's theory in his analysis of Wright's abolitionist commitment.

5. EW, Sr., "A Sketch of the Wright Ancestry," Frederick C. Waite Papers, University Archives, Case Western Reserve University; "Canaan, Births-Marriages-Deaths," *Connecticut Vital Records* (1927), Connecticut State Library, Hartford, hereafter cited as *Conn. Vital Records.*

6. EW, "Reminiscences of Groton during the Years 1826 and 1827," *Historical Series* (Groton, Mass., 1884), 2:1–2; Franklin B. Dexter, *Biographical Sketches of the Graduates of Yale College with Annals of the College History* (New York: Holt, 1907), 210–12; *Conn. Vital Records,* 77; *History of Litchfield County, Connecticut* (Philadelphia: J. W. Lewis, 1881), 264–65, 268; EW, Sr., "Wright Ancestry," Frederick C. Waite Papers; and "Biographical Sketch of EW, Sr.," *Proceedings in Commemoration of the Fiftieth Anniversary of the Settlement of Tallmadge* (Akron: Burke and Elkins, 1857), 82–85. See also David C. French, "Puritan Conservatism and the Frontier: The Elizur Wright Family on the Connecticut Western Reserve," *The Old Northwest* 1 (1975): 85–95; Charles Miller, "Puritan Yankee and Father: An Intellectual Portrait of Elizur Wright, Esq. (1762-1845)," *Connecticut Historical Society Bulletin* 44 (1979): 117–28.

EW, Sr.'s publications include "A Method of Finding the Area of a Field Arithmetically, 1792," box 5, folder 239, John Hosmer Penniman Papers, Archives and Manuscripts, Sterling Library, Yale University; "Essay on Evaporation," Connecticut Academy Papers, Beinecke Library, Yale University; and "Description of an Air Pump Invented (By Himself)," *Memoirs of the Connecticut Academy of Arts and Sciences* 1 (1810): 120–30.

7. EW to Parents, Brothers, and Sister, Sept. 30, 1822, EWP, LC; Barbara M. Solomon, ed., *Timothy Dwight, Travels in New England and New York,* 4 vols. (Cambridge: Harvard Univ. Press, 1969), 2:260–61; Richard J. Purcell, *Connecticut in Transition, 1775–1818* (Washington, D.C.: American Historical Association, 1918), 175–76, 190–91; Kenneth Lockridge, "Land, Population and the Evolution of New England Society, 1630–1790," *Past and Present* 39 (1968): 62–80.

8. Purcell, *Connecticut,* 97–105, 139–51; Percy W. Bidwell, "Rural Economy in New England at the Beginning of the Nineteenth Century," *Transactions of the Connecticut Academy of Arts and Sciences* 20 (1916): 241–339; Charles S. Grant, *Democracy in the Connecticut Frontier Town of Kent* (New York: AMS Press, 1961), 98–103; Bruce C. Daniels, *The Connecticut Town: Growth and Development* (Middletown: Wesleyan Univ. Press, 1979), 53, 171–72, 187–90; Charles R. Keller, *The Second Great Awakening in Connecticut* (New Haven: Yale Univ. Press, 1942), 88.

9. EW, Sr., to Jeremiah Day, Jeremiah Day Papers, Beinecke Library, Yale University; E. O. Randall, "Tallmadge Township," *Ohio Archaeological and Historical Publication* 17 (1918): 275–305; *Proceedings. . . of the Settlement of Tallmadge,* 13–14; Charles Whittlesey, *A Sketch of the Settlement and Progress of the Township of Tallmadge, (No. 2, Range 10), Summit County, Ohio* (Cleveland: Sanford, 1842). See also Harlan H. Hatcher, *The Western Reserve: The Story of New Connecticut in Ohio* (Indianapolis: Bobbs-Merrill, 1949); R. Carlyle Buley, *The Old Northwest: Pioneer Period, 1815–1840,* Vol. 1 (Bloomington: Indiana Univ. Press, 1951); Beverly Bond, Jr., *The Civilization of the Old Northwest: A Study of Political, Social and Economic Development, 1788–1812* (New York: Macmillan, 1934); Lois K. Mathews, *The Expansion of New England: The Spread of New England Settlement and Institutions to the Mississippi, 1620–1865,* vol. 1 (New York: Russell and Russell, 1962); Kenneth V. Lottich, *New England Transplanted* (Dallas: Royal, 1964); Malcolm J. Rohrbough, *The Trans-Appalachian Frontier: People, Societies, Institutions, 1775–1850* (New York: Oxford Univ. Press, 1978).

10. Bidwell judged a small freehold to be 50 to 150 acres; "Rural Economy," 103. See James A. Henretta, "Families and Farms: Mentalité in Pre-Industrial America," *William and Mary Quarterly* 35 (1978): 3–32.

11. Connecticut Land Records, Canaan, Deeds, 5(1773–97): 44, 358, 359, 372, 377–78, 7(1797–1810): 182, 8(1810–18): 10, 18, 26, Connecticut State Library; Land Deed of Feb. 7, 1810, EW, Sr., Papers, Western Reserve Historical Society; *Portage County [Ohio] Recorder. Index to Deeds, 1795–1917,* 380–82, Ohio Historical Center; William B. Doyle, ed., *A Centennial History of Summit County, Ohio and Representative Citizens,* 2 vols. (Chicago: Biographical Publishing, 1908), 2:665; Dexter, *Biographical Sketches,* 210–12; Purcell, *Connecticut,* 97–98.

12. EW to Brother and Sister Hanford, May 8, 1869, C. C. Bronson to EW, Nov. 18, 1875, EWP, LC; EW, Sr., "Wright Ancestry,"; *Proceedings. . . of the Settlement of Tallmadge,* 83; Dexter, *Biographical Sketches,* 210–11; Philip G. Wright and Elizabeth Q. Wright, *Elizur Wright: The Father of Life Insurance* (Chicago: Univ. of Chicago Press, 1937), 6; Selden Haines, *A Biographical Sketch of the Class of 1826, Yale College* (Utica: Roberts, 1866), 1:940; William H. Perrin, ed., *History of Summit County* (Chicago: Baskin and Battey, 1881), 881.

13. M. B. Romegh to EW, Sr., July 1, 1817, EW, Sr., to EW, June 10, 1823, June 10, 1824, Jan. 13, 1825, EWP, LC; EW, Sr., to Simeon Baldwin, Aug. 27, 1837, Baldwin Family Pa-

pers, Archives and Manuscripts, Sterling Library, Yale University; *Ninetieth Anniversary of the First Congregational Church, Tallmadge, Ohio* (n.p., Jan. 21, 1899), 20; Western Reserve Bible Society, "Constitution, Records of the Meetings and Transactions, May 18, 1814–Oct. 1831," Society Papers, University Archives, Case Western Reserve University; *Proceedings . . . of the Settlement of Tallmadge*, 26; Randall, "Tallmadge Township," 290–91; Whittlesey, *Tallmadge*, 9–12, 23–29.

EW, Sr.'s publications at this time include *The District School, According to the Lancasterian Method of Teaching* (Oberlin: Printed at the Evangelical Office, 1843); "A Theory of Fluxions," *American Journal of Science and Arts* 14 (1828): 330–50; "A Discourse on the Different Views That Have Been Taken of the Theory of Fluxions," *American Journal of Science and Arts* 16 (1829): 53–60; "On the Application of Fluxional Ratio to Particular Cases," *American Journal of Science and Arts* 25 (1834): 93–103. See also the following letters: EW, Sr., to Benjamin Silliman, Dec. 20, 1831, Silliman Family Papers, Archives and Manuscripts, Sterling Library, Yale University; EW, Sr., to Jeremiah Day, Apr. 23, Aug. 25, 1821, Aug. 22, 1826, Jeremiah Day Papers.

14. Bernard A. Weisberger, *They Gathered at the River: The Story of the Great Revivalists and Their Impact on Religion in America* (Chicago: Quadrangle, 1966), 3–19; Donald G. Mathews, "The Second Great Awakening as an Organizing Process, 1780–1830: An Hypothesis," *American Quarterly* 21 (1969): 23–43; William G. McLoughlin, *Revivals, Awakenings and Reform: An Essay on Religion and Social Change in America, 1607–1977* (Chicago: Univ. of Chicago Press, 1978), 2–13; Donald M. Scott, *From Office to Profession: The New England Ministry, 1750–1850* (Philadelphia: Univ. of Pennsylvania Press, 1978), 36–51.

15. Keller, *Connecticut,* 13–35; Sidney E. Mead, *Nathaniel William Taylor: A Connecticut Liberal* (Chicago: Univ. of Chicago Press, 1942), 25–47; William W. Sweet, *Religion in the Development of American Culture* (New York: Scribner, 1952), 198–200; Stephen J. Novak, *The Rights of Youth* (Cambridge: Harvard Univ. Press, 1977), 133–37.

16. Lyman Beecher listed twelve points of orthodoxy in *Autobiography and Correspondence of Lyman Beecher,* ed. Charles Beecher, 2 vols. (New York: Harper, 1865), 2:125–27. See also Buley, *Old Northwest* 2:429–30; Charles C. Cole, *The Social Ideas of Northern Evangelists* (New York: Columbia Univ. Press, 1954), 5; Charles I. Foster, *An Errand of Mercy: The Evangelical United Front, 1790–1837* (Chapel Hill: Univ. of North Carolina Press, 1960), viii.

17. EW to Rev. Jonathan Blanchard, [c. 1874], EWP, LC; EW, "Reminiscences," 2; *Massachusetts Abolitionist,* Oct. 3, 1839; EW, Sr., *District School,* 13.

18. EW to Parents, Aug. 3, 1839, EW to Mrs. Lawrence, Apr. 21, 1885, C. C. Bronson to EW, Nov. 18, 1875, EWP, LC; EW, "My Father," *Household Stuff and Some Other Things* (Boston: Privately Printed, 1866), 108; Cotton Mather, *Bonifacius: Or Essay To Do Good* (Cambridge: Harvard Univ. Press, 1966), 47–48; Philip J. Greven, ed., *Childrearing Concepts, 1628–1861* (Itasca: Peacock Press, 1973), 18–41.

For examples of parents breaking the child's will, see Gordon R. Taylor, *The Angel-Makers: A Study in the Psychological Origins of Historical Change, 1750–1850* (London: Heinemann, 1958); John Demos, *A Little Commonwealth: Family Life in Plymouth Colony* (New York: Oxford Univ. Press, 1970); and William G. McLoughlin, "Evangelical Childrearing in the Age of Jackson: Francis Wayland's View on When and How to Subdue the Willfulness of Children," *Journal of Social History* 9 (1975): 21–34.

19. EW, Sr., *District School,* 3–9; Joseph Kett, *Rites of Passage: Adolescence in America, 1790 to the Present* (New York: Basic Books, 1977), 46–47; Fliegelman, *Prodigals and Prophets,* 9–35. Joseph Lancaster urged shaming instead of corporal punishment.

20. *Western Reserve Chronicle,* May 18, 1819; Sanford Fleming, *Children and Puritanism: The Place of Children in the Life and Thought of the New England Churches, 1620–1847* (New Haven: Yale Univ. Press, 1933), 69–70, 104–77; Peter G. Slater, "Views of Children and of Childrearing during the Early National Period: A Study in the New England Intellect" (Ph.D. diss., University of California, Berkeley, 1970), 115–30; McLoughlin, *Revivals,* 106–22; and Ann Douglas, *The Feminization of American Culture* (New York: Knopf, 1977).

21. EW to Brother James, Nov. 30, 1823, EW to Sister Harriet, Apr. 5, 1858, EWP, LC; *Western Reserve Chronicle,* May 18, 1819; *Liberator* quoted in *HOT,* June 15, 1833. See Lawrence Kohlberg, "Development of Moral Character and Moral Ideology," in *Review of Child Development Research,* ed. Martin L. Hoffman and Lois W. Hoffman (New York: Russell Sage, 1964), 383–431; Wesley C. Becker, "Consequences of Different Kinds of Parental Discipline," *ibid.,* 169–208; John W. M. Whiting and Arvin L. Child, *Child Training and Personality: A Cross-Cultural Study* (New Haven: Yale Univ. Press, 1953), 218–62; Gerald Handel, "The Psychological Study of Whole Families," in *The Psychosocial Interior of the Family,* ed. Handel (Chicago: Aldine, 1967), 529–30.

22. EW to Sister Polly, Feb. 16, 1862, EWP, LC. See Kett, *Rites,* 4–16; Anne L. Kuhn, *Th Mother's Role in Childhood Education* (New Haven: Yale Univ. Press, 1947), 27; Erik H. Erikson, *Childhood and Society* (New York: Norton, 1950), 219–22; Joseph Kett, "Growing Up in Rural New England," in *Anonymous Americans,* ed. Tamara Haraven (Englewood Cliffs: Prentice Hall, 1971), 2; Nancy Cott, *The Bonds of Womanhood: "Woman's Sphere" in New England, 1780–1835* (New Haven: Yale Univ. Press, 1977), 46–47, 86–87; Mary P. Ryan, *Cradle of the Middle Class: The Family in Oneida County, New York, 1790–1865* (Cambridge: Cambridge Univ. Press, 1981), 89–91; Richrad A. Meckel, "Educating a Ministry of Mothers: Evangelical Maternal Associations, 1815–1860," *Journal of the Early Republic* 2 (1982): 403–23.

23. James Fisher, ed., *The Westminster Assembly's Shorter Catechism Explained by Way of Question and Answers* (Philadelphia: Presbyterian Board of Publishers, 1765), 85, 88–89, 168, 193; Kett, "Growing Up," 4–5; and Fleming, *Children and Puritanism,* 153.

24. Wrights, *Wright,* 5, 7–8. There were four iron furnances in Litchfield County in 1810; Bidwell, "Rural Economy," 270–71.

For EW's assertions that he "always" disagreed with and "never" accepted specific theological doctrines, see: *Chronotype,* Dec. 1, 1846; EW to Harriet, Apr. 5, 1858, EW to Rev. Jonathan Blanchard, [c. 1874], EW to the Editor of the *Christian Press,* [n.d., vol. 19], EW to Mrs. Lawrence, Apr. 21, 1885, EWP, LC; EW, "Reminiscences," 3; EW, *A Curiosity of Law* (Boston: By Author, 1866), 15.

The metaphor of hell as a fiery furnace was not uncommon in New England theology. For Jonathan Edwards's use of the image, see "Sinners in the Hands of an Angry God," in *Sources of the American Mind,* ed. Loren Baritz (New York: Wiley, 1966), 1:83.

25. The Rev. Spring is quoted in Slater, "Views of Children," 173; Greven, *Protestant Temperament,* 52; McLoughlin, *Revivals,* 115–16; J. C. Flugel, *The Psycho-Analytic Study of the Family* (London: Hogarth Press, 1921), 133–54; Philip M. Helfaer, *The Psychology of Religious Doubt* (Boston: Beacon Press, 1972), 3–52.

26. EW, Sr., to Philo Wright, Oct. 14, 21, 1827, EW, Sr., Papers, Western Reserve Historical Society; EW, Sr., to EW, Aug. 20, 1825, Jan. 25, 1828, Clarissa to EW, Jan. 3, 1837, EWP, LC; EW to Rufus Griswold, Aug. 8, 1842, Rufus W. Griswold Papers, Boston Public Library.

27. The only detailed account of the conversion is in Wrights, *Wright,* 9. See EW, Sr., to EW, Oct. 13, 1826, EW to Rev. Jonathan Blanchard, [c. 1874], EWP, LC; EW, Sr., to Jeremiah Day, Aug. 22, 1822, Jeremiah Day Papers; EW, *Curiosity of Law,* 15; Julian M. Sturtevant, *Julian M. Sturtevant: An Autobiography* (New York: F. H. Revell, 1896), 60–61.

28. EW to Parents, Jan. 25, 1821, EWP, LC. See also William James, *The Varieties of Religious Experience* (New York: Longmans Green, 1904), 189–258; Kett, *Rites,* 83–84; Peter Blos, *On Adolescence: A Psychoanalytic Interpretation* (New York: Free Press of Glencoe, 1962), 134–35, 186–91; Carl W. Christensen, "Religious Conversion to Adolescence," *Pastoral Psychology* 16 (1965): 17–28; Norman Pettit, *The Heart Prepared: Grace and Conversion in Puritan Spiritual Life* (New Haven: Yale Univ. Press, 1966); Howard M. Feinstein, "The Prepared Heart: A Comparative Study of Puritan Theology and Psycholanalysis," *American Quarterly* 22 (1970): 166–76.

2. Yale Years

1. EW, Sr., to Jeremiah Day, Apr. 23, 1821, Aug. 22, 1822, Aug. 22, 1826, Simeon Woodruff to Dear Friends, Aug. 19, 1822, Jeremiah Day Papers; EW to Parents, Brothers, and Sisters, Sept. 30, 1822, EW, Sr., to EW, Oct. 22, 1822, June 19, Aug. 4, 1823, Aug. 21, 1824, Jan. 13, Feb. 17, Apr. 5, Aug. 20, 1825, Parents to EW, Nov. 1, 1823, EW to Mary, July 27, 1862, EWP, LC; EW to Rufus W. Griswold, Aug. 8, 1842, Rufus W. Griswold Papers; *Insurance Monitor* 16 (1868): 237; *Annual Catalogue of Yale College, 1822,* 26–27; Sturtevant, *Autobiography,* 69–70; David F. Allmendinger, Jr., *Paupers and Scholars: The Transformation of Student Life in Nineteenth-Century New England* (New York: St. Martin's Press, 1975), 28–43, 61–62.

2. Clarissa to EW, Apr. 26, 1823, Dec. 13, 1842, Harriet to EW, Apr. 17, 1823, EWP, LC.

3. EW, Sr., to EW, Apr. 26, Aug. 4, 21, 30, Sept. 29, 1823, Jan. 13, Apr. 25, Oct. 22, 1825, May 26, 1826, Nov. 29, 1827, EWP, LC; EW, Sr., to EW, Aug. 20, 1825, EW, Sr., Papers, University Archives, Case Western Reserve University. See also Joseph S. C. Frey, "The Jews and Early Nineteenth-Century Millennarianism," *Journal of the Early Republic* 1 (1981): 27–49.

4. Clarissa to EW, Apr. 26, 1823, EW, Sr., Papers, University Archives, Case Western Reserve University; Clarissa to EW, Aug. 9, 1827, EW, Sr., to EW, Aug. 21, 1824, Apr. 25, 1825, EWP, LC.

5. EW, Sr., to EW, Jan. 18, Apr. 25, 1825, Nov. 29, 1827, Nov. 20, 1829, EW, Sr., Papers, University Archives, Case Western Reserve University; EW, Sr., to EW, Sept. 29, 1823, Aug. 21, 1824, EWP, LC; Frank P. Stearns, *Cambridge Sketches* (1905; Freeport: Books for Libraries Press, 1968), 289.

6. EW to Reverend [William Hanford], May 29, 1826, EWP, LC. EW clarified his biblical interpretation in *HOT,* Apr. 12, 19, 26, May 10, 1832, and *Chronotype,* May 29, 1849.

See Wrights, *Wright,* 55–56, and Conrad Wright, "The Religion of Geology," *New England Quarterly* 14 (1941): 335–58.

7. EW to EW, Sr., June 27, 1823, EW to Parents, Brothers, and Sisters, Sept. 30, 1822, and EW to Parents, May 12, 1823, EW, Sr., to EW, Oct. 13, 1825, EWP, LC.

8. EW to Parents, Nov. 30, 1823, EW to Reverend [William Hanford], May 29, 1826, EW to EW, Sr., June 19, 1823, letter of Eleazar T. Fitch, Feb. 5, 1827, EWP, LC.

The psychology of anxiety is discussed in Roy Schafer, "Ideals, The Ego Ideal, and The Ideal Self," in *Motives and Thought: Essays in Honor of David Rapaport,* ed. Robert R. Holt (New York: International Univ. Press, 1967), 129–74; Abraham H. Maslow, *Toward a Psychology of Being* (New York: Van Nostrand Reinhold, 1968), 10; Erik H. Erikson, *Young Man Luther: A Study in Psychoanalysis and History* (New York: Norton, 1958), 14; Keniston, *Young Radicals,* 73–74.

9. EW to Reverend [William Hanford], May 29, 1826, EWP, LC.

10. *Catalogue of the Officers and Graduates of Yale University in New Haven, Connecticut, 1701–1904* (New Haven: Tuttle, Morehouse and Taylor, 1905), 1–20; *Annual Catalogue of Yale College, 1825;* H. Shelton Smith, *Changing Conceptions of Original Sin: A Study in American Theology since 1750* (New York: Scribner, 1955), 86–98; Roland H. Bainton, *Yale and the Ministry* (New York: Harper, 1957), 81–83; Ralph H. Gabriel, *Religion and Learning at Yale: The Church of Christ in the College and University, 1757–1957* (New Haven: Yale Univ. Press, 1958), 132–41; Mead, *Taylor,* 111.

11. EW, Sr., to EW, Apr. 13, July 6, 1827, Clarissa to EW, Aug. 9, 18, 1827, EWP, LC; Beecher, *Lyman Beecher* 1:554–56; Cole, *Social Ideas,* 58–133; Scott, *From Office to Profession,* 82–84; William G. McLoughlin, *Modern Revivalism: Charles Grandison Finney to Billy Graham* (New York: Ronald Press, 1959), 11–25. See also Whitney R. Cross, *The Burned-Over District* (New York: Harper and Row, 1965), and Paul Johnson, *Shopkeeper's Millennium: Society and Revivals in Rochester, N.Y., 1815–1837* (New York: Hill and Wang, 1978).

12. EW to Reverend [William Hanford], May 29, 1826, EW to Parents, Brothers, and Sisters, Sept. 30, 1822, EWP, LC; *Annual Catalogue of Yale College, 1822,* 25; Chauncey Goodrich, "Narrative of Revivals of Religion in Yale College," *American Quarterly Register* 10 (1838): 305; James B. Reynolds, Samuel H. Fisher, Henry B. Wright, eds., *Two Centuries of Christian Activity at Yale* (New York: Putnams, 1901), 73, 77, 80, 313.

13. EW, Sr., to EW, Aug. 20, Oct. 13, 1825, EW, Sr., Papers, University·Archives, Case Western Reserve University. For the theological cleavage among Congregationalists, see Lewis Perry, *Childhood, Marriage, and Reform: Henry Clarke Wright, 1797–1870* (Chicago: Univ. of Chicago Press, 1980), 108–28.

14. EW, "Reminiscences," 6; *Chronotype,* Aug. 20, 1846; Wrights, *Wright,* 21. *Annual Catalogue of Yale College, 1822* identifies an Edward Laurens of Charleston in EW, Jr.'s class, while the Wrights speak of a Henry Laurens. I have opted for the Yale register, the primary source, and Edward Laurens.

15. EW, "Statement of His Principles about Giving Information against Fellow Students, December 1823," and Faculty Meeting, Oct. 28, Nov. 17, 1823, MS. 1, Papers on College Discipline, 1821–30, Archives and Manuscripts, Sterling Library, Yale University; Reuben Hitchcock to Father, Apr. 10, 1824, Peter Hitchcock Family Papers, Western Reserve Historical Society; EW, Sr., to EW, Mar. 26, 1824, Frederic W. Chapman to EW, Apr. 28, 1824, EWP, LC; Reynolds, *Two Centuries,* 78–79; Allmendinger, *Paupers,* 89–90; Ketts, *Rites,* 51–59.

16. Sturtevant, *Sturtevant,* 69–101. Various student fracases are described by Brooks M. Kelley, *Yale: A History* (New Haven: Yale Univ. Press, 1974), 209–13.

3. Career Choices

1. EW to Parents, Apr. 4, 1825, EW to Reverend [William Hanford], May 29, 1826, J. M. Sturtevant to EW, Oct. 5, 1826, E. T. Sturtevant to EW, Nov. 3, 1826, letter of Eleazar T. Fitch, Feb. 5, 1827, EWP, LC; EW, "Reminiscences," 2–3; Stearns, *Cambridge Sketches,* 289.
2. For the concept of a "psychosocial moratorium," see Erikson, *Luther,* 100–104.
3. *Baker v. Fales, Massachusetts Reports* 16 (1820): 487–522; Williston Walker, *A History of the Congregational Churches in the United States* (Boston: Pilgrim Press, 1894), 329–47; George W. Cooke, *Unitarianism in America: A History of Its Origin and Development* (Boston: American Unitarian Association, 1902), 92–103; Earl M. Wilbur, *A History of Unitarianism: In Transylvania, England and America* (Cambridge: Harvard Univ. Press, 1952), 401–54; Jacob C. Meyer, *Church and State in Massachusetts from 1740–1830* (New York: Russell and Russell, 1968), 168–83; Leonard W. Levy, *The Law of the Commonwealth and Chief Justice Shaw* (Cambridge: Harvard Univ. Press, 1957), 29–32; William G. McLoughlin, *New England Dissent: The Baptists and Separation of Church and State,* 2 vols. (Cambridge: Harvard Univ. Press, 1971), 2:1189–1206.
4. Beecher, *Lyman Beecher* 2:79, 124; Sidney E. Mead, "Lyman Beecher and Connecticut Orthodoxy's Campaign against the Unitarians, 1819–1826," *Church History* 19 (1940): 218–34.
5. *The Spirit of the Pilgrims* 1(1828): 240–48, 449–74, 505–13; Smith, *Conceptions of Sin,* 72–79. See also George E. Ellis, *A Half-Century of the Unitarian Controversy with Particular Reference to Its Origins, Its Course, and Its Prominent Subjects among the Congregationalists of Man* (Boston: Crosby, Nichols, 1857); Joseph Haroutinian, *Piety Versus Moralism: The Passing of the New England Theology* (New York: Harper and Row, 1970); Conrad Wright, *The Beginnings of Unitarianism in America* (Boston: Starr King Press, 1955); Daniel W. Howe, *The Unitarian Conscience: Harvard Moral Philosophy, 1805–1861* (Cambridge: Harvard Univ. Press, 1970). For the cultural aspects of the controversy, see Lawrence B. Goodheart and Richard O. Curry, eds., "The Trinitarian Indictment of Unitarianism: The Letters of Elizur Wright, Jr., 1826–1827," *Journal of the Early Republic* 3 (1983): 280–96.
6. EW, "Reminiscences," 2; *The Rights of the Congregational Churches of Massachusetts. The Results of an Ecclesiastical Council Convened at Groton, Massachusetts, July 17, 1826* (Boston: T. R. Marvin, 1827); Beecher, *Lyman Beecher* 2: 79–80; *Covenant of the First Church, Groton, Massachusetts* (Groton: George H. Brown, 1826); John Todd, *John Todd: The Story of His Life Told Mainly by Himself* (New York: Harper, 1876), 176; John Todd, *Religious Teachers Tested* (Cambridge: Hilliard and Brown, 1827), 44.
7. EW, "Reminiscences," 8; *The Confession of Faith, Covenant, and Principles of Discipline and Practice of the Union Church in Groton, Massachusetts* (Lancaster: Carter, An-

drews, 1831), 2; *Historical Addresses Delivered at the Union Congregational Church, Groton, Mass., Wednesday, Jan. 1, 1902* (n.p., n.d.), 7–15.

8. EW, "Reminiscences," 8. Erik H. Erikson defines a negative identity as "all self-images, even those of a highly idealistic nature, which are diametrically opposed to the dominant values of an individual's upbringing"; *Luther,* 102. See Anna Freud, *The Ego and the Mechanism of Defense* (New York: International Univ. Press, 1946), and David B. Davis, "Some Ideological Functions of Prejudice in Ante-Bellum America," *American Quarterly* 15 (1963): 115–25.

9. EW to Parents, May 12, 1823, Mar. 15, 1827, EWP, LC.

10. EW to Parents, Nov. 16, 1826, Jan. 9, 1827, EWP, LC. The evangelical indictment of Unitarianism was in part a protest against the subversion of traditional values by modernization, of which urbanization was a highly visible component; see Wilson Smith, "John Locke in the Great Unitarian Controversy," in *Freedom and Reform: Essays in Honor of Henry Steel Commager,* ed. Harold M. Hyman and Leonard W. Levy, (New York: Harper and Row, 1967), 88, and Richard D. Brown, "The Emergence of Urban Society in Rural Massachusetts, 1760–1820," *Journal of American History* 41 (1974): 29–51.

11. EW to Parents, Oct. 19, Nov. 16, 1827, EWP, LC.

12. EW to Parents, Jan. 9, Mar. 15, Dec. 25, 1827, Feb. 16, 1828, and EW, to Susan Clarke, Feb. 13, 1828, EWP, LC; EW to Dear Chum, Dec. 7, 1826, Peter Hitchcock Papers. With disestablishment in Connecticut in 1818, evangelicals saw that orthodoxy must be viable apart from the state, hence there was an added incentive for revivalism; see Mead, "Lyman Beecher," 218–34; McLoughlin, *Dissent* 2:1207–29; Bertram Wyatt-Brown, *Lewis Tappan and the Evangelical War against Slavery* (New York: Atheneum, 1971), 17–40.

13. Clarissa to EW, Dec. 22, 1826, EW, Sr., to EW, Dec. 9, 1826, EWP, LC.

14. EW, "Reminiscences," 7; EW to Parents, Oct. 15, Nov. 16, 1827, Jan. 25, 1828, EWP, LC; EW to Friend [Reuben Hitchcock], Feb. 24, 1828, Peter Hitchcock Papers; Wrights, *Wright,* 25–27.

15. EW, "Reminiscences," 6–7; EW to Friend [Reuben Hitchcock], Feb. 24, 1828, Peter Hitchcock Papers; Lyman Beecher, *Six Sermons on Intemperance, On the Nature, Occasions, Signs, Evils of Intemperance* (1826; Boston: T. R. Marvin, 1828). See William J. Rorabaugh, *The Alcholic Republic: An American Tradition* (New York: Oxford Univ. Press, 1979).

16. EW, Sr., to EW, Sept. 29, 1826, Feb. 17, Aug. 28, 1827, Jan. 25, Apr. 18, 1828, Clarissa to EW, Apr. 18, 1828 (compare the following maternal letters: Aug. 28, 1826, "I hope you are the Lord's servant"; Feb. 17, 1827, "that you may be kipt [*sic*] from all evil especialy [*sic*] sin is the daily prayer of your mother"; Aug. 9, 1827, "they [her children] may be ready to give up all for Christ"), EWP, LC. In 1820 there was a call for twenty additional ministers in Elizur's home county; Frederick C. Waite, *Western Reserve University: The Hudson Era* (Cleveland: Western Reserve Univ. Press, 1943), 32.

17. EW to Parents, Nov. 16, 1826, and J. M. Sturtevant to EW, Nov. 9, 1826, E. T. Sturtevant to EW, Dec. 4, 1826, EWP, LC; EW to Dearest Chum [Reuben Hitchcock], Oct. 21, Dec. 7, 1826, Mar. 20, 1827, Peter Hitchcock Papers; Smith, *Conceptions of Sin,* 76n.

18. See French, "Conversion," 81–82; Mead, *Taylor,* 200–232; Perry, *Henry C. Wright,* 108–13; Robert H. Abzug, *Passionate Liberator: Theodore Dwight Weld and the Dilemma of Reform* (New York: Oxford Univ. Press, 1980), 23–24.

19. See Scott, *From Office to Profession,* 52–75; Daniel Calhoun, *Professional Lives in America: Structure and Aspiration, 1750–1850* (Cambridge: Harvard Univ. Press, 1965), 88–177.

20. EW to [Reuben Hitchcock], Oct. 21, Dec. 7, 1826, Mar. 20, 1827, Feb. 24, 1828, Peter Hitchcock Papers; Perry, *Henry C. Wright,* 108–13; Abzug, *Weld,* 23–25.

21. E. T. Sturtevant to EW, Dec. 4, 1826, EW to Martha, Jan. 25, 1828, EWP, LC; Todd, *Story,* 188.

22. EW to Susan, Jan. 31, Feb. 7, 1828, EWP, LC; Wrights, *Wright,* 27–31; Abzug, *Weld,* 166; Lewis Perry, " 'We Have Had Conversation with the World': The Abolitionists and Spontaneity," *Canadian Review of American Studies* 6 (1975): 3–26.

23. Rev. William Hanford to EW, Apr. 24, 1827, E. T. Sturtevant to EW, July 20, 1827, EW to Parents, Oct. 15, 1827, Feb. 16, 1828, EWP, LC; EW, Sr., to EW, Nov. 29, 1827, Jan. 25, 1828, EW, Sr., Papers, University Archives, Case Western Reserve University; Wrights, *Wright,* 31–32.

24. EW to Susan, Oct. 12, Dec. 12, 30, 1828, EW to Martha, Jan. 25, 1828, EWP, LC; EW to [Reuben Hitchcock], Feb. 24, 1828, Peter Hitchcock Papers; Wrights, *Wright,* 32.

25. EW to Susan, Oct. 12, 1828, EWP, LC.

26. EW to Susan, Oct. 12, Nov. 1, 1828, EWP, LC. F. W. B. Bullock, *Evangelical Conversion in Great Britain, 1696–1845* (St. Leonards-on-the Sea, Eng.: Budd and Gillett, 1959), 169–72, has a sketch of Legh Richardson.

Elizur's imperative to evangelize is nicely captured in revivalist Charles G. Finney's "Instructions to Converts": "They should set out with a determination to aim at being useful in the highest possible degree. They should not rest satisfied with merely being useful, or remaining in a situation where they can do some good. But if they see an opportunity where they can do more good, they must embrace it, whatever may be the sacrifice to themselves. No matter what it may cost them, no matter what danger or what suffering, no matter what change in their outward circumstances, or habits, or employments it may lead to." William G. McLoughlin, ed., *Charles G. Finney, Lectures on Revivals of Religion* (Cambridge: Harvard Univ. Press, 1960), 404.

27. On the benevolent societies see Cole, *Social Ideas;* John R. Bodo, *The Protestant Clergy and Public Issues, 1812–1848* (Princeton: Princeton Univ. Press, 1954); Foster, *Errand of Mercy;* Clifford S. Griffin, *Their Brothers' Keeper: Moral Stewardship in the United States, 1800–1865* (New Brunswick: Rutgers Univ. Press, 1960); Ronald Walters, *American Reformers, 1815–1860* (New York: Hill and Wang, 1978), 29–35; Clifford S. Griffin, "Religious Benevolence as Social Control, 1815–1860," *Mississippi Valley Historical Review* 44 (1957): 423–44; W. David Lewis, "The Reformer as Conservative: Protestant Counter-Subversion in the Early Republic," in *The Development of an American Culture,* ed. Stanley Coben and Lorman Ratner (Englewood Cliffs: Prentice Hall, 1970), 64–91. For a revisionist view see Lois Banner, "Religious Benevolence as Social Control: A Critique of an Interpretation," *Journal of American History* 60 (1973): 23–41.

28. Lyman Beecher, *A Plea for the West* (Cincinnati: Truman and Smith, 1835), 3–36. On the trans-Appalachian West, see Ray A. Billington, *The Protestant Crusade, 1800–1860: A Study of the Origins of American Nativism* (New York: Macmillan, 1938), 118–41; Louis B. Wright, *Culture on the Moving Frontier* (Bloomington: Indiana Univ. Press, 1955), 168–97; Dwight L. Dumond, "The Mississippi: Valley of Decision," *Mississippi Valley Historical Review* 36 (1940): 3–26; Richard L. Power, "A Crusade to Extend Yankee Culture, 1820–

1865," *New England Quarterly* 13 (1940): 638–53; Arthur E. Bestor, "Patent Office Models of the Good Society," *American Historical Review* 58 (1953): 505–26; Rush Welter, "The Frontier West as Image of American Society: Conservative Attitudes before the Civil War," *Mississippi Valley Historical Review* 46 (1959–60): 593–614; Loren Baritz, "The Idea of the West," *American Historical Review* 46 (1961): 618–40; David B. Davis, "Some Themes of Counter-Subversion: An Analysis of Anti-Masonic, Anti-Catholic and Anti-Mormon Literature," *Mississippi Valley Historical Review* 47 (1960): 205–24.

29. See *The American Colporteur System* (New York: American Tract Society, 1836), 1–28; Orin J. Oliphant, "The American Missionary Spirit, 1828–1835," *Church History* 7 (1938): 125–37; Elizabeth Twadell, "The American Tract Society, 1814–1860," *Church History* 15 (1946): 116–32; Lawrence Thompson, "The Printing and Publishing Activities of the American Tract Society from 1825 to 1850," *Papers of the Bibliographical Society of America* 35 (1941): 81–114; Harvey G. Neufeldt, "The American Tract Society, 1825–1865: An Examination of Its Religious, Economic, Social, and Political Ideas" (Ph.D. diss., Michigan State University, 1971).

30. EW to Susan, Nov. 6, 1828, Feb. 26, 1829, EWP, LC.

31. EW to Susan, Feb. 7, 20, 1829, EWP, LC.

32. EW to Susan, Oct. 12, Dec. 12, 30, 1828, Jan. 29, Apr. 29, 1829, EWP, LC.

33. EW to Susan, Dec. 12, 1828, Jan. 29, 1829, EW to Rev. Jonathan Blanchard, [c. 1874], EW to the Editor of the *Christian Press,* [n.d., vol. 19], EWP, LC; *Chronotype,* May 29, 1849; EW to Theodore Weld, July 28, 1836, *Weld Letters* 1:320; EW to Rev. R. M. Walker, Dec. 5, 1875, Carroll Cutler Papers, University Archives, Case Western Reserve University; Wrights, *Wright,* 38–39.

34. EW, Sr., to EW, Jan. 25, 1829, EW to Susan, Feb. 26, 1829, EWP, LC; EW to Jeremiah Day, Feb. 25, 1829, Jeremiah Day Papers.

35. EW, Sr., to EW, Apr. 10, 1829, EW to Susan, Mar. 28, 1829, EWP, LC; EW to Jeremiah Day, Mar. 19, 1829, Jeremiah Day Papers. *The Vital Records of Groton to the End of the Year 1849* (Salem: Essex Institute, 1927), 2:192, cited Sept. 12, 1829 as the wedding day, but the Wrights, *Wright,* indicated Sept. 13. I have used the date in the primary source, Sept. 12.

Part II ABOLITIONIST

4. From Colonizationist to Immediatist

1. EW to Leonard Bacon, Apr. 29, 1837, and Leonard Bacon to EW, May 1, 1837, Bacon Family Papers. See also Leonard Bacon, *Slavery Discussed in Occasional Essays, 1833–1846* (New York: Baker and Scribner, 1846).

2. Scholarship dealing with the psychology of immediatism has gone through two major stages in the last generation. Challenging the lingering negative portrait of abolitionists left by Civil War revisionists of the 1930s and 1940s, Martin Duberman's "The Abolitionists and

Psychology," *Journal of Negro History* 47 (1962): 183–91, argues that the abolitionists' high ethical standards indicated great ego strength. Other studies reflecting a psychological rehabilitation of the abolitionists include Silvan Tomkins, "The Psychology of Commitment: The Constructive Role of Violence and Suffering for the Individual and for His Society," in *The Antislavery Vanguard: New Essays on the Abolitionists,* ed. Martin Duberman (Princeton: Princeton Univ. Press, 1965), 270–98; French, "Conversion"; Gerald Sorin, *The New York Abolitionists: A Case Study of Political Radicalism* (Westport: Greenwood Press, 1971).

Current historiography is less concerned with the question of whether abolitionists were emotional saints or neurotic sinners, but with the creative role of personality and character in shaping their reform commitment. Lewis Perry announced the new departure with "Psychology and the Abolitionists: Reflections on Martin Duberman and the Neoabolitionism of the 1960s," *Reviews in American History* 2 (1974): 309–22. Subsequent studies include Peter F. Walker, *Moral Choices: Memory, Desire, and Imagination in Nineteenth-Century Abolition* (Baton Rouge: Louisiana State Univ. Press, 1978); Perry, *Childhood;* Abzug, *Weld;* Goodheart, "Childrearing"; Charles A. Jarvis, "Admission to Abolition: The Case of John Greenleaf Whittier," *Journal of the Early Republic* 4 (1984): 161–76.

Recent studies of group psychology include Wyatt-Brown, "Conscience and Career"; Lawrence J. Friedman, *Gregarious Saints: Self and Community in American Abolitionism, 1830–1870* (Cambridge: Cambridge Univ. Press, 1982). For an overview see Richard O. Curry and Lawrence B. Goodheart, " 'Knives in Their Heads': Passionate Self-Analysis and the Search for Identity in Recent Abolitionist Historiography," *Canadian Review of American Studies* 14 (1983): 401–14.

3. EW, *A Lecture on Tobacco, Delivered in the Chapel of the Western Reserve College, Hudson, Ohio, May 29, 1832* (Cleveland: Published by the Request of the Students, 1832); EW to Susan, June 15, July 13, 1829, EWP, LC; *HOT,* Sept. 12, Oct. 6, 1831, July 12, Nov. 8, 1832; *Western Intelligencer,* July 14, 1829; *American Tract Magazine* 6 (1831): [back cover].

4. See P. J. Staudenraus, *The African Colonization Society, 1816–1865* (New York: Columbia Univ. Press, 1961); Bodo, *Protestant Clergy,* 112–50; George M. Fredrickson, *The Black Image in the White Mind: Debate on Afro-American Character and Destiny, 1817–1914* (New York: Harper and Row, 1971), 1–42; Charles I. Foster, "The Colonization of Free Negroes in Liberia, 1816–1835," *Journal of Negro History* 38 (1953): 41–66.

5. For instance, *HOT,* Dec. 22, 1831, reprinted "The Confessions of Nat Turner." See Arthur Zilversmit, *The First Emancipation: The Abolition of Slavery in the North* (Chicago: Univ. of Chicago Press, 1970); Betty Fladeland, *Men and Brothers: Anglo-American Antislavery Cooperation* (Urbana: Univ. of Illinois Press, 1972); Clare Taylor, *British American Abolitionists: An Episode in Transatlantic Understanding* (Edinburgh: Edinburgh Univ. Press, 1974); David B. Davis, *The Problem of Slavery in the Age of Revolution, 1770–1823* (Ithaca: Cornell Univ. Press, 1975); James B. Stewart, *Holy Warriors: The Abolitionists and American Slavery* (New York: Hill and Wang, 1976), 3–32.

6. William Lloyd Garrison, *Thoughts on African Colonization* (Boston: Garrison and Knapp, 1832), i, 79; *Liberator,* Feb. 2, 1833. See also John L. Thomas, *The Liberator: William Lloyd Garrison, A Biography* (Boston: Little, Brown, 1963), 114–28; David B. Davis, "The Emergence of Immediatism in British and American Antislavery Thought," *Mississippi Valley Historical Review* 49 (1962): 209–30; Anne C. Loveland, "Evangelicalism and 'Immediate Emancipation' in American Antislavery Thought," *Journal of Southern History* 32 (1966): 172–88.

7. *HOT,* Feb. 2, 1832; *Liberator,* Jan. 5, 1833. See also Louis J. Filler, *The Crusade against Slavery, 1830–1860* (New York: Harper, 1960), 23–52; Dwight L. Dumond, *Antislavery: The Crusade for Freedom in America* (New York: Norton, 1961), 131; Leonard J. Richards, *"Gentlemen of Property and Standing": Anti-Abolition Mobs in Jacksonian America* (New York: Oxford Univ. Press, 1970), 92–100, 122–29, 134–50.

8. David Hudson to R. R. Gurley, July 23, 1830, American Colonization Society Papers, Library of Congress; *HOT,* Dec. 1, 15, 1831; Charles B. Storrs, *An Address Delivered at Western Reserve College, Hudson, Ohio, February 9, 1831* (Boston, 1831), 6.

9. Gilbert H. Barnes, *The Antislavery Impulse, 1830–1844* (New York: Harcourt, Brace and World, 1933); *Weld Letters* 1:v–xxviii; *Birney Letters* 1:xxvii–xxviii; Dumond, *Antislavery,* 151–74; Friedman, *Gregarious Saints,* 11–40.

10. *HOT,* June 24, Sept. 2, 9, and Aug. 8, 1830, carried news about Garrison's activities; Isaac Israel Bigelow to Carroll Cutler, [c. 1876], Carroll Cutler Papers. See also Carroll Cutler, *A History of Western Reserve College during Its First Half Century, 1826–1876* (Cleveland: Crockers Publishing House, 1876), 24; Waite, *Western Reserve University,* 95.

11. *HOT,* Oct. 11, Nov. 15, 1832.

12. *Liberator,* Jan. 5, 1833; Wendell P. Garrison and Francis J. Garrison, *William Lloyd Garrison, 1805–1879: The Story of His Life Told By His Children,* 4 vols. (Boston: Houghton Mifflin, 1894), 1:249; Wrights, *Wright,* 61–62.

13. EW to Reuben Hitchcock, Dec. 13, 25, 1832, Reuben Hitchcock to EW, Dec. 16, 1832, Peter Hitchcock Family Papers.

14. *HOT,* Sept. 20, Oct. 4, Nov. 22, 1832.

15. EW, *Lecture on Tobacco,* 12; *HOT,* Sept. 20, 1832.

16. *HOT,* Aug. 16, Nov. 22, 1832.

17. *HOT,* Aug. 16, 1832.

18. John L. Thomas, "Romantic Reform in America, 1815–1865," *American Quarterly* 17 (1965): 656–81.

19. *HOT,* Nov. 8, 22, 1832; *First Annual Report of the American Anti-Slavery Society* (New York: Dorr and Butterfield, 1834), 49.

20. EW to Beriah Green, May 6, 1833, EWP, LC; EW to Reuben Hitchcock, Peter Hitchcock Family Papers. For the psychology of conversion see Gordon Allport, *Becoming: Basic Considerations for a Psychology of Personality* (New Haven: Yale Univ. Press, 1955), 73; Schafer, "Ideals," 150–51; Leon Salzman, "The Psychology of Religious and Ideological Conversion," *Psychiatry* 16 (1953): 177–87.

21. EW to Theodore Weld, Dec. 7, 1832, Weld to William Lloyd Garrison, Jan. 2, 1833, Theodore Weld to Arthur Tappan, Joshua Leavitt, EW, Nov. 22, 1833, *Weld Letters* 1: 97–98, 120; EW, *The Sin of Slavery and Its Remedy: Containing Some Reflections on the Moral Influence of African Colonization* (New York: Printed for the Author, 1833), 10.

22. EW, *Sin of Slavery,* 21–22, 24; EW, to Theodore Weld, Sept. 5, 1833, *Weld Letters* 1:114.

23. EW to Theodore Weld, Sept. 5, 1833, *Weld Letters,* 1:114; EW, *Sin of Slavery,* 9; Simeon S. Jocelyn to EW, May 24, 1833, EWP, LC.

24. See McLoughlin, *Modern Revivalism,* 21; David Hackett Fischer, *Growing Old in America* (New York: Oxford Univ. Press, 1978), 113–22; Lois Banner, "Religion and Reform in the Early Republic: The Role of Youth," *American Quarterly* 23 (1971): 677–95. On the psychology of generational change, see Fred Weinstein and Gerald M. Platt, *Psychoanalytic Sociology: An Essay on the Interpretation of Historical Data and the Phenomena of Col-*

lective Behavior (Baltimore: Johns Hopkins Univ. Press, 1973), 84; Erik H. Erikson, *Life History and the Historical Moment* (New York: Norton, 1978), 113–22.

25. EW, Sr., to EW, Oct. 8, 1832, July 22, 1839, Jan. 7, 1840, Clarissa to EW, Jan. 29, 1833, Clarissa [sister] to EW, Apr. 2, 1835, Sept. 16, 1837, EW to Beriah Green, Oct. 4, 1833, EWP, LC; EW, Sr., to EW, Oct. 11, 1833, EW, Sr., Papers, University Archives, Case Western Reserve University; *HOT,* May, 30, 1833.

26. EW to Theodore Weld, Sept. 5, 1833, *Weld Letters* 1:117; EW to Rufus W. Griswold, Aug. 8, 1842, Rufus Griswold Papers: EW, *Sin of Slavery,* 10. See also French, "Conversion," 107–8; Wrights, *Wright,* 601, 62–63.

27. Emerson quoted in Perry, *Henry Clarke Wright,* 62.

5. The Western Reserve College Controversy

1. For an extended analysis, see Lawrence B. Goodheart, "Abolitionists as Academics: The Controversy at Western Reserve College, 1832–1833," *History of Education Quarterly* 22 (1982): 421–33. Related essays include David C. French, "Elizur Wright, Jr., and the Emergence of Anti-Colonization Sentiments on the Connecticut Western Reserve," *Ohio History* 85 (1976): 49–66, and Bertram Wyatt-Brown, "Abolition and Antislavery in Hudson and Cleveland: Contrasts in Reform Styles," in *Cleveland: A Tradition of Reform,* ed. David D. Van Tassel and John J. Grabowski (Kent: Kent State Univ. Press, 1986), 91–112.

2. See Michael A. McManis, "Range Ten, Town Four: A Social History of Hudson, Ohio, 1799–1840" (Ph.D. diss., Case Western Reserve University, 1976), 148; Betty Fladeland, "Who Were the Abolitionists?" *Journal of Negro History* 59 (1964): 99–115; Banner, "Religion and Reform," 175–86; John L. Hammond, "Revival Religion and Anti-Slavery Politics," *American Sociological Review* 39 (1974): 175–86; Scott, *From Office to Profession,* 95–111.

3. EW to Rev. R. M. Walker, Dec. 5, 1875, Carroll Cutler Papers, EW to Theodore Weld, Feb. 1, 1833, *Weld Letters* 1:103.

4. EW to Rev. R. M. Walker, Dec. 5, 1875, Carroll Cutler Papers.

For Elizur's essays on geology and Genesis, see *HOT,* Apr. 12, 19, 26, May 10, 1832. Conrad Wright, "The Religion of Geology," argues that geology was generally an aid to faith before midcentury. Nevertheless old-school evangelicals in Ohio were uneasy about Elizur's modernization of the biblical story of creation. Elizur's essays on conscience started in the *HOT* on July 13, 1832 and appeared regularly until superseded by his advocacy of immediatism on Sept. 6, 1832.

5. Cutler, *Western Reserve College,* 7–19; Donald G. Tewsbury, *The Founding of American Colleges and Universities before the Civil War* (New York: Teachers College, Columbia University, 1932), 8–9; Waite, *Western Reserve University,* 23–28; John S. Millis, *Western Reserve of Cleveland: One Hundred Thirty-Two Years of a Venture in Faith* (New York: Newcomen Society in North America, 1957), 10–12; Mathews, *The Expansion of New England,* 171–94; Clarence H. Cramer, *Case Western Reserve: A History of the University, 1826–1876* (Boston: Little, Brown, 1976), 4–10.

6. On Storrs, see *Ohio Observer,* Sept. 28, 1833; [Richard Salter Storrs, II], "Sketch of the Life of the Reverend Charles Backus Storrs, President of Western Reserve College," *American Quarterly Register* 6 (Nov. 1833): 84–89; Rev. R. S. Storrs, to Henry [Storrs], Dec. 15, 1853, Charles B. Storrs Papers, University Archives, Case Western Reserve University.

On Green, see *HOT,* Sept. 2, 1830; Samuel Worcester Green, *Beriah Green* (New York: S. W. Green, 1875), 3; Muriel Block, "Beriah Green, The Reformer" (master's thesis, Syracuse University, 1935), 1–36; Milton C. Sernett, *Abolition's Axe: Beriah Green, Oneida Institute, and the Black Freedom Struggle* (Syracuse: Syracuse Univ. Press, 1986), 3–18.

On Nutting, see EW, Sr., to EW, Apr. 10, 1829, EWP, LC; Trustee Records, 1826–34, Western Reserve College, University Archives, Case Western Reserve University; Caleb Pitkin to R. R. Gurley, Mar. 27, 1832, American Colonization Society Papers.

7. *Liberator,* Aug. 11, 1832, reprinted in *HOT,* Aug. 30, 1832; EW, "Reminiscences," 9; Isaac Israel Bigelow to Carroll Cutler, [1875], Carroll Cutler Papers; Oliver Johnson, *William Lloyd Garrison and His Times* (Boston: B. B. Russell, 1881), 141–42.

8. *Liberator,* Aug. 11, 1832, reprinted in *HOT,* Aug. 30, 1832. No black students attended Yale until after 1865; George W. Pierson, *Yale: A Short History* (New Haven, Conn.: Yale Univ. Press, 1976), 53–54.

9. *Liberator,* Aug. 11, 1832, reprinted in *HOT,* Aug. 30, 1832.

10. Isaac Israel Bigelow to Carroll Cutler, [1875], Carroll Cutler Papers; Green is quoted in Wrights, *Wright,* 60; Tomkins, "Psychology of Commitment," 270. The important concept of abolitionist affinity groups is well developed in Friedman, *Gregarious Saints.*

11. Johnson, *Garrison and His Times,* 142.

12. *HOT,* Sept. 6, 13, 27, Oct. 4, 1832.

13. *HOT,* Oct. 11, Nov. 1, 22, 1832.

14. *HOT,* Nov. 8, 1832.

15. *HOT,* Jan. 17, 1833; *Liberator,* Jan. 5, 1833; EW to Theodore Weld, Dec. 7, 1832, *Weld Letters* 1:96; EW to Rev. R. M. Walker, Dec. 5, 1875, Carroll Cutler papers.

16. Horace Taylor to Ralph R. Gurley, Oct. 29, 1832, American Colonization Society Papers; Waite, *Western Reserve University,* 98, 101.

17. *HOT,* Feb. 7, 1833; Beriah Green, *Four Sermons, Preached in the Chapel of the Western Reserve College, on the Lord's Days, November 18 and 25, December 2 and 9, 1832* (Cleveland: Printed at the Office of the Herald, 1833), preface, 18; Beriah Green, *Sermons and Other Discourses with Brief Biographical Hints* (New York: S. W. Green, 1860), 34.

18. Cutler, *Western Reserve College,* 31–32; Waite, *Western Reserve University,* 92–99; the quotations are from Staudenraus, *African Colonization Society,* 201, 203.

19. Green, *Four Sermons,* prefacing note; *HOT,* Jan. 3, 1833; *Liberator,* Jan. 5, 1833; EW to Theodore Weld, Dec. 7, 1832, *Weld Letters* 1:95–96, 101–2; Stephen B. Oates, *To Purge This Land with Blood: A Biography of John Brown* (New York: Harper and Row, 1970), 28–29.

20. *HOT,* Dec. 27, 1832.

21. EW to Reuben Hitchcock, Dec. 13, 1832, Peter Hitchcock Family Papers. Elizur published his letter, dated Dec. 11, 1832, in *Liberator,* Jan. 5, 1833.

22. "Committee Report on Abolitionist Agitation, 1832," University Archives, Case Western Reserve University; [untitled typescript of a Charles B. Storrs MS of Jan. 11, 13, 1833], Charles B. Storrs Papers; *HOT,* Feb. 14, 21, 1833.

23. *Liberator,* Jan. 5, 1833; the latter quotation by Garrison of Nov. 26, 1832 is quoted in Wrights, *Wright,* 62.

24. *Liberator,* Feb. 9, June 15, 1833. Elizur's essays indicting *Christian Spectator* originally appeared in *Genius of Temperance* but were reprinted in *Liberator* on Apr. 27, May 4, June 1, 8, 15, 22, 1833.

25. *Liberator,* Jan. 5, May 25, June 1, 8, 22, 1833; EW to Theodore Weld, Sept. 5, 1833, *Weld Letters* 1:114–15. Additional accounts of Elizur's Boston speaking engagements are in George W. Benson to Isaac Knapp, May 27, 1833, Weston Papers, Boston Public Library; *Boston Recorder,* June 5, 1833; *Emancipator,* June 8, 1833.

26. *Liberator,* June 8, 19, 1833. For the New Haven lecture of June 5, see Simeon S. Jocelyn to EW, May 24, 1833, New Haven Anti-Slavery Society to EW, June 18, 1833, EWP, LC; EW to Theodore Weld, Sept. 5, 1833, *Weld Letters* 1:115. See also *Emancipator,* June 22, 1833; EW to Beriah Green, June 7, 1833, EWP, LC.

27. *Liberator,* July 20, 1833; EW, *Sin of Slavery,* 3, 39, 47.

28. EW to Theodore Weld, Dec. 7, 1832, *Weld Letters* 1:97; John Seward to EW, July 24, 1833, EWP, LC.

29. *HOT,* Aug. 1, 8, 15, Sept. 5, 12, 1833; *Ohio Observer,* Oct. 12, 1833; *Emancipator,* Sept. 21, Oct. 26, 1833; EW to Charles B. Storrs, Aug. 31, 1833, Charles B. Storrs Papers; EW to Theodore Weld, Sept. 5, 1833, *Weld Letters* 1:117.

30. EW to Charles B. Storrs, Aug. 31, 1833, Charles B. Storrs Papers; EW to Rev. R. M. Walker, Dec. 5, 1875, Carroll Cutler Papers; EW to Beriah Green, Sept. 18, 1833, quoted in Wrights, *Wright,* 63; *HOT,* Sept. 12, 1833; Waite, *Western Reserve University,* 103.

31. EW and Beriah Green to Theodore Weld, Feb. 1, 1833, *Weld Letters* 1:103; EW to Theodore Weld, Sept. 5, 1833, *Weld Letters* 1:116; Trustee Records, 1826–34, Western Reserve College, pp. 58, 103, University Archives, Case Western Reserve University; EW to Beriah Green, May 6, June 7, 1833, EWP, LC; EW to Amos Phelps, [between June 7 and Oct. 4, 1833], EWP, LC; *HOT,* July 4, 1833; *Ohio Observer,* Sept. 28, 1833; EW to Beriah Green, Sept. 18, 1833, quoted in Wrights, *Wright* 62, 65.

32. *African Repository* 9 (Aug. 1833): 186–87, 9 (Oct. 1833): 245, 266; *HOT,* Sept. 5, 12, 1833; EW to Amos Phelps, [between June 7 and Oct. 4, 1833], EWP, LC; EW to Theodore Weld, Sept. 5, 1833, *Weld Letters* 1:116.

33. EW to Charles B. Storrs, Aug. 31, 1833, Charles B. Storrs Papers; EW to Theodore Weld, Sept. 5, 1833, *Weld Letters* 1: 116; Theodore Weld to James G. Birney, Aug. 19, 1835, *Birney Letters* 1:239. [Ravenna] *Western Courier,* Sept. 12, 1833, concluded that the immediatist controversy had left "an unfortunate state of things" on campus. On Elizur's role in converting Theodore Weld to immediatism, see Goodheart, "Abolitionists as Academics," 429, 433n.

6. Secretary of the American Anti-Slavery Society

1. EW to Amos Phelps, Dec. 31, 1833, EWP, LC.

2. Insightful characterizations of Elizur's "plain, common sense view" are in Jane H. Pease and William H. Pease, *Bound with Them in Chains: A Biographical History of the American Antislavery Movement* (Westport: Greenwood Press, 1972), 227; and Lawrence J.

Friedman, " 'Pious Fellowship' and Modernity: A Psychosocial Interpretation," in *Crusaders and Compromisers: Essays on the Relationship of the Antislavery Struggle to the Antebellum Party System,* ed. Alan M. Kraut (Westport: Greenwood Press, 1983), 247–48.

3. EW to Theodore Weld, Jan. 10, Sept. 3, Nov. 2, 1833, *Weld Letters* 1:100, 116–19; *Emancipator,* Sept. 14, Oct. 5, 1833; *Liberator,* Oct. 12, 19, 1833; Lewis Tappan, *The Life of Arthur Tappan* (New York: Hurd and Houghton, 1870), 168–75; Dumond, *Antislavery,* 175–76; Wyatt-Brown, *Lewis Tappan,* 101–7; Richards, *"Gentlemen of Property and Standing,"* 26–30.

4. EW to EW, Sr., Nov. 2, 1833, EWP, LC; *Emancipator,* Oct. 5, 1833; *Liberator,* Oct. 1, 19, 1833; *Anti-Slavery Reporter* 1 (Oct. 1833): 79.

5. EW to William Lloyd Garrison, Oct. 31, 1833, American Anti-Slavery Society Papers, Boston Public Library; EW to EW, Sr., Nov. 2, 1833, EWP, LC; Arthur Tappan, Joshua Leavitt, and EW to Theodore Weld, Oct. 29, 1833, and EW to Theodore Weld, Nov. 2, 1833, *Weld Letters* 1:117–20.

6. EW to EW, Sr., Nov. 2, 1833, EWP, LC. "The Declaration of Sentiments" is in *Liberator,* Dec. 14, 1833, and the constitution is in *Second Annual Report of the American Anti-Slavery Society* (New York: Dorr and Butterfield, 1835), 73–74.

7. *Second Annual Report,* 73–74.

8. John Greenleaf Whittier, "The Anti-Slavery Convention of 1833," *Atlantic Monthly* 33 (Feb. 1874), 166; *Second Annual Report,* 4; *Liberator,* Dec. 21, 1833; Stewart, *Holy Warriors,* 50–51.

9. EW to Theodore Weld, Dec. 31, 1833, *Weld Letters* 1:121–28, which includes "particular instructions to agents"; Committee on Agency, Minutes, 1833–38, American Anti-Slavery Society Papers.

10. EW to Theodore Weld, Dec. 31, 1833, Feb. 20, 1834, *Weld Letters* 1:121, 129; EW to Amos Phelps, Dec. 31, 1833, Jan. 16, 1834, EWP, LC; *First Annual Report of the American Anti-Slavery Society* (New York: Dorr and Butterfield, 1834), 40; John L. Meyers, "The Beginning of the Anti-Slavery Agencies in New York State, 1833–1836," *New York History* 43 (1962): 162.

11. EW to William Lloyd Garrison, Jan. 30, 1834, EW to Amos Phelps, Feb. 20, 1834, EW to Beriah Green, Nov. 18, 1833, EWP, LC; EW to Theodore Weld, Feb. 20, 1834, *Weld Letters* 1:129.

12. EW to Beriah Green, Sept. 19, 1834, EWP, LC. On Arthur Tappan, see Wyatt-Brown, *Lewis Tappan,* 99–148.

13. EW to Amos Phelps, Aug. 8, 1834, EWP, LC; EW to Theodore Weld, June 10, 1834, *Weld Letters* 1:150; *Emancipator,* Aug. 12, 1834, Jan. 29, 1835; *Second Annual Report,* 34.

14. EW to Theodore Weld, June 10, 1834, Jan. 9, 1835, *Weld Letters* 1:150, 194–95; EW to William Lloyd Garrison, Nov. 12, 1834, EWP, LC.

15. EW to Amos Phelps, Aug. 8, 1834, Clarissa to EW, Jan. 1, 1835, EWP, LC; *First Annual Report,* 60; EW to Theodore Weld, Jan. 9, 1835, *Weld Letters* 1:195–96; *The Liberator,* June 14, 1834; *Emancipator,* Nov. 25, 1834, Feb. 3, 1835.

16. *First Annual Report,* 38; *Second Annual Report,* 34; *Third Annual Report of the American Anti-Slavery Society* (New York: Dorr and Butterfield, 1836), 32; *Fourth Annual Report of the American Anti-Slavery Society* (New York: Dorr and Butterfield, 1837), 30; *Fifth Annual Report of the American Anti-Slavery Society* (New York: Dorr and Butterfield, 1838), 43, 46; *Sixth Annual Report of the American Anti-Slavery Society* (New York: Dorr and Butterfield, 1839), 50; EW to Theodore Weld, Nov. 4, 1836, *Weld Letters* 1:347;

EW to EW, Sr., Oct. 21, 1837, EWP, LC; James G. Birney to J. M. McKim, Nov. 8, 1839, American Anti-Slavery Society Papers; Wyatt-Brown, *Lewis Tappan,* 174; Benjamin Quarles, "Sources of Abolitionist Income," *Mississippi Valley Historical Review* 32 (1945): 76.

17. EW to Theodore Weld, Dec. 31, 1833, Lewis Tappan to Theodore Weld, Dec. 31, 1833, July 10, 1834, *Weld Letters* 1:153–56; H. E. Benson to G. W. Benson, Aug. 19, 1835, Weston Papers: Stephen English to EW, July 26, 1878, EWP, BL; Lydia Maria Child, *Letters of Lydia Maria Child* (Boston: Houghton Mifflin, 1883), 16; Richards, *"Gentlemen of Property and Standing,"* 113–20, 150–55; Linda Kerber, "Abolitionists and Amalgamators: The New York City Race Riots of 1834," *New York History* 48 (1967): 28–39.

18. The disclaimer is in Lewis Tappan, *Arthur Tappan,* 215–16; "Lookout for Kidnappers, July 8, 1834," American Periodical Series, no. 968, reel 391; *Emancipator,* Apr. 1, 1834, Sept. 16, 1834; *First Annual Report,* 55; *Commercial Advertiser* quoted in French, "Conversion," 197.

19. Lewis Tappan, *Arthur Tappan,* 216; EW to Beriah Green, July 30, 1834, EW to Clarissa, Sept. 16, 1834, EW to Parents, July 31, 1834, EWP, LC; *Liberator,* Aug. 23, 1834.

20. EW to Theodore Weld, Aug. 14, 1834, *Weld Letters* 1:166–67; EW to EW, Sr., Aug. 20, 1834, EW to Amos Phelps, Aug. 20, 1834, EWP, LC; Theodore Weld to James G. Birney, Aug. 25, Sept. 4, 10, 1834, *Birney Letters* 1:130–35; Committee on Agency, Minutes of Aug. 5, 19, 1834, American Anti-Slavery Society Papers; Betty Fladeland, *James Gillespie Birney: Slaveholder to Abolitionist* (Ithaca: Cornell Univ. Press, 1955), 88–89.

21. EW to Parents, Mar. 14, 1834, EW to Beriah Green, Sept. 19, 1834, EWP, LC; to Theodore Weld, Aug. 14, 1834, *Weld Letters* 1:167.

22. EW to Theodore Weld, Feb. 20, 1834, July 16, 1835, Mar. 3, 1836, *Weld Letters* 1:129, 228, 270; Wyatt-Brown, *Lewis Tappan,* 100–101, 110–11.

23. EW to Theodore Weld, July 28, 1836, *Weld Letters* 1:320; EW to Clarissa, Mar. 2, 1835, EWP, LC.

24. EW to Clarissa, Mar. 2, 1835, EWP, LC.

25. EW to Clarissa, Mar. 2, 1835, EW to Parents, May 24, 1835, EWP, LC; EW to Theodore Weld, May 26, 1835, July 28, 1836, *Weld Letters* 1:221, 321.

26. EW to Amos Phelps, Jan. 5, 1835, EW to Beriah Green, Mar. 7, 16, 1835, EWP, LC; EW to Theodore Weld, Mar. 16, 1835, *Weld Letters* 1:210; Wyatt-Brown, *Lewis Tappan,* 138–42; James B. Stern, "Urgent Gradualism: The Case of the American Union for the Relief and Improvement of the Colored Race," *Civil War History* 25 (1979): 309–28; Friedman, *Gregarious Saints,* 38–39.

27. EW to Theodore Weld, Mar. 16, 1835, June 10, 1835, *Weld Letters* 1: 208–9, 225; *Second Annual Report,* 3, 8, 16, 28, 30, 32, 47–48.

28. First Annual Report, 11, 41; *Emancipator,* Nov. 25, 1834; EW to Beriah Green, Nov. 4, 1836, EWP, LC; EW to Theodore Weld, Jan. 9, Mar. 16, June 10, 1835, *Weld Letters* 1:195–96, 209, 225–26; Garrison quoted in Garrisons, *Garrison* 1:461; Dumond, *Antislavery,* 266–67; Wyatt-Brown, *Lewis Tappan,* 143–45.

29. Theodore Weld to Lewis Tappan, Feb. 22, 1836, EW to Theodore Weld, Jan. 9, 1835, Mar. 3, 24, Jan. 22, 1836, *Weld Letters* 1:254, 262–63, 270, 279–80; Dumond, *Antislavery,* 266.

30. EW to Theodore Weld, June 10, Sept. 16, 1835, *Weld Letters* 1:225, 231–32; *Emancipator,* Feb. 3, 1836; *Slave's Friend* 5 [n.d.]: 15–16; *Third Annual Report,* 35.

31. *Third Annual Report,* 42–54; EW, Jr., to Clarissa, Mar. 2, 1835, EWP, LC.

32. EW to Theodore Weld, Sept. 16, 1835, *Weld Letters* 1:233; EW to Beriah Green, Aug. 4, 1835, EWP, LC; *Third Annual Report,* 36, 66.

33. *Third Annual Report,* 27; James B. Stewart, "Peaceful Hopes and Violent Experiences: The Evolution of Reforming and Radical Abolitionism, 1831–1837," *Civil War History* 17 (1971): 293–309.

34. *Third Annual Report,* 62, 80, 87; EW to Clarissa, Sept. 16, 1834, EWP, LC.

35. *Second Annual Report,* 60, 65–66; *Third Annual Report,* 29, 66–73, 82; EW to Theodore Weld, Apr. 21, 1836, *Weld Letters* 1:292; EW to James G. Birney, Nov. 5, 1835, *Birney Letters* 1:256.

36. Dumond, *Antislavery,* 242–48; Wyatt-Brown, *Lewis Tappan,* 170–71; Stewart, *Holy Warriors,* 81–85.

37. *Third Annual Report,* 84; *Fourth Annual Report,* 26, 97; *Fifth Annual Report,* 48; EW to Theodore Weld, Jan. 9, 22, 1836, "American Anti-Slavery Society's Directions to County Anti-Slavery Societies," *Weld Letters* 1:196, 256, 403–404n, 404; Edward Magdol, "A Window on the Abolitionist Constituency: Antislavery Petitions, 1836–1839," in *Crusaders and Compromisers,* ed. Kraut, 46.

38. *Second Annual Report,* 48; EW to Theodore Weld, June 10, 1835, *Weld Letters* 1:225–26; EW to James G. Birney, Sept. 15, 1836, *Birney Letters* 1:357, 365; Dumond, *Antislavery,* 183–89; John L. Meyers, "Organization of the 'Seventy': To Arouse the North against Slavery," *Mid-America* 48 (1966): 29–46; Abzug, *Passionate Liberator,* 150–52.

39. Committee on Agency, Minutes 1833–38, American Anti-Slavery Society Papers; EW to James G. Birney, Sept. 15, Oct. 12, 1836, *Birney Letters* 1:357, 365; EW to Theodore Weld, Sept. 22, Nov. 4, 1836, *Weld Letters* 1:337–38, 346.

40. *Fourth Annual Report,* 31–32; Meyers, "Organization of the 'Seventy,' " 46.

41. EW to Beriah Green, Jan. 13, Oct. 31, 1835, Dec. 15, 1838, EWP, LC; *Second Annual Report,* 40; EW, "Slavery and Its Ecclesiastical Defenders," *Quarterly Anti-Slavery Magazine* 1 (July 1836): 353; EW to Theodore Weld, July 28, 1836, *Weld Letters* 1:320–21.

42. EW to Beriah Green, Mar. 8, 1834, Mar. 29, 1839, EW to James Wright, Oct. 10, 1837, EWP, LC; EW to Leonard Bacon, Apr. 29, 1837, Bacon Family Papers; Charles G. Finney to Theodore Weld, July 21, 1836, *Weld Letters* 1:319; EW, [Preface], *Quarterly Anti-Slavery Magazine* 2 (Apr. 1837): 217.

43. *Fourth Annual Report,* 61–77. For an overview, see John R. McKivigan, *The War against Proslavery Religion: Abolitionism and the Northern Churches, 1830–1865* (Ithaca: Cornell Univ. Press, 1984).

44. EW, [untitled], *Quarterly Anti-Slavery Magazine* 2 (Jan. 1837): 113–14; *Fourth Annual Report,* 113.

45. *Fourth Annual Report,* 113–14.

46. EW to Theodore Weld, Jan. 9, 1835, Apr. 21, Nov. 4, 1836, Theodore Weld to Sarah and Angelina Grimké, Aug. 26, 1837, *Weld Letters* 1:197, 291, 347, 436; Theodore Weld to James G. Birney, May 23, June 26, 1837, *Birney Letters* 1:383, 390; EW to Parents, July 20, 1837, EW to James Wright, Oct. 10, 12, 1837, EW to EW, Sr., Oct. 21, 1837, EWP, LC.

47. Theodore Weld to EW, Mar. 2, 1835, EW to Theodore Weld, May 26, 1835, July 28, 1836, Theodore Weld to Sarah and Angelina Grimké, Dec. 15, 28, 1837, *Weld Letters* 1:205–8, 221, 320, 496, 509; Theodore Weld to James G. Birney, June 26, 1837, *Birney Letters* 1:391; Charles Stuart, "On the Use of Slave Labor," *Quarterly Anti-Slavery Magazine* 2

(Jan. 1837): 153–70, and EW's rejoinder on p. 175. See also Abzug, *Passionate Liberator,* 144, 158; Anthony J. Barker, *Captain Charles Stuart: Anglo-American Abolitionist* (Baton Rouge: Louisiana State Univ. Press, 1986), 126–28.

    48. Theodore Weld to James G. Birney, June 26, July 10, 1837, *Birney Letters* 1:390–91, 395.

    49. Theodore Weld to James G. Birney, May 23, Aug. 7, 1837, *Birney Letters* 1:383, 405–7; Charles Stuart to Theodore Weld, Feb. 7, 1837, *Weld Letters* 1:359.

7. Free Men, Free Labor

    1. *Emancipator,* Mar. 25, Apr. 1, 15, 1834; *First Annual Report,* 56; EW to Beriah Green, July 8, Dec. 10, 1842, EWP, LC. See also Lawrence B. Goodheart, " 'Chronicles of Kidnapping in New York': Resistance to the Fugitive Slave Law, 1834–1835," *Afro-Americans in New York Life and History* 8 (1984): 7–15.

    2. *Emancipator,* Apr. 1, 1834.

    3. For the Fugitive Slave Law of 1793, see *Annals of the Congress of the United States, 1791–1793;* 2d Cong. (Washington, D.C., 1849), 1414–15, and *U.S. Statutes at Large, 1789–99* (Boston, 1853), 1:302–5. See also C. W. A. David, "The Fugitive Slave Law of 1793," *Journal of Negro History* 9 (1924): 18–25; William R. Leslie, "A Study in the Origins of Interstate Rendition: The Big Beaver Creek Murders," *American Historical Review* 57 (1951): 63–76; Robert M. Cover, *Justice Accused: Antislavery and the Judicial Process* (New Haven: Yale Univ. Press, 1975), 159–75.

    4. New York State statutes on fugitive slaves are in John C. Hurd, *The Law of Freedom and Bondage in the United States,* 2 vols. (Boston: Little, Brown, 1858–62), 1:51–59. See also Edgar J. McManus, *A History of Negro Slavery in New York* (Syracuse: Syracuse Univ. Press, 1966), 101–19; Leo H. Hirsch, Jr., "The Negro and New York, 1783–1865," *Journal of Negro History* 16(1931): 406–9; George Walker, "The Afro-American in New York City, 1827–1860" (Ph.D. diss., Columbia University, 1975).

    5. Quoted in Wrights, *Wright,* 94; *Laws of the State of New York* (Albany, 1840), 174–77. See also William M. Wiecek, *The Sources of Antislavery Constitutionalism in America, 1760–1848* (Itahca: Cornell Univ. Press, 1977), 199, 204.

    6. EW to EW, Sr., Nov. 26, 1833, Jan. 5, 1835, EW to Parents, Mar. 14, 1835, EW to Wife, Feb. 1, 1841, EWP, LC. See also Leon F. Litwack, "The Abolitionist Dilemma: The Antislavery Movement and the Northern Negro," *New England Quarterly* 34 (1961): 50–73.

    7. *Emancipator,* Apr. 1, Sept. 16, 1834; *First Annual Report,* 55; *Anti-Slavery Record* 1 (June 1835): 62.

    8. *Emancipator,* Sept. 16, Nov. 4, 1834; *American Anti-Slavery Reporter* 1 (June 1834): 93, 94; *Anti-Slavery Record* (July 1835): 74.

    9. *Anti-Slavery Record* 1 (June 1835): 61–62; *Emancipator,* Sept. 16, 1834; EW to Wife, Feb. 1, 1841, EWP, LC.

10. EW to Beriah Green, Mar. 8, 1834, EW to Wife, Feb. 1, 1841, EWP, LC; *Emancipator,* Sept. 16, 1834. See also Jane H. Pease and William H. Pease, *The Fugitive Slave Law and Anthony Burns: A Problem in Law Enforcement* (Philadelphia: Lippincott, 1975).

11. *Emancipator,* Sept. 16, 1834; *American Anti-Slavery Reporter* (June 1834): 93; *Anti-Slavery Record* 3 (Aug. 1837): 1–12; *Laws of New York* (1840), 174–77; *Colored American,* May 23, 1840.

12. *Emancipator,* Sept. 16, 1834; Walter M. Merrill, ed., *The Letters of William Lloyd Garrison: I Will Be Heard, 1822–1835,* 6 vols. (Cambridge: Harvard Univ. Press, 1971–81), 1:452; Wrights, *Wright,* 95; Wyatt-Brown, *Lewis Tappan,* 179.

13. *Emancipator,* Sept. 16, 1834, May 5, 1835; *First Annual Report,* 58; *Massachusetts Abolitionist,* Jan. 23, 1840; Wrights, *Wright,* 95. See also Merrill, *Garrison Letters* 1:461, which includes Garrison's defense of Elizur from Gerrit Smith's accusation.

14. *Quarterly Anti-Slavery Magazine* 2 (Apr. 1939): 94–97, 218; *Human Rights,* Aug. 1835; *Fifth Annual Report,* 96.

15. *Third Annual Report,* 40; *Fourth Annual Report,* 116–17. See also William Freehling, "The Founding Fathers and Slavery," *American Historical Review* 77 (1972): 81–94; Staughton Lynd, "The Abolitionist Critique of the United States Constitution," in *Antislavery Vanguard,* ed. Duberman, 209–39; Wiecek, *Sources of Antislavery Constitutionalism,* 198.

16. *Third Annual Report,* 46; *Fourth Annual Report,* 89; *Fifth Annual Report,* 48, 59; *Georgia Journal* quoted in *Emancipator,* Oct. 20, 1835; EW to Beriah Green, Aug. 4, 1835, EWP, LC; *Congressional Globe,* 24th Cong., 1st sess., 1836, pt. 3:10. See also Bertram Wyatt-Brown, "The Abolitionists' Postal Campaign of 1835," *Journal of Negro History* 50 (1965): 227–38; Gerald S. Henig, "The Jacksonian Attitude Toward Abolitionism in the 1830s," *Tennessee Historical Quarterly* 28 (1969): 42–56.

17. *Anti-Slavery Examiner* 1 (Aug. 1836): 7, 8; "Speech of Henry Clay to the Senate," *Congressional Globe,* 25th Cong., 3d sess., 1838–39, pt. 7:355; EW, "Advance of the Abolitionist Cause," *Quarterly Anti-Slavery Magazine* 1 (Oct. 1835): 104.

18. Theodore Weld to J. F. Robinson, May 1 [?], 1836, *Weld Letters* 1:297; Louis S. Gerteis, *Morality and Utility in American Antislavery Reform* (Chapel Hill: Univ. of North Carolina Press, 1987), 62–85.

19. *HOT,* Sept. 6, 1832.

20. *HOT,* Oct. 11, Nov. 15, 1832; EW, *Sin of Slavery,* 39; *Genius of Temperance* quoted in *Liberator,* May 18, 1833.

21. *Quarterly Anti-Slavery Magazine* 1 (Apr. 1837): 300; *Liberator,* Aug. 25, 1837; *Anti-Slavery Record* 1 (Jan. 1835): 4; EW to Samuel E. Sewall, Feb. 26, 1836, Norcross Papers, Massachusetts Historical Society.

22. *Quarterly Anti-Slavery Magazine* 1 (July 1836): 364. See also Max Weber, *The Protestant Ethic and the Spirit of Capitalism* (New York: Scribner, 1958), 176–77; Douglass C. North, *Economic Growth of the United States, 1790–1860* (Englewood Cliffs: Prentice Hall, 1961), 189; Stuart Bruchey, *The Roots of American Economic Growth, 1607–1861: An Essay in Social Causation* (New York: Harper and Row, 1965), 85–86, 90; Thomas C. Cochran, *Frontiers of Change: Early Industrialism in America* (New York: Oxford Univ. Press,

1981), 98; William L. Barney, *The Passage of the Republic: An Interdisciplinary History of Nineteenth-Century America* (Lexington: Heath, 1987), 31–45.

23. *Quarterly Anti-Slavery Magazine* 1 (July 1836): 315-16, 2 (Apr. 1837), 242–43; *Human Rights,* Aug. 1835; Adam Smith, *An Inquiry into the Nature and Causes of the Wealth of Nations,* 2 vols. (Oxford: Clarendon Press, 1976), 1:98, 387–89. Robert W. Fogel and Stanley L. Engerman, *Time on the Cross: The Economics of American Negro Slavery* (Boston: Little, Brown, 1974), exemplify the current argument for the economic efficiency of antebellum slavery, including the Calvinist-like work ethic of slaves.

24. *Anti-Slavery Record* 1 (Jan. 1835): 8; *Quarterly Anti-Slavery Magazine* 2 (Jan. 1837): 199; *First Annual Report,* 45–46; *Massachusetts Abolitionist,* Oct. 10, 17, 1839. See Jane H. Pease and William H. Pease, *They Who Would Be Free: Blacks' Search for Freedom, 1830–1861* (New York: Atheneum, 1974), 7-9, 82–92, on the general failure of white abolitionists to employ trained blacks.

25. *Emancipator,* Oct. 21, 1834; *Third Annual Report,* 28; *Fourth Annual Report,* 60. See also Philip S. Foner, *Business and Slavery: The New York Merchants and the Irrepressible Conflict* (Chapel Hill: Univ. of North Carolina Press, 1941), 4, 13–14, 318–19; Barrington Moore, Jr., *Social Origins of Dictatorship and Democracy* (Boston: Beacon Press, 1966), 112–15; Richards, "Gentlemen of Property and Standing," 149.

26. *Fourth Annual Report,* 53-57; *Fifth Annual Report,* 110–11; *Massachusetts Abolitionist,* Jan. 9, Mar. 5, 1840.

27. *Fourth Annual Report,* 53-57; *Fifth Annual Report,* 110–11; *Massachusetts Abolitionist,* Apr. 23, 1840.

28. *Free American,* June 24, July 29, 1841; *Massachusetts Abolitionist,* Mar. 5, May 7, 1840; EW, *Myron Holley and What He Did for Liberty and True Religion* (Boston: Elizur Wright, 1882), 372-73.

29. *Emancipator,* Nov. 2, 1836; *Second Annual Report,* 67; *Third Annual Report,* 51, 59–60, 81–82; *Fourth Annual Report,* 106; *Sixth Annual Report,* 102.

30. *Human Rights,* Oct. 1837; *Liberator,* Mar. 18, 1837. See also Joseph G. Rayback, "The American Workingman and the Anti-Slavery Crusade," *Journal of Economic History* 3 (1943): 152–63; Williston H. Lofton, "Abolition and Labor," *Journal of Negro History* 33 (1948): 249–83; Bernard Mandel, *Labor—Free and Slave: Workingmen and the Anti-Slavery Movement in the United States* (New York: Associated Authors, 1955); Jonathan A. Glickstein, " 'Poverty Is Not Slavery': American Abolitionists and the Competitive Labor Market," in *Antislavery Reconsidered: New Perspectives on the Abolitionists,* ed. Lewis Perry and Michael Fellman (Baton Rouge: Louisiana State Univ. Press, 1979), 195–218; Eric Foner, "Abolitionism and the Labor Movement in Antebellum America," in his *Politics and Ideology in the Age of the Civil War* (New York: Oxford Univ. Press, 1980), 57–76.

31. See Aileen Kraditor, "American Radical Historians on Their Heritage," *Past and Present* 56 (1972): 147–50; Eric Foner, *Free Soil, Free Labor, Free Men: The Ideology of the Republican Party before the Civil War* (New York: Oxford Univ. Press, 1970), 316–17; Alan Dawley, *Class and Community: The Industrial Revolution in Lynn* (Cambridge: Harvard Univ. Press, 1976), 65; John B. Jentz, "The Antislavery Constituency in Jacksonian New York City," *Civil War History* 27 (1981): 101–22; Magdol, "Window on the Abolitionist Constituency," 45–70; and Magdol, *The Antislavery Rank and File: A Social Profile of the Abolitionists' Constituency* (Westport: Greenwood Press, 1986).

Part III TRANSITIONS

8. Tripartite Schism

1. EW quoted in William Lloyd Garrison to George Benson, Sept. 23, 1837, Garrisons, *Garrison* 2:168–69, 178n.

2. *Liberator,* Sept. 1, 1837. On nonresistant thought see Lewis Perry, *Radical Abolitionism: Anarchy and the Government of God in Antislavery Thought* (Ithaca: Cornell Univ. Press, 1973). For the abolitionist schism, see Aileen S. Kraditor, *Means and Ends in American Abolitionism: Garrison and His Critics on Strategy and Tactics, 1834–1850* (New York: Pantheon, 1967); Bertram Wyatt-Brown, "William Lloyd Garrison and Antislavery Unity: A Reappraisal," *Civil War History* 13 (1967): 5–24; Stewart, "Peaceful Hopes," 293–309; Richard O. Curry and Lawrence B. Goodheart, eds., "The Complexities of Factionalism: Letters of Elizur Wright, Jr. on the Abolitionist Schism, 1837–1840," *Civil War History* 29 (1983): 245–59.

3. *Emancipator,* Aug. 24, 1837.

4. EW to James G. Birney, Aug. 14, 1837, *Birney Letters* 1:414; EW to Amos Phelps, Sept. 5, 1837, Amos Phelps Papers, Boston Public Library.

5. William Lloyd Garrison to George Benson, Sept. 23, 1837, William Lloyd Garrison to EW, Oct. 23, 1837, Garrisons, *Garrison* 2:305, 321–22; EW to William Lloyd Garrison, Oct. 10, 1837, EWP, LC.

6. EW to William Lloyd Garrison, Nov. 6, 1837, EW to Amos Phelps, Oct. 20, 29, 1837, EWP, LC; John Humphrey Noyes to William Lloyd Garrison, Mar. 27, 1837, Garrisons, *Garrison* 2:145–48.

7. EW, *A Poem Delivered before the Phi Beta Kappa Society in Yale College, August 20, 1845* (New Haven: B. L. Hamlem, 1846), 16; EW to William Lloyd Garrison, Oct. 10, 1837, EW to Beriah Green, Oct. 17, 1837, EW to EW, Sr., Oct. 21, 1837, EWP, LC.

8. EW to Amos Phelps, Oct. 29, 1837, EW to Beriah Green, Oct. 17, 1837, EW to EW, Sr., Oct. 21, 1837, EW to William Lloyd Garrison, Nov. 6, 1837, EWP, LC.

9. EW to Amos Phelps, Sept. 5, 1837, July 11, Aug. 17, 1838, EWP, LC; *Chronotype,* Oct. 20, 1846.

10. *Emancipator,* May 5, 1835; *Quarterly Anti-Slavery Magazine* 2 (Jan. 1837): 193; *Massachusetts Abolitionist,* Nov. 21, 1839; *Ninth Annual Report of the Massachusetts Anti-Slavery Society, January 27, 1841* (Westport: Negro Univ. Press, 1970), 26, 41–42; *Third Annual Report* [American Anti-Slavery Society], 82; *Fourth Annual Report* [American Anti-Slavery Society], 114.

11. Executive Committee Minutes, p. 103, American Anti-Slavery Society Papers; *Emancipator,* Sept. 20, 1838; *Fifth Annual Report,* 126–27; *Human Rights,* Aug. 1838.

12. Executive Committee Minutes, pp. 116–17, American Anti-Slavery Society Papers.

13. EW to Beriah Green, Apr. 2, 1839, EWP, LC; *Seventh Annual Report of the Massachusetts Anti-Slavery Society, January 24, 1839* (Westport: Negro Univ. Press, 1970). See Elaine Brooks, "Massachusetts Anti-Slavery Society," *Journal of Negro History* 30 (1945):

311–30; Richard H. Sewell, *Ballots for Freedom: Antislavery Politics in the United States, 1837–1860* (New York: Oxford Univ. Press, 1976), 24–32.

14. Executive Committee Minutes, p. 125, American Anti-Slavery Society Papers; Henry Stanton to EW, Jan. 23, Feb. [?], 1839, Amos Phelps to EW, Jan. 22, 1839, EW to Beriah Green, Feb. 9, 1839, EWP, LC; EW, Sr., to EW, Mar. 7, 1839, EW, Sr., Papers, University Archives, Case Western Reserve University. See also Lawrence J. Friedman, "The Gerrit Smith Circle: Abolitionism in the Burned-Over District," *Civil War History* 26 (1980): 19–38.

15. *Liberator,* May 24, 1839; Henry Stanton to Amos Phelps, Sept. 2, [1839], Phelps Papers; EW to Maria Weston Chapman, Feb. 18, 1839, EW to Beriah Green, Feb. 9, 1839, EWP, LC.

16. *Massachusetts Abolitionist,* May 23, June 13, Nov. 7, 1839; *Liberator,* June 7, 1839.

17. *Massachusetts Abolitionist,* Jan. 9, May 7, 1840; EW, *A Poem,* 16.

18. *Massachusetts Abolitionist,* Oct. 31, Nov. 21, 1839; *Chronotype,* Oct. 20, 1846. For Clay's speech see *Congressional Globe,* 25th Cong., 3d sess., 1838–39, pt. 7:354–59.

19. Garrisons, *Garrison* 2:307–11; EW, *Myron Holley,* 234; *Emancipator,* Aug. 8, 1839.

20. Lewis Tappan to John Scoble, Dec. 10, 1839, in *A Sidelight on Anglo-American Relations, 1839–1858,* ed. Frank J. Klineberg and Annie H. Abel (New York: A. M. Kelley, 1970), 62; William Jay to I. S. Norton, A. H. Williams, and S. S. Cowles, Apr. 17, 1840, John Jay Papers, Columbia University Library. See also Lawrence J. Friedman, "Confidence and Pertinacity in Evangelical Abolitionism: Lewis Tappan's Circle," *American Quarterly* 31 (1979): 81–106.

21. *Massachusetts Abolitionist,* Oct. 17, 1839.

22. EW to Henry Stanton, Oct. 12, 1839, EW to Beriah Green, Oct. 10, 1839, EWP, LC.

23. EW to Henry Stanton, Oct. 12, 1839, Henry Stanton to EW, Oct. 28, 1839, EWP, LC; EW, Sr., to EW, Nov. 6, 1839, EW, Sr., Papers, University Archives, Case Western Reserve University.

24. *Liberator,* Nov. 29, Dec. 13, 1839, Jan. 10, 1840; *Massachusetts Abolitionist,* Dec. 5, 12, 19, 26, 1839.

25. Garrisons, *Garrison* 2:315–16; *Massachusetts Abolitionist,* Oct. 17, Dec. 5, 12, 19, 1839; [?] to EW, Apr. 19, 1881, EWP, LC. The anonymous author denied Elizur's allegation that the "streak letter" was stolen.

26. *Massachusetts Abolitionist,* Oct. 17, 24, Dec. 19, 1839, Jan. 9, 16, Mar. 13, 1840; EW, *Myron Holley,* 256; Garrisons, *Garrison* 2:319–20, 339–45; See Ralph V. Harlow, *Gerrit Smith, Philanthropist and Reformer* (New York: Holt, 1939), 147–48.

27. *Massachusetts Abolitionist,* Apr. 9, 16, May 7, 1840; EW, *Household Stuff,* 144.

28. EW to Gerrit Smith, Mar. 20, 1840, Gerrit Smith Papers, George Arents Research Library, Syracuse University; EW to Beriah Green, Jan. 1, 1840, EWP, LC.

29. *Massachusetts Abolitionist,* Mar. 26, 1840; *Chronotype,* Oct. 20, 1846, Oct. 23, 1847; EW to Beriah Green, Aug. 10, 1840, EW to Brother Scobel, Dec. 29, 1840, EWP, LC.

30. EW to Parents, Brother, and Sister, June 7, 1841, EW to Beriah Green, Aug. 19, 1841, EW to Brother, Sept. 25, 1841, EWP, LC; *Free American,* June 24, Sept. 18, 1841; Gerrit Smith to Amos Phelps, Aug. 28, 1841, Phelps Papers. Smith commented to Phelps, "What a prime paper is *The Free American!* It can have no better editor."

31. *Free American,* July 1, 1841.

32. *Free American,* July 1, 8, Aug. 5, Nov. 25, 1841; *Liberator,* Nov. 26, 1841; EW to Beriah Green, Dec. 18, 1943, EWP, LC; Wendell Phillips to Elizabeth Pease, Oct. [?], 1841, Garrison Papers, Boston Public Library; EW, *Curiosity of the Law,* 16.

9. The Sisterhood of Reforms

1. EW to Wife, Aug. 27, 1843, EWP, LC.
2. *Liberator,* May 21, 1841 (reprinted from *Friend of Man*), Aug. 12, 1842; Lewis Tappan to EW, July 9, 1844, Lewis Tappan Papers, Library of Congress. See also Samuel May to Mary Carpenter, Oct. 28, 1844, Taylor, *British and American Abolitionists,* 229–30.
3. *Chronotype,* Sept. 8, 1846.
4. EW to Wife, July 3, Dec. 14, 1844, EW to Francis, Mar. 10, 1847, EW to James, Mar. 30, 1847, EW to Beriah Green, Aug. 19, 1841, Oct. 10, Dec. 18, 1843, EW to Brother and Sisters, May 3, 1858, EW to Parents, Dec. 10, 1839, EWP, LC.
5. EW, *Household Stuff,* iv, 25; EW to Wife Apr. 9, 12, 1833, May 24, 1844, EW, Sr., to EW, Apr. 8, 1833, EW to Beriah Green, May 6, 1833, Aug. 26, 1837, Sept. 17, 1838, EW to Parents, July 20, Aug. 9, 1837, EW to Amos Phelps, Oct. 9, 1837, EW to EW, Sr., Oct. 21, 1837, EW to James, Feb. 5, 1841, EW to Philo, July 1, 1845, EWP, LC; *Chronotype,* Feb. 14, 1846. See also Daniel S. Smith, "Family Limitation, Sexual Control, and Domestic Feminism in Victorian America," *Feminist Studies* 1 (1973): 40–57; Robert V. Wells, "Family History and Demographic Transition," *Journal of Social History* 9 (1975): 1–20; Harry B. Weiss and Howard R. Kemble, *The Great American Water-Cure Craze: A History of Hydropathy in the United States* (Trenton: Past Times Press, 1967).
6. EW to Beriah Green, Jan. 21, Mar. 4, Aug, 10, 1840, Mar. 26, 1841, EW to Parents, Aug. 3, 1839, Sept. 30, Nov. 12, 1840, EW to Parents, Brother, and Sisters, June 7, 1841, Clarissa to Children, Apr. 20, 1841, EWP, LC; EW, "Thanksgiving Stanzas," *Household Stuff.*
7. EW to Beriah Green, Aug. 10, 1840, EW to Brother Scoble, Dec. 29, 1840, EWP, LC.
8. EW, trans., *The Fables of La Fontaine,* 2 vols. (Boston: Elizur Wright, Jr., and Tappan and Dennet, 1842), 1:v; EW to Beriah Green, Jan. 21, 1840, EW to Parents, Nov. 12, 1840, EW to Brother Scoble, Dec. 29, 1840, EWP, LC; *North American Review* 113 (Oct. 1, 1841): 506–11.
9. *Free American,* Nov. 11, 1841; EW to *New York Observer,* [1841], EWP, LC; EW to Brother, May 24, 1843, EW to Parents, Brother, and Sisters, June 18, 1843, EWP, LC; *The Nation* 41 (Nov. 26, 1885): 448; Stearns, *Cambridge Sketches,* 292; Wrights, *Wright,* 136.
10. EW to Wife, Jan. 16, 18, 26, Feb. 1, 3, 27, 1841, EW to Beriah Green, Jan. 29, Mar. 26, 1841, EWP, LC; EW, *Fables* 1:vi.
11. EW to Wife, Dec. 23, 1841, July 6, Aug. 5, Nov. 5, 1842, EW to Beriah Green, Apr. 9, July 8, Nov. 11, 1842, EW to James, Feb. 5, 1841, EWP, LC.
12. EW to Wife, Jan. 6, Feb. 1, 3, 14, 27, Dec. 23, 1841, Aug. 27, 1843, EW to John, July 6, 1842, EW to EW, Sr., Sept. 8, 1843, EW to Beriah Green, Dec. 18, 1843, EWP, LC.
13. EW to Parents, Brother, and Sisters, June 18, 1843, EW to Wife, Aug. 3, 7, 27, 1843, EW to Beriah Green, Aug. 31, 1843, EW to EW, Sr., Sept. 8, 1843, EWP, LC; EW, "Inventions," box 24, EWP, LC.

14. EW to Wife, Aug. 3, 7, 1843, EW to Beriah Green, Dec. 18, 1843, EWP, LC; press clippings, no. 340, EWP, LC.

15. EW to Wife, July 3, 18, 1844, EW to Beriah Green, May 17, 1844, EWP, LC.

16. See Eric J. Hobsbawm, *The Age of Revolution, 1789–1848* (New York: New American Library, 1962), 27–52.

17. Quoted in Wrights, *Wright,* 150–51, 166.

18. Ibid., 151, 156; EW to Wife, Apr. 17, May 24, 1844, EWP, LC; EW, *Appeals for the Middlesex Fells and the Forests* (Medford: Medford Public Domain Club, 1893), iv.

19. EW to Beriah Green, May 17, 1844, EW to Wife, July 18, 1844, EWP, LC; Wrights, *Wright,* 157, 160, 163, 165, 168.

20. Wrights, *Wright,* 158, 171, 173–74.

21. EW to Wife, Apr. 3, 17, 18, May 24, July 3, 18, 1844, EW to Beriah Green, May 17, 1844, EWP, LC; EW, *Middlesex Fells,* v; Wrights, *Wright,* 146.

22. EW to Wife, Sept. 4, 1844, EWP, LC; EW, *Household Stuff,* 67; Wrights, *Wright,* 145.

23. Gerrit Smith to Amos Phelps, May 22, 1844, Lewis Tappan to Amos Phelps, Oct. 24, 1844, Phelps Papers; Lewis Tappan to EW, Nov. 1, 1845, Lewis Tappan to Theodore Weld, July 17, 1844, Lewis Tappan Papers; EW to Beriah Green, Nov. 11, 1844, EW to Philo, July 1, 1845, EW to Wife, Nov. 6, 11, 1844, Lewis Tappan to EW, Nov. 11, 1844, C. D. Cleveland to EW, Nov. 14, 1844, EWP, LC.

24. EW to Parents, Dec. 5, 1839, June 18, 1843, EW to Jonathan Blanchard, [1874?], EWP, LC.

25. EW to James, Oct. 10, 12, 1837, EW to EW, Sr., Oct. 21, 1837, James to EW, June 10, 1843, Mar. 11, 1851, Clarissa to Elizur and Susan, June 16, 1840, May 8, Aug. 28, 1841, EW, Sr., to EW, Jan. 7, 1840, Apr. 20, 1841, EW to Mrs. Lawrence, Apr. 21, 1885, EWP, LC; EW, *Household Stuff,* 108.

26. EW to Beriah Green, July 8, 1842, EWP, LC; EW to Gerrit Smith, Nov. 18, 1842, Gerrit Smith Papers. See also Reinhard O. Johnson, "The Liberty Party in Massachusetts, 1840–1848: Antislavery Third Party Politics in the Bay State," *Civil War History* 28 (1982): 237–65; Sewell, *Ballots for Freedom,* 43–79.

27. EW to Gerrit Smith, Mar. 20, 1840, Gerrit Smith Papers; EW to James G. Birney, Sept. 16, 1843, *Birney Letters* 2:759–60; EW to Beriah Green, Oct. 10, 1843, EW to EW, Sr., Sept. 8, 1843, Henry B. Stanton to EW, July 4, 1843, EWP, LC; EW, *A Poem,* 16.

28. EW to Friend, May [?], 1844, EW to Beriah Green, May 17, 1844, EW to Wife, Nov. 10, 1844, EWP, LC; *Chronotype,* Nov. 9, 1846, May 26, Nov. 1, 1847; EW, *Curiosity of the Law,* 18–19.

29. EW to Brother, May 24, 1843, EW to EW, Sr., Sept. 8, 1843, EW to Beriah Green, Dec. 18, 1843, EWP, LC; EW, *Curiosity of the Law,* 19; Stearns, *Cambridge Sketches,* 166; Wrights, *Wright,* 200.

30. EW, *Curiosity of the Law,* 19; *Chronotype,* Aug. 25, 1847, June 8, 1848; Stearns, *Cambridge Sketches,* 292.

31. EW to Francis, Mar. 10, 1847, EW to James, Aug. 26, 1850, EWP, LC; *Chronotype,* Sept. 8, Dec. 19, 29, 1846, Jan. 2, 5, Aug. 25, 1847, Sept. 23, 1848, Nov. 10, 1849; *The Nation* 14 (Nov. 26, 1885): 448; Anne Warren Weston to Samuel May, Sept. 5, 1849, Samuel May Papers, Boston Public Library; Stearns, *Cambridge Sketches,* 166.

32. EW to Wife, Jan. 18, 1841, EW to Harriet, Apr. 5, 1858, EWP, LC; *Free American,* July 8, 1841; *Chronotype,* Mar. 3, 4, 18, 19, July 20, Aug. 12, Sept. 29, Nov. 11, 1846, June

17, 29, July 24, 26, 28, Aug. 31, Sept. 30, Oct. 15, 1847, Jan. 13, May 19, 1848, June 16, 1849; *Commonwealth,* June 3, 1851.

33. Lewis Tappan to EW, Nov. 25, 1846, Lewis Tappan Papers; EW to James, Mar. 30, 1847, EW to Rev. Hibbard Wilson, Nov. 12, 1846, EWP, LC; *Chronotype,* Oct. 26, Nov. 12, Dec. 1, 2, 1846, May 28, Sept. 24, 27, 1847, Feb. 12, 1848, Apr. 9, Mar. 21, 1849.

34. EW to Brothers and Sisters, Feb. 27, 1853, May 3, 1858, EW to Harriet, Apr. 5, 1858, EW to Brother and Sister Hanford, May 8, 1859, EWP, LC; *Chronotype,* Sept. 27, 1847.

35. *Chronotype,* Mar. 4, 1846.

36. *Chronotype,* June 11, Oct. 10, 1846, Dec. 24, 1847.

37. *Chronotype,* Aug. 22, 1846, Dec. 17, 1847, Jan. 25, 1848.

38. *Chronotype,* Mar. 4, June 23, July 29, Oct. 10, Nov. 19, 1846, Dec. 17, 1847.

39. *Chronotype,* May 2, July 10, 18, 22, 23, 29, Aug. 3, 5, 13, 20, Oct. 30, Nov. 19, 21, 26, Dec. 31, 1846, Nov. 15, 1847, May 3, 30, June 20, 1848, Feb. 10, Mar. 19, Dec. 20, 1849.

40. *Chronotype,* Nov. 9, 1846, May 26, Nov. 1, 1847.

41. *Chronotype,* May 11, 14, Nov. 3, 9, 24, 1846, Jan. 27, Feb. 5, 6, 11, Apr. 9, June 19, 1847, June 9, Dec. 19, 1848.

42. *Chronotype,* Sept. 15, Dec. 5, 1846, July 8, 1847, Feb. 1, 1848; *Emancipator,* Dec. 16, 1846; EW to James G. Birney, Feb. 8, 1847, *Birney Letters* 2:1038–40.

43. *Chronotype,* June 19, July 8, Nov. 12, 1847, Jan. 6, 22, 27, Feb. 1, 1848. See also Friedman, "The Gerrit Smith Circle," 18–38.

44. *Chronotype,* Jan. 29, June 1, 12, 17, 21, July 1, 10, Aug. 1, 5, 1848.

45. *Chronotype,* Aug. 12, 13, Sept. 20, Nov. 1, 7, 13, 1848. See also Sewell, *Ballots for Freedom,* 170–201.

46. EW to Brothers and Sisters, July 23, 1851, EWP, LC; Laura E. Richards, ed., *Letters and Journals of Samuel Gridley Howe,* 2 vols. (Boston: Dana Estes, 1909), 1:331; Wrights, *Wright,* 201.

47. EW to Brothers and Sisters, July 23, 1851, EWP, LC; *Commonwealth,* June 16, 1851; Harold Schwartz, *Samuel Gridley Howe: Social Reformer, 1801–1876* (Cambridge: Harvard Univ. Press, 1956), 177–82; Frank O. Gattell, *John Gorham Palfrey and the New England Conscience* (Cambridge: Harvard Univ. Press, 1963), 200–203.

48. EW quoted in Stearns, *Cambridge Sketches,* 292–93; EW to Wife, Feb. 27, 1841, EW to Beriah Green, Mar. 26, 1841, July 8, 1842, EW to John, July 6, 1842, EW to Friend, May [?], 1844, EWP, LC; press clippings, no. 340, EWP, LC; *Chronotype,* Sept. 11, 12, 15, 18, 21, Oct. 5, 9, 12, 1846; *Commonwealth,* Apr. 15, Nov. 25, 1851; EW, *Household Stuff,* 157.

49. Richards, *Howe Letters* 2:340–41; William Davis to EW, Mar. 11, 1851, James R. Wright to EW, Mar. 11, 1851, EW to James, Mar. 21, 1851 (EW told his brother, "I merely witnessed the rescue of Shadrack without lifting a finger or uttering a word to aid it"), EW to Brothers and Sisters, July 23, 1851, EWP, LC; *Liberator,* Feb. 21, 28, 1851.

50. *Commonwealth,* Dec. 20, 1851; Robert F. Lucid, ed., *The Journal of Richard Henry Dana, Jr.,* 3 vols. (Cambridge: Harvard Univ. Press, 1968), 2:413–14, 492, 511, 513; Charles Francis Adams, *Richard Henry Dana: A Biography,* 2 vols. (Boston: Houghton Mifflin, 1890), 1:216–17.

51. EW to Brother and Sister Hanford, Dec. 31, 1855, Samuel Sewall to EW, May 13, 1852, EWP, LC; *Commonwealth,* Nov. 25, 1851, May 26, 1852; Richards, *Howe Letters* 2:389; Wrights, *Wright,* 201–2; John Mayfield, *Rehearsal for Republicanism: Free Soil and the Politics of Antislavery* (Port Washington: Kennikat Press, 1980), 161–65; Lawrence J. Friedman, " 'Pious Fellowship,' " 253–54.

52. Beriah Green quoted in Wrights, *Wright,* 212; EW to Beriah Green, Oct. 8, 1860, EWP, LC.

53. EW to Beriah Green, Oct. 8, 1860, EWP, LC; *Liberator,* Aug. 15, 1856.

54. Henry Wilson, *History of the Rise and Fall of the Slave Power in America,* 3 vols. (Boston: James R. Osgood, 1872–77), 1:259–60. For an insightful analysis of Elizur's relationship to the Bird Club that has informed this study, see Friedman, *Gregarious Saints,* 244–52; and his " 'Pious Fellowship,' " 252–55.

55. EW to Charles Scribner, May 19, 1854, EWP, LC.

Part IV ACTUARY

10. Commissioner of Life Insurance

1. *North American Review* 143 (1886): 144–45.

2. Ibid.

3. Ibid.; *Massachusetts Insurance Reports* 4(1859): 3, 10(1865): 304; EW, *Curiosity of Law,* 20; *Chronotype,* May 17, 1847; *Hunt's Merchants' Magazine* 27 (1852): 541; Wrights, *Wright,* 221–23; R. Carlyle Buley, *The American Life Convention, 1906–1952: A Study in the History of Life Insurance,* 2 vols. (New York: Appleton-Century-Crofts, 1953), 1:57.

4. EW to Wife, Mar. 3, 1844, EWP, LC; *North American Review* 143 (1886): 144–45.

5. F. Julius Le Moyne to EW, Sept. 12, 1845, EWP, LC. See also Henretta, "Families and Farms"; Viviana Zelizer, *Morals and Markets: The Development of Life Insurance in the United States* (New York: Columbia Univ. Press, 1979), 25–88.

6. *Insurance Monitor* 19 (1871): 587; *North American Review* 143 (1886): 144–45; Charles Dickens, *The Life and Adventures of Martin Chuzzlewit* (Baltimore: Penguin, 1968), 495–517; J. Owen Stalson, *Marketing Life Insurance: Its History in America* (Cambridge: Harvard Univ. Press, 1942), 287.

7. EW, *Curiosity of Law,* 18, 20; *Chronotype,* Feb. 11, 17, 1846; EW to Philo, July 1, 1845, EWP, LC.

8. EW, *The "Bible of Life Insurance"* (Chicago: American Conservation Co., 1932), 76; *Chronotype,* Feb. 18, July 13, 1846, May 17, 1847, Feb. 17, 1849; George Atwood to EW, Oct. 18, 1845, EW to Philo, July 1, 1854, EWP, LC.

9. *Mass. Insurance Reports* 7 (1862): 132; *Chronotype,* Apr. 7, 10, 23, 1846, May 17, June 8, 1847.

10. *Chronotype* Feb. 18, Mar. 17, 24, 28, Apr. 3, 7, 22, 23, 30, June 3, Nov. 3, 1846, Mar. 26, May 16, June 8, 12, 16, 1847.

11. EW to Brothers and Sisters, Feb. 22, 1853, EWP, LC; *Insurance Monitor* 19 (1871): 587; EW, *Valuation Tables on the Combined Experience Rate of Mortality, for the Use of Life Insurance Companies* (Boston: William White, 1853), 3–4; R. Carlyle Buley, *The Equitable Life Assurance Society of the United States, 1859–1964,* 2 vols. (New York: Appleton-Century-Crofts, 1967), 1:58–59; Wrights, *Wright,* 221–22, 229–31; Morton Keller, *The Life Insurance Enterprise, 1885–1910: A Study in the Limits of Corporate Power* (Cambridge: Harvard Univ. Press, 1963), 60–61.

12. EW, *Valuation Tables,* 3–4; *Hunt's Merchants' Magazine* 3 (1854): 734.

13. EW to Brother and Sister Hanford, Dec. 31, 1855, EW to Wife and Children, Dec. 24, 1857, "Circular, 1855," [advertisement for the *Valuation Tables*], EWP, LC; EW, *Curiosity of Law,* 20.

14. *Hunt's Merchants' Magazine* 27 (1852): 544.

15. [EW], "House...No. 91," *Report of the Committee on Mercantile Affairs and Insurance* (Boston, 1855); EW, *Curiosity of Law,* 21; *Massachusetts Acts and Resolves, 1854,* chap. 453, sec. 42, pp. 395–96; *Mass. Acts and Resolves, 1855,* chap. 124, pp. 569–72; Wrights, *Wright,* 232n; Charles K. Knight, *The History of Life Insurance in the United States to 1870* (Philadelphia: University of Pennsylvania, 1920), 128; H. Roger Grant, *Insurance Reform: Consumer Action in the Progressive Era* (Ames: Iowa State Univ. Press, 1979), 172n.

16. *Mass. Acts and Resolves, 1858,* chap. 177, pp. 152–53; EW, *Curiosity of Law,* 21; EW to Brothers and Sisters, May 3, 1858, EWP, LC.

17. *Mass. Insurance Reports* 6(1861):130, 9(1864):282, 10(1865):245; *North American Review* 97 (1863): 317; Stalson, *Marketing Life Insurance,* 347.

18. *Mass. Insurance Reports* 4(1859):17; 7(1862):137, 10(1865):288; EW, *Curiosity of Law,* 8.

19. *Annual Report of the Commissioner of Patents for the Year 1853* (Washington, 1854), 1:100; "Industrial Exhibition, Sept. 15, 1855," EW to Brothers and Sisters, Feb. 22, 1853, EW to G. L. Whittley, Nov. 5, 1855, EW to Hanford, June 17, 1857, EW to Brother and Sister Hanford, Dec. 31, 1855, EWP, LC; *Annual Report of the Commissioner of Patents for the Year 1869* (Washington, 1871), 1:305; EW, *"Bible of Life Insurance,"* 78–79; Stearns, *Cambridge Sketches,* 301; Buley, *Equitable* 2:1270.

20. *Mass. Insurance Reports,* "Introduction," iii, 4(1859):17–18, 7(1862):136; EW, *"Bible of Life Insurance,"* 78; *Insurance Times* 1 (Oct.–Nov. 1868): 448.

21. EW to E. K. Foster, Nov. 18, 1861, Benjamin Silliman to EW, July 5, 17, 26, 1862, EW to Benjamin Silliman, July 7, 19, 1862, Case 1, EWP, BL; EW, *"Bible of Life Insurance,"* 80; *Mass. Insurance Reports* 4(1859):31–32, 7(1962):137, 8 (1863):215–20; Stalson, *Marketing Life Insurance,* 348; Buley, *Equitable* 1:78; Wrights, *Wright,* 234.

22. *Mass. Insurance Reports* 4 (1859): suppl., 36–49, 5(1860): app., 97, 87–101; Wrights, *Wright,* 234–35.

23. *Mass. Insurance Reports* 4(1859):14, 18, 21, 7 (1862):136; 8(1863):225, 231, 9(1864):234–35, 269–70, 273, 283–84, 10(1865):298–302; Stalson, *Marketing Life Insurance,* 348; Knight, *History,* 153.

24. "Was John Brown Right?" Oct. 12, 1860, box 22, vol. 1, [unknown newspaper editorial], Mar. 8, 1862, EWP, LC; EW, *An Eye Opener for the Wide Awakes* (Boston: Thayer and Eldridge, 1860), 8, 15–16, 22–24, 32–39; Wrights, *Wright,* 213.

25. *New York Tribune,* Dec. 6, 1860, box 22, vol. 1, "To the Young Men of Massachusetts, Sept. 10, 1861," [press clipping], EWP, LC; EW, *Household Stuff,* 138; EW, *The Lesson of St. Domingo: How to Make the War Short and the Peace Long* (Boston: A. Williams, 1861), 21.

26. EW to Salmon Chase, May 4, 1861, EWP, LC; *Commonwealth,* Feb. 27, Apr. 10, 1863, Mar. 5, 11, 1864; EW, *Household Stuff,* 138–39; EW, *The Programme of Peace. By a Democrat of the Old School* (Boston: Ticknor and Fields, 1862), 15–21.

27. EW, *Programme,* 14; EW to N. P. Banks, Jan. 3, 1861, EW to Mary, May 18, 1862, EW to The Honorable Alexander H. Rice, May 29, 1862, EW to the *New York Tribune,*

Mar. 22, 1863, "The Moral Effect, 1864," EWP, LC; *Commonwealth,* June 19, 1863, May 1, 13, 27, Dec. 17, 1864; EW to Salmon P. Chase quoted in Gerteis, *Morality and Utility,* 185.

28. EW, *Programme,* 22; *The Equality of All Men before the Law Claimed and Defended in Speeches by the Honorable William D. Kelley, Wendell Phillips, and Frederick Douglass, and Letters from Elizur Wright and William Heighton* (Boston: George C. Rand and Avery, 1865), 40–41; EW to Salmon P. Chase quoted in Gerteis, *Morality and Utility,* 154.

29. *Daily Advertiser,* June 27, 1867, "The Fire in the Rear, Oct. 5, 1868," "What the Matter Is," "Did the Proclamation Emancipate," box 22, vol. 1, EWP, LC; EW to Lysander Spooner, Apr. 10, 1866, Lysander Spooner Papers, New York Historical Society.

30. EW to Salmon Chase, Nov. 13, 1868, "Removing a Non-Executive," scrapbook, box 24, *New York Tribune,* Mar. 26, 1868, box 22, "Some Questions," box 22, "A Good Samaritan Wanted," box 22, "Let Us Have Peace, Nov. 9, 1868," box 22, EWP, LC. See Merton L. Dillon, "The Failure of the American Abolitionists," *Journal of Southern History* 25 (1959): 159–77.

31. *Mass. Insurance Reports* 4(1959):24–27, 5(1860):67–69, 72, 86; 6(1861):125–31, 7(1862):165–69; Stearns, *Cambridge Sketches,* 301.

32. EW to George B. Ayer, Aug. 5, 1864, Case 1, EWP, BL; *Mass. Acts and Resolves, 1861,* chap. 186, pp. 495–96; *Mass. Insurance Reports* 5 (1860): 72–86; Wrights, *Wright,* 237–38; Knight, *History,* 147–48; J. David Cummins, *Development of Life Insurance Surrender Values in the United States* (Philadelphia: S. S. Huebner Foundation for Insurance Education, 1973), 19–23.

33. EW, *Curiosity of Law,* 24–41, 57–58; EW, [Untitled MS of Oct. 29, 1864], case 3, EWP, BL; "Massachusetts Retrograding," *Insurance Monitor,* [n.d.], scrapbook, box 24, EWP, LC.

34. EW, *Curiosity of Law,* 56–60.

35. *Insurance Times* 8 (1875): 239; EW, *Curiosity of Law,* 56–60.

36. EW, *Curiosity of Law,* 51.

37. EW, *Curiosity of Law,* 4, 61; EW and George Sargent, "Memorial to the House of Representatives of Massachusetts, May 21, 1866," case 3, EWP, LC; *Mass. Acts and Resolves, 1866,* Chap. 255, p. 243; *Mass. Acts and Resolves, 1867,* chap. 267, pp. 663–65; *Daily Advertiser,* May 17, 1866.

38. EW, "Petition to the Senate and the House of Representatives of Massachusetts, Jan. 22, 1867," case 3, EWP, BL; EW, *Curiosity of Law,* 68–69; Burton J. Hendrick, *The Story of Life Insurance* (New York: McClure, Phillips, 1907), 79.

39. I. Eadie to EW, July 18, 1866, J. L. Halsey to EW, July 18, 1866, Samuel R. Shipley to EW, July 30, 1866, Frederick Winston to EW, Nov. 6, 1866, J. E. Sanford to Alexander H. Bullock, July 24, 1867, Bullock to Sanford, July 27, 1867, Sanford to EW, July 31, 1867, Stephen English to EW, Sept. 2, 1869, case 1, EWP, BL; EW, *Curiosity of Law,* 13, 68–69.

40. EW, *Curiosity of Law,* 68–69; EW, *Myron Holley;* Wrights, *Wright,* 239.

11. Independent Life Insurance Reformer

1. EW, MS of July 7, 1882, case 3, EWP, BL; EW, *The Politics and Mysteries of Life Insurance* (Boston: Lee and Shepard, 1873), 17–18; EW, *Elements of Life Insurance for the*

Use of Family Banks (Boston: Wright and Potter, 1876), 28–29; *North American Review* 143 (1886): 147; Wrights, *Wright,* 250.

2. EW, *Elements,* 3–6, 20, 26; EW, *Traps Baited with Orphan; Or, What is the Matter with Life Insurance* (Boston: James R. Osgood, 1877), 17–19, 54; EW, *Politics,* 175–78; *Insurance Times* 2 (1869); Cummins, *Development,* 29–30; Wrights, *Wright,* 243.

3. EW, *Life Insurance: The Way to Make It a Public Benefit with the Least Injury to Individuals* [n.p., 1871], 21; EW, *Insurance and Self-Insurance: What Is Meant by Chapter 232 of the Acts of 1880* (Boston: A. Williams, 1880), 21–22; EW, *Traps,* 79; *Insurance Times* 2(1869):45–46, 339–40, 4(1871):193–99, 342a–c, 5(1872):574–574a, 815, 6(1873):783–84; *Insurance Monitor* 19(1871):586–90; *Boston Herald,* Feb. 14, Mar. 8, 1877, Apr. 27, 1880, Mar. 13, 1881, EW, MS of July 7, 1882, case 3, EWP, BL.

4. EW to S. H. White, Jan. 10, 1873, *Boston Herald,* Oct. 24, 1874, June 22, 1878, *Boston Evening Transcript,* Mar. 1, 1877, *Boston Commonwealth Bulletin,* Dec. 9, 1876, *Hartford Courant,* May 4, 1882, *New York Tribune,* Oct. 27, 1873, Mar. 9, 1874, May 6, 1879, *New York Daily Indicator,* Nov. 12, 1880, *Insurance World* 7 (1880): 35–36, *Baltimore Underwriter,* July 16, 1874, case 3, EWP, BL; *Insurance Monitor* 19 (1871):586–90, 27(1879):604; *Insurance Times* 6(1873):675–76, 783–84.

5. "To the Voters of the Second Middlesex Senatorial District," EW to A. H. Rice, Sept. 13, 1875, A. H. Rice to EW, Sept. 16, 1875, *Boston Evening Transcript,* Oct. 26, 1875, *Daily Advertiser,* Oct. 27, 1875, *Boston Herald,* Oct. 29, 1875, case 3, EWP, BL; *Insurance Times* 8 (1875): 691, 776.

6. *U.S. Reports* 93 (1876): 35–47; *Insurance Times* 9 (1876): 805–8; J. W. Foard to EW, Jan. 15, Sept. 22, 1875, May 5, 1876, case 1, EWP, BL; *Boston Daily Globe,* Nov. 17, 1877; *Boston Evening Transcript,* Nov. 13, 1876; *Boston Herald,* Oct. 26, 1876; *Commonwealth,* June 10, 1878, case 3, EWP, BL.

7. EW, *Traps,* 67–70, 79; EW, *Politics,* 93–140, 160–61; EW, *Savings Bank Life Insurance with Illustrative Tables, Analyzing the Premiums...* (Boston: Wright and Potter, 1872); "A Prize of One Thousand Dollars, Jan. 13, 1873," EW, MS of July 7, 1882, case 3, EWP, BL.

8. *New York Evening Post,* May 14, 1872; *New York Tribune,* Apr. 5, 1872; *Daily Advertiser,* Feb. 21, 1872, Feb. 24, 1874; *Chicago Chronicle,* Apr. 18, 1872, case 3, EWP, BL; Henry W. Johnson to EW, Feb. 1, Aug. 8, 1872, Erastus Lyman to EW, May 11, 1872, Charles M. Hibbard to EW, May 6, Sept. 3, 19, 1873, July 16, 1874, Oct. 31, 1876, J. A. Nichols to EW, Jan. 10, 1876, case 1, EWP, BL.

9. EW, *Report on the Union of Savings Bank and Life Insurance, to the Boston Board of Trade, Presented December 17, 1874* (Boston: Wright and Potter, 1874); "Meeting of Feb. 17, 1874, at the Boston Board of Trade," "Petition—American Family Bank—Sept. 7, 1874," case 3, EWP, BL.

10. *Mass. Acts and Resolves, 1876,* chap. 142, pp. 116–18; "The Best Investment for the Future, Nov. 4, 1876," [MSS on insurance matters, stray leaves], case 3, EWP, BL; *Insurance Journal,* Nov. 22, 1879, case 3, EWP, BL; *Mass. Insurance Reports* 8(1863):220–21, 9(1864):266–69, 10(1865):291.

11. EW, *Savings Bank Life Insurance,* 18.

12. EW, "Life Insurance for the Poor," *Journal of Social Science* 8 (May 1876): 154; EW, *Elements,* 30; *Mass. Insurance Reports* 10(1865):303; "Remarks of Elizur Wright before the Committee on Expenditures, April 5, 1870," case 3, EWP, BL; EW, *Insurance and Self-Insurance,* 1–2.

13. "Circular—Massachusetts Family Bank," case 3, EWP, BL; EW, *Traps,* 11. See also David Montgomery, *Beyond Equality: Labor and the Radical Republicans, 1862–1872* (New York: Knopf, 1967), 266–68, 275–77.

14. Ibid.

15. *Chronicle* 14 (1874):57.

16. *Insurance Times* 7(1874):43–44, 95–96, 421–22, 740, 8(1875):417, 9(1876):22–24, 10(1877):257, 436–38, 645; *Chronicle* 14 (1874): 57; *Insurance Monitor* 27 (1879): 238–39, 298–99, 538; *Safeguard,* Feb. 1875, *Hartford Courant,* Dec. 30, 1872, *New York Times* (from the *Hudson River Chronicle),* Dec. 18, 1878, case 3, EWP, BL. For EW's rejoinders, see *Boston Herald,* May 8, 1875, "An Open Letter to Frederick S. Winston, President of the Mutual Life Insurance Company of New York, Oct. 27, 1875," EW to Frederick S. Winston, Jan. 2, 1879, *New York Times,* Dec. 26, 1878, case 3, EWP, BL; Stephen English to EW, Aug. 13, 1874, EW to Stephen English, July 8, 1874, Emory McClintock, to EW, Dec. 23, 1879, case 1, EWP, BL.

17. EW, MS of Nov. 19, 1878, "Act to Amend the Charter of the Massachusetts Family Bank, April 26, 1877," case 3, EWP, BL; Stalson, *Marketing Life Insurance,* 497, 566–67; Louis Brandeis, "The Greatest Insurance Wrong," *Independent* 41 (Dec. 20, 1906): 1480. See Allan Gal, *Brandeis of Boston* (Cambridge: Harvard Univ. Press, 1980), 96–97.

18. *Boston Herald,* Feb. 19, Mar. 3, 1880, Feb. 20, 1881, "Arguments in Favor of Mr. Hastings' Surrender Value Bill as Compared with Commissioner Clarke's, March 25, 1880," "An Act to Regulate the Valuation and Fix the Minimum Cash Surrender Value of Life Insurance Policies [1879]," case 3, EWP, BL; *Mass. Acts and Resolves, 1880,* chap. 232, pp. 182–83.

19. Cummins, *Development,* 22–29, 71–72; David Brown Houston, "An Analysis of Elizur Wright's Life Insurance Reforms" (Ph.D. diss., University of Pennsylvania, 1959), 103–4, 110.

20. *Insurance Times* 10 (1877): 704; EW to W. D. Gibson, Dec. 16, 1881, EW to William A. Brewer, Jr., June 27, 1878, Brewer to EW, June 28, 1878, EW, MS of July 7, 1883, "Policyholders' Association of the United States [n.d.]," case 3, EWP, BL.

21. Emory McClintock to EW, Oct. 5, 1869, Apr. 1, 1871, Erastus Lyman to EW, Feb. 6, 1876, Sheppard Homans to EW, Mar. 14, May 5, 13, Dec. 10, 1870, J. F. Hopper to EW, May 15, 1885, case 1, EWP, BL; EW to Erastus Lyman, June 8, 1863, EW to James G. Batterson, May 11, 22, June 22, 1882, *Hartford Evening Post,* Dec. 14, 1880, *Hartford Courant,* May 4, 1882, [Broadside of Apr. 14, 1882 on the Hartford Life and Annuity Insurance Company], case 3, EWP, LC; Henry B. Hyde to EW, Apr. 17, 1883, VA19, 267, Henry Hyde Papers, Baker Library, Harvard University; Harold F. Williamson and Orange A. Smalley, *Northwestern Mutual Life: A Century of Trusteeship* (Evanston: Northwestern Univ. Press, 1957), 29–30, 60; Richard Hooker, *Aetna Life Insurance Company: Its First Hundred Years* (Hartford: Aetna Life Insurance Co., 1956), 73, 111.

22. EW, *Life Insurance,* 21; EW, *Traps,* 10; EW, *Politics,* 2–3, 68, 91.

23. Hendrick, *Story of Life Insurance,* 129–33; Keller, *Life Insurance,* 56; Roger L. Ranson and Richard Sutch, "Tontine Insurance and the Armstrong Investigation: A Case of Stifled Innovation, 1868–1905," *Journal of Economic History* 47 (1987): 379–90.

24. The charge is in Keller, *Life Insurance,* 58. See also Robert W. Cooper, *A Historical Analysis of the Tontine Principle with Emphasis on Tontine and Semi-Tontine Life Insurance Policies* (Philadelphia: S. S. Huebner Foundation for Insurance Education, 1972), 21; Buley, *Equitable,* 101–2, 296; Stalson, *Marketing Life Insurance,* 490; Houston, "Analysis,"

128; William Cahn, *A Matter of Life and Death: The Connecticut Mutual Story* (New York: Random House, 1970), 107–33.

25. *North American Review* 143 (1886): 148–49; *Insurance Times* 5(1872):509, 6(1873):769; EW, *Politics,* 204–5; Stephen English to EW, Aug. 21, 1872, D. P. Fackler to EW, Mar. 15, 1872, case 1, EWP, BL; EW, [Reprint of the New York County Anti-Monopoly League Letter of Jan. 29, 1883), box 2, EWP, BL; *Boston Herald,* Dec. 27, 1878, Oct. 30, 1881, *New York Daily Indicator,* June 19, 1882, *Chronicle,* Apr. 9, 1877, *Daily Advertiser,* Apr. 2, 1884, case 3, EWP, BL; Hendrick, *Story of Life Insurance,* 159; Houston, "Analysis," 129–30.

26. Hendrick, *Story of Life Insurance,* 133–58; Keller, *Life Insurance,* 16–18, 56–57; Buley, *American Life Convention* 1:101; Cooper, *Tontine Principle,* 10–14; Stalson, *Marketing Life Insurance,* 487–95.

27. H. P. Duclos to EW, Dec. 21, 1880, case 1, EWP, BL.

28. EW to Wife, [?], 1862, EWP, LC; EW to the Insurance Committee of the Mutual Life Insurance Company of New York, July 11, 1862, EW, MS of July 7, 1882, EW, "About That Projected Pension," n.d., *Hartford Courant,* May 4, 1882, EW, "An Open Letter to Frederick S. Winston, President of the Mutual Life Insurance Company of New York," n.d., case 3, EWP, BL; EW, *"Bible of Life Insurance,"* 82; *Insurance Times* 2(1869):709, 6(1873):566–69. After a bitter controversy with EW, Stephen English reneged on his 1873 confession; *Insurance Times* 15 (May 1882):282–83.

29. EW, "The Mutual Life," Nov. 19, 1878, case 1, EWP, BL; *Hartford Courant,* Dec. 18, 1872, *Daily Advertiser,* Sept. 6, 1873, EW, MS of July 7, 1882, case 3, EWP, BL; *Insurance Times Extra,* Jan. 20, 1873, 429; EW, *Politics,* 162–69; Houston, "Analysis," 111–17.

30. EW, MS of July 7, 1882, case 3, EWP, BL; *Insurance Times* 6(1873):567–69.

31. EW, Sheppard Homans, and David Parks Fackler, MS of Dec. 4, 1872, *Daily Advertiser,* Aug. 27, Sept. 6, 8, 12, 13, 18, 25, 1873, case 3, EWP, BL; Shepard B. Clough, *A Century of American Life Insurance: A History of the Mutual Life Insurance Company of New York, 1843–1943* (New York: Columbia Univ. Press, 1946), 141–42; Keller, *Life Insurance,* 16–17.

32. Sheppard Homans to EW, July 19, Aug. 20, Sept. 5, 16, Oct. 9, 1873, "Reply of Mr. Sheppard Homans to the Communication of Mr. Winston over the Signature of John M. Stuart, Secretary, Sept. 1, 1873," case 1, EWP, BL.

33. *Boston Herald,* Nov. 19, 1878, Hazron A. Johnson, Conrad N. Jordan, James W. McCullock to EW, Sheppard Homans, and David Parks Fackler, Dec. 26, 1878, case 3, EWP, BL; EW, "Remarks of Elizur Wright before the Judiciary Committee of the General Assembly of New York, On the 'Rebate Plan' of the Mutual Life Insurance Company, Feb. 19, 1879," EW, [Broadside in the Scrapbook Given by the Mutual Life Insurance Company of Newark, N.J., n.d.], case 3, EWP, BL; *New York Times,* Feb. 20, 1879.

34. *Insurance Times* 6 (1873): 233–34; Stephen English to EW, Jan. 12, 1874, EWP, BL.

35. *Insurance World* 7(1880); 35–36, *Republican,* July 13, 1874, case 3, EWP, BL; Stephen English to EW, Aug. 13, 18, Nov. 18, 1874, July 18, 1879, case 1, EWP, BL; *Insurance Times* 7 (1874):487–88, 561–64, 803–4, 9(1876):5; EW, *Politics,* 153–54.

36. H. B. Hyde to EW, Aug. 22, Sept. 6, 1873, EW to W. D. Gibson, Dec. 16, 1881, case 1, EWP, BL; H. B. Hyde to EW, Aug. 25, Sept. 6, 1873, Henry Hyde Papers; Hendrick, *Story of Life Insurance,* 90–91.

37. H. B. Hyde to Samuel G. Goodrich, Feb. 13, 1882, H. B. Hyde to Thomas Jordan, Apr. 17, 1883, Henry Hyde Papers; James W. Alexander to EW, Oct. 30, 1883, Apr. 1, July 3,

1884, Apr. 5, July 1, 1885, H. B. Hyde to EW, Oct. 3, 1884, Apr. 6, July 1, 1885, T. Doordan to EW, Oct. 3, 1885, Stephen English to EW, Nov. 20, 1883, case 2, EWP, BL.

38. James W. Alexander to EW, Apr. 1, 1884, Jan. 9, Mar. 12, 14, Oct. 24, 1885, case 2, EWP, BL.

39. *Insurance Monitor* 27(1879):298; *Mass. Insurance Reports* 6(1861):130, 10(1865):288, 345.

40. "Act to Incorporate the Chamber of Life Insurance of the United States, Dec. 11, 1867," "Report of the Committee on National Legislation to the Chamber of Life Insurance of the United States, Dec. 11, 1867," case 3, EWP, BL; R. Garrigas to EW, Mar. 20, 1865, Sheppard Homans to EW, May 5, 1865, Oct. 24, 1867, A. W. Kellog to EW, Jan. 31, Nov. 6, 1866, case 1, EWP, BL; EW, *Curiosity of Law,* 68–69; *Insurance Times* 1 (1868); 263–65, 459; Keller, *Life Insurance,* 194–242; Buley, *Equitable* 1:87–88; Stalson, *Marketing Life Insurance,* 781–83.

41. *U.S. Reports* 75 (1868): 86–76, 183; *Insurance Times* 3(1870):331–33, 847–49, 5(1872):29; *North American Review* 143(1886):142–50; *World Today* 15(1908):1276–83.

42. *Mass. Insurance Reports* 10(1865):345–46; *Insurance Times* 1(1868):324; "Report of the Committee on National Legislation to the Chamber of Life Insurance of the United States, Dec. 11, 1867," case 3, EWP, BL; Buley, *Equitable* 1:129.

43. Houston, "Analysis," 111.

44. EW, *Politics,* 114.

45. Ibid., 113.

Part V ATHEIST

12. President of the National Liberal League

1. EW, "Speech at the Heywood Indignation Meeting, Aug. 1, 1878," box 22, vol. 2, EWP, LC; *Proceedings of the Indignation Meeting Held in Faneuil Hall, Thursday Evening, August 1, 1878...*(Boston: Benjamin R. Tucker, 1878), 3–9, 51.

2. Stephen English, "Honorable Elizur Wright," *Insurance Times* 18 (1885): 637; James Bryce, *American Commonwealth* (New York: Macmillan, 1894), 718–19; James Turner, *Without God, Without Creed: The Origins of Unbelief in America* (Baltimore: Johns Hopkins Univ. Press, 1985), 114–15, 134, 260.

3. EW, *Myron Holley,* 234; C. P. Farrell, ed., *The Works of Robert G. Ingersoll,* 12 vols. (New York: Ingersoll, 1900), 12:409–10.

4. EW to Parents, Brothers, and Sisters, June 7, 1841, June 18, 1843, EW to James, Aug. 26, 1850, EW to Brothers and Sisters, May 3, 1858, EW to Beriah Green, Oct. 8, 1860, EWP, LC; *Chronotype,* Apr. 9, 1847.

5. *Insurance Times* 5 (1872):734–35; *Reformer,* Aug. 17, 1872, *Republican,* Oct. 2, 1872, *Medford Journal,* July 20, Sept. 7, 1872, "Civil Service Reform—Purify the Fountain, 1872," "About Political Conversion," EWP, LC.

6. *Medford Journal,* July 20, 1872, *Reformer,* Aug. 17, 1872, EWP, LC; EW quoted on the Klan in Gerteis, *Morality and Utility,* 203.

7. R. G. Ingersoll to EW, Aug. 19, 1879, EWP, LC; Gerteis, *Morality and Utility,* 207–8.

8. *Centennial Congress of Liberals* (Boston: National Liberal League, 1876), 7; "Confidential Circular," box 22, vol. 2, Pa to [?], Feb. 4, 1872, Francis E. Abbot to EW, Jan. 28, 1870, Jan. 1, 1872, May 5, 1873, Apr. 4, 1874, EWP, LC; *Index,* Mar. 7, 1878; Fred M. Rivers, "Francis Ellingwood Abbot: Free Religionist and Cosmic Philosopher," (Ph.D. diss., University of Maryland, 1970), 78–80.

9. *Index,* Apr. 6, 1872, Jan. 1, 1874, July 13, 1876; *Centennial Congress,* 6–8, 19–21, 64–68, 114–18, 169, 175; *Patriotic Address to the People of the United States, Adopted at Philadelphia on the Fourth of July, 1876 by the National Liberal League* (Boston: National Liberal League, 1876), 7–13, 15–16, 20, 22–23; Francis E. Abbot to EW, May 4, 1876, EWP, LC; Rivers, "Abbot," 168; Sydney Ahlstrom, "Francis Ellingwood Abbot: His Education and Active Career," 2 vols. (Ph.D. diss., Harvard University, 1952), 1:191–18; Sidney Warren, *American Freethought, 1860–1914* (New York: Columbia Univ. Press, 1943), 162.

10. Rivers, "Abbot," 74; EW, "Clippings," case 3, EWP, BL.

11. Robert Bremner, ed., *Traps for the Young by Anthony Comstock* (Cambridge: Harvard Univ. Press, 1967), vii–xxxi.

12. *Congressional Globe,* 42d Cong., 3d sess., 1871–72, 46, pts. 2 and 3, pp. 1240, 1436–37, 1525–26, 1571, 2004–5, and Appendix, vol. 42, pt. 3, p. 297; *U.S. Statutes,* vol. 19, chap. 186, p. 90.

13. Ibid.

14. James C. N. Paul and Murray L. Schwartz, *Federal Censorship: Obscenity in the Mail* (New York: Free Press of Glencoe, 1961), 18–29; Anthony Comstock, *Frauds Exposed* (New York: J. H. Brown, 1880), 526–39.

15. Bremner, *Anthony Comstock,* 186; Comstock, *Frauds,* 440; Comstock, "Vampire Literature," *North American Review* 153 (1891): 162. On the religious ferment of the age, see Paul Carter, *The Spiritual Crisis of the Gilded Age* (DeKalb: Northern Illinois Univ. Press, 1971).

16. Comstock, *Frauds,* 556; Comstock, "Vampire Literature," 160–71.

17. *Centennial Congress,* 157–62, 170.

18. Ezra H. Heywood, *Cupid's Yokes* (Princeton: Co-operative Publishing, 1876), 5–27; Ezra H. Heywood, *Free Speech* (Princeton: Co-operative Publishing, 1883?), 51; New York Society for the Suppression of Vice Papers, "Arrests, 1872–1884," 103–4, MS Room, LC; DeRobigne Mortimer Bennett, *Anthony Comstock: His Career of Cruelty and Crime* (New York: Liberal and Scientific Publishing House, 1878), 1060–61; Heywood Broun and Margaret Leech, *Anthony Comstock: Roundsman of the Lord* (New York: Albert and Charles Boni, 1927), 173–74, 179; Ahlstrom, "Abbot," 266n.

19. New York Society for the Suppression of Vice Papers, "Arrests, 1872–1884," 105–6; Bennett, *Comstock,* 1063–64.

20. *Index,* Dec. 20, 1877, May 23, 30, Sept. 19, Oct. 17, 1878; Ahlstrom, "Abbot," 219–28; Rivers, "Abbot," 105–8; Farrell, *Ingersoll* 12: 216; Orvin Larson, *American Infidel: Robert G. Ingersoll* (Secaucus: Citadel Press, 1967), 150.

21. *Index,* Dec. 22, 1877, Nov. 7, 1878; S. W. Green to EW, Oct. 29, 1878, "Letter Accepting the Presidency of the National Liberal League," box 22, vol. 2, EWP, LC; Farrell, *Ingersoll* 12: 216; Larson, *American Infidel,* 152.

22. EW to Nelly, Dec. 18, 1878, EWP, LC; *Index,* Mar. 20, Apr. 3, July 17, Oct. 16, Nov. 30, 1879; Ahlstrom, "Abbot," 239; Rivers, "Abbot," 108–9.

23. *Index,* May 15, Oct. 16, 1879; Francis E. Abbot to EW, July 31, 1879, Thaddeus B. Wakeman to EW, Nov. 20, 1879, *Boston Herald,* May 14, 1880, box 22, vol. 2, EWP, LC; Comstock, *Frauds,* 477–84.

24. *Index,* Apr. 3, May 15, July 17, Oct. 16. 1879; Comstock, *Frauds,* 392–93.

25. EW to Rev. Joseph Cook, n.d., box 24, "Free Thought," folder, EW to Rev. Joseph Cook, Jan. 2, 1880, box 22, vol. 2, EW to Timothy O. Howe, Feb. 15, 1882, "Address at the Chicago Convention of the National Liberal League in 1881," box 22, vol. 2, "Address at Paine Hall, March 30, 1879," press clipping no. 84, EWP, LC; *Index,* Dec. 27, 1877, May 15, 1879.

26. Francis E. Abbot to EW, Sept. 24, Nov. 5, 1879, Feb. 14, 16, 1880, A. L. Rawson to EW, June 2, Oct. 29, 1879, H. L. Green to EW, Nov. 2, 1879, EWP, LC; *Index,* Nov. 30, 1879.

27. *Index,* Oct. 16, Nov. 6, 1879; W. S. Bush to EW, Nov. 1, 1879, Robert G. Ingersoll to EW, Nov. 4, 1879, T. B. Wakeman to EW, Nov. 20, 1879, J. Winslow to EW, Nov. 27, Dec. 18, 1879, A. L. Rawson to EW, Oct. 29, 1879, EWP, LC.

28. *Index,* June 19, 1879; New York Society for the Suppression of Vice Papers, "Arrests, 1872–1884," 103–4; EW to the President of the U.S., Oct. 30, 1878, A. L. Rawson to EW, Nov. 16, 1878, Charles Devins to EW, Jan. 13, 1879, press clipping no. 338, EWP, LC; Charles R. Williams, ed., *Diary and Letters of Rutherford Burchard Hayes,* 5 vols. (Columbus: The Ohio State Archaeological and Historical Society, 1924), 3:518, 522–23.

29. Comstock, *Frauds,* 494; New York Society for the Supression of Vice Papers, "Arrests, 1872–1884," 1278; D. M. Bennett, *The Trial of D. M. Bennett... Upon the Charge of Depositing Prohibited Matter in the Mail* (New York: Truth Seeker, 1879), 165; A. L. Rawson to EW, June 2, 1879, EWP, LC.

30. EW to President Hayes, June 25, 1879, press clipping no. 338, D. M. Bennett to EW, June 28, 1879, T. B. Wakeman to EW, June 1, July 28, 1879, EWP, LC; *Index,* Oct. 16, 1879; Williams, *Hayes Letters* 3:563, 567, 5:67–68.

31. *New York Times,* May 3, 1880.

32. *Index,* Aug. 21, 1879; "A Convention for a Free People to Make a Free Land," box 22, vol. 2, press clipping no. 338, "Equality of Taxation and Inviolability of the Mails," box 22, vol. 2, EWP, LC; *The Third Annual Congress of the National Liberal League* (New York, n.d.), 1–11; Samuel P. Putnam, *Four Hundred Years of Freethought* (New York: Truth Seeker, 1894), 528–32.

33. *Third Annual Congress,* 28; "A Convention for a Free People to Make a Free Land," box 22, vol. 2, "Meeting of Liberals," press clipping no. 83, "Fourth Annual Congress," box 22, vol. 2, EWP, LC; "About Platforms, Nov. 29, 1880," case 3, EWP, BL; National Liberal League Records, 1876–79, pp. 90, 92, Pusey Library, Harvard University; *Index,* Oct. 2, 1879.

34. EW to Leland, Sept. 27, 1882, box 22, vol. 2, E. B. Foote to EW, Oct. 27, 1885, EWP, LC; *Third Annual Congress,* 45–48; Putnam, *Four Hundred Years,* 528–32, 538, 542–43; Ahlstrom, "Abbot," 243.

35. EW to Leland, Sept. 27, 1882, box 22, vol. 2, E. B. Foote to EW, Oct. 27, 1885, EWP, LC; *Third Annual Congress,* 45–48; Putnam, *Four Hundred Years,* 528–32, 538, 542–43.

36. Heywood, *Cupid's Yokes,* 4; Josephine S. Tilton to EW, Sept. 12, 1879, EWP, LC.

37. *Index,* Sept. 12, 1878; "Equal Taxation," press clippings nos. 145–47, EW to Francis E. Abbot, May 20, 1877, EWP, LC; "About Platforms, Nov. 29, 1880," case 3, EWP, BL.

38. *Index,* Feb. 28, 1873, July 5, 1877, Dec. 5, Sept. 12, 1878; "Letter Accepting the Presidency of the National Liberal League," box 22, vol. 2, EW to George Williams, Jan. 6, 1882, "Second Address at the Third Annual Congress of the National Liberal League," box 22, vol. 2, EWP, LC; Wrights, *Wright,* 307.

13. The Family, Death, and Nature

1. Selden Haines, *A Supplement to the Biographical Sketch of the Class of 1826, Yale College* (Rome: Sanford and Carr, 1876), 2:38.
2. EW to Leland, Sept. 27, 1882, box 22, vol. 2, EWP, LC; Stearns, *Cambridge Sketches,* 307–8; George E. Davenport, *A Lecture on the Middlesex Fells* (Medford: Press of Medford City News, 1893), 6–9; *Round about Middlesex Fells: Historical Guide Book* (Medford: Medford Historical Society, 1935), 4–5, 11.
3. EW to Brother James, Nov. 30, 1823, EWP, LC; H. P. Duclos to EW, Mar. 31, 1882, box 2, EWP, BL.
4. EW, *Middlesex Fells,* vii; Farrell, *Ingersoll* 12:411; Wrights, *Wright,* 325.
5. EW, *Myron Holley,* 306.
6. "Circular—Massachusetts Family Bank," case 3, EWP, BL; EW, *Household Stuff,* 32–33; EW to Wife, Feb. 3, 1841, EWP, LC.
7. *Insurance Times* 8 (1875): 239; Stephen English to EW, Feb. 15, 1873, Mar. 19, 1875, EWP, LC; EW, *Household Stuff,* 110 LC; Wrights, *Wright,* 277.
8. *Chronotype,* Oct. 23, 1846; EW to Sister Polly, Feb. 16, 1862, EW to Mary, May 18, 1862, EW to James, Aug. 26, 1850, press clippings, no. 243, no. 290, EWP, LC; EW, *Household Stuff,* 3, 9, 44, 64; *Index,* Feb. 7, 1878.
9. *Insurance Times* 8 (1875): 239; EW to Parents, Brothers, and Sisters, June 7, 1841, EW to James, Aug. 26, 1850, EW, *"Bible of Life Insurance,"* 75, Haines, *Supplement,* 95; EW, *Household Stuff,* 75.
10. EW to Wife, Apr. 17, 1844, EWP, LC; Wrights, *Wright,* 143.
11. EW to Beriah Green, Feb. 7, 1837, EW to Sister Polly, Feb. 16, 1862, EWP, LC; Wrights, *Wright,* 277. See also Sigmund Freud, "Mourning and Melancholia," in *Standard Edition of the Complete Psychological Work of Sigmund Freud,* 24 vols. (London: Hogarth Press and The Institute of Psycho-Analysis, 1955–74), 14:239–58; Erikson, *Childhood and Society,* 268–69; Erikson, *Adulthood* (New York: Norton, 1978), 26; Elizabeth Kübler-Ross, *On Death and Dying* (New York: Macmillan, 1969), 139–59; Adrian Vervoerdt, "Death and the Family," *Medical Opinion and Review* 1 (1966): 38–43; Albert Solnet and Morris Green, "Psychologic Considerations in the Management of Deaths in Pediatric Hospital Services: Part I, The Doctor and the Child's Family," *Pediatrics* 24 (1959): 106–12.
12. EW to Brother and Sister, May 3, 1858, EWP, LC.
13. EW, Sr., to EW, July 25, 1836, Jan. 7, 1840, Apr. 20, 1841, EW to Parents, May 24, 1835, EWP, LC; EW to Theodore Weld, Aug. 15, 1836, *Weld Letters* 1:323. Among Robert Jay Lifton's numerous writings, see *The Broken Connection: On Death and The Continuity of Life* (New York: Simon and Schuster, 1979).
14. EW to [fragment of a letter], Aug. 7, 1878, EWP, LC; Wrights, *Wright,* 346–47. See also Fischer, *Growing Old,* 108.

15. EW, *Middlesex Fells,* iii–iv. See also Donald J. Pisani, "Forests and Conservation," *Journal of American History* 72 (1985): 340–59.

16. EW, *Middlesex Fells,* 11, 16–23, 29, 47–48.

17. EW, *Middlesex Fells,* xi, 12–68; *Daily Advertiser,* Jan. 27, 1881; Wrights, *Wright,* 324.

18. EW, *Middlesex Fells*, xx–xxi, 77–119; *Mass. Acts and Resolves* (Boston, 1883), 200–202; Wrights, *Wright,* 321–22.

19. EW, *Middlesex Fells,* 77–119; *Round about Middlesex Fells,* 11, 15; Wrights, *Wright,* 319–23.

20. *Insurance Times* 1 (1868): 383; EW, *Middlesex Fells,* xxi, 136–39; J. B. Douglas to EW, Jan. 21, 1885, Charles A. Pillsbury to EW, Aug. 29, 1884, box 2, EWP, BL; Wrights, *Wright,* 327–30.

21. *Massachusetts Vital Statistics (Medford)* 14: 307, McCormick Building, Boston; H. S. Carruth to Ellen Martha Wright, Mar. 29, 1894, Ellen Martha Wright to Metropolitan Park Commission, Mar. 31, 1894, box 24, EWP, LC; Wrights, *Wright,* 325–26.

Epilogue: The Evolution of an Evangelical

1. *The Nation* 41 (Nov. 26, 1885): 448; Emerson, *Selected Writings,* 449–50.

Bibliography

PRIMARY SOURCES

Manuscript Collections

George Arents Research Library, Syracuse University, Syracuse, N.Y.
    Gerrit Smith Papers
Baker Library, Harvard Business School, Cambridge, Mass.
    Henry Hyde Papers
    Elizur Wright Papers
Beinecke Library, Yale University, New Haven, Conn.
    Connecticut Academy Papers
    Jeremiah Day Papers
Boston Public Library, Boston, Mass.
    American Anti-Slavery Society Papers
    William Lloyd Garrison Papers
    Rufus W. Griswold Papers
    Samuel May Papers
    Amos Phelps Papers
    Weston Family Papers
    Elizur Wright Papers
Case Western Reserve University Archives, Cleveland, Ohio
    Carroll Cutler Papers
    Charles B. Storrs Papers
    Case Western Reserve University Trustee Records
    Frederick C. Waite Papers
    Western Reserve Bible Society Papers
    Western Reserve College Church Papers
    Elizur Wright, Sr., Papers

Columbia University Library, New York, N.Y.
    John Jay Papers
Connecticut State Library, Hartford, Conn.
    Connecticut Land Records
    Connecticut Vital Records
Library of Congress, Washington, D.C.
    American Colonization Society Papers
    New York Society for the Suppression of Vice Papers
    Lewis Tappan Papers
    Elizur Wright Papers
Massachusetts Historical Society, Boston, Mass.
    Norcross Papers
New York Historical Society, New York, N.Y.
    Lysander Spooner Papers
Ohio Historical Center, Columbus, Ohio
    Portage County Recorder. Index to Deeds, 1795–1917
Nathan Marsh Pusey Library, Harvard University, Cambridge, Mass.
    Francis E. Abbott Papers
    National Liberal League Papers
Sterling Library, Yale University, New Haven, Conn.
    Bacon Family Papers
    Baldwin Family Papers
    College Discipline Papers
    John Hosmer Penniman Papers
    Silliman Family Papers
Western Reserve Historical Society, Cleveland, Ohio
    Peter Hitchcock Family Papers
    Elizur Wright, Sr., Papers

Newspapers and Periodicals

African Repository (Washington, D.C.)
American Tract Magazine (New York City)
Anti-Slavery Examiner (New York City)
Anti-Slavery Record (New York City)
Anti-Slavery Reporter (New York City)
Boston Evening Transcript
Boston Herald
Boston Recorder
Chicago Chronicle
Chronicle (New York City)
Chronotype (Boston)

Colored American (New York City)
Commonwealth (Boston)
Daily Advertiser (Boston)
Emancipator (New York City and Boston)
Free American (Boston)
Hartford Courant
Hartford Evening Post
Hudson Observer and Telegraph (Hudson, Ohio)
Human Rights (New York City)
Index (Toledo, Ohio, and Boston)
Insurance Monitor (New York City)
Insurance Times (New York City)
Insurance World (Pittsburgh)
Liberator (Boston)
Massachusetts Abolitionist (Boston)
Medford Journal (Medford, Mass.)
New York Daily Indicator (New York City)
New York Evening Post (New York City)
New York Times (New York City)
New York Tribune (New York City)
Ohio Observer (Hudson, Ohio)
Pennsylvania Freeman (Philadelphia)
Philanthropist (Cincinnati)
Quarterly Anti-Slavery Magazine (New York City)
Republican (Springfield, Mass.)
Rochester Freeman (Rochester, N.Y.)
Spirit of the Pilgrims (Boston)
Western Courier (Ravenna, Ohio)
Western Reserve Chronicle (Warren, Ohio)

Published Literature

Adams, Charles Francis. *Richard Henry Dana: A Biography.* 2 vols. Boston: Houghton Mifflin, 1890.

American Anti-Slavery Almanac for 1838. Boston: Isaac Knapp, n.d.

American Anti-Slavery Society Annual Reports. Vols. 1–8. New York: Dorr and Butterfield, 1834–40.

American Colporteur System. New York: American Tract Society, 1836.

Annals of the Congress of the United States, 1791–1793, 2nd Congress. Washington, D.C.: Gales and Seaton, 1849.

Annual Catalogues of Yale College, 1813–1836. N.p., n.d. Sterling Library, Yale University.

Annual Report of the Commissioner of Patents for the Year 1869. Vol. 1. Washington, D.C.: GPO, 1871.

Annual Reports of the Massachusetts Anti-Slavery Society, 1833–1842. Vols. 1–10. Westport: Negro Univ. Press, 1970.

Atkinson, Brooks, ed. *Selected Writings of Emerson.* New York: Random House, 1950.

Bacon, Leonard. *Slavery Discussed in Occasional Essays, 1833–1846.* New York: Baker and Scribner, 1846.

Baker v. Fales. Massachusetts Reports 16 (1820). Boston: Little, Brown, 1864.

Baritz, Loren, ed. *Sources of the American Mind.* 2 vols. New York: Wiley, 1966.

Barnes, Gilbert H., and Dwight L. Dumond, eds. *Letters of Theodore Dwight Weld, Angelina Grimké Weld, and Sarah Grimké, 1822–1844.* 2 vols. New York: Appleton-Century, 1934.

Beecher, Charles, ed. *Autobiography and Correspondence of Lyman Beecher.* 2 vols. New York: Harper, 1865.

Beecher, Lyman. *A Plea for the West.* Cincinnati: Truman and Smith, 1835.

_____. *Six Sermons on Intemperance, On the Nature, Occasions, Signs, Evils of Intemperance.* 1826. Boston: T. R. Marvin, 1828.

Bennett, DeRobigne Mortimer. *Anthony Comstock: His Career of Cruelty and Crime.* New York: Liberal and Scientific Publishing House, 1878.

_____. *The Trial of D. M. Bennett... Upon the Charge of Depositing Prohibited Matter in the Mail.* New Yorker: Truth Seeker, 1879.

Birney, Catherine H. *The Grimké Sisters, Sarah and Angelina Grimké.* Boston: Lee and Shepard, 1885.

Bremner, Robert, ed. *Traps for the Young by Anthony Comstock.* Cambridge: Harvard Univ. Press, 1967.

Catalogue of the Officers and Graduates of Yale University in New Haven, Connecticut, 1701–1904. New Haven: Tuttle, Morehouse and Taylor, 1905.

Centennial Congress of Liberals. Boston: National Liberal League, 1876.

Charter and By-Laws of the Massachusetts Family Bank. Boston: Albert J. Wright, 1877.

Child, Lydia Maria. *Letters of Lydia Maria Child.* Boston: Houghton Mifflin, 1883.

Comstock, Anthony. *Frauds Exposed.* New York: J. H. Brown, 1880.

Confession of Faith, Covenant, and Principles of Discipline and Practice of the Union Church in Groton, Massachusetts. Lancaster: Carter, Andrews, 1831.

Congressional Globe and Appendix. 42d Cong., 3d sess., pts. 2 and 3. Washington, D.C.: Office of Congressional Globe, 1873.

Covenant of the First Church, Groton, Massachusetts. Groton: George H. Brown, 1826.

Davenport, George E. *A Lecture on the Middlesex Fells.* Medford: Press of Medford City News, 1893.

Dexter, Franklin Bowditch. *Biographical Sketches of the Graduates of Yale College with Annals of the College History.* Vol. 4. New York: Henry Holt, 1907.

Dickens, Charles. *The Life and Adventures of Martin Chuzzlewit.* Baltimore: Penguin, 1968.

Dumond, Dwight L., ed. *Letters of James Gillespie Birney, 1831-1857.* 2 vols. New York: Appleton-Century, 1938.

The Equality of All Men before the Law Claimed and Defended in Speeches by the Honorable William D. Kelley, Wendell Phillips, and Frederick Douglass, and Letters from Elizur Wright and William Heighton. Boston: George C. Rand and Avery, 1865.

Farrell, C. P. *The Works of Robert G. Ingersoll.* 12 vols. New York: Ingersoll, 1900.

Fisher, James, ed. *The Westminster Assembly's Shorter Catechism Explained by Way of Questions and Answers.* Philadelphia: Presbyterian Board of Publishers, 1765.

Garrison, Wendell P., and Francis J. Garrison. *William Lloyd Garrison, 1805-1879: The Story of His Life Told by His Children.* 4 vols. Boston: Houghton Mifflin, 1894.

Garrison, William Lloyd. *Thoughts on African Colonization.* Boston: Garrison and Knapp, 1832.

Green, Beriah. *Four Sermons, Preached in the Chapel of the Western Reserve College, on the Lord's Days, November 18 and 25, December 2 and 9, 1832.* Cleveland: Printed at the Office of the Herald, 1833.

————. *Sermons and Other Discourses with Brief Biographical Hints.* New York: S. W. Green, 1860.

Green, Samuel Worcester. *Beriah Green.* New York: S. W. Green, 1875.

Goodell, William. *Slavery and Anti-Slavery.* New York: William Harned, 1852.

Goodrich, Chauncey. "Narrative of Revivals of Religion in Yale College." *American Quarterly Register* 10 (1838): 289-310.

Haines, Selden. *A Biographical Sketch of the Class of 1826, Yale College.* Utica: Roberts, 1876.

————. *A Supplement to the Biographical Sketch of the Class of 1826, Yale College.* Rome: Sanford and Carr, 1876.

Heywood, Ezra H. *Cupid's Yokes.* Princeton: Co-operative Publishing, 1876.

————. *Free Speech.* Princeton: Co-operative Publishing, 1883.

Historical Addresses Delivered at the Union Congregational Church, Groton, Mass., Wednesday, Jan. 1, 1902. N.p., n.d.

History of Litchfield County, Connecticut. Philadelphia: J. W. Lewis, 1881.

Homans, Sheppard. "The Insurance Crisis." *North American Review* 124 (1877): 254-64.

————. "Life Insurance in the United States." *Bankers' Magazine* 24 (1869): 447-53.

Hurd, John C. *The Law of Freedom and Bondage in the United States.* 2 vols. Boston: Little, Brown, 1858–62.

Johnson, Oliver. *William Lloyd Garrison and His Times.* Boston: B. B. Russell, 1881.

"Life Insurance." *North American Review* 97 (1863): 301–24.

"Life Insurance—Wright's Tables." *Hunt's Merchants' Magazine* 21 (1854): 734–36.

Lucid, Robert. F., ed. *The Journal of Richard Henry Dana, Jr.* 3 vols. Cambridge: Harvard Univ. Press, 1968.

McLoughlin, William G., ed. *Charles G. Finney: Lectures on Revivals of Religion.* Cambridge: Harvard Univ. Press, 1960.

Massachusetts Acts and Resolves, 1854. "An Act Concerning Insurance Companies." Chapter 453. Boston: Wright and Potter, 1854.

————, *1855.* "An Act to Establish a Board of Insurance Commissioners." Chapter 124. Boston: Wright and Potter, 1855.

————, *1858.* "An Act for the Better Establishment of the Board of Insurance Commissioners." Chapter 177. Boston: William White, 1858.

————, *1861.* "An Act to Regulate the Forfeitures of Policies of Life Insurance." Chapter 186. Boston: William White, 1861.

————, *1866.* "An Act in Relation to the Appointment of an Insurance Commissioner." Chapter 255. Boston: Wright and Potter, 1866.

————, *1867.* "An Act Relating to Insurance Companies." Chapter 267. Boston: Wright and Potter, 1867.

————, *1876.* "An Act to Incorporate the Massachusetts Family Bank." Chapter 142. Boston: Rand, Avery, 1877.

————, *1880.* "An Act Limiting the Forfeiture of Policies in Life Insurance Companies." Chapter 232. Boston: Rand, Avery, 1880.

————, *1883.* "An Act Authorizing Towns and Cities to Provide for the Preservation and Reproduction of Forests May 25, 1882." Chapter 255. Boston: Wright and Potter, 1883.

Mather, Cotton. *Bonifacius: Or Essay To Do Good.* Cambridge: Harvard Univ. Press, 1966.

Merrill, Walter M., ed. *The Letters of William Lloyd Garrison: I Will Be Heard, 1822–1835.* 6 vols. Cambridge: Harvard Univ. Press, 1971–81.

Minutes of the First Congregational Church, Hudson, Ohio, 1802–1837. Hudson: Hudson Library and Historical Society, 1966.

Ninetieth Anniversary of the First Congregational Church, Tallmadge, Ohio. N.p.: Jan. 21, 1899.

Patriotic Address to the People of the United States Adopted at Philadelphia on the Fourth of July, 1876 By the National Liberal League. Boston: National Liberal League, 1876.

Paul v. Virginia. 75 United States Reports, 1868. New York: Banks Law, 1911.

Proceedings in Commemoration of the Fiftieth Anniversary of the Settlement of Tallmadge. Akron: Beebe and Elkins, 1857.

Proceedings of the 56th Anniversary of the Settlement of Hudson. Hudson: E. F. Chittenden and Brother, 1856.

Proceedings of the Indignation Meeting Held in Faneuil Hall, Thursday Evening, August 1, 1878 to Protest against the Injury Done to the Freedom of the Press by the Conviction and Imprisonment of Ezra H. Heywood. Boston: Benjamin R. Tucker, 1878.

Proceedings of the New England Anti-Slavery Convention Held in Boston, May 24, 25, 26, 1836. Boston: Isaac Knapp, 1836.

Putnam, Samuel P. *Four Hundred Years of Freethought.* New York: Truth Seeker, 1894.

Report of the Commissioner of Patents for the Year 1853, Part I, Arts and Manufactures. Washington, D.C.: Beverly Tucker, 1854.

Richards, Laura E., ed. *Letters and Journals of Samuel Gridley Howe.* 2 vols. Boston: Dana Estes, 1909.

The Rights of the Congregational Churches of Massachusetts. The Results of an Ecclesiastical Council Convened at Groton, Massachusetts, July 17, 1826. Boston: T. R. Marvin, 1827.

Ruchames, Louis, ed. *The Letters of William Lloyd Garrison: A House Dividing against Itself, 1836–1840.* Vol. 2. Cambridge: Belknap Press, Harvard Univ. Press, 1971.

Smith, Adam. *An Inquiry into the Nature and Causes of the Wealth of Nations.* 2 vols. Oxford: Clarendon Press, 1976.

Solomon, Barbara M., ed. *Timothy Dwight: Travels in New England and New York.* 4 vols. Cambridge: Harvard Univ. Press, 1969.

Stearns, Frank P. *Cambridge Sketches.* 1905. Freeport: Books for Libraries Press, 1968.

Storrs, Charles Backus. *An Address Delivered at Western Reserve College, Hudson, Ohio, February 9, 1831.* Boston, 1831.

[Storrs, Richard Salter, II.] "Sketch of the Life of the Reverend Charles Backus Storrs, President of Western Reserve College." *American Quarterly Register* 6 (Nov. 1833): 84–89.

Stuart, Charles. "On the Use of Slave Labor." *Quarterly Anti-Slavery Magazine* 2 (Jan. 1837):153–70.

Sturtevant, Julian M. *Julian M. Sturtevant: An Autobiography.* New York: F. H. Revell, 1896.

Tappan, Lewis. *The Life of Arthur Tappan.* New York: Hurd and Houghton, 1870.

Todd, John. *John Todd: The Story of His Life Told Mainly by Himself.* New York: Harper, 1876.

———. *Religious Teachers Tested.* Cambridge: Hilliard and Brown, 1827.

Vital Records of Groton to the End of the Year 1849. Vol. 2. Salem: Essex Institute, 1927.

Wakeman, Thaddeus B. *The Comstock Laws Considered as to Their Constitutionality.* New York: D. M. Bennett, 1880.

Weld, Theodore, ed. "In Memory: Angelina Grimké Weld." [Includes Elizur Wright's Eulogy.] Boston: George H. Ellis, 1880.

Whittier, John Greenleaf. "The Anti-Slavery Convention of 1833." *Atlantic Monthly* 33 (Feb. 1874): 166–72.

Whittlesey, Charles. *A Sketch of the Settlement and Progress of the Township of Tallmadge, (No. 2, Range 10), Summit County, Ohio.* Cleveland: Sanford, 1842.

Williams, Charles Richard, ed. *Diary and Letters of Rutherford Burchard Hayes.* 5 vols. Columbus: Ohio State Archaeological and Historical Society, 1924.

Wilson, Henry. *History of the Rise and Fall of the Slave Power in America.* 3 vols. Boston: James R. Osgood, 1872–77.

Wright, Elizur. "Advance of the Abolition Cause." *Quarterly Anti-Slavery Magazine* 1 (Oct. 1835): 103–4.

_____. *Appeals for the Middlesex Fells and the Forests.* Medford: Medford Public Domain Club, 1893.

_____. *The "Bible of Life Insurance."* Chicago: American Conservation Co., 1932.

_____. *A Curiosity of Law: Or, A Respondent in the Supreme Judicial Court As a Judge in the General Court; And What Possibly Came of It.* Boston: By the Author, 1866.

_____. *Elements of Life Insurance for the Use of the Family Banks.* Boston: Wright and Potter, 1876.

_____. *An Eye Opener for the Wide Awakes.* Boston: Thayer and Eldridge, 1860.

_____, trans. *The Fables of La Fontaine.* 2 vols. Boston: Elizur Wright, Jr., and Tappan and Dennet, 1842.

_____. "House...No. 91." *Report of the Committee on Mercantile Affairs and Insurance.* Boston: House of Representatives, 1855.

_____. *Household Stuff and Some Other Things.* Boston: Privately printed, 1866.

_____. *Insurance and Self-Insurance: What Is Meant by Chapter 232 of the Acts of 1880.* Boston: A. Williams, 1880.

_____. *A Lecture on Tobacco, Delivered in the Chapel of the Western Reserve College, Hudson, Ohio, May 29, 1832* (Cleveland: Published by the Request of the Students, 1832.

_____. *The Lesson of St. Domingo: How to Make the War Short and the Peace Long.* Boston: A. Williams, 1861.

_____. "Life Insurance." *North American Review* 143 (July 1886): 142–50.

_____. *Life Insurance: The Way to Make It a Public Benefit with the Least Injury to Individuals.* N.p., 1871.

_____. "Life Insurance for the Poor." *Journal of Social Science Containing the Transactions of the American Association* 8 (May 1876): 147–57.

_____. *Massachusetts Reports on Life Insurance, 1859–1865. By the Insurance Commissioners. With an Appendix by Elizur Wright.* Boston: Wright and Potter, 1865.

_____. *Myron Holley and What He Did for Liberty and True Religion.* Boston: Elizur Wright, 1882.

_____. *The Northern Pacific Railroad: By a Friend of the Road and An Enemy of Placing Stock, Be It Cash or Water, Where It Will Do the Most Good.* Boston: Lee and Shepard, 1874.

_____. Obituary. *Nation* 41 (Nov. 26, 1885): 448.

_____. *Perforations in the "Latter-Day Pamphlets," By One of the Eighteen Millions of Bores.* Boston: Phillips, Sampson, 1850.

_____. *A Poem Delivered before the Phi Beta Kappa Society in Yale College, August 20, 1845.* New Haven: B. L. Hamlen, 1846.

_____. *The Politics and Mysteries of Life Insurance.* Boston: Lee and Shepard, 1873.

_____. *The Programme of Peace. By a Democrat of the Old School.* Boston: Ticknor and Fields, 1862.

_____. "The Regulation of Life Insurance." *Hunt's Merchants' Magazine* 28 (Nov. 1852): 541–46.

_____. "The Relations of Debt and Money." *North American Review* 124 (Jan. 1877): 417–34.

_____. "Reminiscences of Groton during the Years 1826 and 1827." *Groton Historical Series.* No. 2. Groton, Mass., 1884. 1–14.

_____. *Report on the Union of Savings Bank and Life Insurance, to the Boston Board of Trade, Presented December 17, 1874.* Boston: Wright and Potter, 1874.

_____. *Savings Bank Life Insurance with Illustrative Tables, Analyzing the Premiums....* Boston: Wright and Potter, 1872.

_____. *The Sin of Slavery and Its Remedy: Containing Some Reflections on the Moral Influence of African Colonization.* New York: Printed for the Author, 1833.

_____. "Slavery and Its Ecclesiastical Defenders." *Quarterly Anti-Slavery Magazine* 1 (July 1836): 341–74.

_____. "Some Aspects of Life Insurance." *North American Review* 136 (Jan. 1883): 277–83.

_____. *Tables on the "American" Rate of Mortality, at $4^1/_2$ Per Cent, for Calculating Reserves and Insurance Values.* Boston: Wright and Potter, 1872.

_____. *Traps Baited with Orphan; Or, What is the Matter with Life Insurance.* Boston: James R. Osgood, 1877.

_____ . *Valuation Tables on the Combined Experience Rate of Mortality, for the Use of Life Insurance Companies.* Boston: William White, 1853.

Wright, Elizur, Sr. "Description of an Air Pump Invented (By Himself)." *Memoirs of the Connecticut Academy of Arts and Sciences* 1 (1810): 120–30.

_____ . "A Discourse on the Different Views That Have Been Taken of the Theory of Fluxions." *American Journal of Science and Arts* 16 (1829): 53–60.

_____ . *The District School, According to the Lancasterian Method of Teaching.* Oberlin: Printed at the Evangelist Office, 1843.

_____ . "On the Application of Fluxional Ratio to Particular Cases." *American Journal of Science and Arts* 25 (1834): 93–103.

_____ . "A Theory of Fluxions." *American Journal of Science and Arts* 14 (1828): 330–50.

SECONDARY SOURCES

Books

Abzug, Robert H. *Passionate Liberator: Theodore Dwight Weld and the Dilemma of Reform.* New York: Oxford Univ. Press, 1980.

Allmendinger, David F., Jr. *Paupers and Scholars: The Transformation of Student Life in Nineteenth-Century New England.* New York: St. Martin's Press, 1975.

Allport, Gordon. *Becoming: Basic Considerations for a Psychology of Personality.* New Haven: Yale Univ. Press, 1955.

Bailyn, Bernard. *The Ideological Origins of the American Revolution.* Cambridge: Harvard Univ. Press, 1967.

Bainton, Roland H. *Yale and the Ministry.* New York: Harper, 1957.

Barker, Anthony J. *Captain Charles Stuart: Anglo-American Abolitionist.* Baton Rouge: Louisiana State Univ. Press, 1986.

Barnes, Gilbert H. *The Antislavery Impulse, 1830–1844.* New York: Harcourt, Brace and World, 1933.

Barney, William L. *The Passage of the Republic: An Interdisciplinary History of Nineteenth-Century America.* Lexington: Heath, 1987.

Billington, Ray A. *The Protestant Crusade, 1800–1860: A Study of the Origins of American Nativism.* New York: Macmillan, 1938.

Blos, Peter. *On Adolescence: A Psychoanalytic Interpretation.* New York: Free Press of Glencoe, 1962.

Bodo, John R. *The Protestant Clergy and Public Issues, 1812–1848.* Princeton: Princeton Univ. Press, 1954.

Bolt, Christine, and Seymour Dresher, eds. *Antislavery Religion and Reform: Essays in Memory of Roger Anstey.* Folkestone, Eng.: W. Dawson, 1980.

Bond, Beverly, Jr. *The Civilization of the Old Northwest: A Study of Political, Social and Economic Development, 1788-1812*. New York: Macmillan, 1934.

Boyer, Paul S. *Purity in Print: The Vice-Society Movement and Book Censorship in America*. New York: Scribner, 1968.

Broun, Heywood, and Margaret Leech. *Anthony Comstock: Roundsman of the Lord*. New York: Albert and Charles Boni, 1927.

Brown, Richard D. *Modernization: The Transformation of American Life, 1600-1865*. New York: Hill and Wang, 1976.

Bruchey, Stuart. *The Roots of American Economic Growth, 1607-1861: An Essay in Social Causation*. New York: Harper and Row, 1965.

Buley, R. Carlyle. *The American Life Convention, 1906-1952: A Study in the History of Life Insurance*. 2 vols. New York: Appleton-Century-Crofts, 1953.

_____. *The Equitable Life Assurance Society of the United States, 1859-1964*. 2 vols. New York: Appleton-Century-Crofts, 1967.

_____. *The Old Northwest: Pioneer Period, 1815-1840*. Vol. 1. Bloomington: Indiana Univ. Press, 1951.

Bullock, F. W. B. *Evangelical Conversion in Great Britain, 1696-1845*. St. Leonards-on-the-Sea, Eng.: Budd and Gillett, 1959.

Bushman, Richard L. *From Puritan to Yankee: Character and the Social Order in Connecticut, 1690-1765*. New York: Norton, 1967.

Byrce, James. *American Commonwealth*. New York: Macmillan, 1894.

Cahn, William. *A Matter of Life and Death: The Connecticut Mutual Story*. New York: Random House, 1970.

Calhoun, Daniel. *Professional Lives in America: Structure and Aspiration, 1750-1850*. Cambridge: Harvard Univ. Press, 1965.

Carter, Paul. *The Spiritual Crisis of the Gilded Age*. DeKalb: Northern Illinois Univ. Press, 1971.

Clark, Sydney A. *The First Hundred Years of the New England Mutual Life Insurance Company, 1835-1935*. Concord: New England Mutual Life Insurance Co., 1935.

Clough, Shepard B. *A Century of American Life Insurance: A History of the Mutual Life Insurance Co. of New York, 1843-1943*. New York: Columbia Univ. Press, 1946.

Coben, Stanley, and Lorman Ratner, eds. *The Development of an American Culture*. Englewood Cliffs: Prentice Hall, 1970.

Cochran, Thomas C. *Frontiers of Change: Early Industrialism in America*. New York: Oxford Univ. Press, 1981.

Cole, Charles C. *The Social Ideas of Northern Evangelists*. New York: Columbia Univ. Press, 1954.

Cooke, George W. *Unitarianism in America: A History of Its Origin and Development*. Boston: American Unitarian Association, 1902.

Cooper, Robert W. *A Historical Analysis of the Tontine Principle with Emphasis on Tontine and Semi-Tontine Life Insurance Policies.* Philadelphia: S. S. Huebner Foundation for Insurance Education, 1972.

Cott, Nancy. *The Bonds of Womanhood: "Woman's Sphere" in New England, 1780–1835.* New Haven: Yale Univ. Press, 1977.

Cover, Robert M. *Justice Accused: Antislavery and the Judicial Process.* New Haven: Yale Univ. Press, 1975.

Cramer, Clarence H. *Case Western Reserve: A History of the University, 1826–1876.* Boston: Little, Brown, 1976.

Cross, Whitney R. *The Burned-Over District.* New York: Harper and Row, 1965.

Cummins, J. David. *The Development of Life Insurance Surrender Values in the United States.* Philadelphia: S. S. Huebner Foundation for Insurance Education, 1973.

Cutler, Carroll. *A History of Western Reserve College during Its First Half Century, 1826–1876.* Cleveland: Crockers Publishing House, 1876.

Daniels, Bruce C. *The Connecticut Town: Growth and Development.* Middletown: Wesleyan Univ. Press, 1979.

Davis, David B. *The Problem of Slavery in the Age of Revolution, 1770–1823.* Ithaca: Cornell Univ. Press, 1975.

Dawley, Alan. *Class and Community: The Industrial Revolution in Lynn.* Cambridge: Harvard Univ. Press, 1976.

Degler, Carl N. *At Odds: Women and the Family in America from the Revolution to the Present.* New York: Oxford Univ. Press, 1980.

DeMause, Lloyd, ed. *The History of Childhood.* New York: Psychohistory Press, 1974.

Demos, John. *A Little Commonwealth: Family Life in Plymouth Colony.* New York: Oxford Univ. Press, 1970.

Douglas, Ann. *The Feminization of American Culture.* New York: Knopf, 1977.

Doyle, William B., ed. *A Centennial History of Summit County, Ohio and Representative Citizens.* 2 vols. Chicago: Biographical Publishing, 1908.

Duberman, Martin, ed. *The Antislavery Vanguard: New Essays on the Abolitionists.* Princeton: Princeton Univ. Press, 1965.

Dumond, Dwight L. *Antislavery: The Crusade for Freedom in America.* New York: Norton, 1961.

Ellis, George E. *A Half-Century of the Unitarian Controversy with Particular Reference to Its Origins, Its Course, and Its Prominent Subjects among the Congregationalists of Massachusetts.* Boston: Crosby, Nichols, 1857.

Erikson, Erik H., *Childhood and Society.* New York: Norton, 1950.

_____. *Life History and the Historical Moment.* New York: Norton, 1978.

_____. *Young Man Luther: A Study in Psychoanalysis and History.* New York: Norton, 1958.

_____, ed. *Adulthood.* New York: Norton, 1978.

Filler, Louis J. *The Crusade against Slavery, 1830–1860.* New York: Harper, 1960.

Fischer, David Hackett. *Growing Old In America.* New York: Oxford Univ. Press, 1978.

Fladeland, Betty. *James Gillespie Birney: Slaveholder to Abolitionist.* Ithaca: Cornell Univ. Press,.1955.

————. *Men and Brothers: Anglo-American Antislavery Cooperation.* Urbana: Univ. of Illinois Press, 1972.

Fleming, Sanford. *Children and Puritanism: The Place of Children in the Life and Thought of the New England Churches, 1620–1847.* New Haven: Yale Univ. Press, 1933.

Fliegelman, Jay. *Prodigals and Prophets: The American Revolution against Patriarchal Authority.* Cambridge: Harvard Univ. Press, 1982.

Flugel, J. C. *The Psycho-Analytic Study of the Family.* London: Hogarth Press, 1921.

Fogel, Robert W., and Stanley L. Engerman. *Time on the Cross: The Economics of American Negro Slavery.* Boston: Little, Brown, 1974.

Foner, Eric. *Free Soil, Free Labor, Free Men: The Ideology of the Republican Party before the Civil War.* New York: Oxford Univ. Press, 1970.

————. *Politics and Ideology in the Age of the Civil War.* New York: Oxford Univ. Press, 1980.

Foner, Philip S. *Business and Slavery: The New York Merchants and the Irrepressible Conflict.* Chapel Hill: Univ. of North Carolina Press, 1941.

Foster, Charles I. *An Errand of Mercy: The Evangelical United Front, 1790–1837.* Chapel Hill: Univ. of North Carolina Press, 1960.

Fredrickson, George M. *The Black Image in the White Mind: Debate on Afro-American Character and Destiny, 1817–1914.* New York: Harper and Row, 1971.

Freud, Anna. *The Ego and the Mechanism of Defense.* New York: International Univ. Press, 1946.

Freud, Sigmund. *Standard Edition of the Complete Psychological Works of Sigmund Freud.* 24 vols. London: Hogarth Press and The Institute of Psycho-Analysis, 1955–74.

Friedman, Lawrence J. *Gregarious Saints: Self and Community in American Abolitionism, 1830–1870.* Cambridge: Cambridge Univ. Press, 1982.

Gabriel, Ralph H. *Religion and Learning at Yale: The Church of Christ in the College and University, 1757–1957.* New Haven: Yale Univ. Press, 1958.

Gal, Allon. *Brandeis of Boston.* Cambridge: Harvard Univ. Press, 1980.

Gattell, Frank O. *John Gorham Palfrey and the New England Conscience.* Cambridge: Harvard Univ. Press, 1963.

Gerteis, Louis S. *Morality and Utility in American Antislavery Reform.* Chapel Hill: Univ. of North Carolina Press, 1987.

Grant, Charles S. *Democracy in the Connecticut Frontier Town of Kent.* New York: AMS Press, 1961.

Grant, H. Roger. *Insurance Reform: Consumer Action in the Progressive Era.* Ames: Iowa State Univ. Press, 1979.

Greven, Philip J. *Childrearing Concepts, 1628-1861.* Itasca: Peacock Press, 1973.

———. *The Protestant Temperament: Patterns of Childrearing, Religious Experience, and the Self in Early America.* New York: Knopf, 1977.

Griffin, Clifford S. *Their Brothers' Keeper: Moral Stewardship in the United States, 1800-1865.* New Brunswick: Rutgers Univ. Press, 1960.

Handel, Gerald, ed. *The Psychosocial Interior of the Family.* Chicago: Aldine, 1967.

Haraven, Tamara, ed. *Anonymous Americans.* Englewood Cliffs: Prentice Hall, 1971.

Harlow, Ralph V. *Gerrit Smith, Philanthropist and Reformer.* New York: Holt, 1939.

Haroutinian, Joseph. *Piety Versus Moralism: The Passing of the New England Theology.* New York: Harper and Row, 1970.

Hatcher, Harlan H. *The Western Reserve: The Story of New Connecticut in Ohio.* Indianapolis: Bobbs-Merrill, 1949.

Helfaer, Philip M. *The Psychology of Religious Doubt.* Boston: Beacon Press, 1972.

Hendrick, Burton J. *The Story of Life Insurance.* New York: McClure, Phillips, 1907.

Henretta, James A. *The Evolution of American Society, 1700-1815: An Interdisciplinary Analysis.* Lexington: D.C. Heath, 1973.

Hobsbawm, Eric J. *The Age of Revolution, 1789-1848.* New York: New American Library, 1962.

Hoffman, Martin L., and Lois W. Hoffman, eds. *Review of Child Development Research.* New York: Russell Sage, 1964.

Holt, Robert, ed. *Motives and Thought: Essays in Honor of David Rapaport.* New York: International Univ. Press, 1967.

Hooker, Richard. *Aetna Life Insurance Company: Its First Hundred Years.* Hartford: Aetna Life Insurance Co., 1956.

Howe, Daniel W. *The Unitarian Conscience: Harvard Moral Philosophy, 1805-1861.* Cambridge: Harvard Univ. Press, 1970.

Hyman, Harold M., and Leonard W. Levy, eds. *Freedom and Reform: Essays in Honor of Henry Steele Commager.* New York: Harper and Row, 1967.

James, William. *The Varieties of Religious Experience.* New York: Longmans Green, 1904.

Johnson, Paul. *Shopkeeper's Millennium: Society and Revivals in Rochester, N.Y., 1815-1837.* New York: Hill and Wang, 1978.

Keller, Charles R. *The Second Great Awakening in Connecticut.* New Haven: Yale Univ. Press, 1942.

Keller, Morton. *The Life Insurance Enterprise, 1885-1910: A Study in the Limits of Corporate Power.* Cambridge: Harvard Univ. Press, 1961.

Kelley, Brooks M. *Yale: A History.* New Haven: Yale Univ. Press, 1974.

Keniston, Kenneth. *Young Radicals: Notes on Committed Youth.* New York: Harcourt, Brace and World, 1968.

Kett, Joseph. *Rites of Passage: Adolescence in America, 1790 to the Present.* New York: Basic Books, 1977.

Klineberg, Frank J., and Annie H. Abel, eds. *A Sidelight on Anglo-American Relations, 1839–1858.* New York: A. M. Kelley, 1970.

Knight, Charles K. *The History of Life Insurance in the United States to 1870.* Philadelphia: University of Pennsylvania, 1920.

Kraditor, Aileen S. *Means and Ends in American Abolitionism: Garrison and His Critics on Strategy and Tactics, 1834–1850.* New York: Pantheon, 1967.

Kraut, Alan M., ed. *Crusaders and Compromisers: Essays on the Relationship of the Antislavery Struggle to the Antebellum Party System.* Westport: Greenwood Press, 1983.

Kübler-Ross, Elizabeth. *On Death and Dying.* New York: Macmillan, 1969.

Kuhn, Anne L. *The Mother's Role in Childhood Education.* New Haven: Yale Univ. Press, 1947.

Larson, Orvin. *American Infidel: Robert G. Ingersoll.* Secaucus: Citadel Press, 1967.

Levy, Leonard W. *The Law of the Commonwealth and Chief Justice Shaw.* Cambridge: Harvard Univ. Press, 1957.

Library of Congress Symposia on the American Revolution: Leadership in the American Revolution. Washington, D.C.: Library of Congress, 1974.

Lifton, Robert Jay. *The Broken Connection: On Death and the Continuity of Life.* New York: Simon and Schuster, 1979.

Lottich, Kenneth V. *New England Transplanted.* Dallas: Royal, 1964.

McKivigan, John R. *The War against Proslavery Religion: Abolitionism and the Northern Churches, 1830–1865.* Ithaca: Cornell Univ. Press, 1984.

McLoughlin, William G. *Modern Revivalism: Charles Grandison Finney to Billy Graham.* New York: Ronald Press, 1959.

_____. *New England Dissent: The Baptists and Separation of Church and State.* 2 vols. Cambridge: Harvard Univ. Press, 1971.

_____. *Revivals, Awakenings and Reform: An Essay on Religion and Social Change in America, 1607–1977.* Chicago: Univ. of Chicago Press, 1978.

McManus, Edgar. *A History of Negro Slavery in New York.* Syracuse: Syracuse Univ. Press, 1966.

Magdol, Edward. *The Antislavery Rank and File: A Social Profile of the Abolitionists' Constituency.* Westport: Greenwood Press, 1986.

Mandel, Bernard. *Labor—Free and Slave: Workingmen and the Anti-Slavery Movement in the United States.* New York: Associated Authors, 1955.

Maslow, Abraham H. *Toward a Psychology of Being.* New York: Van Nostrand Reinhold, 1968.

Mathews, Lois K. *The Expansion of New England: The Spread of New England Settlement and Institutions to the Mississippi, 1620–1865.* Vol. 1. New York: Russell and Russell, 1962.

Mayfield, John. *Rehearsal for Republicanism: Free Soil and the Politics of Antislavery.* Port Washington: Kennikat Press, 1980.

Mead, Sidney E. *Nathaniel William Taylor: A Connecticut Liberal.* Chicago: Univ. of Chicago Press, 1942.

Meyer, Jacob C. *Church and State in Massachusetts from 1740–1830.* New York: Russell and Russell, 1968.

Millis, John S. *Western Reserve of Cleveland: One Hundred Thirty-Two Years of a Venture in Faith.* New York: Newcomen Society in North America, 1957.

Montgomery, David. *Beyond Equality: Labor and the Radical Republicans, 1862–1872.* New York: Knopf, 1967.

Moore, Barrington, Jr. *Social Origins of Dictatorship and Democracy.* Boston: Beacon Press, 1966.

North, Douglas C. *Economic Growth of the United States, 1790–1860.* Englewood Cliffs: Prentice Hall, 1961.

Norton, Mary Beth. *Liberty's Daughter: The Revolutionary Experience of American Women, 1750–1800.* Boston: Little, Brown, 1980.

Novak, Stephen J. *The Rights of Youth.* Cambridge: Harvard Univ. Press, 1977.

Oates, Stephen B. *To Purge This Land with Blood: A Biography of John Brown.* New York: Harper and Row, 1970.

Patterson, Edwin W. *The Insurance Commissioner in the United States.* Cambridge: Harvard Univ. Press, 1929.

Paul, James C. N., and Murray L. Schwartz. *Federal Censorship: Obscenity in the Mail.* New York: Free Press of Glencoe, 1961.

Pease, Jane H., and William H. Pease. *Bound with Them in Chains: A Biographical History of the American Antislavery Movement.* Westport: Greenwood Press, 1972.

———. *The Fugitive Slave Law and Anthony Burns: A Problem in Law Enforcement.* Philadelphia: Lippincott, 1975.

———. *They Who Would Be Free: Blacks' Search for Freedom, 1830–1861.* New York: Atheneum, 1974.

Perrin, William H., ed. *History of Summit County.* Chicago: Baskin and Battey, 1881.

Perry, Lewis. *Childhood, Marriage, and Reform: Henry Clarke Wright, 1797–1870.* Chicago: Univ. of Chicago Press, 1980.

———. *Radical Abolitionism: Anarchy and the Government of God in Antislavery Thought.* Ithaca: Cornell Univ. Press, 1973.

Perry, Lewis, and Michael Fellman, eds. *Antislavery Reconsidered: New Perspectives on the Abolitionists.* Baton Rouge: Louisiana State Univ. Press, 1979.

Persons, Stow. *Free Religion: An American Faith.* New Haven: Yale Univ. Press, 1947.

Pettit, Norman. *The Heart Prepared: Grace and Conversion in Puritan Spiritual Life.* New Haven: Yale Univ. Press, 1966.

Pierson, George W. *Yale: A Short History.* New Haven: Yale Univ. Press, 1976.

Pivar, David J. *Purity Crusade: Sexual Morality and Social Control, 1868-1900.* Westport: Greenwood Press, 1973.

Post, Albert. *Popular Freethought in America, 1825-1850.* New York: Columbia Univ. Press, 1943.

Purcell, Richard J. *Connecticut in Transition, 1775-1818.* Washington, D.C.: American Historical Association, 1918.

Reynolds, James B., Samuel H. Fisher, and Henry B. Wright, eds. *Two Centuries of Christian Activity at Yale.* New York: Putnams, 1901.

Richards, Leonard J. *"Gentlemen of Property and Standing": Anti-Abolition Mobs in Jacksonian America.* New York: Oxford Univ. Press, 1970.

Rohrbough, Malcolm J. *The Trans-Appalachian Frontier: People, Societies, Institutions, 1775-1850.* New York: Oxford Univ. Press, 1978.

Rorabaugh, William J. *The Alcoholic Republic: An American Tradition.* New York: Oxford Univ. Press, 1979.

Round About Middlesex Fells: Historical Guide Book. Medford: Medford Historical Society, 1935.

Runyan, William M. *Life Histories and Psychobiography: Explorations in Theory and Method.* New York: Oxford Univ. Press, 1982.

Ryan, Mary P. *Cradle of the Middle Class: The Family in Oneida County, New York, 1790-1865.* Cambridge: Cambridge Univ. Press, 1981.

Schwartz, Harold. *Samuel Gridley Howe: Social Reformer, 1801-1876.* Cambridge: Harvard Univ. Press, 1956.

Scott, Donald M. *From Office to Profession: The New England Ministry, 1750-1850.* Philadelphia: Univ. of Pennsylvania Press, 1978.

Sears, Hal D. *The Sex Radicals: Free Love in High Victorian America.* Lawrence: Regents Press of Kansas, 1977.

Sernett, Milton C. *Abolition's Axe: Beriah Green, Oneida Institute, and the Black Freedom Struggle.* Syracuse: Syracuse Univ. Press, 1986.

Sewell, Richard H. *Ballots for Freedom: Antislavery Politics in the United States, 1837-1860.* New York: Oxford Univ. Press, 1976.

Smith, Daniel B. *Inside the Great House: Planter Family Life in Eighteenth-Century Chesapeake Society.* Ithaca: Cornell Univ. Press, 1980.

Smith, H. Shelton. *Changing Conceptions of Original Sin: A Study in American Theology since 1750.* New York: Scribner, 1955.

Sorin, Gerald. *The New York Abolitionists: A Case Study of Political Radicalism.* Westport: Greenwood Press, 1971.

Stalson, J. Owen. *Marketing Life Insurance: Its History in America.* Cambridge: Harvard Univ. Press, 1942.

Staudenraus, P. J. *The African Colonization Society, 1816-1865.* New York: Columbia Univ. Press, 1961.

Stewart, James B. *Holy Warriors: The Abolitionists and American Slavery.* New York: Hill and Wang, 1976.

Sweet, William W. *Religion in the Development of American Culture.* New York: Scribner, 1952.

Taylor, Clare. *British American Abolitionists: An Episode in Transatlantic Understanding.* Edinburgh: Edinburgh Univ. Press, 1974.

Taylor, Gordon R. *The Angel-Makers: A Study in the Psychological Origins of Historical Change, 1750–1850.* London: Heinemann, 1958.

Tewsbury, Donald G. *The Founding of American Colleges and Universities before the Civil War.* New York: Teachers College, Columbia Univ., 1932.

Thomas, John L. *The Liberator: William Lloyd Garrison, A Biography.* Boston: Little, Brown, 1963.

Turner, James. *Without God, Without Creed: The Origins of Unbelief in America.* Baltimore: Johns Hopkins Univ. Press, 1985.

U.S. Statutes at Large, 1789–99. Vol. 1. Boston: Little, Brown, 1853.

Van Tassel, David D., and John J. Grabowski, eds. *Cleveland: A Tradition of Reform.* Kent, Ohio: Kent State Univ. Press, 1986.

Waite, Frederick C. *Western Reserve University: The Hudson Era.* Cleveland: Western Reserve Univ. Press, 1943.

Walker, Peter F. *Moral Choices: Memory, Desire, and Imagination in Nineteenth-Century Abolition.* Baton Rouge: Louisiana State Univ. Press, 1978.

Walker, Williston. *A History of the Congregational Churches in the United States.* Boston: Pilgrim Press, 1894.

Walters, Ronald. *American Reformers, 1815–1860.* New York: Hill and Wang, 1978.

Warren, Sidney. *American Freethought, 1860–1914.* New York: Columbia Univ. Press, 1943.

Weber, Max. *The Protestant Ethic and the Spirit of Capitalism.* New York: Scribner, 1958.

Weinstein, Fred, and Gerald M. Platt. *Psychoanalytic Sociology: An Essay on the Interpretation of Historical Data and the Phenomena of Collective Behavior.* Baltimore: Johns Hopkins Univ. Press, 1973.

Weisberger, Bernard A. *They Gathered at the River: The Story of the Great Revivalists and Their Impact on Religion in America.* Chicago: Quadrangle, 1966.

Weiss, Harry B., and Howard R. Kemble. *The Great American Water-Cure Craze: A History of Hydropathy in the United States.* Trenton: Past Times Press, 1967.

Whiting, John W. M., and Arvin L. Child. *Child Training and Personality: A Cross-Cultural Study.* New Haven: Yale Univ. Press, 1953.

Wiecek, William M. *The Sources of Antislavery Constitutionalism in America, 1760–1848.* Ithaca: Cornell Univ. Press, 1977.

Wilbur, Earl M. *A History of Unitarianism: In Transylvania, England and America.* Cambridge: Harvard Univ. Press, 1952.

Williamson, Harold F., and Orange A. Smalley. *Northwestern Mutual Life: A Century of Trusteeship.* Evanston: Northwestern Univ. Press, 1957.

Wright, Conrad. *The Beginnings of Unitarianism in America.* Boston: Starr King Press, 1955.

Wright, Louis B. *Culture on the Moving Frontier.* Bloomington: Indiana Univ. Press, 1955.

Wright, Philip G., and Elizabeth Q. Wright. *Elizur Wright: The Father of Life Insurance.* Chicago: Univ. of Chicago Press, 1937.

Wyatt-Brown, Bertram. *Lewis Tappan and the Evangelical War against Slavery.* New York: Atheneum, 1971.

Zelizer, Viviana. *Morals and Markets: The Development of Life Insurance in the United States.* New York: Columbia Univ. Press, 1979.

Zilversmit, Arthur. *The First Emancipation: The Abolition of Slavery in the North.* Chicago: Univ. of Chicago Press, 1970.

Articles

Banner, Lois. "Religion and Reform in the Early Republic: The Role of Youth." *American Quarterly* 23 (1971): 677–95.

_____. "Religious Benevolence as Social Control: A Critique of an Interpretation." *Journal of American History* 60 (1973): 23–41.

Baritz, Loren. "The Idea of the West." *American Historical Review* 46 (1961): 618–40.

Bestor, Arthur E. "Patent Office Models of the Good Society." *American Historical Review* 58 (1953): 505–26.

Bidwell, Percy W. "Rural Economy in New England at the Beginning of the Nineteenth Century." *Transactions of the Connecticut Academy of Arts and Sciences* 20 (1916): 241–339.

Brandeis, Louis. "The Greatest Insurance Wrong." *Independent* 41 (Dec. 20, 1906): 1475–80.

Brooks, Elaine. "Massachusetts Anti-Slavery Society." *Journal of Negro History* 30 (1945): 311–30.

Brown, Richard D. "The Emergence of Urban Society in Rural Massachusetts, 1760–1820." *Journal of American History* 41 (1974): 29–51.

Christensen, Carl W. "Religious Conversion in Adolescence." *Pastoral Psychology* 16 (1965): 17–28.

Cott, Nancy F. "Notes toward an Explanation of Antebellum Childrearing." *Psychohistory Review* 6 (1978): 4–20.

Curry, Richard O., and Lawrence B. Goodheart, eds. "The Complexities of Factionalism: Letters of Elizur Wright, Jr. on the Abolitionist Schism, 1837–1840." *Civil War History* 29 (1983): 245–59.

————. "'Knives in Their Heads': Passionate Self-Analysis and the Search for Identity in Recent Abolitionist Historiography." *Canadian Review of American Studies* 14 (1983): 401–14.

David, C. W. A. "The Fugitive Slave Law of 1793." *Journal of Negro History* 9 (1924): 18–25.

Davis, David B. "The Emergence of Immediatism in British and American Antislavery Thought." *Mississippi Valley Historical Review* 49 (1962): 209–30.

————. "Some Ideological Functions of Prejudice in Ante-Bellum America." *American Quarterly* 15 (1963): 115–25.

————. "Some Recent Directions in Cultural History." *American Historical Review* 73 (1968): 696–707.

————. "Some Themes of Counter-Subversion: An Analysis of Anti-Masonic, Anti-Catholic and Anti-Mormon Literature." *Mississippi Valley Historical Review* 47 (1960): 205–24.

Dillon, Merton L. "The Failure of the American Abolitionists." *Journal of Southern History* 25 (1959): 159–77.

Duberman, Martin. "The Abolitionists and Psychology." *Journal of Negro History* 47 (1962): 183–91.

Dumond, Dwight L. "The Mississippi: Valley of Decision." *Mississippi Valley Historical Review* 36 (1940): 3–26.

Feinstein, Howard M. "The Prepared Heart: A Comparative Study of Puritan Theology and Psychoanalysis." *American Quarterly* 22 (1970): 166–76.

Fladeland, Betty. "Who Were the Abolitionists?" *Journal of Negro History* 59 (1964): 99–115.

Foster, Charles I. "The Colonization of Free Negroes in Liberia, 1816–1835." *Journal of Negro History* 38 (1953): 41–66.

Freehling, William. "The Founding Fathers and Slavery." *American Historical Review* 77 (1972): 81–93.

French, David C. "Elizur Wright, Jr., and the Emergence of Anti-Colonization Sentiments on the Connecticut Western Reserve." *Ohio History* 85 (1976): 49–66.

————. "Puritan Conservatism and the Frontier: The Elizur Wright Family on the Connecticut Western Reserve." *The Old Northwest* 1 (1975): 85–95.

Frey, Joseph S. C. "The Jews and Early Nineteenth-Century Millennarianism." *Journal of the Early Republic* 1 (1981): 27–49.

Friedman, Lawrence J. "Confidence and Pertinacity in Evangelical Abolitionism: Lewis Tappan's Circle. *American Quarterly* 31 (1979): 81–106.

————. "The Gerrit Smith Circle: Abolitionism in the Burned Over District." *Civil War History* 26 (1980): 19–38.

Goodheart, Lawrence B. "Abolitionists as Academics: The Controversy at Western Reserve College, 1832–1833." *History of Education Quarterly* 22 (1982): 421–33.

————. "Childrearing, Conscience, and Conversion to Abolitionism: The Example of Elizur Wright, Jr." *Psychohistory Review* 12 (1984): 24–33.

————. " 'Chronicles of Kidnapping in New York': Resistance to the Fugitive Slave Law, 1834–1835." *Afro-Americans in New York Life and History* 8 (1984): 7–15.

Goodheart, Lawrence B., and Richard O. Curry, eds. "The Trinitarian Indictment of Unitarianism: The Letters of Elizur Wright, Jr., 1826–1827." *Journal of the Early Republic* 3 (1983): 280–96.

Graham, William J. "The Romance of Life Insurance." *The World Today* 15 (1908): 1276–83.

Griffin, Clifford S. "Religious Benevolence as Social Control, 1815–1860." *Mississippi Valley Historical Review* 44 (1957): 423–44.

Hammond, John. "Revival Religion and Anti-Slavery Politics." *American Sociological Review* 39 (1974): 175–86.

Henig, Gerald S. "The Jacksonian Attitude Toward Abolitionism in the 1830s." *Tennessee Historical Quarterly* 28 (1969): 42–56.

Henretta, James A. "Families and Farms: Mentalité in Pre-Industrial America." *William and Mary Quarterly* 35 (1978): 3–32.

Hirsch, Leo H., Jr. "The Negro and New York, 1783–1865." *Journal of Negro History* 16 (1931): 383–423.

Hoffman, Frederick L. "Fifty Years of American Life Insurance Progress." *Publications of the American Statistical Association* 12 (1911): 667–764.

Jarvis, Charles A. "Admission to Abolition: The Case of John Greenleaf Whittier." *Journal of the Early Republic* 4 (1984): 161–76.

Jentz, John B. "The Antislavery Constituency in Jacksonian New York City." *Civil War History* 27 (1981): 101–22.

Johnson, Reinhard O. "The Liberty Party in Massachusetts, 1840–1848: Antislavery Third Party Politics in the Bay State." *Civil War History* 28 (1982): 237–65.

Kerber, Linda. "Abolitionists and Amalgamators: The New York City Race Riots of 1834." *New York History* 48 (1967): 28–39.

Kraditor, Aileen. "American Radical Historians on Their Heritage." *Past and Present* 56 (1972): 136–53.

Leslie, William R. "A Study in the Origins of Interstate Rendition: The Big Beaver Creek Murders." *American Historical Review* 57 (1951): 63–76.

Litwack, Leon F. "The Abolitionist Dilemma: The Antislavery Movement and the Northern Negro." *New England Quarterly* 34 (1961): 50–73.

Lockridge, Kenneth. "Land, Population and Evolution of New England Society, 1630–1790." *Past and Present* 39 (1968): 62–80.

Lofton, Williston H. "Abolition and Labor." *Journal of Negro History* 33 (1948): 249–83.

Loveland, Anne C. "Evangelicalism and 'Immediate Emancipation' in American Antislavery Thought." *Journal of Southern History* 32 (1966): 172-88.

McLoughlin, William G. "Evangelical Childrearing in the Age of Jackson: Francis Weyland's View on When and How to Subdue the Willfulness of Children." *Journal of Social History* 9 (1975): 21-34.

Mathews, Donald G. "The Second Great Awakening as an Organizing Process, 1780-1830: An Hypothesis." *American Quarterly* 21 (1969): 24-43.

Mead, Sidney E. "Lyman Beecher and Connecticut Orthodoxy's Campaign against the Unitarians, 1819-1826." *Church History* 19 (1940): 218-34.

Meckel, Richard A. "Educating a Ministry of Mothers: Evangelical Maternal Associations, 1815-1860." *Journal of the Early Republic* 2 (1982): 403-23.

Mendenhall, T. C. "The Town of Tallmadge—The Bacons and Shakespeare." *Ohio Archaeological and Historical Publications* 22 (1923): 590-612.

Miller, Charles. "Puritan Yankee and Father: An Intellectual Portrait of Elizur Wright, Esq. (1762-1845)." *The Connecticut Historical Society Bulletin* 44 (1979): 117-28.

Myers, John L. "The Beginning of Anti-Slavery Agencies in New York State, 1833-1836." *New York History* 43 (1962): 149-81.

————. "Organization of the 'Seventy': To Arouse the North against Slavery." *Mid-America* 48 (1966): 29-46.

Oliphant, Orin J. "The American Missionary Spirit, 1828-1835." *Church History* 7 (1938): 125-37.

Perry, Lewis. "Psychology and the Abolitionists: Reflections on Martin Duberman and the Neo-Abolitionism of the 1960s." *Reviews in American History* 2 (1974): 309-22.

————. " 'We Have Had Conversation with the World': The Abolitionists and Spontaneity." *Canadian Review of American Studies* 6 (1975): 3-26.

Pisani, Donald J. "Forests and Conservation." *Journal of American History* 72 (1985): 340-59.

Power, Richard L. "A Crusade to Extend Yankee Culture, 1820-1865." *New England Quarterly* 13 (1940): 638-53.

Quarles, Benjamin. "Sources of Abolitionist Income." *Mississippi Valley Historical Review* 32 (1945): 63-76.

Randall, E. O. "Tallmadge Township." *Ohio Archaelogical and Historical Publication* 17 (1918): 275-305.

Ranson, Roger L., and Richard Sutch. "Tontine Insurance and the Armstrong Investigation: A Case of Stifled Innovation, 1868-1905." *Journal of Economic History* 47 (1987): 379-90.

Rayback, Joseph. "The American Workingman and the Anti-Slavery Crusade." *Journal of Economic History* 3 (1943): 152-63.

Salzman, Leon. "The Psychology of Religious and Ideological Conversion." *Psychiatry* 16 (1953): 177-87.

Smith, Daniel S. "Family Limitation, Sexual Control, and Domestic Feminism in Victorian America." *Feminist Studies* 1 (1973): 40–57.

Solnet, Albert, and Morris Green. "Psychologic Considerations in the Management of Deaths in Pediatric Hospital Services: Part I, The Doctor and the Child's Family." *Pediatrics* 24 (1959): 106–12.

Stern, James B. "Urgent Gradualism: The Case of the Amerian Union for the Relief and Improvement of the Colored Race." *Civil War History* 25 (1979): 309–28.

Stewart, James B. "Peaceful Hopes and Violent Experiences: The Evolution of Reforming and Radical Abolitionism, 1831–1837." *Civil War History* 17 (1971): 293–309.

Thomas, John L. "Romantic Reform in America, 1815–1865." *American Quarterly* 17 (1965): 656–81.

Thompson, Lawrence. "The Printing and Publishing Activities of the American Tract Society from 1825 to 1850." *The Papers of the Bibliographical Society of America* 35 (1941): 81–114.

Twadell, Elizabeth. "The American Tract Society, 1814–1860." *Church History* 15 (1946): 116–32.

Vervoerdt, Adrian. "Death and the Family." *Medical Opinion and Review* 1 (1966): 38–43.

Wells, Robert V. "Family History and Demographic Transition." *Journal of Social History* 9 (1975): 1–20.

Welter, Rush. "The Frontier West as Image of American Society: Conservative Attitudes before the Civil War." *Mississippi Valley Historical Review* 46 (1959–60): 593–614.

Wright, Conrad. "The Religion of Geology." *New England Quarterly* 14 (1941): 335–58.

Wyatt-Brown, Bertram. "The Abolitionists' Postal Campaign of 1835." *Journal of Negro History* 50 (1965): 227–38.

————. "New Leftists and Abolitionists: A Comparison of American Radical Styles." *Wisconsin Magazine of History* 53 (1970): 256–68.

————. "William Lloyd Garrison and Antislavery Unity: A Reappraisal." *Civil War History* 13 (1967): 5–24.

Dissertations

Ahlstorm, Sydney A. "Francis Ellingwood Abbot: His Education and Active Career." 2 vols. Ph.D. diss., Harvard University, 1952.

Block, Muriel L. "Beriah Green, The Reformer." Master's thesis, Syracuse University, 1935.

French, David C. "The Conversion of an American Radical: Elizur Wright, Jr. and the Abolitionist Commitment." Ph.D. diss., Case Western Reserve University, 1970.

Houston, David B. "An Analysis of Elizur Wright's Life Insurance Reforms." Ph.D. diss., University of Pennsylvania, 1959.

McManis, Michael A. "Range Ten, Town Four: A Social History of Hudson, Ohio, 1799–1840." Ph.D. diss., Case Western Reserve University, 1976.

Neufeldt, Harvey G. "The American Tract Society, 1825–1865: An Examination of Its Religious, Economic, Social, and Political Ideas." Ph.D. diss., Michigan State University, 1971.

Plunkett, Margaret L. "A History of the Liberty Party with Emphasis upon Its Activities in the New England States." Ph.D. diss., Cornell University, 1930.

Rivers, Fred M. "Francis Ellingwood Abbot: Free Religionist and Cosmic Philosopher." Ph.D. diss., University of Maryland, 1970.

Slater, Peter G. "Views of Children and of Childrearing during the Early National Period: A Study in the New England Intellect." Ph.D. diss., University of California, Berkeley, 1970.

Walker, George. "The Afro-American in New York City, 1827–1860." Ph.D. diss., Columbia University, 1975.

Index

Union for the Relief and Improvement of the Colored Race, 73

Unions, opposition to, 164–65

Unitarianism: and challenge to established church doctrine, 19–20; condemnation of, 25–27; quarrels with Congregationalism, 23–25; secession in Groton, 25; Wright's curiosity about, 25

Valuation Tables, 146–47

Van Buren, Martin, 110, 120, 127, 133, 134

Vashon, J. B., 58

Vegetarianism, 83

Vesey, Denmark, 39

"Victim of Prejudice, The" (letter), 50

Wakeman, Thaddeus B., 183, 191

Walker, David, 39

Weber, Max, 94

Webster, Daniel, 127

Webster, Joshua, 155, 157

Weld, Theodore: at Andover Theological Seminary, 29; congratulations to Wright on Middlesex Fells success, 201; falling out with Wright, 82–83, 84, 125, 206; as immediatist, 40, 43, 44, 45, 59, 62, 63, 65, 66, 67, 68, 71, 72, 73, 74, 77, 78, 79, 80, 92; prudism of, 197; and women's issues, 104

Western Reserve. *See* Ohio, Western Reserve of

Western Reserve Anti-Slavery and Colonization Society, 57

Western Reserve Anti-Slavery Society, 57–58, 63

Western Reserve Bible Society, 8

Western Reserve College: abolitionist society at, 54; colonizationists versus immediatists at, 47–60; Elizur, Jr.'s employment at, 29–30, 33–34, 38, 47, 57, 58–59; Elizur, Sr., as trustee of, 8, 33, 54, 55, 57; establishment of (1826), 48–49

West Indies, emancipation in, 93, 179

Weston, Anne Warren, 128

Whig party, conscience members of, 132–33

Whitney, Eli, 6

Whittier, John Greenleaf, 64, 72, 77, 104, 161, 201

Wiecek, William M., 91

Wilberforce, William, 40

Williams, E. D., 173

Williams, Peter, 68

Wilmot Proviso, 133

Wilson, Henry, 127, 137

Winston, Frederick, 160, 165, 170–71, 175

Wise, Rabbi Isaac, 182

Women's rights, 102, 104, 107, 110, 117, 128, 133, 190

Wood, Leonard, 28

Woodbury, James T., 102

Wordsworth, William, 123

Working Men's party, 97

Wright, Amelia (half-sister), 5, 12

Wright, Anne Carroll (daughter), 195, 199

Wright, Arthur Tappan (son), 121, 195, 199

Wright, Charles Storrs (son), 117, 195, 198, 199

Wright, Clara Richards (daughter), 73, 195, 199

Wright, Clarissa Richards (mother): childrearing by, 12; marriage to Elizur, Sr., 4, 5; migration to Ohio by, 8; religious views of, 20, 27; support of Elizur, Jr., by, 45; worries about Elizur, Jr., by, 17, 126

Wright, Clarissa (sister), 5

Wright, Edward Kittredge (son), 195, 199

Wright, Elizur, Jr.: as actuarial, 167–68; in American Anti-Slavery Society, 61–84 passim; anticlericalism of, 62, 82, 84, 107, 117, 125, 176; as atheist, 179–80, 192–93, 203–4, 206; as biographer of Holley, 158; birth of, 4; childrearing by, 128–29, 197–98; and civil rights for blacks, 86; as colonizationist, 37, 38, 40, 41, 43, 204; as colporteur, 30, 31–33, 34; as commissioner of life insurance,